The Sexual Harassment of Women
in the Workplace, 1600 to 1993

The Sexual Harassment of Women in the Workplace, 1600 to 1993

by

KERRY SEGRAVE

McFarland & Company, Inc., Publishers
Jefferson, North Carolina, and London

British Library Cataloguing-in-Publication data are available

Library of Congress Cataloguing-in-Publication Data

Segrave, Kerry, 1944–
    The sexual harassment of women in the workplace, 1600 to 1993 / by
Kerry Segrave.
        p.   cm.
    Includes bibliographical references and index. ∞
    ISBN 0-7864-0007-2 (lib. bdg. : 50# alk. paper)
    1. Sexual harassment of women — History.   2. Sex discrimination in
employment — History.   I. Title.
HD6060.3.S43 1994
331.4133′09 — dc20   94-2803
                                                                CIP

Manufactured in the United States of America

McFarland & Company, Inc., Publishers
  Box 611, Jefferson, North Carolina 28640

Contents

Preface

This book examines the history of the phenomenon of sexual harassment of women in the workplace. While the emphasis is on the United States, sources from around the world are included. Coverage ranges, occupationally, from the domestic servant of the 1600s to the professional female worker of the 1990s. Generally each chapter looks at one occupation. Chapter Four, for instance, covers industrial workers in the 1800s; Chapter Eight discusses clerical workers across time.

The intent is to look at the issue from a global and historical perspective as a complement to the now fairly large body of material on workplace sexual harassment in the United States which has been generated since the late 1970s. One of the striking aspects is the universality of the phenomenon—compare the abuse of female workers in the U.S. textile industry in the 1830s to the abuse of female workers in the Japanese textile industry in the 1900 era with other periods in the development of the industry.

This book should be regarded as a survey of conditions from the 1600s to 1993. By no means is it exhaustive. The surprising amount of historical material, particularly pre–1960, is a testament to the determination of people around the world and across time who persevered in getting abuses on record, even if they could not stop the abuse. The exploited and abused rarely get to participate in the writing of history, a task usurped by the exploiters and abusers.

Research for this book was conducted in Los Angeles at the UCLA library system, the USC library system and at the Los Angeles Public Library. While journal and newspaper articles were useful for some older material, they were of most use for recent events. Books were the major source material for the bulk of the research involved in this book. Basically I went through every book on the shelves in subject areas such as "Women—Employment" and "Women—History," and selectively in other areas, such as women and trade unions.

It is my hope that the information in this book facilitates understanding of this ageless abomination.

1
Introduction

One writer stated in 1982 that all women who worked outside the home had to do so with the expectation that they would likely experience sexual harassment on the job at some time in their working lives. For many women it was something they would be subjected to on a daily basis as a part of their standard work environment.[1]

In 1979 militant feminist Andrea Dworkin said of the issue, "The debilitating, insidious violence of sexual harassment is pervasive in the workplace. It is part of nearly every working environment. Women shuffle; women placate; women submit; women leave; the rare brave women fight and are tied up in the courts, often without jobs, for years. There is also rape in the workplace."[2]

Today those statements remain true. They are also true of the past as far back as one can see. If anything those statements understate the pervasiveness of sexual harassment in the workplace. Compare them with the 1918 utterance of industrial psychologist Ordway Tead, who wrote that the presence of women in the workplace was a sexual fringe benefit for male coworkers and supervisors. Tead placed sex along with security and recognition as major incentives for male workers.[3] Unfortunately many of Tead's sentiments are still the order of the day, just as they were many decades ago. Tead was unusual to the extent that he was candid about the issue. In the past and into the present the overwhelming response by males has been to deny the existence of sexual harassment, whether it was an "official" report of some type in 1900 or a panel of United States senators meeting in 1991 to hear a complaint. Always the game was fixed; always the decision was reached before the facts were heard. So effective were male control and domination of this issue that it was not publicized to any extent in the media until the mid– to late 1970s and then only in response to increasing pressure, lobbying, and surveying done by the women's movement as part of an overall effort to redress a variety of grievances. Women, of course, have always been aware of the problem, at least any who have ever worked outside the home. Often they were conditioned to believe they were overreacting to friendly overtures, or if that were not so, the situation must have been their fault. Complaints usually had to be initiated with a report to a direct supervisor, who, as often as not, was the harasser. Beyond that, a woman would have to face a board of male managers or male unionists who were at best not receptive and at worst, hostile. Having launched an almost bound-to-fail complaint, the woman left herself open to retaliation at work, which was not a rare happening. If a woman needed the job and income, it was often a case of submit or get out.

Michael Korda's book *Male Chauvinism*, published in 1972, was designed to explain how chauvinism worked. When he talked about sexual harassment in the office—he didn't call it that, for the term would not come into general usage until near the end of that decade—he dealt with it in condescending terms. Explaining that the idea of men and women working together in the same place was fairly recent, hardly a hundred years old, he noted, "Until then men and women worked together only in circumstances of such degradation and slavery that sex cannot have represented a major problem—after all, in Victorian England, women, even children hauled coal in the mines, stripped naked, and harnessed to wagons, and worked sixteen or more hours a day in the 'dark satanic mills' of the Industrial Revolution."[4] What Korda noted was correct except that sex was indeed a problem even under the conditions that were as bad as Korda described them. He missed the point entirely and adopted a self-serving male revisionist historical approach by linking sexual activity in the workplace with desire, libido, lust.

Sexual harassment has nothing whatsoever to do with libido and lust. It has everything to do with exploiting, objectifying, and dominating women. It is a manifestation of the extreme loathing so many men bear toward women, which can also be seen in sexual harassment outside the workplace—rape, child sexual abuse, incest, pornography, and sexist behavior in general. Linking sexual harassment with libido laid the groundwork for excusing, accepting, and forgiving male violence against women. If sexual harassment is libido, then men cannot help it; if it is libido, then women must be at least partly to blame; if it is libido, then claiming that women must have done something to provoke it is easier to do. If it is libido, then nature is the culprit, and what can be done about nature? This same reasoning was applied to rape—why was the victim there at that time? why was she wearing that? and so on—until recently, when society began to recognize rape for what it is, an act of violence and hatred designed to dominate and control women.

So it is with sexual harassment in the workplace. The woman in the Victorian coal mines was indeed harassed on the job—most tried to work with a male relative such as a brother for some measure of safety. When she worked underground in the mines in the suffocating heat, she very infrequently worked naked to the waist, as did the men. It was more usual for her to work head to foot in her underwear. This caused her to be branded as immoral, as indeed were working women who removed their outer garments ony above the waist. Public sentiment grew against the woman coal miner in Victorian England until she and other women were banned from working underground in English coal mines. They had been employed there for at least half a century before the ban. Subjected to inhuman working conditions for subsistence wages doing backbreaking work, subjected to sexual harassment by coworkers and supervisors, these women, who had absolutely no recourse or redress of this sexual abuse, were finally banned from this work. Why? They were sluts; it was all their fault. When Korda was coyly explaining the inner mechanisms of male chauvinism, he should have included his own book.

The idea of the slut—the loose, immoral, promiscuous female—occurred over and over again in connection with sexual harassment from the early 1600s right up to the early 1990s. Female reputations were scored all the way from an illiterate indentured servant in New England in the 1620s right up to the educated, articulate law professor Anita Hill in 1991. This took the idea of libido a step further. Under the libido idea a female could passively cause sexual harassment just by being there. However, at times it could be difficult to convince others that such passivity was the cause of all that trouble. Enter the active, aggressive slut. This loose woman would actively entice the male, making him all the more blameless and her all the more blameworthy for her abuse.

To this end much was made of the connection between working women and prostitution. With low wages and periods of unemployment, many working women did indeed drift in and out of prostitution. Wages paid to women were lower than those paid to men. They were not designed to allow a female to support herself, and any children, independently. They were designed to be for women who still lived at home or who were married and lived with their husbands. This money was designed to be supplemental income only, not the sole or primary income. Many women did not fit these categories of dependency and found it next to impossible to survive even though they were fully employed and worked virtually every waking hour. The drift to prostitution occurred through economic necessity. However, the overclass viewed this move as one of inclination and moral perversion. Thus by putting a spin on economics, men were able to brand working women as corrupters of men in the workplace. Workplace abuse became even more of a nonissue, even more the fault of women. Clearly these insatiable sluts were forcing themselves on males, vulnerable men who could not help but yield.

When an 1866 report claimed that much of the prostitution then said to be rampant in Detroit began in the tobacco factories, it was used as an argument to adopt "protective" legislation for women. In other words, limit their employment opportunities. James W. Jack, president of the Missouri Press Association, declared in 1895 of African-American females that they all "were prostitutes and all were natural thieves and liars." In a now classic book published in 1858, *A History of Prostitution*, William Sanger questioned a number of prostitutes as to why they turned to that occupation. The most frequent answer received, he said, was "inclination," which Sanger understood "as meaning a voluntary resort to prostitution in order to gratify the sexual passions."[5]

To the male overclass this connection between female workers and prostitution was used to reinforce the idea that women's morals went downhill in paid employment. Women entered factories, became loose, and in some cases went further downhill by becoming prostitutes. The idea that a woman who had lost her virginity at work — female virginity was then considered important — by agreeing to sex to keep her job might turn to prostitution when she was dismissed, because she needed money and her virginity had been sacrificed, was not considered or even mentioned. Domestic servants were particularly vulnerable since when dismissed they lost their job, income, and housing all at once.

Some voices did raise the thought that the ranks of prostitutes were perhaps increased because some women workers were corrupted, sexually harassed, by supervisors who had threatened to fire them or promised them a pay raise. To quiet such thoughts the federal government stepped forward. In 1887 the U.S. Bureau of Labor concluded after an investigation of working females, "They are not corrupted by their employers nor do their employers seek to corrupt them."[6]

Combining the idea of looseness with that of paying lower wages to women than to men was an employer who told the Minnesota Department of Labor in 1904 that lower pay was justified because females only worked for "extra luxuries." Besides, he said, the women worked only for "the excitement, the opportunity for ogling customers, and display of cheap finery."[7]

Employers in 1850s England, and the working class itself, regularly judged factory women as "common," with its connotations of disreputability. Some employers segregated the sexes into separate workrooms; some imposed a no talking rule between the sexes. A mill worker in 1830s Scotland complained that the lack of education of factory women "makes them looser and more dissolute in their manners than they otherwise would be; that there is a great deal of promiscuous intercourse of the sexes at these works; that illegitimate children are not uncommon."[8]

One observer noted that in American stores and factories of 1900 foremen could pinch and fondle female workers without their having any redress; inspectors could promise fewer rejections of work in exchange for sexual favors. "Few could afford to refuse — and then the women were blamed as enticers . . . . No one cared."[9]

In Pakistan during the early 1960s a survey was undertaken that showed that many people felt that women should not work outside the home. Twenty-one percent of those who felt that way believed that the morals or reputation of females could be adversely affected on the job. Somehow this brought up images of females being at fault if indeed their morals were affected. Pakistani women who worked outside the home knew differently. When asked what problems they faced at work, one replied, "Men take undue advantage" of them, while a second complained of the "difficulty of having a loose character boss."[10]

Many, many other examples of female workers being branded as loose, as promiscuous, as in moral danger if they entered employment, will be found in this book. Never was it stated or even implied that females were being harassed at work, subjected to coerced sex, or even raped by male employers and supervisors. This silence allowed the solution to the problem of female morality to be presented exclusively as removing women from the workplace or regulating their hours and conditions. Never was the focus placed on male behavior. The idea that male behavior might be the problem was rarely raised, even to be refuted and dismissed as a silly suggestion. However, the overclass needed women in the workplace in order to maximize profits. How badly women were needed depended on time and circumstances. For instance, females were badly needed in the work force during World Wars I and II. At times like those there tended to be much less publicity given to the idea that work and female immorality went hand in hand. Such a need for female workers existed much earlier as well. Secretary of the Treasury Alexander Hamilton, who urged females to take employment outside the home in response to industrialization, especially in the cotton industry, said in 1791, "In general, women and children are rendered more useful . . . by manufacturing establishments, than they would otherwise be." With industrialization getting well under way there was a shortage of male labor at the time. Public moralists of the 1790s also acclaimed the factory employment of women. These men felt that females who didn't respond to the call would be "doomed to idleness and its inescapable attendants, vice and guilt."[11]

When New England textile mills recruited in the early part of the 1800s, notably the 1830s, they targeted daughters of the impoverished middle classes with promises of a very moral factory atmosphere. The overclass could alter its propaganda quickly when need be, but the masses could not be stripped of their old beliefs so easily or rapidly. In this case it successfully countered the idea, already then well entrenched, that females became immoral from factory employment. These promises consisted essentially of locking the women up in dorms in their few off-hours and forcing them to go to church every Sunday. It was never clear whether employers were locking up the women so the men could not get at them or so the women could not throw themselves at the men.

Making it difficult for women to report incidents of sexual harassment was the idea that women should not talk about certain subjects or use certain words. This was particularly true in the past but perhaps has not altogether vanished even today. It would have been difficult for a woman to tell a man, or a group of them, that a coworker or supervisor had grabbed her breast and so on.

The prevailing idea of sexual intercourse at the turn of the century was that respectable women had no sex drive, did not enjoy sex, did not initiate sexual activity, but surrendered to it for the sake of their husbands and for reproduction. Also commonly held was the idea that the sex drive was a powerful and difficult force to control among males. A book published in 1982 reported that working women saw themselves as responsible for preventing any unwanted sexual advances. Both sexes, it added, shared a belief in the myth of the uncontrollable male sex drive, thus leaving it to women to repulse harassing males.[12] Under this concept rape is thus more or less uncontrollable by men since their drive is so strong; in turn this concept is used to let them off with lesser punishment or none at all. It also excuses sexual harassment in the same way.

Of course this kind of ideology of women disliking sex did not fit in with the loose factory women idea. If sex was so unappealing to women, why would they engage in it? The best the male overclass could do here was to claim class difference. Respectable, middle- and upper-class, women were sexless, but lower-class women were loose and immoral, insatiable sluts. By definition a lower-class woman was one who accepted employment. Also never mentioned or explained was why prostitutes, presumably making more money than factory workers, would from time to time spend stints working in factories—10 or 12 or more hours a day, six days a week, for starvation wages. But then these myths were a hodge-podge of contradictions and inconsistencies tossed out on the run as the overclass tried to explain, dismiss, or justify unpleasantness—such as sexual harassment at work. Such explanations were not supposed to make sense, be logical, or relate to each other. The myth of the sexless woman, however, did help to "explain" harassment from a male point of view: it wasn't harassment at all, of course. If women did not desire sex, did not enjoy it, and did not initiate it, then how did a man get a female to engage in sex? Well, he had to hound her, pester her, and so on. Since females did not like sex, when approached they could be expected to say no most of the time, if not always. Herein lies the idea that no means yes. If intercourse was not pleasurable but painful as a matter of course, then painful intercourse would not by itself be a sign of rape or coerced sex.

Women wanting to complain about sexual harassment on the job often found themselves in a dilemma. For example, victims feared suggestions of complicity from employers. Suspicion of collusion or spite made complaining a risky business. Thus the idea of complicity kept women from complaining quickly and readily to other people. This undermined their credibility when they finally did object. The charge of complicity became more believable if complaints were made only after much time had passed. Somehow the assaults came to look less objectionable, or the complaints would be interpreted as grudges, settling perhaps other old scores by slander. Anita Hill faced just such charges when she spoke up about Clarence Thomas. All of this was in addition to the very real fear of retaliation. Also, sexual harassment rarely involved witnesses.

Typical of the reports that condemned the female workers in the early years and not the harassers was a 1911 study done by the federal government. One task was to determine if there was a link between women's occupations and criminality. In this case criminality was essentially limited to prostitution and drunkenness, what were called moral crimes. Acknowledged initially was the fact that these moral crimes were often blamed on new occupations that had recently opened up to women, such as factory work, office work, and store work, compared to the long established female occupation of domestic service and other personal service. The study found that the old occupations furnished proportionately nearly twice the number of offenders, leading to the conclusion that lawbreaking among women had no connection with the change in industrial conditions. These newer occupations for women, investigators thought, might even be beneficial since they gave "incentives to right living." Another conclusion was that economic "want seems to have played a very small part in leading women astray but to have had considerable influence in keeping them in the wrong path when once the start had been made." That women went bad was attributable "to moral causes, to their inheritance and early training, or to lack of training," investigators believed. Moral causes referred to "moral perverts," those fond of excitement, those who were indolent, those who were vain, those with no inner strength, and those who were easily influenced.[13]

Despite this somewhat reasonable start, the report went on to list four occupations as especially morally dangerous for women. These were domestic service, low-grade factory trades, waitressing, and nursing. The report felt "the dangers lay not so much in the work itself . . . as in the kind of women who are likely to enter such occupations." Back in 1910 most women workers were employed in one of those four jobs. As examples to illustrate this point, the report discussed two young domestics, 15 and 16, who were seduced and deserted in "cold-blooded" fashion by their employers' husbands. The study noted that "one could not willingly minimize the men's share in the matter." However, this report did just that by declaring that neither girl had any morality to begin with as both were termed "thoroughly degenerate." Upon getting a job in a Boston store a salesclerk entered into a sexual relationship with her employer; she was nevertheless a "thoroughly depraved girl" before that. This incident was the first step to a life of "promiscuous immorality upon which she promptly embarked." A few other cases of that nature were reported. In one case a stenographer was made pregnant by her employer, who promptly denied all responsibility and fired her. Here the report was forced to conclude the employer was at fault as the stenographer had been up until then a "good girl." Even here blame was not affixed fully to the man since the report listed two causes for the stenographer's downfall: "affections, employer." The idea that she was coerced into sex or raped was not considered.

The work in which the cases above appear was one of a 19-volume series that the federal government issued as a study of the working conditions of women and children. Only this volume mentioned anything about what we now call sexual harassment and then only briefly, as the preceding indicates. Yet the conclusion about the harassment situation drawn by this report is such that the investigators indicated indirectly by their wording that they were well aware, at least through rumors, of the extent of the problem, though they did not deal with it directly. They chose to whitewash it in a few pages that more or less blamed the victims. "It will be noticed that the unscrupulous employer does not appear as extensively here as might have been anticipated.... It would appear to indicate that he is not the universal menace to the morals of working girls that he is sometimes represented to be," said this report.[14] But he was. And he is.

The idea that sexual harassment is tied to libido has not abated since Korda's book was published. In the wake of the Clarence Thomas hearings the magazine *Christianity Today* published an editorial that, naturally enough, came out strongly against harassment on the job. This December 1991 editorial was titled "Lust on the Job."[15]

Along similar lines was an editorial in the *Times* of London that was politically correct in not condoning sexual harassment and superficially was against it, but in subtle ways equated it with libido, blamed the victim, and suggested why laws against it would not work or were perhaps not necessary. Drawing a red herring across the matter, the editor talked about not wanting sex banished from the workplace since many pairings resulted from office meetings. True of course, but he refused to see that one is normal sexual and mutual attraction, while the other is sexual violence, unwanted by one party. They are no more similar than those proverbial apples and oranges that can never be compared. Another red herring was the editor's statement that "much of female dress and make-up still seems designed to attract the opposite sex." Although he didn't suggest that wearing certain clothes triggered sexual harassment, the idea that the victim was to blame was firmly planted. (Historically rape victims were often blamed the same way, allowing the male to escape punishment.) In fact, having broached the idea of clothes, he simply let it die without giving any reason for bringing it up in the first place. This editor agreed there was a role for law, "yet statute law is likely to prove a clumsy means" of resolution. This is not so, except to harassers. It is easier to harass if nothing is on the statute books and the only guidelines are those incorporated into company policy manuals, as the harasser would like. The editor suggested that, instead of a law, society should have recourse first "to modern skills of informal advice and communication between those who cannot adjust to sexual strains at work, and second to old fashioned restraint and good manners." If the latter prevailed, there would not be sexual harassment in the first place. Note in this proposal that again sexual harassment is equated with libido and again the victim is blamed. If a person at work is being subjected to violence — and that is how the matter should be worded — for absolutely no reason other than the twisted motives of the harasser, why should that person have to adjust? Why should a victim be expected to adjust to pawing or attempted rape at work? The solution is to control and stop the perpetrator. That is where the adjustment must take place. By suggesting a good-manners method in place of a formal law, the editor trivialized the problem, downplaying it from serious to at best minor. Yet this editorial can in some ways be considered a model. While it was obviously antifemale and trivialized a problem of very serious concern to all women, it made those points often but only indirectly. On its face it was "against" sexual harassment and set out to propose ways to stop it.[16]

Continuing this line of reasoning was Helen Gurley Brown, editor of *Cosmopolitan,* who said in late 1992, "I have this possibly benighted idea that when a man finds you sexually attractive, he is paying you a compliment. . . . When he doesn't, that's when you have to worry." Then she trivialized the problem by adding, "Most unwanted sexual advances can and are turned away without dire results." Apparently Brown had determined the topic would never grace the pages of her magazine for she stated, "Many people have suggested articles on sexual harassment to *Cosmo.* Though a devout feminist, I have resisted."[17]

Harassed women were also regularly scored in recent times when the complaint was not made at the time of the incident. In commenting on the charges against Senator Bob Packwood and other politicians, *The Economist* wondered, "The most curious feature of these stories is the lapse of time in every case between incident and allegation, which surely cannot always be explained away by fear of coming forward." As will be seen throughout this book, it certainly can. *The Economist* drew no conclusion from its musings but definitely planted the idea that perhaps something was not quite right with such accusations.[18]

Carrying on this theme and extending it was Gretchen Morgenson, a senior editor at *Forbes,* writing in the *National Review.* Citing the low rate of harassment reporting at the time of happening, she wrote, "Could it be that these women did not report their 'harassment' because they themselves did not regard a sexual advance as harassment?" Wondering if it was really a big problem, she mused, "Or is it largely a product of hype and hysteria?" In her mind it was possible that many stories saying harassment was a severe problem stemmed from consultants whose livelihood depended on exaggerating its extent. Using the idea that as females appeared in greater proportion in departments, on assembly lines, or in companies, say 30 percent, harassment went away, she predicted sexual harassment would decline in the coming years.[19] There is no evidence to support that idea and much to discredit it.

One of the odder articles to blame the victim was one study in which a group of male and female undergrads were shown one of three colored photos of a model wearing either heavy, moderate, or no cosmetics and then indicated how likely the model was to "provoke" sexual harassment and to be sexually harassed. When the model wore heavy makeup, she was rated significantly more likely to provoke harassment than when she was not wearing cosmetics. The model wearing heavy or moderate cosmetics was rated more likely to be harassed than when she wore no makeup.[20] This experiment started off showing its bias by equating harassment with sexual attractiveness. The use of the word *provoke* implied the female was somehow at least partly responsible.

A study conducted in India in the early 1990s showed that blaming the victim was not limited to the Western world. Suresh Kanekar considered harassment to be more blatant and endemic in that country than in the West. This study presented a hypothetical workplace harassment situation varied by type of harassment (stared at, commented on, or touched on the breast), by status of the harasser (superior, inferior, or equal), and by the victim's response (formal complaint made or incident ignored). Five hundred and forty male and female students at the University of Bombay then attributed blame to the victims and recommended punishment for the harasser, both on a seven-point scale. There were no significant interactions on any two variables. In all cases male subjects attributed more blame to the victim than did female respondents. Overall blame attributed was higher for victims who complained than for victims who ignored the harassment. Male respondents recommended less punishment in all cases than did female respondents.[21]

As the discussion of sexual harassment has become more open and as it has been recognized as a serious and pervasive problem, at least by females, the number of articles attacking and blaming the victims, such as the foregoing examples, has increased. One of the more extreme ones appeared in the journal *Society* in 1991 and was written by Nicholas Davidson. He saw harassment as part of a larger effort by feminists "to wrench power from the male oppressors and create an egalitarian society." Since he felt the sexual revolution had wrought changes in society and that feminism bore responsibility for that revolution, then "in this sense, women's liberation has produced women's oppression." That is, women were responsible for sexual harassment. Of course to argue that he had to claim that harassment was greater over the previous couple of decades than in the past—a totally false idea. "Nothing could be clearer . . . than that disappointed female lovers sometimes make real trouble for the men who reject them," he warned. "Endless phone calls, threats, and even violence are hardly unknown behaviors for either gender." Actually they are almost unknown among women. The "stalker" laws that have been enacted recently in various jurisdictions, such as California, have been enacted because men commit these behaviors against women. If a female was being harassed, Davidson had a simple solution: "After all, could a woman not just say no?" He worried that the "threat of punishment for sexual harassment constitutes a growing element in the lives of Americans."[22]

Actually the likelihood of being punished even when a person has been adjudged to have been a blatant harasser is only very slightly above zero. Examples can be found throughout this book, especially in the last chapter, outlining the difficulties of bringing a complaint. For every 1,000 incidents of sexual harassment, perhaps 250 complaints will be made, sometimes less, sometimes more. With a success rate of 5 percent, an estimate which may be too high, that means 12 of the 1,000 harassed women will have their complaint upheld. A few of those 12 men might be punished. Most of them will not be punished; some will be promoted. Of those 250 women who complain, many more than 12 will suffer retaliation.

2
Indentured Servants, Serfs, and Slaves

Indentured servants arrived in America from Europe beginning in the 1620s and continued to come for well over a century. These were white women who lacked sufficient funds to pay for their passage across to the New World. In exchange for having their fare paid, these women were indentured to work as domestics for a period of time, usually two or three years. At the end of that time they became free women. However, during the course of their service they were subjected to various onerous rules. One rule stipulated that they could not leave their employment, or marry, without permission from their owner. He was reluctant to grant such permission, fearing a loss of the woman's service through pregnancy and the lying-in period when she could not perform her duties. Such regulations of course tended to foster more unconventional liaisons. In turn these liaisons were used against the woman to question her morality. If an indentured servant violated any of the rules — such as getting married, bearing an illegitimate child, or failing to show up for work for any reason — then her term of service was extended as a punishment.

Laws making illegitimate births a crime applied equally to free women and indentured servants. When a servant gave birth to an illegitimate child, she was viewed as having committed a great dishonor to God and an injury to the community and as having damaged her master. Bastardy legislation existed partly for moral purposes but also to try saving the parish the money involved in the upkeep of large numbers of bastards. Children had to be supported only up to the age of ten in that era. An indentured servant guilty of bastardy could be fined and whipped. Since she invariably had no money to pay a fine, the term of service to her master was extended. These fines were levied as well against free, unmarried women. In addition to this punishment, the indentured servant was hit a second time since her pregnancy and lying-in had cost her owner in service. Therefore she was required to indemnify her master. Once again a fine was charged, which once again she could not pay. Her term of service was extended. It was thus possible for a master to gain two service extensions from his servant's one illegitimate birth. If she could not prove to the court's satisfaction that the man she accused of being the child's father was in fact the father, she could be subjected to a public whipping. Not surprisingly servants in this position often attempted to hide their pregnancies to the greatest possible extent, to give birth alone, then resort to infanticide.[1]

The problem of masters sexually abusing their indentured servants was sufficiently widespread that Governor Nicholson of Virginia called attention to the getting of servants pregnant by their masters, labeling it a serious grievance. This was in the 1670s. In many bastardy case reports, the name of the reputed father was absent. Some of these may have involved a master who was rewarding his servant for her silence or threatening to make her life miserable should she expose him. Women having bastards fathered by their masters were likely not often brought into court since it was usually the owner who reported such delinquency in order to be compensated for his loss of service. Some owners wished to avoid the stigma of being publicly linked to such an event. When Elizabeth Phillips had a child by her master, she was ordered sold after the expiration of her term for the use of the parish. This meant she was indentured to the highest bidder, for two years or so, with the proceeds going to the state. Elizabeth's master went unpunished. The same thing happened to Mary Rogers, who at first refused to reveal her master as the father of her child.[2]

Virginia had a particularly perverse law on its statute books that allowed a master who fathered his servant's child to demand compensation from her for her bastardy in the form of extra service. A new law passed in 1672 made it impossible for the master to do so any longer. The new act declared that "late experiments shew that some dissolute masters have gotten their maides with child, and yet claime the benefitt of their service." Under the new provision when the term of indenture expired, the servant who had given birth to her master's bastard could be sold by the church wardens for the use of the parish for two years. The obvious implication that these powerless female servants were the victims of rape or coerced sex was simply never raised in public. Invariably these indentured servants were severely punished one way or another.[3]

With infanticide at a troublingly high level, the authorities wanted to take action to stem it; however, they were technologically limited. It was not then possible to tell if a child had been born dead or murdered shortly thereafter. The response to this state of affairs by the authorities was to pass acts that provided the death penalty for any woman who concealed the death of her bastard, regardless of whether it was born dead or alive.[4]

Female serfs in Russia during the 1600s and 1700s were subjected to similar treatment. One serf wrote to his owner complaining that a steward was guilty of sexual abuse: "[He] demands young girls for himself and has deprived many of their maidenhood." It was not uncommon for a master to keep a harem. Owner P. A. Koshkarov put 12 to 15 young girls under the watchful eye of a trusted female relative and placed them in a wing of his residence. General L. D. Izmailov kept 30 young servant girls at his estate for the "amusement" of himself and his guests. An owner named Pastukhov "forcibly compelled peasant women and servant girls to engage in lecherous relations with him."[5]

Australia had its system of indentured servitude in operation by the 1790s. Women convicts transported to that country from England were initially housed in what were called female factories—basically prisons—where they performed work such as laundering until they were assigned as domestic servants to private families that had put in requests for household help. Masters were required to feed, clothe, and satisfactorily maintain these servants for the period of their assignment—usually two or three years—after which these women obtained their freedom. Any unsatisfactory performance on the job would lead to the woman being returned to the factory by the master, where she would await reassignment to another family. The government had an interest in keeping these women in private employment to reduce its own expense of maintaining them when they were quartered and sustained in the female factories. Theoretically the women could be assigned to any type of employment; however, domestic work was about all that was available for females.[6]

Coming from the lower classes of British society, these women arrived in Australia with a reputation already in place that painted them as loose and immoral. Government officials and others considered them "damned whores." The Australian government's 1812 Select Committee on Transportation viewed these females as "of the most abandoned description and that in many instances they are likely to whet and to encourage the vices of men."[7]

All of this provided a very convenient cover for the sexual abuse of these women. Such sentiments were both excuse and rationale for sexual harassment. As one writer noted, the majority of masters received these people "rather as prostitutes than as servants." Infrequently the odd official in the government spoke out about the reality of the situation. The country's secretary of state commented that while assigned as servants the women were often subjected to "criminal solicitation, to grievous oppression, and often to personal violence." After such experiences in their assigned workplaces, many were returned to the female factories, often pregnant, to be confined "at the public expense," before they would "again go forth . . . to return again, in many cases, under similar circumstances."[8]

In theory a servant who was subjected to such abuse could appeal to a magistrate, bringing her harasser to court on charges. In practice it was just about impossible for a servant to get any redress for charges of molestation. A contemporary observer noted, "There was little probability that magistrates would inflict any punishment [on masters], or even give the complaint [of assigned servants] consideration." The worst that could happen to a master who proved to be irresponsible, cruel, or excessively exploitative was the denial of the assignment of any more servants by the government. Mr. and Mrs. Robert Harvey were denied any more servants after their servant Georgiana Baxter complained that she had been given insufficient food and that her mistress had "solicited her to be unchaste." Nothing prevented the Harveys from obtaining a servant from a nongovernmental source.[9]

Mary Ann Carberry was transported to Tasmania, Australia, around 1830, from Dublin, Ireland. Her offense was arson—house burning. Some people in the British Isles who had little or no money committed such offenses in the hope that they would be transported to what they thought would be a better life. In her first job a month after her arrival, Carberry alleged sexual impropriety against her master. One day when her mistress was ill in bed, Carberry said her master had taken "indecent liberties" with her. She related this incident to her mistress, adding that she could no longer remain at that job. A few days after that Carberry refused to work—an offense for which the police were called in to arrest her. Appearing in court, her master denied all the allegations, saying in reply to prisoner Carberry's charges, "I did not put my hand in your bosom and blow the lights out." The court decided the master had done no wrong. Carberry was given six months in the female factory with hard labor, every other month to be spent in solitary. When that sentence was completed, Carberry was transported to the interior, an uninviting area that attracted few people. All in all it was a harsh set of penalties levied against Carberry.[10]

The already mentioned 1812 government commission showed little or no concern about the masters who had assigned servants, the way the women were treated, or whether they were forced into prostitution. The chief concern was to limit the number of such women whose upkeep expense fell on the government. Denying future servants to particularly unacceptable masters was as far as this commission would go. In addition it took one more equivocal step by deciding women would no longer be assigned as servants to single men, "if possible."[11]

A quarter of a century later little had changed: harassment continued and was pervasive enough to be officially noted. In 1838 an Australian government report stated regarding assigned servants in private families, "A convict woman, frequently the only one in the service, perhaps in the neighbourhood, is surrounded by a number of depraved characters, to whom she becomes an object of constant pursuit and solicitation; she is generally obliged to select one man, as a paramour, to defend her from the importunities of the rest." The government thought the women would prefer being in private service to being in the female factories, yet many women would commit one or more minor offenses in the assigned household just to get sent back. The situation was not good in the factories, but it was often worse in the household.[12]

In India circa 1800 a historian of that era reported that female domestic slaves were kept "almost universally for sexual purposes . . . secluded . . . from all appeal to Courts of Justice, often treated with caprice, frequently punished with much cruelty, and sometimes murdered with impunity." Slavery officially ended in India in 1843. Much of it took place under British rule, but the colonial masters preferred not to see it. Under Hindu law of the early 1800s, if a master sexually abused his minor female slave, it was an offense, but the worst that could happen to the man was to be fined a small sum of money. The child remained with him as his slave. It was also technically unlawful for him to have forced sex with his adult female slaves; however, "in most cases it was well-nigh impossible for a female slave who had been thus injured to secure her master's punishment. Her very condition rendered it difficult to approach the judges, and in a Court of Justice her testimony would not have weighed against her master's bold assertion that she had freely consented to have intercourse with him." In Dacca four brothers purchased a female slave for the sole purpose of using her for "their gratification." The result was that she gave birth to two children. Even if the forced sex with a minor went further than rape, there was no justice. If as a result of the assault the female child was severely injured or died, "the Ruling Power can only punish him by fining him a paltry fifty Kowries." The Muslim master in India had even laxer laws governing his conduct toward his slaves than did the Hindu. The Islamic slave owner had a right to not only use his slaves "for the sensual or rather beastly gratification of unnatural passions . . . but also legally to outrage the very laws of nature."[13] Although slavery may have officially ended in India in 1843, a book on that country's domestics published in 1960 noted that domestic slavery persisted there right into the 1940s, with female domestic slaves still being retained for sexual purposes.[14]

In the institution of American slavery one can see more clearly than in any other area the connection between sex and violence; the use of sexual harassment to degrade not just the women targeted but also their men; the connection between sex and misogyny; the complicity of their courts, which blamed "seductive" women; and the branding of helpless females as devoid of morals and as sexually promiscuous by the harassers and by white society in general. A slave owner's legal rights in America never extended to sanctioned sexual harassment and abuse of his slaves, as in India, but, as might be expected, both were rampant nonetheless. If the American slave owner did not have unlimited sexual rights over his slaves in law, he had them in fact. Due perhaps to the degree of control exercised over the victims, such harassment was particularly vicious and brutal.

That a large proportion of babies born to black slave women had white fathers was obvious to anyone who observed the scene. Traveling through the south in the 1850s, Frederick Law Olmstead, landscape architect and chief planner of New York's Central Park, noted that it was common on plantations to see slaves so white they could not be easily distinguished from whites. At a nursery he visited on one plantation Olmstead observed "some twenty or thirty infants and young children, a number of whom were evidently the offspring of white fathers." During his travels he saw about 100 reward-offering advertisements for runaway slaves described as being so white they could be mistaken for white people. An overseer told Olmstead he had never been on a plantation that did not have at least one such child.[15]

Figures from 1860 classified 10 percent of the slave population as mulatto, an estimate generally regarded as conservative. For the most part what occurred were the extreme forms of sexual harassment—rape and concubinage. However, it was the women who were blamed. Prevailing public sentiment was similar to that held by the plantation manager who told Olmstead that "negro girls are not remarkable for chastity."[16]

Writer Leslie Owen summarized the pervasiveness of this belief during the slave period by noting that even many scholars of later times who studied and wrote of the era doubted the morality of the slaves. Owen added, "Females have borne the brunt of unfavorable conjectures. Scores of mulatto children fathered by masters have been used to support arguments that bondswomen were indiscriminate in their selection of male sex partners." That the aggressive sexual acts of the planters against a population with no way to effectively resist might have been responsible for the rise in the mulatto population was rarely argued.[17]

Only with great difficulty and only infrequently did a black female slave manage to bring a white man into court on a charge of sexual abuse. That white planter or overseer had little to fear, however, for the courts maintained the fiction of promiscuous females. These courts assumed that slaves willingly participated in such liaisons. In 1850s Louisiana a court did note that "it is true, the female slave is particularly exposed . . . to the seductions of an unprincipled master. That is a misfortune; but it is so rare in the case of concubinage that the seduction and temptation are not mutual that exceptions to a general rule cannot be founded on it." Of these particular courts it has been reported that in such cases, "blame, when placed at all, was usually assigned to the 'seductiveness' of the bondswomen."[18]

The reality was that many slave women were driven and beaten without mercy. Some achieved relief only in return for sexual submission. One woman was suspended from a barn rafter and beaten with a horsewhip "nekkid 'til the blood ran down her back to her heels" because she repulsed the advances of a Virginia plantation overseer. Next to family separation this sexual violation of black females by white men was the foremost provocation inserted into black family life by the slaveholders. Women who did not submit might find themselves sold away from their families or whipped. The male partners of these women were well aware of the sexual harassment and abuse directed toward their mates. The resultant humiliation of black men was a reaction deliberately provoked in many cases. One Louisiana white man would enter a slave cabin telling the husband to go outside "til he do what he want to do." The black husband "had to do it and he couldn't do nothing 'bout it." Some husbands chose to run away rather than have to witness such horrors.[19]

Reverend Ishrael Massie, a former Virginia slave, when asked if whites associated with slave women, recalled, "Dat wuz common. Marsters an' overseers use to make slaves dat wuz wid their husbands git up, do as dey say. Send husbands out on de farm, milkin' cows or cuttin' wood. Den he gits in bed wid slave himself. Some women would fight an tussel. Others would be 'umble—feared of dat beatin'. What we saw, couldn't do nothing 'bout it. My blood is bilin' now at the thought of dem times. Ef dey told dey husband he wuz powerless."[20]

Harriet A. Jacobs was herself a slave during the period from her birth in 1813 until about 1840. Around 1825 she was sold into the household of a Dr. Flint, for whom she was a house slave in town. Flint owned a residence in town, several plantations, and about 50 slaves. One night Flint ordered a plantation slave brought to town and tied up in the work house while Flint ate supper. After a leisurely meal the doctor beat the slave mercilessly, with Jacobs hearing "hundreds of blows fall." The likely reason for the beating was that an overseer overheard the slave accuse his wife of giving birth to Flint's child. The slaves were very dark; the child was very fair. A few months later the pair was handed over to a slave trader, with Flint telling the mother, "You have let your tongue run too far; damn you." Jacobs wrote, "She had forgotten that it was a crime for a slave to tell who was the father of her child." In a different episode with a different master a young slave girl lay dying soon after giving birth to an almost white child. The slave owner's wife stood by mocking the expiring slave; "You suffer do you? I am glad of it. You deserve it all, and more too."

When Jacobs was 15 Flint "began to whisper foul words in my ear. . . . He peopled my young mind with unclean images, such as only a vile monster could think of. I turned from him with disgust and hatred." He told her she was made for his use, made to obey his command in everything. She noted that a slave had nowhere to turn to, that she had nothing to protect her from atrocities "inflicted by fiends who bear the shape of men," and that the owners' wives had no feelings toward the slave women "but those of jealousy and rage." Jacobs managed to escape coerced sex by Flint partly because he feared her grandmother, a free woman whom he thought might be able to make trouble for him, and partly because his wife, who watched him closely, foiled his bids to establish Jacobs in a cabin separate from other slaves and all the while despised Jacobs.[21]

Despite the overwhelming odds stacked against a black man in slavery, occasionally one would be unable to stand the pain and the hurt any longer. He would rise and resist. In 1859 a slave killed his overseer after being informed by his wife that she had been forced to have sex with the overseer. Most commonly the outcome was the reverse, as this remembrance of former Virginia slave Charles Grandy illustrated: "Dere was an' ole overseer too, what wanted one o' de slaves wife. Started bothern wid her right fo' de slave's face. De colored man made at him an' he shot 'im wid a gun. Den de colored man come at him wid a hoe. He kept shootin' 'til de man fall dead in his tracks. Nigger ain't got no chance." Although black men could not often resist, mulatto children were regularly scorned in the slave quarters, indicating the black community in general did not regard sexual abuse with equanimity.[22]

Former Virginia slave Robert Ellett recalled, "In those days if you was a slave and had a good looking daughter, she was taken from you. They would put her in the big house where the young masters could have the run of her." May Satterfield remembered, "Ma mama said that in dem times a nigger 'oman couldn't help herself, fo' she had to do what de marster say. Ef he come to de field whar de women workin' an' tell gal to come on, she had to go. He would take one down in de woods an' use her all de time he wanted to, den send her on back to work." One master brought his son to the cabin of slave Ethel Mae; both men raped the woman, with the father using the occasion to give his son his first sexual experience. Virginia Hayes Shepherd told of a slave named Diana who was harassed by her owner, Gaskins. After one of the times Diana fought him off, she complained to Mrs. Gaskins, who offered no help. Resisting once too often, Diana was auctioned off. When mistress Betty came upon her husband Ben preparing to sexually force himself on slave Fannie, the latter was sold off a week later.[23]

Lewis Clarke, a former Kentucky slave, related that his sister was called to the master's house at age 16. "When he sent for her again, she cried and didn't want to go." She complained to her mother, who told her to hold her head up above such things the best she could. The master got so angry at the fact that the girl complained to her mother that he immediately sold her off to Louisiana. Clarke heard later that his sister died there of hard usage. Madison Jefferson, a former slave from Virginia, recounted that "women who refuse to submit themselves to the brutal desires of their owners, are repeatedly whipt to subdue their virtuous repugnance, and in most instances this hellish practice is but too successful—when it fails, the women are frequently sold off to the south." This was a reference to the Deeper South, where work was primarily on cotton plantations. This work was considered harder and more killing than other work, such as on tobacco plantations in northern areas of the South.

Jefferson's master repeatedly beat a slave on his estate for refusing his advances, finally accomplishing his purpose "while she was in a state of insensibility from the effects of a felon blow inflicted by this monster." Thomas Likers, onetime bondsman in Maryland, remembered that his owner Ben Kidd was in the habit of meeting his slaves in the barn to sexually abuse them. "He generally carried a white oak cane, one end very heavy, and if the women did not submit, he would think nothing of knocking them right down." When a Missouri master found his 18-year-old slave to be pregnant by him, he tied her up and whipped her in an attempt to produce a miscarriage. Often the master's wife was as cruel as the master. An Alabama slave recalled being regularly whipped by the master, sometimes at the behest of his wife, who manufactured situations—for example, putting cow hairs into the butter that the slave had churned—to justify the demand that the slave be beaten. When asked if the master had harmed this slave in other ways, she admitted to having borne five children by him. "I didn't want him, but I couldn't do nothin'. I uster say 'What do you want of a woman all cut ter pieces like I is?' But 'twant no use." In this case the wife may have been taking out her anger against her husband by setting up and orchestrating attacks on the slave.[24]

A former slave from Tennessee said, "Old Buford, his darkies had chillun by him, and mammy wouldn't do it; and I've seen him take a paddle with holes in it and beat her." Looking over a slave childhood, the worst whipping John Finnelly recollected was one given to slave woman Clarinda after she hit the master with a hoe while trying to stop him from sexually abusing her.[25]

Emancipation brought little relief from sexual harassment for black women, whether they sharecropped or worked for wages. Some former slaves registered charges of being sexually abused by white men with the Freedmen's Bureau, an agency set up in the 1860s to assist blacks soon after emancipation. Scilla Gedders told the Monck's Corner, South Carolina, bureau that Warren Carson, the white man who managed the farm on which she worked had attempted to rape her in the fields. Jane Harris complained that a white man had beaten her after she had resisted his sexual advances on a farm. During the summer and fall of 1865 the Murfreesboro, Tennessee, bureau received three separate complaints from former slaves against Andrew B. Payne. Sam Neal stated that "Payne hired myself and family altogether to work for the season. He has made several attempts on my daughter; has ordered me off without pay or share of my crop." When Neal refused to leave the land, Payne recruited Miles Ferguson to help him badly beat Neal. Each of them was ordered to pay Neal $25, with Neal also being allowed to gather the crop and keep his share. A woman named Tabby Wheatley and her daughter were both beaten by Payne and Ferguson when the daughter resisted Payne's sexual advances. The same thing happened to former slave Maria Posey in a separate incident. Nathan Sweeney complained to the bureau that the son of his employer had raped his daughter. Sweeney and his family then quit the farm. John Wright of Greenville, South Carolina, lodged a complaint in 1868 with the bureau against his employer, Robin Craig. Wright had contracted to work Craig's land for half the crop but was driven off the land by Craig less than two months later without crop or money because, said Wright, Craig and his two sons "were after his wife."[26]

Whereas sharecropping was dangerous enough work for black women, working for wages under whites was even worse. At least with sharecropping there was less direct white supervision, and a woman's family was usually nearby to offer some protection. Black men in tobacco-growing regions as well as Cotton Belt freedmen "preferred that their womenfolk not perform field work for wages under the direct supervision of whites." Also relying heavily on wage workers was the Louisiana sugar industry. One such sugar plantation owner in 1888 noted in his diary that women working for wages (as opposed to sharecropping) remained vulnerable to rape and other forms of sexual abuse at the hands of white men. Speaking of his own assistant overseer, his owner wrote, "Young Turcuit is very objectionable from his goings on with the colored women on the place."[27]

With the passage of years little change took place. In the Durham, North Carolina, area of the 1930s the more successful of the white farmers and tenants affirmed in their minds their claim to positions of superiority by hiring black females as domestic labor and field hands and "regarding them as sexual prey."[28]

With little money to buy land of their own, blacks were forced into one system or the other, usually wage work since that was what the overclass needed the most. Between 1916 and 1921 blacks moved north in unprecedented numbers. It was a huge migration, with an estimated 5 percent of the total southern black population heading north. It was more than the aggregate number for the preceding 40 years. Interviews at the time showed the reasons for the migration to be varied and to include low wages, lack of educational opportunities for black children, and "the degraded status of [black men's] womenfolk.... Husbands told of sexual harassment of wives and daughters by white men and of other forms of indignities woven into the fabric of southern society."[29]

Slavery in Brazil followed a pattern similar to that found in the United

States. Women were viewed by society as loose and immoral. As an additional abuse Brazilian slaves were often forced to prostitute themselves. Around 1700 Italian Jesuit friar Jorge Benci condemned Brazilian masters for establishing "friendships" with their slave girls, adding, "And is it not much worse yet, and more abominable, to compel her by the use of force to consent to her master's sin, and to punish her when she resists and seeks to avoid this offense against God?" In his travels around Brazil Benci found that many owners forced their slave women to provide for the house. For example, one would be required to supply the bread, another the meat, and so on. As these slaves had no money, Benci noted, "where should it come from, except from sin and the wanton use of their bodies?"[30]

Over 150 years later prostitution remained a serious form of sexual exploitation of Brazilian slave women. As historian Robert Conrad noted, "Many Brazilian towns contained notorious districts where demoralized and physically ravaged slave women offered themselves to the public, no doubt often against their will." In 1871 municipal judge Miguel Jose Tavares wrote to the Rio de Janeiro police chief about this problem, saying, "There has been an increase in the public protests in this city against the immoral scandal of slave women prostituting themselves either by order or with the express consent of their masters, from which the latter gain exorbitant profits. These unfortunate women are forced to satisfy the hellish greed of these masters by practicing acts that are exceedingly offensive to public morality, presenting themselves at windows semi-nude."[31]

The legal system did nothing about the forced prostitution of slaves or about a master's assault on one of his own slaves. In 1882 owner Henriques Ferreira Pontes was accused by his 12-year-old slave Honorata of having "deflowered" her. He was then a known molestor of young black girls. The rape took place on the very day he purchased the child from her previous owner. Slaves older than 16 had essentially no rights, whereas minors could theoretically seek legal protection and redress in cases such as this. Ferreira never denied the charge in court but defended himself by stating that the court had no right to involve itself in a case where a master had deflowered his slave woman. The court held he should be tried. But the trial court ruled in his favor by declaring there was no proof that Honorata was younger than 17 and therefore a minor, this despite medical testimony to the absence of pubic hair, undeveloped breasts, and less than fully developed genitals, which assured doctors she was 11 to 13 years old. The police official who charged Ferreira in this case reported the master had attempted to deflower a young girl four years previously. Two years after that the master deflowered a little mulatto girl. The police official did not indict Ferreira in either of those cases but did when he was accused by Honorata because by then the official had become an abolitionist. A couple of years after this case Brazil abolished slavery.[32]

3

Domestic Servants

In theory domestic servants were not as badly off as indentured servants, slaves, or serfs since they were not legally owned either for a period of time or for life. In practice domestics were subjected to sexual harassment almost as much as any slave, and attempts at redress did little to improve their status. The idea that domestics caused trouble, that they led men on, and that they were promiscuous was already firmly established in the 1600s and 1700s. The victim was blamed for initiating the harassment and then blamed and punished for the consequences. This blaming the victim became the dominant ideology and was applied to all females in the workplace and elsewhere as well. It became a principal way in which the male overclass dealt with the problem, whether it was rape in the street or sexual harassment. The first-used line of defense, of course, was denial. The problem did not exist. When denial could not be used—as, for example, with rape in the street—the next line of male defense was to blame the victim. It happens, said the overclass, but it is the fault of females provoking it somehow. The male perpetrators were cast as the real "victims," helplessly ensnared by plotting females.

Whether it was an English domestic servant in the 1600s or Anita Hill appearing before a congressional inquiry in 1991, somehow the female involved was inevitably made to shoulder the blame. After all women were sexually voracious. Blaming the victim still works to some degree, and many females believe it. Person-in-the-street interviews appearing on television during the Clarence Thomas hearings confirmed that. When a female is, for example, subjected to sexual harassment, it is just as likely for another woman to see the victim as somehow different than to think, "It could have been me." Such responses markedly lower the likelihood of females banding together as a solid unit to protest.

During the 1600s in England there was an unnamed married couple that could never agree on a maid because the wife refused to accept a pretty one, while the husband would have no other kind. A compromise was reached when he agreed to accept a "liquorish" girl, hoping "to have a lick at her honeypot." When later she was found drinking her employer's wine in the cellar, he forced her to submit to his advances under threat of sending her to prison for theft. The earl of Sussex ordered six of his housemaids to dance naked. Only one refused. When the earl's wife pressed this housemaid to comply, she immediately quit. The Stuart royal family, which ruled England from 1603 to 1714, was reported to have "debauched their own and everybody else's servants."[1]

One historian of this period noted that society "expected pretty young women to put old gentlemen to bed and could hardly complain if the morals of pretty young women suffered in the process." Handbooks of the time for serving maids warned them that the master of the house and his sons were liable "to fall foul on the wench in the scullery." To reduce these risks domestics were urged "to discount the flatteries of gentlemen, to beware of idleness, wanton looks and gestures, to wear no bright ribbons, feathers or other inducements to lust."[2]

Writer Daniel Defoe made his position clear on domestics when he wrote, "Many good families are impoverished and disgraced by these pert sluts who, taking the advantage of a young man's simplicity and unruly desires, draw many heedless youths, nay, some of good estates, into their snares." Defoe had no doubt of the link between servants and prostitution, writing, "Many of 'em rove from place to place, from bawdy-house to service and from service to bawdy-house again . . . nothing being more common than to find these creatures one week in a good family and the next in a brothel." Jonathan Swift was less misogynistic on the subject, giving servants the following advice: "I must caution you particularly against my Lord's eldest son. . . . After ten thousand promises you will get nothing from him, but a big belly or a clap, and probably both together." With tongue in cheek Swift advised domestics to allow their masters no liberties unless they were paid extra, starting with 1 guinea for holding hands, to 5 guineas for fondling of the breasts, to 100 guineas for sexual intercourse.[3]

Infanticide was a major problem for these domestics, just as it was for the indentured servants in America. Given that these women were subject to rape by their employers, lacked effective birth control methods, and would usually be summarily fired if they had a child, infanticide became an obvious solution. These women would try to conceal their pregnancy, give birth, murder the child, and be back at work within a few hours.

When Defoe tied domestics to prostitution, he seemed to imply that this was by choice, that it was due to their "slutty" nature. In turn this allowed him to blame these servants for vamping the master of the house. What Defoe did not consider, or perhaps did not want to consider, was the enormous power wielded by the employer. In addition to being fired for sex activity, a servant was often fired for totally trivial reasons, on a whim of the master. There was no redress against this and virtually none against employer rape. In the space of an hour a servant could find herself out of a job, with very likely little or no money saved from an inadequate salary. Not only did she lose her job, but in that same hour she also lost her living quarters — the vast majority of servants were live-in. Often she may have turned to prostitution not due to her "promiscuous" nature but due to the nature of an economic order structured by the male overclass that wanted the institution of prostitution and orchestrated the societal order to ensure it existed. Employers looked at the matter differently. As one source noted, once the servant had been dismissed, the employer "thought nothing more of her; if she later heard that the girl had exchanged hunger for prostitution it was easy to assume that she had a natural disposition to vice."[4]

Despite the enormous odds against obtaining justice in the legal system, domestics did sometimes prosecute their employers for rape. Anna Clark studied court records of sexual assault in England during the period 1700–1799. She found that 29 percent of London rapes and 9 percent of the northeast assize cases involved masters and servants. Clark thought the difference in percentages was due to the relative labor shortage in London, making it easier to get another job, whereas "in rural areas, a woman could be blacklisted and never find another place if she dared protest a rape." Even though a number of domestics did not accept their masters' right to sexually harass and abuse them, juries did. In all of the cases examined by Clark not one master was punished for raping his servant.[5]

In 1772 Sarah Bishop, who was 16, told her mistress that her master, publican George Carter, had raped her. The woman told Sarah, "He always served all his servants on the night they came into the house." Jeremiah Amenet was tried for raping his 13-year-old apprentice Mary Martin, who had immediately told neighboring women about the attack. A midwife testified that the girl had been ill-used. Despite this Amenet was found not guilty on the strength of testimony by his friends as to his "good character." After raping a 16-year-old servant in the late 1700s, William Hodge boasted of the deed to his neighbors. The judge summed up the acquittal of Hodge by commenting, "It is a very brutal thing, for which this fellow deserves to be punished in a way more severe than he has been, or will be; to be sure, taking any method to persuade a girl, his servant, of this age, in his house, under his protection, he having a wife and three children, one cannot assume anything more brutal and beastly than his conduct, but as to a rape there is no pretence."[6]

For French domestics in the 1700s, one writer stated, "the most abiding threat that a female servant faced was sexual. . . . Once a woman was known to have lost her virtue, whether willingly or not, her chances of finding a husband were destroyed or at least seriously curtailed." French domestics were often accused of prostitution and were assumed to carry on affairs with their masters. They were often insulted by men in the streets, who shouted remarks such as "I know her; I want my share" as they passed by.[7]

The idea that servants were promiscuous was equally pervasive in America. A 1790s observer of Philadelphia noted of the free white servants he saw, "They are usually libertines and there are hardly any women servants in Philadelphia who could not be enjoyed for a very small sum."[8]

Domestic work was always looked down on as an occupation. (It remains a low-status job today.) Partly this was due to the nature of the work, which consisted mainly of cooking, cleaning, and child tending, pursuits that were traditionally unpaid labor done by housewives for no direct remuneration. Also involved were the long hours of work, the infrequent time off, and the lack of privacy, as most domestic servants were live-in employees, at least until well into this century. All of this gave the employer enormous power over the domestic, including power to sexually harass and abuse her. Throughout the 1800s and early 1900s female chastity remained important. The loss of virginity in an unmarried female was of more concern to a woman than it is today. A woman in that circumstance faced a diminished chance of being married. If a servant had a baby, no matter what the circumstances of conception might have been, she continued to face a likely termination of employment as well as a loss of housing. Given a choice between factory work and domestic service, most women opted for the former despite its marked shortcomings. In a book on domestics David Katzman noted of the period 1865 to 1918, "The one area of great power of men over servants was in sexual contact. . . . The success of the master or of other men of the household in using a maid as a sexual object reflected the powerlessness of servant girls. Afraid of dismissal, some submitted to private indignities." This was true both before and after the period of time that Katzman dealt with.[9]

Despite the obvious inequities in the master-servant relationship, or more likely because of them, the domestic remained widely viewed as loose and promiscuous. Established in several cities in 1904 was a women's group called the Inter-Municipal Committee on Household Research to Study the Servant Situation. One of the committee members argued that employers needed to be protected from their servants, claiming that the effects of "promiscuous mingling" on the ships that brought immigrants to North America, in the boarding houses, and in employment offices created situations in which "the girl passes from these surroundings with their increment of dishonesty, promiscuousness and vice directly into the presence of an American family. . . . Since she . . . becomes a member of our households, it is a grave question as to how far the atmosphere of lax morality which she brings with her may extend."[10]

David Sutherland noted that in the early 1900s charges of theft were often raised by masters against their servants but that "a more serious charge against female servants was sexual immorality and . . . sexual promiscuity. Servant girls had reputations as flirts."[11]

When the U.S. Congress studied the conditions of female and child wage earners in 1910, one aspect studied was the relationship between occupation and criminality of women. With regard to "offenses against chastity," the study concluded that domestics made a poor showing. Mostly, the study decided, it was because many of the domestics were "of too low grade to be employed elsewhere." Nevertheless, so many succumbed to these vices, including a "number of better-class servants," that the investigators were forced to consider other possibilities. One of these was that "if the men of her employer's family have any desire to mislead her, her position makes it peculiarly easy to do so, while if the girl herself happens to be one of the moral imbeciles before discussed, her position likewise gives her peculiar opportunities for spreading moral contagion." Overall, however, congressional investigators concluded that "the dangers lay not so much in the work itself . . . as in the kind of women who are likely to enter such occupations."[12]

Much was made of the purported connection between prostitution and servants in these later periods, with some studies claiming that one third to one half of prostitutes had first been domestic servants. Even though this connection may have been true, it resulted from economic pressures placed on a domestic who had lost both job and home when she had been terminated. Those who cited such connections implied it showed servants to be inherently promiscuous and used it as proof of the lack of morality on the part of domestics. In cities like New York up to two thirds of servants were hired through employment agencies, which were often unscrupulous places that sent unsuspecting women to houses of prostitution instead of regular domestic work. Between 1904 and 1907 in New York 14 such agencies had their licenses revoked for sending women to brothels and "immoral places."[13]

England harbored the same view of servants as America did, seeing them as loose and blameworthy. Around 1850 one writer complained that in small families the servants often gave themselves up to the sons. He concluded that "female servants are far from being a virtuous class." In 1889 Charles Booth, famous for his tome *Life and Labour in London*, wondered about servants in that a "curious feature is the frequency with which girls will run away from their places instead of giving notice of leaving." This is a normal response to an incident of extreme harassment for which the victim realizes there will be no redress and likely future episodes. However, all a puzzled Booth could offer as a reason was that this flight was due "to a feeling of alarm at the formality of giving notice."[14]

Sometime earlier in that country between 1800 and 1830, servant Isabella Roberts, aged 14, complained that her master, Cornelius Hancock, had attempted to kiss her while she poured out his tea for him at the table. When Roberts told her mother about this, Hancock fired the girl. The matter

ended up in court, where Hancock explained himself by telling the magistrate, "I owe there was some little liberty taken, I pulled her on my knee
and kissed her . . . but . . . she is a very loose girl." Masters, male servants,
and boarders all knew they were unlikely to suffer any consequences as a
result of their sexual attacks because females thought twice about complaining to their mistresses lest they found themselves fired for immorality.
If a servant accused somebody of rape, she immediately labeled herself as
"unchaste." This "spoiled her character" for future employment opportunities, not to mention diminishing her marriage prospects. All of this
could transpire even when the rape charge was true and the female shown
to be blameless. Isolated in homes by class position, servants were particularly vulnerable to sexual harassment.[15]

Another teenager faced sexual harassment in Dedham, England, in
1851. When she heard that an elderly gentleman from Dedham was looking
for a companion for his sister, the 19-year-old Louisa May Alcott, then unknown and in need of money, took the position. The employer, lawyer
James Richardson, assured her she would be one of the family and would
be required only to help out with the lighter work around the house in addition to her main duties as companion to his sister. As it turned out he
harassed her by inviting her into his study. His attentions intensified as he
plied her with poems while she washed the dishes. He left a stream of notes
under her door. Unable to stand this any longer, Alcott confronted Richardson, reminding him that she was hired as companion to his sister, not
to him. Retaliation was swift: all the household work was suddenly assigned
to her. Louisa was required to shovel a path through the snow, bring water
from the well, chop up the kindling, and take out the ashes. The last straw
came when she was ordered to polish Richardson's muddy boots. After
seven weeks on this job Alcott quit. She used this incident in one of her
stories and of course went on to international fame by writing works such
as *Little Women*.[16]

Women who spent part of their lives as domestics in Germany during
the period 1840s–1880s routinely reported the danger of rape by their employers. Anna Mosegard left three jobs in a row after being the victim of
unwanted sexual advances from her masters. Angela Langer told of being
driven from a well-paid post as a governess because she refused to comply
with her employer's sexual demands. Despite these reports the bourgeois
press of Germany sang the same old universal song when it persisted in
reporting "the threat to the morality of children that the employment of
servants represented."[17]

While the ruling class spread the fiction that servants tempted and
lured their sons, the reality was the reverse. In the late 1800s Juliet Sauget
left her impoverished rural French family for a hoped for better life in
Paris. Shortly after starting her first job as a domestic, she complained one

night at supper that the family's teenage son had come into her room with the intention of having sex with her. The family just laughed in reply. Juliet quit. About the same time and from the same kind of background Marie Renard journeyed to Paris, where she quickly got a job as a servant. Soon Renard asked her employers for a key to her room. When asked why she explained it was to protect herself from the advances of the family's teenage son. The request was denied. The son came to her room again and forced her to have sex with him even though she tried to prevent him. Forced intercourse continued after that occasion, with the result that Renard became pregnant within four months of her arrival in Paris. Often a servant had a room that could not be locked. Even if it could—in any country—it was rare for the servant to have a key.[18]

With servants becoming pregnant in all countries, observers sometimes commented on this fact but generally expressed their surprise. In England circa 1890 professional do-gooder Dinah Mulock Craik and her Victorian friends could only conclude that "stranger still to account for is, that women who thus fall are by no means the worst of their station." Nearly a century later when the Craik account appeared in a 1979 *Feminist Studies* article by John Gillis, he came to the bizarre and overclass-serving conclusion that of the 1800s period, "although exploitation of servant girls by their masters appears to have been far from common, nevertheless, the lecherous employer or rakish lodger did present a danger."[19]

Perhaps the best known case of servant abuse was that of Hester Vaughan (sometimes Vaughn). It combined every element: sexual abuse; pregnancy; loss of job, home and income; death of a child; and punishment of the servant. Every misfortune hit the hapless woman. However, there was a reasonably happy ending in this case but only because the servant's abuse coincided with a brief period of militant feminism. Vaughan was an English immigrant who arrived full of hope in Pennsylvania, where she took a job as a domestic. Her employer forced her into having sex soon thereafter. Hester became pregnant, which led to her employer firing her. Without money or family the physically ailing Vaughan gave birth alone in an unheated room and was found, still very ill, three days later with a dead child. Nothing indicated that the infant had died from an act of commission on Vaughan's part. She was likely unconscious or at least too ill to care for the child, who expired for that reason plus being in an unheated room. Nevertheless, the woman was arrested, convicted of infanticide, and sentenced to death in Philadelphia. The year was 1868. The feminist newspaper *The Revolution*, started by Elizabeth Cady Stanton and Susan B. Anthony and published from 1868 to 1871, heard of the case and took up Vaughan's cause. In editorials the paper condemned a system of sexual and economic oppression that would put her in such circumstances and then convict her of them. The Working Women's Association sent a delegation to visit her in prison. Stanton personally visited the Pennsylvania governor to lobby for a pardon, which was ultimately granted. After the Working Women's Association raised the money for the fare, the penniless Vaughan was returned to her family in England. *The Revolution* saw infanticide as an example not of women's depravity but of women's insubordinate relation to men, which made them, among other things, subject to sexual abuse due to the economic blackmail of employment.[20]

One of the few contemporary writers who clearly understood the situation a century ago was Helen Campbell, who in 1887 published an investigative report of working conditions of females in the United States. She wrote, "Household service has become synonymous with the worst degradation that comes to women." Servants themselves felt, Campbell said, "that only here and there is a young girl safe, and that domestic service is the cover for more licentiousness than can be found in any other trade in which women are at work."[21]

This view of servants as promiscuous was the popular image of an outgroup. Such images are not a function of the outgroup's characteristics but more a function of the way the overclass wishes to see that group and wishes it to be seen by society in general. Illustrating this is a comparison between black servants in the United States and Northern Rhodesia. In America it has always been the black male who has been portrayed as sexually hyperactive. Yet in Northern Rhodesia (now Zambia) circa 1910 it was the black female who was viewed as oversexed and aggressive, lacking in any moral code. So pervasive was this view that black females were almost never employed as house servants there, in comparison house servants in the United States were almost always females, while black men were field servants and outside slaves, partly due to the "oversexed" nature of black men. In Northern Rhodesia the idea of oversexed black males did not exist; they were viewed more as large, simple children. It was said to be axiomatic that "an Englishman neither marries, employs, nor befriends an African woman."

This ideology developed as a sort of check against the wholesale sexual abuse of black women that was taking place. Writer Karen Hansen noted that most white men did not keep African women on a long-term basis but that "most white men took African women in the way they had taken everything else, land and labour, and when it was not forthcoming, then by force." White men took black females out of their villages against their will, sometimes coercing a village chief to part with one woman or sometimes sending out their houseboys to use their powers of persuasion or coercion to procure one. By keeping black women out of the house as servants, these white men could more easily maintain the fiction that nothing was going on and claim that they actually showed their virtuous nature by officially barring the house door to these oversexed black women. Whether a group such as black males is regarded as being oversexed, as having a singleminded determination to sexually possess white women, as in the United States; or as being asexual children perfectly safe to have around the house, as in much of Africa, not just Northern Rhodesia, depended on the needs and wants of the overclass and not on the behavior of the group and its members.[22]

Once in a while a master was punished for abusing his servant. In 1818 in Hinckley, England, a "man of property" was convicted of administering the drug laudanum to the governess of his three daughters with the view to "rendering her subservient to his passions." He was fined £100 and jailed for 12 months. Twenty-five years later near Broadway, England, a farmer was ordered to pay £300 to the father of his 14-year-old governess, whom the farmer had raped in reply to her query about what he wanted for supper. By way of defense the farmer claimed the girl was guilty of "conduct as shameless as would have disgraced a cyprian in the Metropolis."[23]

Mostly, however, there was no justice for servants in any country. William Avery Rockefeller was born around 1809. On July 23, 1849, the court in Auburn, New York, indicted Rockefeller for rape on the basis of evidence furnished by victim Anne Vanderbeak, a hired girl in the Rockefeller household. Allegedly the incident took place in 1848 on the Rockefeller estate at Moravia, New York. At the time Rockefeller's son John D. Rockefeller was ten years old. Getting tipped off in advance, the elder Rockefeller fled Moravia a few hours ahead of a sheriff on his way to make the arrest. As Rockefeller took pains to stay out of the jurisdiction of this court for years, the case never came to trial. Many historians of the family do not believe this story—but then women are rarely believed. If Rockefeller was not guilty, why did he run? And why did he stay away for years? Adding support to the idea that something ugly happened at that time was the hostility shown him then by his father-in-law, John Davison. He brought suit against Rockefeller for a $1,200 debt and early in 1850 changed his will to place Eliza's (his daughter and William's wife) share of his estate in the hands of trustees.[24]

When missionary Sidney Gulick traveled through Japan in the early 1910s, he observed the condition of Japanese domestics who worked in hotels, teahouses, and restaurants. A provincial chief of police told Gulick that the police considered 75 percent of these women to be prostitutes. In return for working from 4 or 5 A.M. to midnight, these women were given food, two dresses a year, and a small amount of cash, but principal earnings were expected to come from tips. At the poorest of these establishments the women did not have a private room but were forced to sleep in reception rooms and entryways. It was reported that "few traveling men in Japan feel any special hesitation in taking advantage—with financial compensation of course—of such opportunities afforded them." One of these servants rushed into Gulick's room one day to escape the advances of a guest. She had worked there for only one week but was going to quit as she found it all unendurable.[25]

An 1898 writer spoke to a number of adolescent boys in Toronto, Canada, who claimed to have had sexual relations with the domestic servants working in their homes. One boy claimed that over the previous five years he had slept with every domestic employed by his father.[26]

In America in the 1880s there was a domestic who worked in a boardinghouse. One boarder kept after her but got nowhere until "one Sunday when she was alone in the house and none to hear or help, he had his will." When the owner of this boardinghouse heard about what had happened, she fired the servant, exclaiming, "Such things don't happen unless the girl is to blame."[27]

During the middle of the 19th century Elizabeth Blackwell, the first woman medical doctor, worked in a Philadelphia almshouse, where she found that "most of the women are unmarried, a large proportion having lived at service and been seduced by their masters, though, on the whole, about as many seducers are unmarried as married." In Elmira, New York, a rescue and rehabilitation organization for young women named the Anchorage found much the same story, "In the privacy of their records, the Anchorage administrators recorded a number of cases when girls came to them from service pregnant and named a member of the employing family as the father." Using a word such as seducer was a circumspect way of dealing with the issue as it left open the idea of consent. In most cases forced sex or rape was a more appropriate label for the activity than seduction. Use of such words greatly mitigated the employer's responsibility, changing his image from that of a power-abusing, violent assaulter to a more innocuous, irresistible Don Juan.[28]

Other charitable institutions were aware of what was happening but chose to do nothing. In the period 1870–1900 several private asylums in Boston, Massachusetts, including the Boston Female Asylum, looked after orphaned or otherwise needy children. By the time girls in the asylums' care reached 15 or so, they were sent out for a period of years to work as domestic servants in private households that had put in requests to these asylums for maids. At these asylums only domestic skills were taught to the female inmates. In one of these places a staff member volunteered to teach the girls bookkeeping as an extra or her own time as she felt it was a better skill to have. This request was denied by the administration on the grounds that it would "encroach" on some of her time that was due the others. This institution also refused to teach the girls typing as "it would unfit them for domestic services." When placement of the girls was made, it was often followed by problems. Sometimes the condition of the family changed, affecting the girl. "More often, however, the Asylum was to make an error in judgment about the man of the house, later to be upset by complaints of his sexual advances to the girl." Records were filled with complaints of sexual misconduct by the husband, or sons, of the employing family. As a result a girl often had to be moved from one job to another anywhere from four to eight times during her adolescence. In at least one case the employing husband and wife complained about their servant Lizzie's "gross immorality" with their own children. Recognizing that her wrongdoing was the result of "the bad influence and bad practices" of the man to whom she was formerly bound, the couple urged criminal action against him. But as the asylum had no proof against this man and only Lizzie's word to go on, its administrators "did not feel they could interfere in the matter."[29]

Mary Findlay worked as a live-in domestic in New Zealand during the 1930s. When she was in her room one night almost undressed for bed, her employer, Mr. Mitchell, came in and tried to have sex with her, telling her, "Don't fight m'dear. All the girls love me. Servants should be obedient to their masters. I've had every girl who ever worked here." Another time she was employed by a dentist who promised to double her wages if she would have sex with him. She fled without her pay and told her father, who went and had it out with the dentist and demanded her pay. Said Findlay, "Oh, yes. Girls had it expected of them. To get extra money or to keep their jobs." Wages were so low that some men reasoned their servants would be glad to make a little extra by submitting to sex along with the household chores.[30]

In that same decade the British government steered women toward domestic servant jobs at the expense of other employment, which they had been pushed out of after World War I. Young girls from depressed areas became servants in London and other large English cities. According to a group organized to protect individual rights, the National Vigilance Association (NVA), they faced moral dangers. The records of that group, said one observer, "make harrowing reading and reveal how misleading job advertisements turned out to be when the girl arrived." One girl from South Wales arrived at a bachelor's home in the Midlands to find only a see-through partition separating her "bedroom" from his and a nude photograph on her side of the partition. NVA workers frequently had to rescue young women from exploitative households and send them home by train.[31]

Although in the American south white servants did face sexual harassment from their employers, for southern black women sexual harassment was a major problem. Blacks of both sexes were outspoken in calling this a major abuse of the southern caste system. Domestic work compounded male sexual abuse since it placed black females even more directly under white power within a system that condoned white male–black female relations. Writing in 1898, W. E. B. DuBois told of black hatred for domestic work, saying, "Parents hate to expose . . . their daughters to the ever-possible fate of concubinage." At the same time a middle-class black woman stated, "There is no sacrifice I would not make, no hardship I would not undergo rather than allow my daughters to go in service where they will be thrown constantly in contact with Southern white men for they considered the colored girl their special prey."[32]

A white woman sexually abused at work could only rarely expect any justice. A black woman could expect even less. A Georgia servant tried to resist the sexual advances of her employer in 1912 and later told her husband about the incident. Confronting the tormentor, this black man found himself cursed and slapped by the white employer and then arrested. The presiding judge fined the black man $25 after stating, "This court will never take the word of a nigger against the word of a white man."[33]

Little changed for black domestics over the years. Verta Mae, a servant, published a book in 1972 detailing her experiences and those of her friends as servants. She wrote, "I remember many stories from Black women who talked of how 'the mister' of the house would bother them." Her friend Carolyn worked for a rich southern family. One time she got an odd feeling about a party and decided not to work it for her employers. The next day Carolyn heard that one of the maids had been raped by a male guest who had got drunk and "had to have a black woman." Mae's cousin Zipporah was sent at age 13 to fill in as a servant for one day to replace her ailing mother. She arrived home earlier than expected, crying, saying the man of the house had tried to rape her. Her mother's first words were, "Child, for God's sake, don't tell your father. You'll get him kilted." To Mae the mother said, "What could a poor Black man do legally or physically to a rich white man who had tried to molest his daughter? What could he do and get away with—alive?" The father was never told about the attempted rape.[34]

In Canada in 1979 one case investigated by the Canadian Advisory Council on the Status of Women was that of a 32-year-old Jamaican woman domestic whose household duties included having sexual intercourse with her Ottawa employer. From this resulted a pregnancy and an abortion. Nevertheless, the woman refused to report her employer and remained in the household. Like many others from Third World countries, she needed the income to send home to her children in Jamaica.[35]

A survey of nonwhite domestics in Toronto, Canada, in the 1980s found that most would refuse to work for a single male employer. One woman spent just four months on a job because the employer's brother would go into her basement room and harass her with promises that he would make his sister give her a raise if she would have sex with him. "I was crying all the time cause I had a feeling that my employer knew about it," she said. A second was harassed by the husband of the family and finally quit when she could not stand any more of his grabbing her and his dirty jokes. When she left she told the wife she was leaving because she was not happy with the pay. Yet another maid was pawed by the husband but refrained from telling the wife because "I did not know what she'll do." Rina Cohen, who conducted the survey, perhaps recognizing the powerlessness of domestics, could offer them no solutions and concluded that "avoidance probably has only a temporary effect and quitting might be the only ultimate solution for a sexually exploited woman domestic worker."[36]

In America Margo Townsend was the director of a support and training program for domestics of all colors in the early 1970s. When one of the domestics complained to her about being sexually harassed by the husband of her employer, Townsend called and explained the problem to the wife, who replied, "What do you think I brought her up here for?" Asked how often sexual harassment happened to women in this program, Margo replied, "It happened to a number of women in our program, mainly to the live-in help. That's why people want to get out." Judith Rollins interviewed a number of domestics in the 1980s, finding they preferred to work for women. The reason given was "the risk of sexual advances from male employers. Most domestics were reluctant to expand on brief remarks like, 'Men tend to get fresh'." One woman elaborated by saying, "And I don't work for any more men. I've tried it a couple of times with these men. They don't seem to act right." An 18-year-old live-in domestic in Alabama, Elizabeth Roy, explained, "The old man was rough.... The reason I left—they had a bad teenage son who was roguish and mean and I didn't trust him. He and the husband made advances. But I didn't report it; I just left.... They were in my room constantly. They'd come in when the wife would leave. I felt very uneasy."[37]

Kimberly Scothorn, who ran a placement agency, Nannies of Georgia, said that 20 percent of nannies who contacted her had been sexually harassed on the job. Mexican nanny Alma Mujica won a paternity suit against her former employer, Ron Lapin, a Santa Ana, California, physician. Lapin's attorney commented, "At the time [Mujica] was a fairly attractive young woman. So this isn't surprising, human nature being what it is." Eighteen-year-old nanny Rebecca McCloud was fresh from Utah when on the night of July 6, 1991, she was horrified to find a hidden video camera pointing at her in the shower in Malden, Massachusetts. She went to the police and filed a suit against her employer, eight-term Democratic representative John C. McNeil. This led to an investigation that resulted in the November 1992 indictment of McNeil for allegedly videotaping another former nanny engaged in sexual acts with his teenage godson. When Deborah Rocks arrived in the United States in 1983 as an 18-year-old from Ireland, she immediately started work for Bill and Maureen Civitello as nanny and housecleaner in their affluent Long Island suburban home. Her salary of $50 a week was paid only sporadically, with the Civitellos always claiming they did not have the money, although Maureen Civitello took an extended European vacation during Rocks's employment. Bill Civitello began to force himself sexually on Rocks at the end of the first year. It was the first of many such instances. Rocks told no one, feeling ashamed and worried she would lose her job and be tossed into the street. At the time she had no friends or contacts in America. A 1985 visit to New York City to see a friend visiting from Ireland led her to contact the expatriate Irish community, which led a few months later to a new nanny job. When she left the Civitellos they still owed her $950 in salary, of which they eventually paid $300. Rocks had felt disempowered, embarrassed, alone, and isolated. In 1993 she said, "Looking back, I think, 'You should have done something!' But back then it was different. I was numb. I thought there was nothing I could do." That same year Civitello, then in California, denied all the allegations. Federal antidiscrimination law applied only to a workplace of 15 or more employees, which excluded virtually all domestics. In New York State human rights legislation that prohibited both sexual harassment and discrimination specifically excluded domestic workers.[38]

The plight of domestic workers employed in the households of foreign diplomats in Washington, D.C., came to public light at the end of the 1970s. Servants working for American employers had little enough protection; these women had even less. Many of them were modern-day indentured servants held as virtual prisoners of the diplomats. These women entered the United States legally on diplomatic passports as employees of embassies and other international organizations. American authorities did not want to hear about their problems, leaving the matter to the foreign governments involved. For one thing the United States did not want to offend another country. Besides workdays of 12 to 19 hours, low pay, beatings, and so on, these women were sexually abused. Rita fled her embassy after being sexually molested by the ambassador. The ambassador falsely reported to the police that she had stolen $2,000 and asked that she be found and deported. In 1977 a woman from the Philippines came to America to work in a foreign diplomat's household. During her nine months on the job she was paid a total of $170—instead of the promised $200 a month—and threatened with deportation when she resisted her employer's sexual advances.[39]

In Third World countries the situation for servants was bleaker still. Many women from the Philippines migrated to other countries to work as domestics in the 1980s. Saudi Arabia had a reputation of being particularly bad in terms of the level of sexual abuse to be expected. Sexual harassment was also reported to abound in Singapore and Hong Kong.[40]

Of the situation in Peru in the 1970s and 1980s one observer noted that sexual exploitation of domestics by members of the employer's household "frequently results in pregnancy and loss of employment." Girls as young as 12 and under served as maids in homes, usually coming from poor families in the countryside. A second writer noted that "it is part of the traditional cultural mores that these female children are also there to be approached by the sons of the employer, or sometimes the employer's husband himself, to fullfil their sexual needs. The small servants sometimes are sexually abused, and often beaten as well." An example was Maria, who at age 10 was given in trust to a *patrona* in Cusco with the understanding she would be fed, clothed, and sent to school in exchange for domestic service. The promises were ignored: Maria worked up to 16 hours a day and was sexually molested regularly by a frequent visitor to the employer's house. He was never stopped. By chance an older sister of Maria's heard what was happening and alerted their mother, who came to Cusco to retrieve her daughter, who was almost without clothes and still illiterate. At 13 Maria was given over to a *patrona* in Lima with the same understanding as before. Maria still received no education. She was abused verbally and physically and forced into a sexual relationship with her employer's brother-in-law. A pregnancy resulted. The man responsible denied paternity and refused to pay child support. [41]

A survey of the situation in India in the mid–1980s by Indira Chauhan led her to conclude that masters thought nothing of taking their servants to bed and that domestic servants were particularly easy targets.[42]

Women of El Salvador employed as servants in the mid–1980s were subjected to physical and verbal abuse and sexual harassment with a frequency that was "all too common," according to one report. Peasant women working as maids were considered "fair game" by the males of the household.[43]

"Democracy" may have been restored to Kuwait in 1991 when the U.S.-led coalition ousted Iraq from that country and reinstalled the Kuwaiti overclass, but these circumstances had no effect on the circumstances of domestic servants, most of whom were Asian women. In May 1992 hundreds of these Asian servants took refuge in their respective embassies in Kuwait. They had been raped and beaten by their Kuwaiti masters, who had also refused to pay them and had confiscated their passports. Five hundred of these servants took refuge in the Philippine Embassy alone, while 200 sought safety in the Indian Embassy. The government of Kuwait was embarrassed enough that the Interior Ministry stopped issuing new visas for Asian domestics until further notice. By then Kuwait had already flown more than 500 Asian maids home for free and was in the process of setting up a repatriation center to deal with the onslaught. The government planned to issue temporary travel documents and provide free flights home to all of these servants who wished to go. This response to the problem apparently was implemented after behind-the-scenes mediation by the United States.[44]

Working in the great outdoors with good, clean air and being close to nature are much praised and romanticized ideals. However, for women working outdoors the atmosphere has been decidedly unhealthy all too often. While technically not slaves, serfs, or servants, their conditions of work have been similar, if not identical.

The agricultural gang system flourished in England in the period 1830–1860, with its peak being in the Midlands from 1850 to 1860. Under this system a farmer would contract with a gangmaster to have a piece of work done on his property for a sum of money. The gangmaster would then mobilize a team, chiefly women and children; supervise and direct their work; and then pay them directly. This system rose and flourished due to a shortage of male labor. The work itself was backbreaking, but what offended the public was not the physical hardship that the women endured but the moral hazards that they faced because some of them were "seduced by gangmasters or fellow male workers." The vicar of Chatteris was an opponent of the gangs, blaming the women of course, because the females were "more immodest and impudent . . . than the boys." He found their language to be "low, debasing and disgusting." After supper these women would "flauntily dress themselves." All of this, said the vicar, led to fornication and bastardy. Another observer of the period called women employed under the gang system as "of the lowest class." When the government investigated the gang system its report of 1862 concluded, "When the sexes are mixed, as is almost always the case, the results are quite as demoralizing. . . . It appears that the casual superintendent of the private gang is often . . . a man of bad character." Public sentiment continued to inveigh against the gangs while blaming the women. Finally the government acted and in 1867 passed a law that no child under eight could be employed and "that no woman or girl could be employed in a gang in which men worked; and that gangmasters should be licensed by Justices of the Peace after enquiries into their character." This law was evaded through the simple expedient of having the farmer pay the members of the gang directly. That turned private gangs into public gangs, with the latter being exempt from the law. Nothing else changed. However, by the time the law was implemented the gang system was on the road to extinction.[45]

Physician Luigi Angeli looked at the condition of female rice workers in the Italian rice fields near Bologna in the 1870s. He concluded that the deterioration of health and morality that he observed was due to the mingling of the sexes in the fields. He called the migratory weeders—women did the weeding—responsible for "enormous excesses of dissoluteness and licentiousness." Another observer of this same period felt these migrant weeders returned to their homes damaged "in their most delicate feelings as a consequence of the promiscuity of the lodgings, and by the loose morals that are its results." When unionist Carlo Vezzani tried to get a wage increase for the weeders in 1902, he also called for better housing for them instead of "the present promiscuous bivouac, cause of immorality and nameless shame." An inquiry into their conditions by the government in 1903 concluded that "many defenceless young women fell prey to the advances of the caporali, who abused their power to 'seduce' the objects of their sexual whims."[46]

During the period 1876–1910 in Mexico workers on the tobacco plantations of the Valle Nacional region were treated as slaves in fact, if not in name, where they worked under a system of contract labor. None of these plantations provided separate dormitories for women and children. Observed one visitor to one of these ranches, "Women of modesty and virtue are sent to Valle Nacional every week and are shoved into a sleeping room with scores and even hundreds of others, most of them men, the door is locked on them and they are left to the mercy of the men." When entire families were taken in as a group, according to this same writer, "if the wife is attractive in appearance she goes to the planter or to one or more of the bosses. The children see their mother being taken away and they know what is to become of her. The husband knows it, but if he makes objection he is answered with a club. Time and time again I have been told that this was so, by masters, by slaves, by officials."[47]

On the farms of the Yucatan, Mexico, area in 1910 the horrendous working conditions of the women campesinas (peasants or agricultural laborers) and the "sexual excesses on the part of hacendados and their sons appalled" outsiders who visited the area. Seventy years later much the same thing was written about El Salvador's peasant women: "Many local caciques or large landowners expect to have sexual access to campesina women, particularly young girls, living on or near their estates. Class relations are such that it would be very difficult for a campesina family to refuse."[48]

4
Industrial Workers, 1800s

Capitalism was in its freest and most unfettered state during the 1800s. At the same time worker exploitation reached a virulent and vicious apex. This was an era of nightmarish working conditions and wages for both male and female industrial workers, adults and children. It was an era that provoked such disparate writers and thinkers as Karl Marx and Charles Dickens to react with appalled horror and to comment on the living and working conditions of the underclass. Whether the country was England, France, Japan, or the United States, conditions were atrocious. Female industrial workers, in addition to sharing all the sufferings and exploitative conditions of their male counterparts, were brutalized still further through even lower wages and sexual harassment.

Women had been employed in British coal mines as far back as the 1700s. Up until the mid–1800s they labored with male miners both above and below the ground. Reportedly this work by women was condemned not on moral grounds but on the grounds that the work was physically debilitating in general and therefore not fit for women. A Lancashire collier girl of 1795 was said to have gone unmolested, with the male miners allowing the "hapless female to sleep her hour in rest and safety" and "return unsullied to the world."[1]

If this was true in general, not just for this one isolated case, conditions soon changed as female miners were harassed, branded as loose, and condemned for their work in the mines more for moral reasons and less for physical reasons alone. A writer by the name of Richard Ayton visited a coal mine in 1813 in Whitehaven, where he was shocked when he found females working underground. He was struck by a "shameless indecency" in their behavior, noting they "became a set of coarse, licentious wretches, scorning all kinds of restraint, and yielding themselves up, with shameless audacity to the most detestable sensuality." Ayton's attack on this employment of women picked up steam and supporters, with the owner of the Whitehead mine being finally persuaded in 1827 to stop hiring female miners altogether. Other investigators began to look into the situation. One such group, when its members saw how little clothing the women wore, sometimes naked to the waist due to the heat and poorly ventilated conditions, pronounced themselves also shocked. "No brothel can beat it," exclaimed one investigator. As to harassment it was said that "many girls claimed that the men respected them, though even if this were not the case, they might not have dared admit otherwise." Apparently it was not the case for a number of colliers hinted at personal knowledge of "immorality below ground." Frequently females worked with close male relatives, which offered them some protection. Miner Selina Ambler declared that the male miners never dared to touch her because if they did, her brother would "plump" them. Male colliers at Barnsley voted in 1841 in favor of a resolution that stated that the employment of "girls in pits is highly injurious to their morals; that it is not proper work for females, and that it is a scandalous practice."[2]

As the issue heated up it moved into the British Parliament, where it was debated and where in 1842 Lord Shaftesbury delivered a speech in the House of Lords advocating the abolition of the employment of women and children in the mines. Especially worried about the mingling of the sexes and female morality, Shaftesbury intoned, "In the male the moral effects of the system are very sad, but in the female they are infinitely worse. . . . It is bad enough if you corrupt the men, but if you corrupt the women, you poison the waters of life at the very fountain." Generally speaking, at that time the suffering of the underclass was attributed to that class. If a person was morally polluted, poor, or unemployed, this was due to his or her own drinking, licentiousness, and so on. No account was taken of underlying and motivating social factors or of unequal power relationships at work, coercion, and so forth. All the agitation against female miners finally bore fruit in 1842 when females were banned from working underground in the British mines, although they were allowed to continue working at the mines above ground at the pit head.[3] Further restrictions were applied in 1872 when the hours females could labor at the pit were limited to those outside the period from 9:00 P.M. to 5:00 A.M. because night work was "attended with evils of a moral character."[4]

In Chester, England, in 1824 a judge remarked that rapes of female children were "an all too common vice . . . above all, in this manufacturing country, where the females were, at a tender age, placed away from the control of their parents, to work at the factories." C. R. Jones, a linen weaver, raped several small girls in the Leeds factory that employed him. A Carlisle weaver named Horsely raped the 13-year-old girl who assisted him at his loom. Drawing on the stereotype of the immoral working female, he successfully defended himself in court against the charge by claiming the victim solicited him by the use of lascivious language. Around the same period Benjamin Haywood was fined £5 for an indecent assault on a girl who was employed in the Hunslet cotton mill where he worked as an overlooker. Jeptha Paver was a 34-year-old married overlooker in a flax mill who raped 15-year-old Eliza Higgins. Not guilty was the verdict. James Blakesley, an overlooker in Bradford, raped and impregnated a 14-year-old girl he superintended. Magistrates decided there was insufficient evidence to commit him for trial. He did lose his job, however. Some local people were so incensed and upset over the legal decision that they turned into a yelling mob that pursued Blakesley in the streets. He escaped a beating.[5]

When men testified before English commissions investigating factory conditions, they usually saw female factory workers as loose women. Even those who should have known better apparently did not. Frances Place, a well-known British working-class radical, said that in factories, "girls are willingly debauched at 12 years of age."[6]

In the wake of such sentiment, and in the wake of the English Factories Enquiry Commission, which reported a lack of morality on the part of both male and female factory workers, it became conventional wisdom to believe moral standards were lower among factory workers due to their general degeneracy, depravity, and so on. Few people stood up to defend women. One of the few who did, and one of the few who made a cogent analysis and assessment of the position of women and their circumstances in factories, was Friedrich Engels. Writing about the 1845 English factory system, Engels argued, "It will, of course, be appreciated that the girls who work in a factory, even more than girls working in other occupations, find that they have to grant to their employers the 'jus primae noctis.' In this respect, too, the factory owner wields complete power over the persons and charms of the girls working for him. Nine times out of ten, nay, in ninety-nine cases out of a hundred, the threat of dismissal is sufficient to break down the resistance of girls who at the best of times have no strong inducement to chastity. If the factory owner is sufficiently debased—and the Report of the Factories Enquiry Commission recounts several such cases—his factory is also his harem. As far as the girls are concerned the situation is not altered by the fact that not all manufacturers take advantage of their opportunities in this matter."[7]

For saying this Engels was heavily scored by many critics, who said there was no evidence for his assertion and that, although there may have been immorality, it came not from the owners of factories but from the female employees. The 1968 edition of Engels's *The Conditions of the Working Class in England*, which contained the foregoing quote, felt compelled to add a footnote to say there was little to support Engels's contention in that Factories Enquiry Commission report. To understand the difficulty of getting females to talk before such boards and commissions—invariably all male—one need only read the section in this book on the New York City department store clerks in 1895. The females who testified there all refused to talk, with very good reasons—fear of job loss, discomfort with men on these panels, working-class versus ruling-class antagonisms. Engels understood sexual harassment was rife.

When men hold such investigations, they set them up in such a manner that no evidence will turn up. If by chance it does, it will be ignored or twisted, as in the infamous Rodney King beating in Los Angeles where what we saw was not what we saw, an advance on Orwell's doublespeak to include doublesee. According to such logic, King was threatening and in control of the situation. However, by having these inquiries at all, the powers that be put an official stamp on things and advance the fiction that nothing happened. The abused and the exploited do not stand a chance taking their grievances before a panel composed solely of members from the same group as the abusers and or exploiters. Not only will the abused and exploited lose; they will also come out of the experience with the blame clearly clinging to them. Rodney King controlled the situation; he orchestrated his beating. Anita Hill was not a harassed female—she was a slut, a liar, a spurned female hysterically seeking revenge. If evidence of sexual harassment does present itself at one of these boards, if it can't be twisted out of context, then it will simply be ignored.

Over the period from the 1840s to the 1890s a variety of sexual harassments were recorded in Germany. Factory worker Marie Sponer, when she refused the sexual demands of her supervisor, was at one point threatened with the loss of her job and also her mother's job if she did not comply. A shoe factory worker related that a high-ranking official of the plant got one of her coworkers pregnant and then abandoned her. "Now, because he had to drop her, he looked for a new victim for his desires and he cast his eye upon me, but didn't have any luck because I refused him sharply. The result of this was that soon I was back on the street." Adelhard Popp became a factory worker around 1880 when she was just 12 or 13 years old. Despite her age she was sexually abused in the factory. According to Popp's account, sexual exploitation of female child workers by their immediate supervisors was a major problem.[8]

At an 1896 German inquiry into industrial working conditions one female witness testified that her foreman was notorious for his ill-treatment of the women. He and some of the other men often beat the females, even women in their fifties. The men called the women "every filthy name possible and tried to look up their dresses when they climbed the ladders. Most women were pressed to have sex with the foreman. As a rule he had one of them living with him for periods of time, until she was discarded."[9]

During the 1880s–1890s period there was an employer at a cotton mill near Manchester, England, who made seduction one of the conditions on which women could work at his plant. "If they decline, they must quit. Single or married makes no difference, and the same rule applies to the girl of sixteen as to the woman of thirty. He has been doing it for years. There are many employers like him," noted a contemporary observer. An over-looker at a Nelson, England, mill was fined in 1893 for using indecent language and for making immoral proposals to the married women employees. This behavior was termed "an offence not uncommon amongst men who have the oversight of the female operatives of the mills."[10]

Yet the idea remained strong that the morals of factory women were low and inferior and that the employment of women in cotton mills was breaking up the moral structure of the working class. This view attacked women for being workers (they should stay home in their place) and branded them as sexually provocative and as initiators in sexual behavior. Contradicting this was the Victorian England idea that women were chaste and pure creatures who did not like sex. If this was true, why did they engage in it, provoke it, and initiate it at work? No mention was made that their participation in sex in the workplace might be a result of coercion or domination by males, especially ones in positions of authority. With birth control either nonexistent or largely ineffectual, the consequences of sexual activity could be disastrous because not all cotton mills were willing to employ mothers of illegitimate children. Although low morality was touted as a fact of factory life, this idea was never put to any test or proved. It was simply presented as fact.[11]

At the plant in Crewe, England, where Ada Chew worked as a tailor in 1894, the foreman passed judgment on completed work, which was paid on a piecework basis, and handed out the next work—an obviously powerful position. Ada reported, "That an evil of favouritism exists to a fearful degree amongst us, not only in the factory in which I work, but in at least one other factory in Crewe, as I know for a fact. . . . This is a very real evil, and I say should not exist at all. It is a pernicious, debasing practice, alike to the favored and the unfavored. . . . Skill and execution are not necessary qualifications for the rank of favourite." Like many writers of the period Ada left little doubt about what was needed to become a favorite but could never bring herself to speak of it in a direct fashion.[12]

Sexual harassment was common enough in the textile mills of France that journalist Jane Dubuisson wrote about it in 1834, commenting, "And do not think that all those women who are exposed to so many horrible seductions give in, oh no! I have seen upright women, however miserable, who, given a choice between vice and hunger, refuse such shameful transactions and, thanks to this refusal, have their work taken away from them. Their work! Their daily bread!"[13] Nineteenth-century supervisors in textile mills in the French towns of Lille, Roubaix, and Tourcoig were reported in another source as resorting to fining those among their women employees who resisted these supervisors' advances.[14]

Throughout the 1880s and 1890s in France numerous reports of incidents ranging from immoral talk to propositions to physical abuse to rape in textile mills appeared in the local socialist press. One article denounced several factory foremen. Another paper criticized one supervisor at the LeBlan factory who was notorious for "favoring certain pretty workers." Noted the reporter, "Everyone knows at what price a girl gains his favor." One day this man's jealous wife turned up at the plant to see what was going on. Deciding her husband was too fond of one young employee, an orphan who had worked there for five years, the wife forced her husband to fire the girl. "We leave it to our readers to figure out why," concluded the paper.[15]

Mill owners used a variety of pressures, economic and otherwise, to keep unruly employees in line. One was a system of fines and bonuses; another was a "sophisticated system of factory surveillance and intimidation—which included the sexual harassment of female workers," as one historian concluded. All of this strengthened the workers' always present fear of unemployment, the final sanction applied to those who deviated too far. For women to object to the sexual advances of male supervisors was to risk "instant chomage" or the lesser penalty of classification as a "difficult worker." Resistance also provoked extra fines "a variety of pretexts was always available." This harassment was so ubiquitous in French mills that the socialist paper *Le Cri du Travailleur* launched a protest campaign in 1887. One success from this effort came when one particularly brutal foreman became so notorious that the mill owners finally fired him for abusing a young girl who worked under his direction.[16]

So-called loose, immoral women were a huge "problem" as well in U.S. factories during the 1800s. In labor leader Samuel Gompers's papers was an 1883 letter from a girl in Boston who applied for a job in a large sewing plant in that city. Told she could have the job only for so many weeks as the work was seasonal, she asked what she should do for the rest of the year. The perspective employer told her, "Oh you can do as many others do; some gentleman will pay your rent in a private room, and pay your board in full or in part, for the privilege of occasionally visiting you in a friendly way."[17]

Rather than analyze this type of situation as one wherein the female worker, through unemployment or inadequate wages, could not support herself and was forced into the sex industry, public opinion all too often portrayed her as entering the sex business voluntarily, out of desire. This, of course, made it easier to damn her for low morals, to blame her for whatever sexual activity took place at work, and to maintain that she should have nothing to complain about. After all, such women were nothing but sluts.

Joseph Cook was a Congregational minister in Lynn, Massachusetts, during the second half of the 1800s when he condemned the labor situation in the shoe town in which he ministered and industrialization in general in the United States. He found himself receiving a lot of publicity and support for his views. Cook argued that the real danger to female workers lay not in the streets or boardinghouses but in the work arrangements in the shoe factories. "The irregulated boarding-house and the street school may strip the flesh from the peach, but the down of the peach was brushed away in the workrooms," lectured the minister. Even though he questioned the morals of both male and female workers, Cook emphasized those of women as especially lax. Mixing the two sets in one workroom was a method he characterized as a "foul system." When Cook visited a mixed workroom he found the women to be "coarse, low, vulgar and bad featured." According to the man who showed Cook around, no virtuous young man could work there for any length of time without staring moral ruin in the face "because the girls were so bad." Cook argued for separation of the sexes in the factories. So much support came his way that the shoe industry felt itself obliged to respond to the minister's agitation. These manufacturers argued that they had considered the moral implications of mixing the sexes back in the 1850s when the shoe industry had instituted the practice. The experiment was successful, said the industry, and "women are employed wherever their labor can be available, and in a large majority of factories, where they are at work with men, better order and decorum is manifest."[18]

Many female workers agreed with Cook, sometimes refusing outright to work with men. One employer remarked that "few American women will work in factories with men." Some Irish women reportedly would not work with men also. A number of German females would go to work only when they were guaranteed a separate workroom for their sex. Some employers on their own initiative did establish separate workrooms for the sexes. When women expressed a reluctance to work in the same area with men, it was sexual harassment that they feared. It was not a worry that their low morals would get the best of them.[19]

The debate over the mixing of the sexes went back a long way, at least to the 1850s. Virginia Penny was a journalist of that era who investigated the condition of women's employment. At an umbrella manufacturing concern that employed some 250 females, management told her that females did indeed become "very immoral" from associating with men at work; but in large plants females had a separate workroom, which meant that while they were at work they never had to see any men, "except the foreman."[20]

Apparently this was an argument that Penny bought because in another book published seven years later she expanded a little on the issue. She worried about the moral consequences of mixing men and women at work in the same room. It depended on the moral character of the workers, she responded. "If they have moral principles and self-respect, there will not be much danger. . . . Some women and girls do not conduct themselves properly in their work-room, and on the street." Penny spoke to a textile factory foreman who told her, "If girls are too free with men, they ought not to be permitted to work with them. . . . If a girl is inclined to be immoral, she will be so." Penny decided the best arrangement was to have separate workrooms for each sex, with forewomen supervising females. Implied here was the idea that this arrangement was best due to the immoral predilection of women rather than men. Also while she looked at factory conditions she seems to have talked only to management to see what was happening, not to the female workers themselves.[21]

It was a topic that was slow to die, for decades later in 1910 Louis Kuppenheimer of Chicago's Kuppenheimer clothing company prided himself on the moral atmosphere of his factory in which there was no mixing of the sexes. In fact he claimed that many parents appealed to him to employ their daughters because of the "protection this afforded them."[22]

Prior to the entrenchment of the factory system whereby workers journeyed from their homes to the plant to perform their labor, homework was the prevalent method of production. For example, a woman did all her needlework at home, starting almost as soon as she got up and continuing until almost time for bed. The employee performing homework would drop off finished material and pick up new work on some regular basis such as daily or weekly. Pay was by the piece. Although not unknown, sexual harassment of homeworkers was likely much less prevalent than under the factory system. With homework the female usually had some or all of her children helping out. Likely she lived in a one- or two-room unit in a crowded tenement with many other families in the same position. Under such conditions privacy was unknown, making opportunities for harassment limited to the times the worker dropped off and picked up material. A factory subjected a woman to that potential of harassment all of her working day. Factories always had small, private offices as well as deserted aisles, storerooms, nooks, and crannies. One example of harassment of homeworkers was that of Rose Haggerty, who was protected in her first work at home by an older woman who would pick up each of their sewing bundles. She did this so "the agent had no opportunity to follow out what had now and then been his method, and hint to the girl that her pretty face entitled her to concessions that would be best made in a private interview."[23]

For a time factories sometimes combined homework with in-plant labor. Since it afforded an opportunity for extra money, such outwork was desired by the employees. Writing in 1859 of this practice, Margaret Sanger said, "There are instances where . . . the sacrifice of a woman's virtue has been required for the privilege of sewing at almost nominal prices. If this is conceded, the victim may be assured of the best work and the most favors."[24]

When 16-year-old Catherine Runnett went to work in an American pen manufacturing plant in 1850, her employer promised to protect her from "insults" by putting her to work in his own office. Her mother was reluctant to let her go to work at all. These objections proved to be well founded for Runnett ended up pregnant in short order. Her father sued in court for monetary damages. After having coerced Runnett into sex, her employer, family man Albert Bagley, disavowed all responsibility for the pregnant teenager. During the trial the lawyer for Bagley attempted to discredit Runnett's character by trying to establish that somebody else could be the father; by getting her to admit she had talked with men in the workroom when she was carrying tea to her father, who was also employed by Bagley; and by bringing out the fact that Runnett had recently read a French novel. Runnett's father was awarded damages of $1,800 after asking for $10,000.[25]

When Helen Campbell published her 1887 investigative work on female working and living conditions, she found evidence of sexual harassment. A worker named Mrs. W said, "So far I've kept decent; I've had to leave three places because they wouldn't let me alone, and I stay where I am now because they're quiet, respectable people, and not outrageous." A young German woman, Lotte Bauer, had her work made more difficult by her employers so she earned only $6 a week instead of her usual $8 or $9. Said Bauer, "He had often done this where girls had refused his advances, yet it was impossible to make complaints. The great house on Canal Street left these matters entirely with him and regarded complaint as mere blackmail."[26]

During the 1880–1885 period it was said of New York City carpet weaving plants that "if a girl is so unfortunate enough to attract the attention of her employer or any of his friends, the boss will endeavor to arrange a meeting between the parties in one of the adjacent cities for a purpose easily surmized and if the young lady refuses to accept the proposition she is told there is no more work for her."[27] About 1880 women wrote pathetic appeals to the "Bintel Brief" advice column in the newspaper the *Jewish Daily Forward* complaining of desertions, bigamous husbands, and sexual harassment in the workplace.[28]

On August 20, 1890, Mrs. Alexander Bremmer, a deputy factory inspector in New York, read a paper to a convention of her peers on the importance of female inspectors, citing certain "immoralities" that existed in New York's factories. James Connolly, the state's chief of factory inspectors, vehemently denied Bremmer's allegations, forbade her to talk to the press, and demanded her resignation. A couple of years later Helen Campbell urged the appointment of female factory inspectors as one remedy for sexual harassment, saying, "The appointment of women inspectors, lately brought about for New York, is imperative at all points, since women will tell women the evils they would never mention to men."[29]

Also considering the idea of having forewomen more often in charge of female factory workers was England's John Milne. He argued, somewhat naïvely, in his 1870 book that more middle-class women should be hired in industry in "foremen-type positions" to serve as an example to lower-class females and to act as a safeguard. Milne muddied the waters by turning the issue more into one of class than gender. He thought these forewomen would set an example to show that advancement was possible and to keep the lower classes on a proper moral path. Under the existing system, Milne argued, female workers in factories were "necessarily" of a rank below that of the men. These women would feel more protected if women of the middle classes were among them, for "there would then be thus afforded a natural check to impropriety. Young men thrown in the company of a girl of humbler rank would be led to protect her in place of misleading her. If they respect female character in the one rank, they will respect it also in the other." To illustrate his naïvete Milne cited domestic service as an example, where, he argued, the servant (lower class) was under the protection of a middle- or high-ranking female. This protection was a "sufficient safeguard" to prevent a lapse from propriety. He considered domestic service to be very moral.[30]

The issue was a universal one for an Australian writer of 1894. This writer lamented the lack of forewomen in factories, "for it must be remembered that this class of girl wants to be saved as much from herself as from the cupidity and brutality of master or overseer, the latter of whom, in the case of a girl anxious to keep her place, can obtain a most undesirable hold over her."[31]

Nowhere was the protection of female morality ostensibly given a higher priority than in the textile mills in and around Lowell, Massachusetts. This reached its zenith around the 1840s and 1850s. Single female employees had to live in company boardinghouses — males did not — where the doors were locked at 10:00 P.M. These girls had to attend church each Sunday. All of these measures were designed to ease the fears of parents and families that their daughters would fall into dens of iniquity in the big city. Many of these employees came from rural areas where parents as well as daughters had to be convinced. They were from families with middle-class values and aspirations, but not money, which was why they were forced to send their daughters to work in the mills. This system waned a few decades later when immigrants took most of these positions. The morality question remained the same, but as native-born American females were involved to a far smaller degree, it did not bother people as much. At the Lowell Corporation textile mill there existed a rule that any person leaving the company's employ was prevented from obtaining work in any other company in the area if, in the opinion of the overseer where the person had previously worked, she or he was not a suitable person to be employed. Even if, as happened, the overseer acted for "the gratification of an envious favorite" or "revenge for disappointed lechery," this rule would drive a woman out of the city if the foreman chose to exercise that power over her.[32]

Writing about the female worker in the factories of Lowell earlier in the century, Harriet Robinson said in 1898 that this worker was the lowest among women and, referring to other mills as well, that "she was represented as subjected to influences that could not fail to destroy her purity and self-respect. In the eyes of her overseer she was but a brute, a slave, to be beaten, pinched and pushed about."[33] Sometime in the 1840s Robinson was fired from her job in a Lowell cotton mill after she spoke to an overseer about his familiar manner with her and the other operatives.[34]

The textile industry in Japan developed in the same fashion as it had in the United States with regard to female workers. The first model textile mill was opened by the government in 1873. It featured dormitories for the female workers, also with locked doors at night. Male employees did not have to stay in dorms. Recruitment was from impoverished rural families. As in the United States these precautions were designed to show families that the factories were safe places for young women since working away from home with men might damage the marriage chances of these young females. This effort worked, and soon private companies were establishing mills with dorms and successfully recruiting in the countryside as initial resistance to the idea was broken.[35]

Young rural women were usually "sold" by their parents to the mill for three to five years, with the daughter obligated to remit a set amount each month to her parents or to the mill if the parents had accepted a "loan" from the mill for the amount. This contract labor system evolved as demand for female labor grew. It was a way for companies to get long-term commitments from workers without cost. The company could dismiss employees at any time, but the worker could not quit. However, there were many runaways. Free-lance recruiters gradually took over most of the recruiting from the companies. As one writer of the period noted, "Often the young girls were also obligated to sexually satisfy the recruiters before being delivered to the mills for work. Indeed the recruiters would boast among themselves of how many women they had conquered."[36]

In the mills themselves women worked 12-hour shifts, day or night, and were subjected to much more sexual harassment on the night shift, a fact that was well known to the employing companies. Despite the evidence some writers blamed the women. One wrote, "Life in the textile industry has been criticized as approximating that of a desert, which drove female factory workers to satisfy their hunger and their sexual desires by having trysts with men." In reality male floor supervisors had total control over the women on their shifts and, wrote one observer, "during night work they often treated these women as a private harem." In larger companies the foremen recommended bonuses, reported tardiness, docked workers' pay for different infractions, and ultimately decided how long the shift would be. "It was extremely important for women working with these men not to displease them."[37]

Other sources confirm harassment in the Japanese textile mills during the last three decades of the 19th century. Harassment was common on the shop floor of both cotton and silk mills. If inducements did not cause the women to submit, then rape might be used, especially on the night shift. The dorm system was well established in Japan in these industries by the 1890s; however, it did not preclude sexual abuse by individual male workers and supervisors. Often recruited from rural areas distant from the plant, these women were especially vulnerable as it meant they had no supportive family around them.

Silk workers were abused on the shop floor by supervisors who administered the factory's overall system of fines and punishments. As one observer noted, "The young operatives, single and vulnerable, were open targets for personal whims and sexual abuse by these low-ranking supervisors." Owners and managers were just as abusive as their male subordinates, and unlike lower-ranked male workers, these men usually had keys to the women's dormitory rooms. One factor that fueled labor disputes in Tenma in 1889 and 1894 as well as in Mie in 1894 was the anger of women employees being discriminated against through unequal pay. Those women who submitted to their superiors were paid more money. If rape or coerced sex ended in pregnancy, the male involved had little to worry about; he paid the woman a small sum of money, and that ended the matter.

5
Strikes and Trade Unions

At times the pressure to submit or get out was so great that sexual harassment became one of the issues, or the major issue, that precipitated a strike. Given that women workers were often not unionized, or not supported by male members on female issues if they were organized, and were generally second-class citizens, these strikes were a measure of the outrage often felt by harassed women. They may have been in a no-win situation, but they were often subjected to such amounts of abuse that they felt compelled to take action of some type. In New York City in 1907 white goods workers struck in protest over the "insults of a male employee whom the company refused to discharge." Around the same time in another plant more than 400 wrappers walked off the job due to "grievances against the foreman."[1]

On the other side of the country that same year several hundred telephone operators went on strike in San Francisco as part of a larger strike movement. In most phone exchanges the female operators were supervised by women, thus having no contact with males except when journeying to and from work. In itself this was considered dangerous and unsavory, especially on the night shift, as many exchanges were located in rough areas, thereby putting females at risk as they were going to and coming from work. It was ideas like this that would eventually lead to the barring of females from night shift work in many jurisdictions to "protect" them from such dangers. These striking San Francisco operators did have male supervisors, however. Among their demands was "the replacement of male chief operators by women" to eliminate sexual harassment. One reason for the failure of this strike was reportedly the lack of support by male telephone workers.[2]

About 800 female corsetmakers struck the Kalamazoo Corset Company in Kalamazoo, Michigan, in March 1912. They were members of the International Ladies Garment Workers' Union (ILGWU). Initially the demands of the strikers were for purely economic gains such as higher wages and for union recognition. The ILGWU sent three organizers in to head the strike, of which Josephine Casey and Pauline Newman played the most important roles. When Casey heard the horror stories of sexual harassment at the plant, she quickly publicized them, thus turning harassment into a major strike issue. Workers complained that the foremen awarded the more desirable jobs to those women who complied with sexual demands. Others told of their supervisors' obsession with achieving sexual relations with the workers. "The management of that concern is run by superintendents, some of them diseased and filthy, whose minds are occupied more with carnal pleasure than with the business of the firm," said the strikers. Not long after her arrival on the scene, Casey led the pickets in a prayer, which included the line "May it please Thee to save the girls now on strike from the wicked city of Sodom." Shortly after that Casey was arrested and jailed.[3]

Casey felt that appeals based on the sexual exploitation of women workers would arouse sympathy and public support for the strikers. That did not happen. When Newman took charge, she downplayed the entire issue. To her, sexual harassment was a national problem that could not be eliminated with solutions specific to the Kalamazoo plant. Moral issues should not become the focus of the strike, she reasoned. She favored a solution involving paying women a living wage and educating them to their vulnerability in the workplace. "I realize there are religious, moral and educational problems, but I firmly believe that each of these, important as it may be, is subsidiary to the economic problem," she commented. Also she was much less optimistic about the power of the public to sway factory owners and of the power of the lower-class women to arouse sympathy among middle- and upper-class women, who often took a patronizing attitude toward them.[4]

Even though she downplayed the harassment issue, Newman was well aware that many female workers were forced into sexual liaisons with bosses or compelled into prostitution in order to survive. In a 1912 private letter to her friend and sister unionist Rose Schneiderman, Newman wrote, "You know as well as I that there is not a factory today where the same immoral conditions do not exist! You remember your factories where you have worked and so do I, and both of us know that the cloak factories and all other shops in the city of New York or Chicago, every one of the men will talk to the girls, take advantage of them if the girls will let them, the foremen and the superintendents will flirt with the girls, and it is nothing new for those who knew that this exists today everywhere.... You find the same old story that the foreman asked a girl to come into his office and hold hands, etc."[5]

Of course foremen did not ask an employee into the office to "hold hands." They did so for forced sex. Yet Newman, a tough organizer, a knowledgeable observer of the industrial scene, and a feminist ahead of her time, could not bring herself to speak bluntly of the problem even in a letter to a close friend, a private letter that Newman thought would never be read by others. The best Newman could do was tiptoe around the subject indirectly. This illustrates just how difficult it would have been in this time period for an average woman—lacking Newman's education, professional status, literacy, facility with the language, and so on—to speak openly of the problem, especially to a superior such as a foreman or manager or to a board or panel of investigators, composed almost always of men, of course.

This strike ended in June 1912 with only a few minor concessions to the workers. When the company reneged, the ILGWU almost immediately called for a national boycott of the company. Apparently it was successful for the Kalamazoo Corset Company went out of business in December 1914, throwing all of its employees into the street.[6]

Buttonmakers walked out on strike in February 1911 in Muscatine, Iowa. These women insisted "that managers used their power to force sexual relations upon the women button makers. One manager, for example, maintained a 'resting room' where women who gave 'in to his devilish demands were reciprocated with a steady job. Those who did not comply with his wishes received discharge notices'." This strike ended 15 months later. In New York City shirtwaist workers walked out in 1909. Strike leader Clara Lemlieh complained of the bosses who "don't use very nice language. They swear at us and sometimes they do worse."[7]

A broom factory strike in 1915 in an unspecified city featured sexual harassment by the foreman as a major issue. As this overseer was described as a man who "did not stop at anything," some of the employees took to carrying knives to protect themselves. Activist Mary Anderson intervened on behalf of the workers. When she spoke to the employer she told him, "I had heard stories about one of his foremen, not only of his brutality in dealing with the women, but also that he was immoral and that immoral conditions existed in the plant because of him. The employer said he knew this was so." According to Anderson, when the strike was finally settled, this foreman was fired.[8]

The tyranny of foremen was also a major precipitator of a Chicago garment workers' strike in 1910. A contemporary account described the workplace as one where "abusive and insulting language is frequently used by those in authority in the shops. This is especially intolerable to the girls, who should have the right to work without surrendering their self-respect. No woman should be subjected by fear of loss of her job to unwarranted insults."[9]

Women did not even have to be employed outside the home to be victimized. In September 1913 the United Mine Workers of America began the 15-month-long Colorado fuel and iron strike best remembered for the April 1914 attack by Colorado National Guard troops on the strikers' tent colony at Ludlow. All of the striking employees were male. One coal mine inspector reported he had been told by the miners' wives that there "was no privacy in their home life, that whenever a representative of the company or deputy sheriff desired, they entered the house unannounced." A mine guard by the name of Bob Lee had been able to terrify some wives and daughters into submitting to him by using the authority of his badge and by threatening the loss of their men's jobs. The National Guard troops treated the women in the same fashion. At a later inquiry before a commission on industrial relations, miner's wife Mary Thomas testified to the prevalence of rape, saying, "It is terrible. . . . It cannot be stated—the insults the women have had to undergo. And since these militiamen have been here there's dozens of young girls who have had to go to homes expecting to become mothers." Commissioners were not too happy to hear such stories at the inquiry for in the midst of her testimony Thomas was told her time was running short. At that point another commissioner changed the topic by asking about the company stores.[10]

The Industrial Workers of the World struck the Pressed Steel Car Company in July 1909 over a number of issues. Once again all the employees were men. This McKees Rocks, Pennsylvania, firm was a subsidiary of U.S. Steel. Through the Fidelity Land Company, Pressed Steel Car owned 200 double houses, which it rented out to its workers. The house boss was a company agent who took advantage of his authority to cheat and terrorize the workers in a number of ways. One, for example, charged a special fee whenever an event such as a wedding or christening took place. One called himself a justice of the peace and collected money that way. Another was described simply as "a specialist in women."[11]

Company foremen made a practice of demanding that wives and daughters of the workers submit sexually to prevent their male relatives from being discharged. After making an on-the-spot investigation, Reverend A. F. Toner, pastor of St. Mary's Roman Catholic Church in McKees Rocks, described the situation at the plant by saying, "Men are persecuted, robbed and slaughtered, and their wives are abused in a manner worse than death—all to obtain or retain positions that barely keep starvation from the door. It is a pit of infamy where men are driven lower than the degradation of slaves and compelled to sacrifice their wives and daughters to the villainous foremen and little bosses to be allowed to work. It is a disgrace to a civilized country." Following a bloody strike a settlement was reached in September. Among other items the striking men obtained a pledge from the company that any foreman or agent found guilty of demanding sexual favors from workers' wives or daughters as a condition of continued employment would be immediately fired. Prior to the strike Frank N. Hoffstot, Press Steel Car president, had only one response to complaints: "If a man is dissatisfied, it is his privilege to quit."[12]

English cotton mill operatives experienced the same harassment as did their American counterparts. Overlooker Houghton Greenwood's behavior led to a strike at Evan and Berry's Walverden Weaving Shed in the town of Nelson, near Manchester, in 1891. Other issues were also involved. Greenwood used unfit language to women workers and made immoral propositions. Replacement workers were hired during the strike. Demonstrations outside the plant against Greenwood and the scabs drew as many as 500 people. Attempting to blame the victims, the president of the Nelson and District Powerloom Overlookers Society explained to the press that he had found operatives with good morals and operatives with bad morals. He remarked, "It could not be denied that overlookers had a great deal of temptation put in their way by those under their charge, but he was proud to say that few of them yielded to such temptation." As a condition to end the strike the Nelson Weavers' Association demanded the unconditional discharge of Greenwood. The company refused. The weavers finally settled for arbitration, with three clergymen ultimately hearing the case. When they found him guilty, the company relented and fired Greenwood. When the strike ended many, but not all, of the strikers were rehired by the firm. Condemning Greenwood's actions the clergymen pointed out that such offenses were "not uncommon among men who have the oversight of . . . female operatives."[13]

A few years prior to that in January 1887, 68 female and male operatives from the card and blowing room walked out of the Spinning Company's mill in the town of Oldham, also near Manchester. These employees refused to go back to work until an investigation into the conduct of a head carder by the name of Robert Yates was carried out. Workers alleged he used his position to sexually pressure and even assault the young females under his authority. Complaints had come to the attention of George Silk, general secretary of the Oldham Provincial Card and Blowing Room and Ring Frame Operatives' Association, beginning in the spring of 1886 and grew more and more pressing as Yates's indecencies increased. Parents of some of the younger females complained to Silk, most of whose union members were women. When Silk attempted to negotiate the issue with plant management, he was totally rebuffed, management added insult to injury by attacking the character and morals of the women employees. With negotiations breaking down completely the workers struck and were immediately replaced by scabs. After this happened Yates was assailed by a crowd as he left work with cries of "Bury Bob" and had to duck into a nearby pub for safety.[14]

An irate father of one victim took matters into his own hands by having Yates brought to court on criminal charges of committing indecent assault. Specifically he was charged with assault on at least three workers aged 15 or 16. In one incident during the summer of 1886 Yates asked two of the females into his house while they were passing by. Once inside he sexually attacked them. Both struggled with him but were wary of screaming in case he would fire them. One threatened to tell on him, but Robert warned her it would be "the worse for her" if she did so. These girls did tell a workmate of the incidents, with the result that a rumor spread through the mill. Soon the females involved found themselves at least partly blamed, for it was reported that "the reputations of both Yates and the girls evidently suffered." During the trial other incidents came to light. One woman told how Yates had once put his hands up her clothes at work. Although advised by a coworker to report this, she did not for fear of being fired. Another time Yates exposed himself before this woman and continually pestered her to meet him after work in a pub. Other women testified that the defendant often tried to get women into an empty storeroom at the plant where "he began to use dirty language, and also behaved indecently." Also fueling the strike was anger at the firings for no reason of many mill operatives. Implicitly these dismissals seemed to be linked to women who refused Yates's advances.[15]

The union seemed to be resigned to the impossibility of stopping him. Silk commented, "He knew that it was absolutely impossible for him to be caught and stopped in his actions if he pursued a similar method from then till doomsday. . . . It has not been possible in any way to bring this man to book, his method in all cases being to make improper overtures, and on refusal to pick a quarrel, which is always easy, and then to either discharge them at once or with a week's notice." So arrogant was Yates that he openly boasted to the men under him, and to Silk, of his power over subordinates, saying, "He would have none working under him but what would comply with his wishes whatever they were." Added Silk of the period before the trial, "The knowledge of the late transactions of this man has not been given by the girls themselves but has principally been told by the man himself."[16]

The defense put forth by Yates's lawyer at the trial consisted of trying to discredit the complainants by calling them "sexually precocious" and by insisting they had been willing partners. In support of this the defense cited the long time lapse between the alleged incidents and the laying of charges of indecent assault and the victims' initial unwillingness to complain to anyone. Yates was not guilty of improprieties, argued his lawyer; the behavior was simply flirting, teasing, or an innocent playfulness. Many of the aspersions cast at the girls apparently stuck for Silk noted that he "found it difficult to convince many Oldham people that the girls involved were blameless."[17]

Robert Yates, 49 and married, was found guilty and fined £5 plus court costs. By the end of February it was all over. The company fired Yates. However, none of the original workers from his department was rehired. All were blacklisted.[18]

Some 1,700 Russian weavers, most of them female, struck the Egorov factory in Riazan province in May 1893. These women broke into the factory office, where they destroyed the books and tore the place up. Next they moved to the company store, looted what they could, and then trashed what remained. They wrecked the looms in the plant and then tried unsuccessfully to find the factory director, whom they wished to kill. After this short but violent one-week-long strike, the workers were pacified by the blandishments of a factory inspector backed by a battalion of soldiers. This inspector concluded that above all the employees were upset that a foreman "used his unlimited power to seduce and rape attractive girls and married women . . . who had the misfortune of appealing to him. If one refused to submit to his bestial desires, she would be unceremoniously fired. And not just she, but her entire family would be kicked out of the factory."[19]

Generally the trade union movement ignored the issue of sexual harassment of its female members. At times it was even openly hostile to female workers. In the 1830s Britain's male National Trades Union constantly alluded to the corruption of women's morals in factories, stating that "their morals frequently depart before their health, in consequence of being often crowded in such large numbers, with all characters and all sexes." It was left unsaid just how this corruption came about, but there was nothing to suggest the labor movement thought it was a result of sexual harassment by male employees. Rather this worry over morals of women was used by the union as a reason to limit the employment of women.[20]

Close to a century and a half later the British labor movement was beginning to change. The Women's Conference brought pressure to bear, and in 1983 the Trades Union Congress published its guidelines on sexual harassment, affirming it as a trade union issue and detailing what action trade unions could take to counter it. Indirectly revealing union attitudes on the issue was the guidelines' opening statement, which read, "Many trade unionists still regard it as a 'fuss about nothing,' something that is an inevitable consequence of men and women working together, or harmless fun. Such attitudes fail to recognize the difference between social interaction at work, which involves social relationships mutually entered into, and sexual harassment, which is the imposition of unwelcome attention or action on one person often by a person in a superior position."[21]

This question of female morality was also of concern to the union movement in Scotland in the 1860s. When the issue of hours and conditions of work for females arose, the unions were silent when it involved trades where only women were employed. However, they became much concerned and very vocal about regulating female labor, due to its effects on morality, when it involved trades that employed both males and females. Once again the reason was to increase the number of jobs available only to men. It was self-interest to protect themselves against competition.[22]

In 1866 a Detroit, Michigan, report claimed that much of the prostitution "which curses this city is the loathsome fruit of the depravity which dates its commencement at the tobacco factories." Trade unions responded to this by using it as ammunition and proof of the need for protective legislation for women—meaning to limit their job opportunities.[23]

When the Knights of Labor held its 1886 general assembly, 660 delegates attended; 16 were women. At the request of these women all 16 were appointed to a committee on women's work. In addition to looking into issues such as securing equal pay for equal work and ending child labor, the group was charged "to investigate the abuses to which our sex is subjected to by unscrupulous employers." Nothing ever came of this charge because this union, although progressive for its time, had a very short life span. At least the Knights of Labor acknowledged the existence of sexual harassment in the workplace, which was not the case for those people or groups in a position to do anything about the problem.[24]

One group that did not do so openly was the Women's Trade Union League (WTUL), which was formed in 1903 in New York City, with chapters then springing up in various other cities. The purpose of the WTUL was to organize females into unions and gain acceptance of them in the male-dominated trade union movement. More often than not the WTUL did so by adopting the male attitude to various issues. As a result all too often the organization lobbied for protective legislation, such as limiting the hours and the shifts females could work.[25]

Just as Pauline Newman steered around sexual harassment in her union work, so did Dorothy Jacobs Bellanca, who organized for the Amalgamated Clothing Workers of America during the 1915–1930 period. Like Newman, Bellanca was aware, as few male organizers were, of the sexual exploitation of women on the job. However, she never confronted male unionists with the issue; "rather, she relied on class solidarity in her quest for recognition of women as valuable trade unionists," reported one source.[26]

All too often sexual harassment occurred within the trade union movement itself. Pauline Newman experienced it herself from the head of her union, the ILGWU, early in this century. Newman left the ILGWU for a brief time in 1911, and returned that same year, because the union wanted to pay her less money than a male organizer and because she had been sexually harassed. Newman, the first female organizer of the union, wrote in a letter to Rose Schneiderman about the two women hired to replace her, saying, "Well they are not bad looking, and one is rather liberal with her body. That is more than enough for Dyche [the executive secretary of the union]." During her union organizing Newman made a conscious decision to downplay the issue of on-the-job sexual harassment, viewing it as bad strategy to raise issues of "morality" when they threatened to interfere with negotiations over wages and hours. Nevertheless Newman always acknowledged the existence of harassment, feeling there was not a single factory that was free from it. But, she reasoned, "this to my mind can be done away with by educating the girls instead of attacking the company."[27]

An ocean away and separated more than half a century in time an American scholar found sexual harassment in Germany in the 1980s when he spent a year working at the German Trade Union office. What surprised him the most was the sexism that he found in that office. He found the male trade union leaders to be ready to accept broad pronouncements of policy against sex discrimination, but "in everyday life, they harass their secretaries."[28]

Chinese women striking a Japanese-owned factory in China in 1925 complained in their strike manifesto that "the Japanese are immoral and rude. They make advances toward the women workers. The clever ones flirt with them; the less clever ones reject their advances and scorn them, so that sometimes they are forced to quit. This drives us to a violent anger that we cannot control." Other complaints included the fact that managers beat the workers for no reason and fined them on a whim.[29]

During the late 1970s a female employed as a cleaner in a New South Wales, Australia, courthouse complained to her union, the Miscellaneous Workers Union, after being sexually harassed at work by another employee. The union took the case to the Justice Department, the man's employer. After a hearing the Justice Department concluded the man was innocent. This prompted all the women in the union to go on strike, demanding that the man be fired. They stayed out until the Justice Department relented and placed the harasser on special leave.[30]

At Thionville, France, in April 1972, 80 women supermarket employees walked off the job. They had many grievances, one of which was "in order to obtain promotion, you have to be nice to the head of personnel and have pretty legs," one of the strikers complained.[31]

About 1,400 members of the International Woodworkers of America shut down three logging camps and five mills in Shelton, Washington, in October 1979. All but 50 of them were men. They walked out in support of a woman member of the union fired for refusing to drop charges of sexual harassment against the Simpson Lumber Company. During the shutdown 7 other women employed at Simpson came forward to sign affidavits stating they had also been harassed during the hiring interview process, as the fired woman alleged in her case. During their hiring interviews they had been "asked to take off their blouses, asked if they wore a bra, asked if they would have sex with their supervisors and had to endure comments about their breasts." Explaining the union's position of support, local president Jim Lowry told the press that "as male chauvinistic as our workers might be, even they don't tolerate that kind of interview process."[32]

6
Industrial Workers, 1900s

Sexual harassment continued unabated in factory work well into the 20th century. Women regularly quit jobs to get away from it. Edward Cadbury reported in 1907 on an inquiry into female working conditions in a large, unnamed American city where several hundred women who applied for jobs were questioned as to why they had left their previous employment. Major reasons given were the low wages and too few hours, "but there remained a considerable number who had no such complaint to make. With these, the reason for leaving was generally that some one in authority was 'forward' or 'spoke as they didn't ought'." Cadbury felt this was only a hint as to how matters stood. He acknowledged that "girls are appallingly helpless if personal favoritism or feeling of any kind are allowed to have influence in the shop."[1]

Yet the old images remained. One report from the early years of this century considered the factory to be more morally protected than other employment but admitted conditions were far from what they should be. A problem was that many female factory employees worked either side by side with men or very near them. As a consequence, said the report, "they sometimes become careless in their conduct, slack in manners and conversation, immodest in dress, and familiar to a degree that lays them open to danger."[2]

During the first decade of the 1900s several females went to find out firsthand the conditions women faced in the workplace. One was Dorothy Richardson, who circa 1900 worked in New York City in a variety of factories and stores before writing up her experiences. While working in a factory that made jewelry cases, Richardson and coworker Eunice discussed their absent coworker Bessie. Eunice worried about her ailing friend because "I've watched the boss following her around with his eyes ever since we came here to work. You didn't see for you don't know as much about their devilment as I do." Richardson later noted to herself, "I had seen more of the manager's advances than Eunice gave me credit for observing."[3]

Later while working in a laundry, Richardson was told by the boss that she was to be promoted to a slightly higher paying job the next day. One coworker congratulated her, but "this opinion was not shared, however, by the rest of my companions, who repeated divers terrible tales of moral ruin and betrayal . . . wherein the boss was inevitably the villain." A foreman who had befriended her slipped her a note that day that read, in part, "You'd better give up this job. It's no place for a girl that wants to do right." He advised her to quit that very day. Before receiving notice of her promotion, Richardson and the other workers had had "jokes [flung] at us [by the boss] all in a manner of insolent familiarity." When he came to Richardson, he "uttered some joking remarks of insulting flattery, and in a moment he had grasped my bare arm and given it a rude pinch." She did quit that day. Summing up her work experiences in general, Richardson admitted, "As to moral conditions, I have not been in every instance so scrupulously truthful — that is, I have not told all the truth. For it is a truth which only too often will not bear the suggestion of telling."[4]

About the same time Mrs. John Van Vorst was doing what Richardson had done. After a stint in a Perry, New York, textile mill, she wrote of mills in general, "The mill owners exert, as far as possible, an influence over the moral tone of their employees, assuming the right to judge their conduct both in and out of the factory and to treat them as they see fit." At a Columbia, South Carolina, cotton plant Van Vorst wrote about Bessie, who, then 18, had entered the mill at age 8, "If she does not feed the passion of the overseer, she may find some mill-hand who will contract a 'mill-marriage' with this daughter of the loom, a marriage little binding to him and which will give her children to give in time to the mill." Minnie had entered the mill at age 14 and, Van Vorst observed, "so much grace and good looks could not go, cannot go, does not go unchallenged by the attention of the men who are put there to run these women's work. The overseer was father of her child, and when she tried to force from him recognition and aid he threw over his position and left Columbia and this behind him. This one instance under my own eyes observed. There are many."[5]

After a union was formed at the Aptheker textile shop around 1908 in New York City, organizer Rose Schneiderman got a call from the chairwoman of the plant union. This woman told Schneiderman that Mr. Aptheker had a habit of pinching the female employees on the bottom whenever he passed by. They wanted it stopped. Schneiderman, along with the chairwoman, went to see Aptheker, telling him the women resented his behavior and asking him to stop it. "Why, Miss Schneiderman," replied the boss, "these girls are like my children." Without missing a beat the chairwoman retorted, "Mr. Aptheker, we'd rather be orphans." According to Schneiderman, the pinching then stopped.[6]

A 17-year-old factory worker was raped by her foreman in the early years of this century. She became pregnant from this assault and underwent an abortion. To make matters worse the cousin with whom she lived threw her out—in a classic example of blaming the victim. Recalled the girl, "I had lost my virginity, my reputation and my job. All I had gotten was older." This woman attributed her entry into prostitution to the sexual harassment at work and its results. She went on to become famed bordello operator Polly Adler.[7]

When New York State had a committee investigating working conditions in factories in 1912 one investigator took an undercover job in a cannery for a firsthand look. She reported that she received several immoral propositions. One foreman, named Gilette, told her, "You can't make enough money up here to pay your board, but I will give you a chance to make two or three dollars on the side any time." Other girls corroborated her experiences and told her, "It was best to keep away from him." One coworker also warned her to stay away from the Italian male workers in the plant "because they were dangerous."[8]

Immigrant women faced the added problem of a language handicap that made it difficult to complain. Not that complaining would have done much good. In a 1907 letter to the "Bintel Brief" advice column in the *Jewish Daily Forward*, an immigrant girl complained of the poor wages she received in a Vineland, New Jersey, factory. In her letter she said about a foreman, "And worse than all of this, in spite of the fact that he has a wife and several children, he often allows himself to 'have fun' with some of the working girls. It was my bad luck to be one of the girls that he tried to make advances to. And woe to any girl who doesn't willingly accept them . . . . He started to pick on me, said my work was no good, and when I proved to him he was wrong, he started to shout at me in the vilest language . . . . The girls in the shop were very upset over the foreman's vulgarity but they don't want him to throw them out, so they are afraid to be witnesses against him." This woman lost her job for unrecorded reasons.[9]

Rebecca Hollard was the only female employed in a small Chicago clothing plant around 1910. She related, "I worked there and I couldn't stand the language of the men. They used to tell dirty sex stories, and I didn't understand anything about that . . . . I was the only girl and I couldn't stand it. I used to come home and cry at night because they always talked about sex relations and stuff." Rose Cohen was one of a few women in another small shop. Of a particular male coworker she said, "Whenever he was not busy he would come and amuse himself by telling obscene stories and jokes." After she requested and received a separate work table for the females, this man took a dislike to Rose. "He talked of the most intimate relations of married people, in a way that made even the men exclaim and curse him while they laughed. We girls as usual sat with our heads hanging." Another male worker understood the impact of this type of behavior when he commented, "For a young woman unaccustomed to such language there was no greater torment than to work in the midst of this vulgarity." Fannie Shapiro was getting up on a table to fix a machine when the boss came along and pinched her behind. In return she gave him a smack, which caused him to fall down. Shapiro was immediately fired. Sarah Rozner worked in a plant where the foremen were especially "mean to the girls." The women were expected to listen to their dirty jokes and put up with their pinches, pats, and tickles. After one grabbed Rozner by the bust, she threatened to stab him with her scissors. Rozner was immediately fired. However, she was quickly reinstated. As a historian noted of this period, "Not uncommonly, young immigrant women were pinched, fondled, patted, or grabbed by a boss or foreman, either in full sight of the other workers or in a hall, corridor, or office."[10]

Immigrant Elizabeth Hasanovitz went into the boss's office in New York City one day in 1913 to get her pay after two and one-half days at a new job. As she had not worked in some time, she needed the money in advance. They were alone in the office when suddenly the boss grabbed her in his arms. She struggled free and fled. At home she recalled, "I stood up before the mirror and studied my face, trying to find out if there was anything in it that awakened men's impudent feelings toward me. . . . If I could only discredit that man so that he could never dare to insult a working girl again! If only I could complain of him in court! But I had no witnesses to testify the truth; with my broken English I could give very little explanation. Besides that, if I were working in a shop and were called to court, the firm might suspect some evil in me and send me away. So I left him alone and never went to collect my money, although I was in a frightful need."[11]

The sexual harassment of 14-year-old Mary Phagan was of the most extreme form — she was raped and then strangled to death in the pencil factory at Marietta, Georgia, where she was employed. This murder took place on a Saturday, April 27, 1913, when there were few people in the plant. On a note Phagan apparently managed to scribble out before she died, she charged an unnamed black man with having assaulted her. Although the name of Mary Phagan is not remembered by most people, the name of the man quickly arrested, convicted, and sentenced to die for this murder is — Leo Frank, who was white, Jewish, and part owner of the factory. On August 16, 1915, while Frank was in jail as his case was under appeal; he was pulled from his Marietta cell by a mob of 25 to 30 men and lynched. No one was ever charged in this lynching. This case became, and remained, famous because no one believed Frank had anything to do with the crime. It was a case of anti–Semitism at work.[12]

Seventeen-year-old Rosie worked in the needle trade in 1914, where she found "the boss from the shop was always fresh with the girls. He liked to see us blush, so we made a society, called 'The Young Ladies Educational

Society,' and we was not to stand the freshness of the boss. But we was afraid of him, and so we couldn't help each other. Once he touch me, very fresh like, and I cried, and he said, 'Let's be good friends, Rosie.'" Needleworker Atta was an expert at dodging the boss and at threatening him with her needle when he tried to grab her. The first English sentence that Rosa, a new immigrant worker, learned from Atta was "Keep your hands off please."[13]

Frieda W. worked in a shirtwaist factory when her boss asked her to stay after hours to "finish up a sample." When everyone else had gone the boss came up to her and told her he wanted her for a "sweetheart." She declined. A week later he told her, "If you won't be my sweetheart, then you don't work here." She got mad and told him, "The hell with you! And the hell with your job too!" Frieda remarked, "That's already three jobs I had already bad experiences with men. That's when I was young. No more now. Thank God!"[14]

Sexual harassment had become so rife by 1917, particularly among single and or newly arrived immigrant women who worked in factories, that the National Council of Jewish Women's Department of Immigrant Aid was taking newly arrived females and their fiancés to City Hall in order to have a civil marriage ceremony performed "for their protection." At the time conventional wisdom held that after a rape or a coerced sex act the path was "down into prostitution as young women felt that they were suited for no other life." The marriages did not prevent sexual harassment but perhaps precluded abandonment by a fiancé after an episode of forced sex took place.[15]

Nowhere was the hypocrisy of what a company said it stood for and what it tolerated unofficially more evident than in the tobacco factories of the Durham, North Carolina area. During the period of 1880 to 1930 these employers tried to monitor their white female employees to ensure their chasteness. Around 1900 Washington Duke of the Duke tobacco company declared his company policy as one that encouraged workers, particularly young white women, to be "self-respecting, religious and chaste." The Liggett and Myers (L & M) company required chastity on the part of its unmarried white female employees on pain of being dismissed. Nevertheless, these employers not only did not bother to guard the virtue of their black female employees but also "tolerated their sexual exploitation by white foremen." This code supposedly protected white women at L & M from the sexual abuse suffered there by black women, but even the white women were sometimes harassed. One example was at American Tobacco, where "love birds" received favors from management. Annie Mack Barbee, a onetime employee of American Tobacco, recalled how a foreman used the women he supervised by offering them as "sexual favors to the visiting officials sent by American Tobacco from New York. They received benefits, such as being able to rest while others were working."[16]

During the 1930s the same thing was happening with black women, who were still the targets of sexual advances by foremen who tried, in the words of one worker, "to fumble your behind." Many of the women felt helpless to repulse the advances out of fear they would lose their jobs if they objected. When a strike at the R. J. Reynolds Tobacco plant at Winston-Salem, North Carolina, ended in 1947, the Food, Tobacco, Agricultural, and Allied Workers of America announced that "women in the Reynolds plant could now resist the humiliation of sexual advances by foremen without fear of losing their jobs."[17]

Rarely did somebody from the enemy camp—the male overclass—admit the extent or existence of the problem. One who did was industrial consultant and business author Ordway Tead, who wrote of the factory conditions for women in the 1915 period. Noting the power of the foremen and employers over the women, who were wholly dependent on them for employment, Tead told of shirtwaist workers in New York who had been forced to strike to put an end to the familiarities of a superior officer in the company. He also mentioned a mill in a small Massachusetts town where it was an established practice for the plant superintendent to "indulge his passions" at the expense of any of his female workers who were anxious to retain their jobs. "And these cases might be multiplied. When a man can prey upon girls sufficiently under cover to allow his intimidation to become complete, he can have his way with pitiful ease," concluded Tead.[18]

Whether women should or should not work the night shift was the cause of much debate early in this century. Night shift meant any stint of employment that ended from about 9:00 P.M. until 5:00 A.M. or so. It was considered dangerous for women who worked these hours because they were subjected to even more harassment than during a day shift. Also it was thought dangerous for a female to return home at a bad hour such as 2:00 or 3:00 A.M. Others said it was difficult for women who worked those shifts to find a respectable boardinghouse as such a place would not admit a female after midnight. The solution sought was not to somehow contain the behavior of male workers on the night shift, rather it was to deal with the issue by barring females from working such hours. Many jurisdictions did just that. A government study of the glass industry in 1911 observed, "The more evil tendencies of the workers, of the men especially, appear most strongly at night, and it is everywhere observed that the character of the conversation and jesting is at its worst on the night shift."[19] During a 1913 court case before the New York Court of Appeals lawyers arguing in defense of a law barring night work for females cited, among other items, "exposure to the increased vulgarity of men night workers."[20]

Also debated was the number of hours per day a woman should be allowed to work. Often presented as saving women from excessive hard work, these attempts were in fact made to drive women out of the workplace so males could have the jobs. Even here women sometimes caught flak for their supposed immorality as a result of night work, long hours, or some other aspect of the working period. In 1908 the U.S. Supreme Court in *Miller* v. *Oregon* upheld an Oregon statute that limited the number of hours females could work. In a brief to the High Court arguing for the state of Oregon, Louis D. Brandeis, later a Supreme Court justice declared that the prevailing ten-hour day "was likely to leave a woman exhausted, her higher instincts dulled, craving only excitement and sexual pleasure."[21]

Other jurisdictions around the world took similar action to regulate female employment. Beginning in 1874 in France females could not work underground in mines, perform night work, or work more than 11 hours per day. Argentina abolished night work and limited hours for females in 1900. Japan took similar action in 1911. If the trade or industry was all or mostly female dominated, then the laws were more likely to be ignored than if it was a male-dominated trade. Inspectors were few and far between, making detection unlikely. Even if caught and convicted, a company faced nothing save a tiny fine. Invariably these regulations were presented to the public as taken to protect female workers. Speaking in 1877, the president of the American union the Cigar Makers' International advocated such regulations. He was a little more forthright when he stated, "We cannot drive the females out of the trade but we can restrict their daily quota of labor through factory laws."[22]

England had also regulated hours, and in the very early 1900s women were limited to a maximum of 55½ hours per week in textile factories and 60 hours in nontextile plants. Hours for males were unregulated, except for miners. Yet writer Jenny Morris presented evidence to show that women worked more hours each week than did men as well as providing examples of how the law was easily evaded by employers. For example, in a laundry a worker could be listed as a washer for 40 hours and then as an ironer for the last 40 hours of her 80-hour week, making her appear on the books to be two employees. Women working the longer hours were in female-dominated occupations. Men organized into unions and shortened their hours to less than those worked by females in all-female industries, whose hours had by law been "shortened" to "protect" them.[23]

Female factory workers in Mexico in the period 1905–1910 started to organize themselves into unions for protection as they were "underpaid, overworked, mistreated and often taken advantage of sexually by male foremen."[24]

Japanese factories apprenticed girls aged 12 or 13 for a period of several years during the 1910–1915 period. A Western missionary in Japan then complained that the "moral conditions are about as bad as can be. It is estimated that one-half of the girls are ruined before the close of their apprenticeship." Seventy percent of the female factory workers in that country were forced to live in company dorms. "Their overseers are too often men of little principle, and frequently constitute one of the gravest dangers to the girls," added the missionary. Half of the women arrested in 1912 in Osaka as prostitutes had worked in factories.[25]

In Russian factories during the period 1900–1915 conditions were much the same for their female employees. The day in many factories began and ended with the humiliation of a physical search of workers, both sexes. Searches of females were conducted by male supervisory personnel. One worker described them by saying, "The searches were disgraceful. Often they took place in the presence of the shop stewards and other male administrative personnel. Of course, it is clear why they all gathered by the women's exit of the factory. During the search . . . they would toss out remarks of such a content that I cannot bring myself to repeat them." A factory owner contended that there is "nothing immoral about women being searched by men: women workers are accustomed to it and see it as an ordinary thing."[26]

In a tobacco factory the plant administrator was notorious for the sadistic pleasure he derived from forcing the search on employees and especially for his lecherous behavior toward female employees. After making repeated and unsuccessful sexual advances to one young woman, he accused her of stealing from the factory and ordered a special search in full view of the entire factory. Two guards conducted the search. "One fumbled in her sleeves, unbuttoned her dress, and exposed her breasts. . . . The other emptied her pockets, searched the pleats of her skirt and groped in her stockings." Nothing was found. Coworkers tried to comfort the girl, who had been left in a state of shock, but worried over what her fiancé might say. The fear was that others would consider the girl as shamed. Vera Karelina, who tried to organize women workers around Russia, used this story as part of the speech she delivered in her travels.[27]

Summer heat combined with poor ventilation made factories unbearable, with female workers in a majority of cases forced to toil in their underwear, as did the men. A Russian factory inspector acknowledged the need of such measures when he noted, "In the extreme heat all the women workers must work half naked." Then he turned around and, dredging up the old stereotype, accused them of immorality because of it.[28]

Sexual harassment and abuse were commonplace on the shop floor. In a rare complaint to a factory inspector in 1901 in St. Petersburg, a woman said of her foreman, "If a woman worker pleases him, he calls her to his office and is not shy about making the most foul propositions. If she refuses she is subjected to pressure, oppression, and even firing. Once a girl ran out of his office screaming, and the very next day she was fired." This foreman also cursed, swore, and was in the habit of pulling the hair of the women. In a wood-processing plant a worker told of an attempted rape. Although she had fought off this attempt by two male coworkers, one had held her down while the other had smeared "the lower part of her torso with black grease." The factory manager refused to hear her complaint, while other male coworkers who had witnessed the entire episode did nothing except "laugh in an unwholesome way." From a carton factory a woman complained that male workers treated females as if they were prostitutes. "All the time one hears from them nothing but insults and obscene propositions." She related how one of these men exhibited his genitals to mock the women and how another raped a woman in a hidden corner of the factory. If a female worker's appearance did not please the machinist, she could just sit and wait until he was ready to fix her machine. If she complained, he would make her wait even longer. This kept the woman without work and income. "It is not unusual for the machinist to make obscene propositions. In most cases the woman submits to them because she is afraid that he will not repair her machine."[29]

Some males did condemn this type of behavior. In St. Petersburg in 1913 representatives from 15 factories in that city reprimanded male workers at the Novyi Bessner plant for stationing themselves at the female employees' exits and hurling "curses and obscenities at them." These representatives threatened to make public the names of the offenders if the practice did not stop. That same year a male employee at a metalworking plant wrote a letter to *Pravda* detailing how his coworkers treated females at the plant. "They insult them, mock them, make disgusting propositions, and beat them up for no reason but to have fun."[30]

When the Weavers' and Winders' Association held a meeting in 1912 in Todmorden, a small weaving town northeast of Manchester, England, someone complained about the ill-treatment of children in the large, local cotton mill, Hoyles' Derdale plant. This led W. J. Tout, the secretary of the union to launch an investigation. He was diligent with the investigation, which lasted some months. Thirty-one women employed at the mill testified at the union office. Perhaps suddenly faced with an opportunity to speak to someone not openly hostile or holding their future in his hands, these women unburdened themselves. But it was not about child abuse, for they told of acts ranging from men's offensive language to some acts deemed to be "unprintable." Almost as soon as the investigation started, it dropped the question of the reported thrashing of boys in the weaving department, with Tout concentrating on the issue of sexual harassment complaints. A number of female winders told of being molested in an artificially lit mill passage. This had become such a regular occurrence that women waited for one another in the morning rather than walk along the passageway alone. If a young woman was walking alone, the light had a habit of going out. Then, said a contemporary account, "in the dark, an arm has been placed round their waist, and worse things have followed." During the two months prior to this investigation six or seven females had been molested in this passage leading to the winding room. Other women who spoke to Tout gave him the impression that they had been subjected to harassment but were too ashamed to publicly admit it. Some of these females had gone to management at the mill to complain about being molested, but they were referred back to their department heads, who did nothing, perhaps being involved in the harassment. One woman had quit the mill twice to get away from the abuse but was forced to return when she could find no other work. Women who had left the plant years earlier came forward to give statements similar to those of the employees of 1912. Tout remarked, "One thing that has surprised me . . . is the number of people who knew or had heard about these things. It must have been a public scandal." When management of the mill was presented with the evidence gathered by Tout, it stonewalled in the normal fashion by promising a full inquiry.[31]

When Liston Pope examined the relationship between Gaston County, North Carolina textile mills and the church, he interviewed pastors of mill village churches, many of whom gave evidence of direct control by mills over churches in the county. One told him that "a prominent official of an uptown church in Gastonia in the early 1920s was superintendent of three mills around the industrial church I was pastor over. He was a notorious whoremonger, and took girls from the night shift out into the grass nearly every night. Because I knew this, and he knew that I did, he undermined me with the uptown church, and I had to leave the pastorate."[32]

The textile mills of the Lowell, Massachusetts, area continued to operate until around 1960, when the last one finally shut down. Sexual harassment continued there throughout the latter period. Emma, a comber in 1940, recalled, "Oh, the boys used to get away with murder!. . . They would be coming up our aisles and squeezing us, and oh, you could not concentrate. One would have the sweeping job and was supposed to sweep in the aisles and at the same time he would be, you know. . . . So one day I got very mad at him. I told him I didn't like that. You know, he used to squeeze me. He didn't care." Harry Dickenson, a loom fixer from 1922 to 1954, remembered, "For instance, this girl — she was a lovely girl, you know what I mean? She was a battery hand. I guess the boss was trying to riga-marole, but she wouldn't come across. What he did, he took her off the job that she was used to and put her on another job. Finally she quit. There was a lot of that done. The boss taking advantage of a person like that. You either come across or nothing." Henry Paradis was a loom fixer from 1937 to 1954 who said, "Actually as far as trouble goes, the trouble was with the supervisors. . . . A girl would come in neat and nice looking, and oh, cripes, you're not going to stay here long. Because the supervisors, the Romeos, they think they can do anything they want to do or have anything they want."[33]

Mary Blewett, who collected the Lowell reminiscences, commented that the network of older family members recruiting younger ones into the mills afforded at least some small protection for women workers but that any presentable young woman who walked into one of these mills looking for work became an easy target. She added, "Taking their cues from the petty tyrannies practiced by the bosses, some male workers felt free to annoy and molest women in the mill. Most bosses remained indifferent to such sexual harassment. Young women who needed to keep their attention on the work and dangerous machinery were taken advantage of. Even then bosses rarely intervened. Many women regarded their bosses as 'hard' and felt that they could make no complaint for fear of being fired.... Male workers sometimes sexually harassed young women, knowing that the boss would look the other way.... Male workers were well aware of the sexual harassment of women by supervisors, which was one good reason to see to it that wives or daughters never entered the mill."[34]

At the Ternstedt General Motors parts plant in Detroit in 1937 most women were subjected to sexual harassment. When some of these women were interviewed years later, virtually all commented on the problem of harassment and the pressure to trade sexual favors for jobs. "Women who refused to participate in this exchange reported receiving poorer work assignments, less work, less tractable machines, and constant harassment from foremen." When the auto workers were unionized that year, sexual harassment diminished as unionization lessened the power of foremen to extract sexual activity in exchange for work. For example, under union conditions layoffs and recalls were done on the basis of seniority. This improvement for women workers was the indirect result of changes designed mainly to improve conditions for men. The issue of sexual harassment of women in the industry was not addressed.[35]

At other plants that the United Auto Workers (UAW) was in the process of organizing in the 1930s similar conditions prevailed. "Women also were subject to sexual harassment by foremen who extorted dates and other favors in exchange for employment," reported one account. After one female worker joined the UAW local at the Midland Steel plant in Detroit, a union official asked what had prompted her to join. Expecting her to respond it was for higher wages, he was surprised to hear her reply, "[Because] when you belong to a union, the foreman can't screw you. Last month my foreman asked me to go out with him and I told him 'to hell with you Charlie, I know what you want.' He got mad but he didn't try to spite me. He knew damn well the union would be on his neck if he did."[36]

Over at the General Electric plant that same decade the United Electrical Workers (UE) instituted seniority systems for layoffs and the rehiring of workers. Sadie Rosenberg of UE local 427 remembered, "I can think of some of the gals who actually had to sleep with some of these guys, and you'd expect the hands to creep as the foremen walked up and down the aisles." Rosenberg acknowledged that the harassment was never eliminated but felt that the situation improved for the better for females once her plant was unionized.[37]

During the 1930s labor agents traveled the countryside around Shanghai, China, where they bought teenage girls from their parents. These girls were contracted to work for the labor agent for a fixed number of years. Eighteen-year-old Tao Kougu was in her dormitory one night when her agent broke into her room and raped her repeatedly over several days. Another girl was beaten by her contractor until her eyes were swollen shut after she refused his demands for sex. Such cases were typical. "These girls frequently lost their virginity, because they either were raped by the contractors themselves or were passed on to other hoodlums."[38]

Many of these girls were contracted out by their agents to Shanghai cotton mills, where they and the regularly hired female employees were subjected to further abuse. Foremen routinely combined sexual harassment with regular discipline. Those who resisted advances risked punishment or firing. Worker Wang Luoying recalled of one of the foremen, "Then if there were young girl workers who did not have a mate, he would want them to be his mate, and sleep with him. If a girl went along with him he would give her more comfortable work. . . . If you did not go along with the male foreman, he could give you lousy and hard work. Because of this situation some women just left the mill to go somewhere else to work." At the Japanese-owned Dong Hua Mill an overseer propositioned a worker. When she refused, he beat her badly, causing serious injuries. Incidents such as that one were frequently reported in the Shanghai press.[39]

Around the same period cotton mill workers in Tianin, China, reportedly were victimized. One such woman employee said, "There were people who played up to the foremen, and people that the foremen took a fancy to. If you didn't go alone, he would always pick on you. Some people couldn't take it and had to leave. There were some the foreman fired if they didn't consent. It was a common thing."[40]

In the 1930s Bengali females who were employed in mills as jute workers in Calcutta, India, were regularly equated by public moralists with prostitutes. The assistant director of public health for that city stated in 1930 that "among female workers, one out of every four owns to being a prostitute." A study of the period suggested that the majority of Calcutta's women jute workers were prostitutes, "especially if they owned jewellery." What was more certain of the time and place was that a female factory laborer had to have male protection in the workplace and in her living quarters because "single women labourers were particularly vulnerable to sexual harassment and women without husbands were thus forced to find a male worker with whom them could cohabit," wrote one source. These jute workers became more militant in the 1940s as a consequence of the double oppression they faced as females. As well as economic oppression, "they constantly faced the moral opprobrium of the wider society and of their male fellow workers, which constituted them as loose."[41]

Workers in South African textile mills were severely exploited economically and sexually harassed. Mostly these employees were lower-class white females. One observer addressed the problem at a tangent when he noted in the 1920s that the difficulties encountered by these women were "not only of an economic order." An examination of the conditions of female textile workers in the early 1930s found that they had many complaints, including sexual harassment. Over a decade later when writer Louis Freed documented the problem of European prostitution in Johannesburg, he argued that the high level of sexual harassment in factories facilitated women taking that "short step" to prostitution. Clothing workers complained in 1931 of "rude and vulgar" treatment and pressure to go out with the foreman or the boss in order to keep their jobs.

While a high degree of segregation kept black male and white female interactions to a minimum in factories, campaigns were nonetheless mounted from outside the plants to "protect" white women. One black male supervisor in 1934 was sentenced to three months' hard labor for an alleged "indecent assault": touching a white female worker on one occasion and putting his arm around her on another. Even though the magistrate found a certain amount of conflict in the evidence, he felt a harsh sentence was necessary because the defendant's actions displayed a lack of respect for the plaintiff. This case resulted in a widespread campaign, led by the white, middle-class South African League of Women Voters, to stop the possibility of "native foremen" controlling "European girls." This agitation led the government's Labour Department to conduct an investigation, which it claimed revealed that only 79 white females worked under nonwhite supervision and that "in no case was the supervisor a native." Soon the focus extended to Asians as well. Those white female textile workers being "protected" expressed anger and indignation when interviewed about the situation. They said that their current Asian employers treated them far better than had former white employers. Likely this was so because the strong taboos against white females interacting with nonwhite males may have afforded them a measure of protection not available under whites. As in so many other cases one response to harassment in the South African mills was to move the complainers. One example occurred in 1939 in the Consolidated Textile Mills at Huguenot, where "at one stage all the work ... was confined to European labour, but owing to the familiar behavior of the European male employers toward the women, the management was compelled to replace a portion of them by Non-European labour."[42]

Factories around the world remained dangerous places for female employees into the modern era. Shanta and Lalita worked in a large textile mill in India in the 1970s. Both claimed females employed there were compelled to have sexual relations with supervisors and management to keep their jobs. Shanta explained that some women in the mill were employed as temporaries. They got 15–20 days' work each month. And the number of days' work they received depended on their supervisor. "If a supervisor wants to have it with a particular woman, he'll give her work for, say, ten days. If she asks him for more, he'll ask her out; and these days people can't fill their stomachs on only ten days' work." Asked how common this sexual abuse was in their mill, Lalita responded, "No one can even estimate the actual number, but it's fairly widespread." In spite of all this Shanta still blamed the victim, saying, "I feel that if a woman wants to avoid it, she can." When she was asked if the union could act in some fashion to stop this abuse, Shanta explained, "Our union people don't think it's a problem — they too feel it can be avoided if women want."[43]

Kamala worked at an Indian tobacco plant but wished she could somehow work at home because "the male workers and owner look at us women with the eyes of hungry wolves. At least we could be free from this at home." Radhika was employed by a garment factory in India, also in the 1970s. She related that "fifteen of us were crowded in one room without ventilation, nothing. One of the women was being wrongly used by our employer. . . . We felt and were made to believe that the other women too had relations with the employer."[44]

Textile worker Clara Thrift was employed in a North Carolina mill in the 1960s when one of the mill bosses was going out with some of the workers. Related Clara, "He had said something to me about going out with him and I had said no. He was married and I knew his wife. I used to work with her. Well, after I had said no, he put me on a bad set of machines. One thing led to another and I quit." This boss openly favored some women over others, giving the ones he liked the best set of machines to operate. Seniority rules were supposed to prevail, but the employees knew the mill did not work that way. "Favoritism meant like, you go out with me and I'll see that you get a good set of machines and make good money," explained Clara. She was upset enough by what was happening that she went to personnel and complained, only to find out later that the man she spoke with, "as it turned out, was also going out with the women."[45]

Of the 85 percent female work force in 1970 of clothing plant Farah Manufacturing in El Paso, Texas, most were Chicanas. Those women who were pretty and willing to date their supervisors received preferential treatment on the job. One seamstress who had worked on a particular job for 20 years received a smaller salary than a young woman who had been on that same job for only 1 year. Less favored females were also subjected to closer supervision, speedups, and so on.[46]

Toward the end of the 1970s male coworkers were asked if females working in American steel mills had problems. In addition to expected comments such as women have lower physical strength, one inspector mentioned that women got harassed a lot. Another man added that females had difficulty in adjusting to the language used in what had been an all-male environment. Observed a mechanic who admitted that his female coworkers had to fight off wolves, "Women should learn to deal with it; that's just how guys are."[47]

When English working women were questioned about their lives, none was routinely asked about sexual harassment, yet several brought it up themselves. Sheila, then in her thirties, related an incident that had occurred almost 20 years before in the 1960s when she was a teenager on her first job in a paper mill. The mill foreman, said Sheila, "used to touch all the young girls. . . . When the young ones used to start they used to start in the cutter house, you know — they was all like fifteen-year-old girls, and he used to — you know — be rude to them." Sheila quit that job due to the harassment, as had the other women who brought the issue up.[48]

When female employees in Pakistan were questioned in 1975, the majority of these factory workers expressed a preference for female supervisors instead of male because, among other reasons, "men consider us sex objects. They accost us. We do not have such problems with women supervisors." One employee complained that a male coworker pursued and harassed her both inside and outside the plant even to the extent that he followed her home. Even though she constantly complained to management, nothing was done. Finally management did speak to him, but he boldly told her that management could not stop him from "loving a woman."[49]

Looking at Peruvian female factory workers in 1978–1979, Carol Andreas did not deal with the sexual harassment issue but did coincidentally shed some indirect light on the problem, albeit without any details. With an economic recession wracking Peru, factory closures increased. Some women workers took over their factories in an effort to keep them operating, while others marched to demand improvements such as better wages and day care. At the same time "demonstrations and pickets denounced rape and harassment of women by managers and bosses."[50]

A privately owned steel mill in Venezuela hired a number of females for its mill in 1976. These 75 were the first women employed in steel production in that country. Reasons given by the company for this step were a shortage of male labor and a belief that women would be more docile. Almost immediately the plant manager complained that problems of seduction and pregnancy had arisen because "confrontations between men and unwilling women on the job led to fooling around in the plant." Blame for this turn of events was placed on "hotblooded young males for whom sex was primordial" and "inexperienced young girls" who allowed the men to take liberties and "didn't know how to command respect." One complaint of sexual harassment against a foreman was lodged with the company and investigated. In the absence of concrete evidence this man was transferred to a section of the plant that had no female workers. A male laborer who attempted to molest a coworker away from the plant was fired.[51]

Venezuela's state-owned steel mill hired its first female production workers in 1979. Reportedly a number of men were fired for harassing these women. In the absence of any official policy for females in the mill, plant supervisors handled each case of harassment on an individual basis. Completely divided on the issue was the labor union, which represented the steelworkers. Only a minority of the all-male executive board of the union was inclined to include women's issues in its agenda. For the majority of the board female employees in the mill "only distract the men and cause trouble at the mill." As a result the union did not involve itself in the issue. By 1981 the situation had become even more intolerable for most women at the mill. Forced to finally move due to rapidly deteriorating conditions, the union denounced what by then was known as "Operation Mattress," whereby "only women who slept with foremen would be allowed to keep their jobs." Under the plant system laborers were required to file any complaints they had with their immediate supervisor. In the case of women with sexual complaints all too often the person who received the complaint was also the harasser. Female engineers in the plant tried to set up support groups for victimized female laborers, but upper-level management which disbelieved or refused to accept the idea that harassment was rife, ordered them to immediately cease their "radical feminist" activities under a threat of loss of their jobs. After a look at the question mill management declared that "Operation Mattress was a fabrication promoted by the union"; no action was taken at all.[52]

Confounding the issue with class distinction, female engineers at the plant reported that sexual harassment was not a problem for them, although several mentioned that they had been approached, but in a very subtle way. Men professionals did not make open demands; instead they couched proposals in jokes or spoke of them as "favors" to the women, they explained. Most female engineers also said that they had sufficient social skills to fend off proposals "without offending the source."[53]

A few of the women production workers at the steel plant did receive promotions; however, the three who rose most quickly in salary and position were not the ones with the most training or the most competence. These women were the ones, as pointed out by coworkers and a male supervisor, who "maintain[ed] sexual relationships with foremen from the production area. In this particular area, promotions of laborers were determined by foremen."[54]

Workers in South African textile plants still had problems in the 1970s, but by that time most were black women. During a strike at the Consolidated Textile Mills in 1973 it was reported that male supervisors might grant permission to go to the bathroom or the "privilege" of resting briefly during working hours in exchange for sexual favors. Women workers reported that male workers had no respect for them. On the factory floor the males mistreated them and became "vulgar by touching the women in embarrassing parts." Others related that if they complained of sexual abuse to supervisors, those managers took the side of the males. Another large strike of textile workers broke out in the Frame factories around Durban in 1980, where the work force was 70 percent female, with 90 percent of those being migrants who lived in hostels. During the strike the hostel security and regulation system broke down. Nonresidents had easier access to the women's rooms. The women became the target of police violence and youth gangs, with many of them being robbed and raped. Some of the women who were sexually assaulted by nonstrikers were then ordered to return to work by their attackers. Many of these females were forced to flee their hostel accommodation for the nearest available safe place—a man's bed. Reported a 1980 study of the strike, "Once again, women found themselves having to choose between the lesser of two abuses—rape by, or involuntary submission to, male coworkers."[55]

The image of loose, immoral, and promiscuous women turned up again in Malaysia in the 1980s and was firmly attached to the female factory workers of that country. The public was said to attribute a "heightened sexuality" to these women. Newspapers and other media outlets regularly ran stories that these factory women were sexually servicing tourists and soldiers. When these women were simply going about their business, such as on the street shopping, clerks, street urchins, and other passersby often yelled names at these women, such as "perumpuan jahat (bad women/prostitutes)." One woman factory worker complained that the public considered factory women on the same low level as streetwalkers. She argued that office workers were also known to be "immoral" but that the public was less concerned because these women had higher academic qualifications than did the factory women. Some of the factories tried to take their female employees who were not living at home, especially the ones from rural areas, and quarter them together in the same group of rooming houses. A personnel manager explained that he felt responsibility for these young women, saying "Since they are exposed to dangers, we have to look after them."[56]

In the factories women who asked for medical leave could be rudely questioned by foremen making humiliating innuendos. In a 1976 incident a foreman at one factory was set upon, beaten, and badly hurt by an unknown gang. When an assistant foreman came to help, he was also assaulted.

According to an informal questioning of workers after the incident, the foreman deserved to be punished "because he refused workers their 15 minute break, insulted them about personal matters, followed women into the locker room, and threatened to terminate their employment whenever he felt necessary." The company retained this foreman but told him to alter his behavior. At a different factory one supervisor reported that he, and all the other male supervisors, had been "warned by Malay youths that reports of their mistreatment of women workers would invite personal retaliation."[57]

When Commissioner for Equal Opportunity Fay Marles delivered her 1979 annual report in Victoria, Australia, she described sexual harassment as a problem of a "particularly serious nature." Considering that many inquiries to her office did not lead to formal complaints, she worried that sexually harassing behavior could be very much more prevalent than originally thought. Talking to welfare groups in Victoria, Marles found that "when it comes to exploitation of migrant women, sexual harassment was one of the most difficult things they faced in the factory."[58]

Around 1982 Paula worked in a San Salvador, El Salvador, biscuit factory. She recounted how the supervisors constantly bothered the women, said insinuating things to them, and made insulting remarks. Living in dire poverty, these women often needed small sums of money to tide them over to payday, and "in many cases, in order to obtain a loan, the women would have to go to bed with one of the supervisors or the boss."[59]

Sonia, of Rio de Janeiro, was interviewed in 1983 about her experiences working in Brazilian factories. "In the factory there were girls who got fired because they wouldn't go along, and the bosses got angry and fired them," she said. "The operators were Black and White women, blondes, mulattos, and the bosses were by and large White.... Yes, they were after the women—for sex, you know, they've got no real preference, it's all the same to them.... Lots of women left because they wouldn't go along."[60]

From South Korea came 1981 reports that in the factories located in the free export zones of that country Japanese supervisors sexually abused the female employees with impunity.[61] Reports from China in the mid–1980s indicated that female factory workers were often forced into having sex with their superiors. One 1984 case was dubbed in the press as "three heads taking liberties with a woman." It involved two superiors from a factory near Loyang and a local government official who made sexual advances to a female employee of the plant while the group was attending meetings in Beijing. The advances were made with implicit threats that made the woman fear offending her superiors. She was saved from rape by hotel security staff who heard her screams. The three men were sent to jail, with the female being rebuked for being afraid to offend her superiors.[62]

By the end of the 1980s a soft-drink factory in Queretaro, Mexico, was employing no women in the production areas. The factory had in the past but had "had" to get rid of them all due to conflicts of a "sexual nature which developed between male and female staff." In 1979 a large multinational cereal factory in Mexico had laid off women employees because of "personal attachments" and the fact that men resented taking orders from women. The following year this company started to hire women again but limited them to female-only departments in the plant. An agricultural machinery plant in Queretaro had no female operatives either as it believed a mixed work force would lead to sexual relations and conflicts. In addition a Mexican turbine plant had no female production workers. The only female employee who had contact with male factory workers was a single woman cleaner, whom this company "had" to get rid of "because she was subjected to so much sexual harassment by the male workers."[63]

Canada's largest steel plant, Stelco, located in Hamilton, Ontario, hired its first women for production work in the mill in 1979. It was a move taken not of the company's own choosing but in response to a variety of pressures brought about by different groups, including militant women who wanted to see equality extended to the integration of this gigantic steel mill. Although the pressure was successful, from the start Stelco tried to make things so unpleasant for these new employees that no woman would want to stay. By 1984 only a handful of females were employed in the plant. Some had quit because of harassment, others had fallen victim to an economic recession and been laid off. One of those hired in 1979 was Bonita Clark, a pump tender then aged 27. What happened to her was typical of how Stelco treated its females. Shortly after being hired, Clark was subjected to repeated sexual harassment by her foreman. He insulted her verbally, physically grabbed her upper body, and followed her around the plant continually. Things just got worse when she complained about this treatment. Male foremen banded together and spread stories of a sexual nature about her around the plant in retaliation. When she took her complaints to higher supervision, the harassment only intensified. She was repeatedly ordered to enter the men's washrooms and change area and clean them. Stelco refused to screen off the men's shower room, with the result that Clark had to see them naked. In response to her complaints, supervisors told her to shut up and enjoy the free show. Plant supervision insisted that each time Clark wished to go to the toilet she ask permission. Male workers were not required to do this. Each complaint about this brought only insults from supervisors. Eventually Clark was told that each time she wanted to go to the toilet, she would have to ask permission over the plant intercom, audible to all. Commented Clark, "Supervisors made any access to the washroom an embarrassing hardship. I felt humiliated." During 1984 she complained about the pornographic graffiti on the walls. She filed grievances with the union over many of these incidents. The union duly put each grievance in and duly dropped each one later on, claiming the contract language in that area was not strong enough for the union to accomplish anything. She went to the Ontario Human Rights Commission to complain. That body wrote up a complaint but never got a reply from Stelco. In September 1985 Clark filed charges with the Ontario Labour Relations Board claiming sexual harassment by Stelco over a six-year period.[64]

Joan Keopple started work at the Stroh's brewery in St. Paul, Minnesota, in 1984. As the first female machinist on the plant floor she was subjected to jokes and catcalls from her first day on the job. Among her many allegations of sexual harassment were that the women's locker room was termed "the beaver lounge" and that a male machinist who worked with several women was called "the mayor of pussyville." In one instance a male coworker asked her to wrap her legs around his neck; male employees would leave porn magazines in her presence, saying what they would do to the pictured females. Often beer was poured into her tool cart, and pornographic pictures were left in her drawer. On the bathroom walls graffiti included "Jean Keopple fucks pigs" and, after she befriended an African-American foreman, "Jean Keopple sucks black dick." Despite her repeated complaints, the harassment against her and other female employees continued. Finally in 1991 she and seven other women employees filed suit against the company, asking more than $350,000 each in damages. Stroh's denied that the brewery condoned sexual harassment. By late 1992 only one of the plaintiffs still worked at Stroh's, with the others taking leaves or other jobs. This case achieved notoriety because the plaintiffs also demanded that the brewery stop sexually exploiting women in its advertising. Specifically cited were the five bikini-clad actresses in commercials for Stroh's brand Old Milwaukee beer—the Swedish Bikini Team. The issue of this jiggle ad quickly overshadowed the harassment aspects of the case.[65]

Working conditions in Honduras in an industrial park free-trade zone containing seven Korean-owned factories were abysmal in all respects in the early 1990s. At the garment assembly factory SP Honduras only 50 of the 900 workers were male. Most female employees were aged 12 to 20. Former employee Irma Malinsy Torres related that every day her supervisor, Mr. Pak, came up behind her and said, "Chici, chici, you are going to have a baby with me." To avoid the harassment she got herself transferred to another area. When her machine jammed, she sent for a mechanic to fix it. He started touching her on the leg. She took his hand away, but he continued to grab at her leg. When she persisted in removing his hand, he finally screamed at her in Korean and left without repairing the machine. Another former employee, Carmen Portillo, said that sometimes when a worker would not let the supervisors touch her, she was suspended without pay or forced to lift a bench and hold it over her head for three hours. If she let it down, Pak hit her in the buttocks with a stick.[66]

7
The Trades
and Blue-Collar Workers

Women in nontraditional, blue-collar, hard-hat–type occupations found sexual harassment prevalent, just as women in factory work did. When Jeffrey Riemer looked at the construction trades in America in 1977, he concluded that females experienced on-the-job harassment and physical abuse at the hands of their male coworkers. Complaints included being the object of graffiti campaigns, finding dildos fashioned from bananas or large screws in their lunch boxes, finding nude centerfolds (male and female) in their toolboxes, and having a full range of sexist and verbal sexual abuse directed at them. The most frequent type of abuse was verbal. Comments between male coworkers after one had worked with a female on a specific task included "Did she give you a good job today?" "How does it feel to have a woman working under you?" and "You mean you were up in that crawlspace with her all day?" These comments were always delivered so the woman in question would hear them. As an example of physical abuse Riemer told of a female apprentice carpenter in California who was cornered after work by two journeymen and told to quit. When she refused, one held her down while the other smashed her thumbs with a hammer.[1]

Jean Schroeder collected the reminiscences of women in the trades during the 1970s and 1980s. Most of them worked in the Pacific Northwest. Truck driver Kathryn Brooke recounted that the male drivers all called her a beaver. (The term *beaver* is an epithet for vagina.) They had bumper stickers about beavers such as "Save our forest. Eat a beaver." Papermaker Beverly Brown recalled there were spaces behind her machine where no one could see anything that was going on. Supervisors would joke to her, "Let's get Beaver [also her nickname] behind the machine." Brown continued, "I've had lots of men try to corner me—just thinking it was fun and jokes. I didn't think it was fun and jokes and I let them know now." Coworkers would make remarks such as "You aren't going to get your tit caught in the winder, are you?" "Gee, you could show a little bit more cleavage there," "Boy we sure like the way you bounce when you bend over," and "Don't bend over like that in front of me; you know better."[2]

Electrician Anna Brinkley was sexually harassed by the lead man on an electrical job. She had entered the trades partly for the higher pay and partly to escape the sexual abuse she had received in her earlier occupation of waitressing. A woman bus driver would find male drivers waiting for her at the terminal when she finished her shift. When she stepped off the bus, they would yell at her in unison, "Do you wanna fuck?" Steel hauler Mary Rathke recalled that her dispatcher was a male chauvinist who was always making suggestive remarks to her. Once in a while Rathke felt as if she had to play along with him a little. If she did not, she feared he would not call her into work. As Rathke was not then on the seniority list, the dispatcher was at liberty not to call her in if he did not want to. Although she never got involved with him, she felt she could not just say, "Knock it off, you idiot," even though she often felt like it. "But I found, like for me, you have to walk on a fence, you have to be willing to put up with a certain amount of teasing and carrying on, and joking. . . . You can't be offended by it," she explained. "Here you are, the only woman in this man's world, and you'd better get along or get out."[3]

Working as an outside machinist in a shipyard, Barbara Shaman had coworkers tell her to go home because she should not be there. They wrote on the bulkheads of ships "outrageous stuff about women." Shaman would go to find an area of the ship that needed work. When she got there and shined her flashlight, all of a sudden she would see on this bulkhead comments "literally engraved in steel, about—really nasty, derogatory comments about women, women's bodies, and what some men would like to do." When Katie Murray first started work as a sheet metal worker, her coworkers gave her a hard time and wrote "dirty words on the ladies-room walls about what they would like me to do for them—sex and like that. . . . And when I would walk up the aisles they would make wise cracks about what they would like to do. I just kept walkin' and pretended I didn't hear 'em. . . . The white men think they can take advantage of a black woman." Teresa Selfe found that when she attended seamanship school, a couple of the teachers made constant references in class to "women's bodies, other women's bodies, my woman's body." She also remembered being called "cutie" or "good-looking" and in general being treated with a very general lack of respect. Selfe likened it to being in the "Green Bay Packers locker room." Later when she was working on ships as a sailor, she found herself subjected continually to such harassment.[4]

Machinist Amy Kelley opened her tool cabinet door one day to find a nude centerfold stuck there. It was just one of many examples of harassment she could cite. "I had one supervisor that used to come up behind me and pat me on the butt, and I didn't even know he was back there. And

I had another supervisor that would come around, when I didn't know it, and snap my bra strap." She told one to stop and filed a complaint on the other. They stopped. Kelley said that other problems came from managers rather than coworkers. Although she admitted the latter subjected her to a lot of joking and teasing, she said that did not bother her.[5]

Another collection of stories about the lives of blue-collar working women in the 1980s included the tale of Gigi Marino, who went to sea as a merchant sailor for the very first time in 1981 on an Exxon ship. She was the only female on board, with the other sailors all regarding her as fair game. Marino said that most of these men considered women on ships to be loose and lascivious creatures. Their most commonly asked question about such women did not concern their ability or competence as sailors but centered around whom the women slept with. Marino cringed with embarrassment on that voyage when a shipmate confided in her that the crew discussed her breast size during coffee breaks. Within the first few days she was propositioned and harassed by a middle-aged officer. Flustered by this, Marino consulted the chief engineer about what to do. This man consoled her by saying that if he were a female on a ship and did not get propositioned, "then he'd start worrying." Marian Swerdlow started work in 1982 as a subway conductor with the New York City Transit Authority. So often was she propositioned that she dealt with it by joking about giving a civil service exam for the position, complete with filing fee and physical. Fai Coffin dealt with her harasser by stomping on his hand. Beth Szillagyi was a sheet metal worker pestered constantly for dates by a married electrician who took to blowing her kisses in front of other people. She got rid of him finally by giving him what was supposed to be her phone number. It turned out to be the number for Dial-a-Devotion.[6]

Rose Melendez started work as a San Francisco police officer in 1974. A decade later between 30 and 40 female cops on that force formed a support group to "address the sexual harassment that was causing life-threatening situations on the street." As examples she cited that a woman calling in for help or needing backup would be cut off, somebody would keep talking so she could not get through, or help would not show up when it was needed. All of these actions were the result of repulsed sexual advances. Some male officers were also getting tired of the situation because they were cut off on the radio as well just because they might be friendly with or work with some of the women. According to Melendez, sexual harassment had been tolerated by the department until then, but the chief started to take the issue seriously when the women approached it as an officers' safety issue.[7]

Policewomen have suffered from a great deal of sexual harassment as their proportion on police forces has risen. Prior to the mid-to-late-1960s they comprised only a token number, being limited to a narrow role dealing with females and minors. Female officers were allowed that token role partly because of sexual harassment in the first place. Initially they broke into the ranks of prison guards, or matrons, because female prisoners were being assaulted by male guards. When New York's City Prison, known as the Tombs, opened in 1838, female detainees were housed in the same building as male prisoners. Following a "brutal outrage" females were housed in a separate building.[8]

Agitation spread to a demand for matrons in police station lockups, with complaints about the "systematic outrage on the sacredness of womanhood which is constantly perpetuated by the Police." The attempted rape of a 15-year-old detainee by a police officer in a New York police station in 1890 caused enough of a stir to help force the city to hire matrons. Even the *New York Times* previously opposed to matrons, came around and editorialized that "recent experience has given new force to the demand for matrons." Many other areas had already hired matrons during the 1870s and especially the 1880s. Among the reasons for opposing the hiring of matrons in police stations, a favorite given by police commissioners was that "a police matron would not be safe from insult by the policemen of the station houses."[9]

Problems for female police officers surfaced publicly around 1975 in Washington, D.C., when they reported harassment. Officer Peggy A. Jackson complained, "You've got to make love to get a day off or make love to get a good beat." Most of the females would not officially complain because they feared retaliation from their superiors. Penny Bolden reported that her male partner pulled their squad car into a Washington park, requested that she have sex with him, and warned her to say nothing about it. Of the District of Columbia's 333 policewomen in 1975, approximately half had been assigned to patrol duty, with interviewed policewomen estimating about half of them had been sexually harassed. One of the most often heard stories these women told "consisted of male officers—many of whom outrank the women—punishing policewomen who would not submit to sexual advances and rewarding those who did with better treatment and assignments." Washington police chief Maurice J. Cullinane termed these charges "unsubstantiated innuendo and back-alley gossip" and dismissed the allegations on the grounds that to that date he had received no official complaints.[10]

When a female officer was assigned with many others to protect a visiting foreign dignitary's hotel, a sergeant came up to her and said in front of other males, "Come on, I have a room. I want a header." At a signing out several male police officers looked at one female officer's chest and remarked, "How long do you think she can float?" This woman said, "I know this is sexism and I try to put them in their place but if I get snippy they'll get me for insubordination." When another female was harassed by a male officer who told her, "I just want you to know that you have the biggest breasts I've ever seen on a policewoman," she did upbraid him in front of his peers. However, she quickly acquired a reputation for being "stuck up, snotty and evil; even being a lesbian." "I preferred it that way. Then they'd leave me alone," she added. Among male and female officers there was a strong feeling that the women harassed had "asked for it." According to many female cops, "It all depends on how a woman carries herself." One commented, "If a person cannot deal with their own sexuality, they have no business having a gun, arresting people or making serious decisions about other people." This was a standard she did not apply to men.[11]

Female police officers arrived later in India than in the United States, with the result that in the late 1970s they still functioned mainly to protect female detainees from the sexual assaults of male police officers. About half of the male officers regarded the female cops as being of easy morals. However, the women said that "generally when policewomen are recruited they are not bad, but are made bad . . . . They sometimes fall prey to the sexual lust of the male officers."[12]

A study of women in English police forces in the mid–1980s when women made up about 11 percent of the total sworn personnel and 1–2 percent of the senior officers found much harassment. The senior officer of a female officer in central London was replaced by a man she termed a "frightful little creep" who made advances to her. When she rebuffed him, "he made life extremely difficult. He blocked any application I made to do anything more interesting." She later resigned. Another woman constable related that being one of the boys meant sleeping around, with the result she was called a "relief bicycle." The one who refused became a "lesbo." If rumors spead that a woman slept around, that might affect promotion. A senior officer might say, "She's a bit free and easy. We don't want her," explained a woman inspector. On a large northern force a female sergeant experienced severe problems because she refused sexual demands on more than one occasion, noting, "I wouldn't sleep with senior officers. If you say no, they take it as a personal insult; and no matter what they say, they really do take it out on you." Commenting on the prevasiveness of harassment, a woman constable said, "It's just a way of life and you have to take it in good part." Harassers were called "canteen cowboys." Another constable stated that having a married male constable ask her out was just "part and parcel" of the job. A married chief inspector in uniform turned up at her door one night with a bottle of wine. She made some excuse, but two nights later the same thing happened. This time she told him no in blunt terms. "And he then made my life hell for two months," she exclaimed.[13]

Peter Horne's 1980 study of women in law enforcement barely acknowledged the problem. He cited one female officer, who said that it was practically an unwritten rule that with certain male supervisors "you've got to make love to get a day off or a good beat and you've definitely got to put out to get a superior performance evaluation." However, Horne devoted less than half a page to sexual harassment in police forces, calling it "a very small problem percentage-wise," while devoting more than a page explaining how female police officers can and do use sexuality to manipulate male supervisors.[14]

Writer Susan Martin interviewed 71 female cops in the late–1980s; 75 percent indicated they had experienced sexual harassment on the job. There was little difference in the rate of harassment whether the woman entered policing prior to 1975, in the 1985–86 period, or in between. Of the 75 percent harassed, 49 percent reported being pressured by fellow officers or supervisors for intercourse. Besides sexual propositions the males harassed the women with frequent pranks, jokes, and comments. One woman said, "There were constant comments and always a 'Hustler' lying around." Many of the women interviewed recalled events that took place over a decade previously, yet still broke down in tears. Some were evasive; some still burned with anger. One, recalling her harasser, exclaimed, "The bastard deserves to die." While walking in the station house parking lot, a female officer was called to a car by a male cop she trusted. When she got there a second officer was exposing his genitals. Another woman rejected her boss's pleas for a date. "Suddenly my work was no longer acceptable; he will not speak to me at all now. Up 'til last May, I had rave evaluations, all of a sudden it changed." She transferred to another squad. Most of those harassed, particularly those hired early, suffered in silence as they tried to fit in. One remarked that before equal employment opportunity and sexual harassment laws, she did not think of what they faced as discrimination. "It was just the cost of doing the job."[15]

Three female sheriff's deputies sued the Santa Clara County, California, Sheriff's Department, alleging an officer demanded sex in exchange for favorable work reviews. They sued after the department failed to investigate their complaints. A federal district court jury upheld their charges in November 1990, awarding them $2.7 million. New York City probationary officer Karen Sorlucco was raped at gunpoint by a fellow officer in 1983. A week after the assault Sorlucco identified Officer John Mielko as her assailant. Police authorities charged Sorlucco with making a false police report, a charge a jury later found her guilty of. This was struck down by an appeals court, which ruled that her conviction was a direct result of a consistent effort by police authorities to refuse any investigation into Sorlucco's charges against Mielko. The court ruled, when it awarded her a little more than $250,000, that the police had treated Sorlucco "harshly." Mielko was never charged and by then had retired on a full pension. Around 1990 a female civilian employee of the Fairfax County, Virginia, police force was discouraged by a male supervisor from leveling a sexual assault charge against a male officer. The complaint was registered, with the male subsequently pleading guilty to a misdemeanor.[16]

In 1992 two female officers complained that they had been harassed by other officers and that their 110th Precinct commander in Queens, New York, Deputy Inspector Hugh Selzer, had failed to take any action in response to their complaints. Incidents included an obscene statement written on a precinct wall, pornographic pictures on their lockers, and lewd phone calls received at home. In October that year Selzer was transferred to the executive office of the 15th Division in Brooklyn. The head of the department's Inspection Service Bureau said the harassment complaint was "part of" the reason for the transfer. Inspector Lawrence Loesch said the transfer was a promotion; "it's the next level of supervision." This division post involved less direct supervision of rank-and-file officers than did a precinct commander's job.[17]

Lost in the Christopher Report on the Los Angeles Police Department (LAPD), which investigated excessive use of force in the wake of the Rodney King beating, was what it had to say about female officers. It concluded that they did a good job and were better at averting physically violent situations than were males. Documented by the report were the messages that went back and forth on computer screens from patrol car to patrol car. Phrases and messages such as "Barbie dolls . . . Sgt. Tits . . . cunt . . . We got rid of our two lovely young ladies. They both need a few rounds with the old baton, wouldn't you say? . . . Pound her into submission . . . Hey slut. . . . I have heard of some guys even getting away with rape because they r ofcrs."[18]

Toward the end of 1992 former LAPD officer Teri Lyons filed suit against the department, alleging she was raped by a superior and then fired for reporting the attack to the LAPD's Internal Affairs Division (IAD). She alleged that Commander Maurice Moore had raped her the previous spring and that when she reported the rape to Moore's superior, she was told, "These things happen." Another superior told her not to discuss the incident. Thereafter she was discharged.[19]

She was one of about six policewomen who alleged they were raped by LAPD policemen over the period of 1989–1993. Another was officer Suzanne Campbell, who alleged she was raped on the grounds of the Police Academy in 1990 by Officer Ernest Hill. In October 1992 she filed a lawsuit claiming the LAPD and the city's unofficial policy was to ignore and even discourage women—sometimes with threats of disciplinary action—from filing complaints of sexual harassment. After making a formal complaint to the department, the LAPD took 15 months to process Campbell's assault charge before sustaining the complaint, which led to the firing of Hill. During that period Campbell claimed she was further harassed for pursuing the case. The first step was an investigation by IAD. After three months IAD sent a report to Chief Daryl Gates with a recommendation to send Hill to a board of rights. Gates reversed this, calling the accusations unsustained. According to Campbell, Moore recommended to Gates that all charges against Hill be dismissed. When Campbell asked LAPD officials for an explanation of this decision, none was given. Detective Kena Brutsch, the force's women's coordinator, told her if she continued to seek action against Hill, she would be charged with "lewd conduct in a public place." Campbell also alleged that IAD captain Jan Carlson told her it was department policy to take no disciplinary action in "one-on-one" incidents of harassment. This woman also reportedly told Campbell that if she persisted, she would be charged with having sex on company grounds. Ignoring standard procedure, Campbell appealed the decision directly to the police commissioners, who ordered a board of inquiry review of the department's handling of the case. This board found IAD negligent in its handling of the case in that it had failed to interview key witnesses. Eventually Hill was fired.[20]

Katherine Spillar, co-chair of the Women's Advisory Council (WAC) to the Police Commission, said that some field-training officers made it clear to recruits that sex could be traded for favors. The number of women reporting sexual assaults to the WAC was termed by Spillar as "disturbing." A male officer speaking anonymously told of a field-training officer who put the lives of sexually noncompliant female recruits at risk by provoking suspects into an altercation with them. When his behavior was finally documented, he was quietly transferred to a different division. Teresa Wallin was another policewoman from Los Angeles suing on an alleged rape charge. Wallin did not report the rape for four weeks because she feared retaliation from the accused and his friends and because she believed that if she reported the assault, her career would be ruined. In the cases of Wallin and Campbell IAD investigators questioned their associates about the officers' social and sexual history. Commander Daniel Watson of the LAPD's Personnel Division said that sexual harassment in the force "is really bad, but it's not as big a problem as women think it is."

IAD made the decision to characterize charges of sexual harassment as "conduct unbecoming an officer," offering the rationale that this charge was easier to prove than harassment charges. Women countered that this perpetuated the idea that harassment was not worthy of consideration on its own merits. They also felt that if harassment charges were entered into a personnel file only as "conduct unbecoming," it would be more difficult to show a pattern of sexual misconduct. When Willie Williams took over as chief in the wake of the Rodney King beating, he reviewed the WAC's recommendations and ordered anti–sexual harassment training for the entire command staff, including himself, which began in 1993. During

Williams's tenure the LAPD's board of rights found that a case in which a male officer pulled a woman's face into his crotch was not harassment as he did not derive gratification. That officer was finally suspended after being found guilty of inappropriate conduct involving the same policewoman. Spillar was not optimistic that the departure of Gates would change the sexist ways of the LAPD. "Willie Williams has a problem," she explained. "He's sitting on top of a department that is philosophically opposed to change."[21]

In 1991 the Los Angeles Sheriff's Department fired five male deputies for harassing a female deputy. It happened at a county jail, where the deputies encouraged male detainees to expose themselves to her and throw eggs, tomatoes, and water balloons at her. The detainees also screamed obscenities at her and threatened her safety. After a five-month internal investigation the deputies were terminated.[22]

Despite this action, the Los Angeles Sheriff's Department has been "plagued for years by allegations of lewd and unfair conduct toward women in the ranks," according to *Los Angeles Times* reporters. In December 1992 the department — 12.5 percent of whose 7,915-member force were women — signed a consent decree that ended 12 years of litigation over two landmark lawsuits. One dated back to 1980, with Deputy Susan Bouman Paolino arguing she had been denied a promotion because she was a female, a charge upheld by courts along the way, although Paolino no longer worked there. Deputy Laura Beard's 1990 suit alleged "almost daily abusive and demeaning remarks and sexually offensive posters and pictures." Both suits potentially affected all female deputies. In the consent decree the department agreed to spend $4.5 million over the coming four years to improve the lot of females in the department by holding gender sensitivity training, establishing an ombudsperson, and so on. One change was to a training film on defensive driving in which a topless female motorist is shown distracting a male deputy who is driving a patrol car.[23]

A jury awarded former Long Beach, California, police officers Lindsey Allison and Melissa Clerkin $3.1 million in damages in the fall of 1991 as a result of their sexual harassment suit. Both had left the department in 1988. At the trial they and other women testified that sexual harassment was "endemic" in the Long Beach Police Department. Male officers often used obscene language to degrade women and then retaliated if they complained of it. Forms of retaliation experienced by Clerkin included having male officers refuse to provide her with backup assistance, being called vulgar names, and receiving offensive messages on the police computer screen. When the trial concluded Clerkin commented, "For so long we were told 'we' were the problem. 'We' couldn't get along. How good it feels to prove it wasn't us." Her fellow officers told her graphic sex stories, urinated outdoors in her presence, and allowed their police dogs to attack her (she was assigned to the canine unit). Detective Estella Martinez said that while she was a cadet in 1985 at the Long Beach Police Academy, she and other recruits were instructed in the presence of supervisors to run and sing in cadence a suggestive rhyme that began, "I wish all women were holes in the road." After the court decision a *Los Angeles Times* reporter contacted several females on the Long Beach force for comment to see if the situation had changed. None would do so for fear of repercussions.[24] As of spring 1993 neither woman had received any money because the case remained on appeal.[25]

In southern California the Newport Beach Police Department was hit by a sexual harassment scandal that began to unfold on September 24, 1992. On that day four current and former department employees filed a sex discrimination lawsuit in Orange County Superior Court naming the city of Newport Beach as defendant and accusing Captain Anthony Villa and Police Chief Arbra "Arb" Campbell of misconduct. The civil suit was brought by Officer Cheryl Vlacilek, records supervisor Mary Jane Ruetz, communications supervisor Margaret McInnis, and Officer Rochell Maier (who had been fired). The women charged Villa with harassment and Campbell with condoning that behavior. Allegedly Villa made sexual advances, which included touching breasts, and made sexually suggestive remarks, which included an explicit description by Villa of a pornographic movie. All of the complainants except McInnis contended they had been disciplined and then fired on spurious charges after rejecting Villa's advances. Vlacilek and Ruetz were reinstated by the Newport Beach Civil Service Commission; Maier's reinstatement appeal was then under consideration. At the time of filing Ruetz was on disability leave, claiming to be suffering from stress due to the sexual harassment.

According to the lawsuit, the women were told to socialize with male officers off duty, especially commanding officers, and to wear short skirts to show off their legs and clothes deemed "desirable" by the men. Some female officers involved with high-ranking male officers were said to receive favorable treatment over the female employees who would not "go along to get along." A number of women had left the department because of sexual harassment and discrimination, according to the suit. After filing the suit, the women told a reporter they were "petrified" of retaliation but filed as they felt the department was an intolerably sexist workplace, describing the department as a "hotbed of sexually offensive conduct at the top levels of the command structure." Vlacilek said, "It's been extremely stressful and very retaliatory. . . . At times, it's very unbearable to work there, and with the powers that be, I worry about what could happen." Ruetz commented that "it's been almost unbearable as far as fear and pressure and retaliatory treatment." The department consisted of 250 employees. Of those, 75 were female, including 7 officers. Around the time of the lawsuit filing the department announced that Villa was being transferred from patrol captain to captain of administration. A police spokesperson said this was just part of a routine rotation.[26]

Both Campbell and Villa declined to comment publicly on the charges, but their attorney stated they denied the accusations and described the women as disgruntled employees who were properly disciplined and fired. The two accused jointly owned property in Riverside County. On October 14 Campbell announced his retirement, effective May 15, 1993, giving no specific reason.[27]

Just one day later a fifth woman, dispatcher Peri Ropke, joined the lawsuit. She alleged that eleven years earlier in 1981, when she was 22, she had been raped and subjected to other sex acts by both Campbell and Villa. After the rape, which had taken place in a vehicle at the end of a department party at a landfill site, Campbell had ordered her out of the vehicle and, claimed Ropke, had told her to never discuss the incident with anyone, threatening retaliation if she did. For the following decade the two men allegedly told Ropke to be "a good girl" and "keep her mouth shut." Villa warned her that Campbell was a force to be reckoned with who fancied the job of chief (which he became in 1986) and that Villa would ride his coattails. Given the six-year statute of limitations for rape, no criminal charges could then be brought. Said Ropke, "Working for Arb and Tony for the last 11 years, it was very difficult. I was constantly living in fear.... I hope that by my coming forward, other women will have the courage to do the same." Later that day Newport Beach city manager Kevin J. Murphy responded to the latest charges by placing Campbell and Villa on paid administrative leave and appointing an acting chief. Bruce Praet, the city-hired attorney for the two men, denied the latest charge on behalf of his clients. He added, "We're going to respond on our own and set these people for independent psychiatric evaluation which, we think, especially in Ropke's case, will be very enlightening." Near the end of October the police employees' association announced an overwhelming vote of no confidence in the chief.[28] In November Campbell and Villa filed a federal civil rights lawsuit against the city of Newport Beach charging that they had been improperly removed from duty when placed on administrative leave. By that time Campbell had withdrawn his resignation.[29]

Early in December four more Newport Beach Police Department female employees joined the lawsuit, bringing the number to nine. They also alleged to have been touched against their will by Villa, told to socialize with male officers off duty, denied promotions because they were female, and in other ways harassed. These women were Officers Shontel Sherwood and Katherine Heinzel, dispatcher Molly Thomson, and Animal Control Officer Michelle LeFay. The latter two had taken medical leaves from the department. Two of the women were able to corroborate Ropke's story to the extent they stated she told them about the assault years before her accusation became public. Sherwood remarked, "I believe that by my actions in joining the lawsuit, other employees will not have to endure the wrong that made me a victim." Praet continued to deny everything on behalf of his clients. Now he contended Ropke confused the party at which she alleged rape with another sexual encounter involving two different men while she was employed by another police department. Regarding the latest four women to join the suit, Praet stated their case had no merit and added, "The more people who jump on the bandwagon, the less credibility it gives the original plaintiffs, if there was any credibility in the first place.... You can cry wolf too many times."[30]

Shortly after the first suit was filed the city of Newport Beach hired an outside attorney, Harold A. Bridges of Los Angeles, to investigate the charges. Bridges reported on his "substantially complete" investigation to the City Council in mid–December after questioning 169 members of the Police Department. Bridges concluded that "the interviews revealed information from which a trier of fact might find that conduct of a sexually harassing nature occurred." However, he added that the women who filed the suit may have themselves "engaged in sexually harassing conduct." Continuing, he stated that apart from sex "a substantial number of those interviewed believed there to be a hostile work environment." Bridges gave no names or specifics for any of his conclusions.[31]

The City Council's response to this report was only to be "saddened." This listless response was enough to anger an editor at the *Los Angeles Times*, who demanded, "Where is the council's outrage about the trouble in the department? Where are the promises to clean it up?" Acknowledging there were serious problems in the department, the newspaper termed the council's reluctance to confront the problem as "disturbing" and urged a stronger response.[32]

This stronger response came on December 22, 1992, when City Manager Murphy fired Campbell. He gave no specific reason other than to say the grounds were "many" and "varied." Four days prior to that steps had begun to also fire Villa. Because Campbell was an at-will employee, it was procedurally easier to terminate him than it was Villa. Reportedly Campbell had also diverted to his personal use a 1985 Mercedes-Benz sedan seized in a drug raid and turned over to his department for law enforcement purposes. Campbell also allegedly granted special favors and police services to a wealthy friend who had sold Campbell some property. The firing had the full support of the council. This move met with approval from the *Los Angeles Times*, which described it as showing admirable decisiveness.[33]

A day later Campbell made his first public statement on the situation. Denying all allegations of sexual harassment, he said that he was the victim of a conspiracy and a "witch hunt" and that "the inmates are now running the asylum." In the face of the overwhelming no-confidence vote in him by the department, he insisted he could effectively run the department if he was reinstated. Campbell accused some of his immediate subordinates in the department, members of the City Council, and the city manager of orchestrating his removal by utilizing sexual harassment complaints as a way to fulfill the city manager's political agenda.[34]

In January 1993 city officials announced they would no longer pay the legal bills of Campbell and Villa in the harassment law suit. The next month four female employees of the Police Department who said they had been sexually harassed on the job—they were not part of the suit—accepted cash settlements ranging from $2,000 to $7,500 in exchange for a promise not to take legal action. Said Mayor Clarence Turner, "We investigated, and made a determination that we think they were harassed, and acted accordingly." The ten women suing (one other had joined the first nine) reportedly rejected a proposed settlement around that time that would have given them a total of between $300,000 and $500,000. While that suit remained outstanding, a settlement was reached between the city and Campbell and Villa in June 1993. In return for a promise to drop their lawsuit, to waive their right to civil service hearings, and to not seek reinstatement to active duty on the force, the two men were reinstated on June 10 and immediately retired that same day. The settlement agreement with Campbell stated that the city had "no corroborated evidence that Campbell sexually harassed any female employee of the department" or that he condoned any misconduct on the part of any others in the department. No such statement was included in the settlement with Villa. Newport Beach agreed to pay all their legal bills. Under the agreements the city would not oppose disability retirements for Campbell, 54, and Villa, 48, who claimed injuries dating back as much as 15 years. Retirement packages would total around $50,000 a year tax free for Villa. In addition the city agreed to pay each man a lump sum of about $30,000 to settle workers' compensation claims. Beno Hernandez, a lawyer representing the ten women, bitterly exclaimed, "They're rewarding the people who have allegedly raped and pillaged their employees. If you're going to be a victim of sexual harassment in Newport Beach, forget it. . . . They're going to protect their own and they don't care how they protect it."[35]

Yet another southern California police department came under attack in June 1993 when a few details of a harassment suit launched the previous February were made public. Four female members of the Irvine Police Department were suing on the basis of alleged harassment and discrimination against women on the force. According to the four women, two of whom were then on medical leave, male officers boasted about their on-duty sexual exploits and formed a "Code Four" club in which membership and pins were awarded to an officer once he had had intercourse with a woman in his patrol car. Code Four means an officer is all right.[36]

Coming under fire as well in 1993 was the federal Bureau of Alcohol, Tobacco, and Firearms (ATF). As an agency of the Treasury Department it collects excise taxes on alcohol, tobacco, and firearms and enforces federal laws on firearms and explosives. Three female ATF agents went public with their claims of harassment in the bureau on the CBS television program "60 Minutes." Chicago agent Sandra Hernandez endured for two years a high-ranking agent who repeatedly pawed her, forcibly kissed her, and propositioned her for sex. The publicity led to an investigation by ATF that verified Hernandez's allegations and recommended the firing of the harasser. Allegations that ATF management turned a blind eye to sexual harassment, and to racial discrimination, forced ATF director Stephen E. Higgins to take action. He appointed a task force to study the situation.[37]

Mary Walshok interviewed 117 women in nontraditional jobs in 1976–1977 and found that actual sexual harassment, such as touching, sexual overtures, and obscene language, was mentioned in many of the interviews; approximately one third of the women at one time or another had had to deal with such conduct. This one-third figure did not include the women who had had to cope with the general "tits and ass" conversation that came from supervisors and coworkers. One woman had had her breast grabbed by a coworker in front of other coworkers. Walshok suggested that the less strange a woman appeared and felt in the workplace, the less strained her relationships would be — that is, a blue-collar male and a female worker with no background or familiarity with blue-collar work would have nothing in common. Given the absence of any such common language or signs, Walshok found it not surprising "that hostility and testing occur, or that sexual harassment occurs."

In an obtuse, reactionary way Walshok really blamed women because she argued that there is less sexual harassment when people can find a common basis for interacting, so "women who can define themselves or present themselves in terms that are familiar to the men help take the pressure off." The best way to deal with harassment, she thought, was with a confrontational style, such as a slap or an angry verbal response. Such a direct strategy was only possible because women in skilled blue-collar employment were not as powerless as many other women, such as secretaries in office situations. Walshok felt this may have been why reported sexual harassment in her study was a lot less than other studies reported. In only one of Walshok's cases did the woman go to her union representative to report harassment, and "she had a difficult time gaining his support." Walshok found blue-collar sexual harassment more direct and upfront than in an office environment, where harassment was more often veiled in innuendo and polite suggestion. A blue-collar workplace she found to be characterized by "rougher language and more physical aggressive-ness." She also thought blue-collar men were less persistent in their sexual harassment of women than were white-collar and professional men.[38]

When Walshok argued there was harassment in the blue-collar world, at least partly due to her nothing-in-common concept, and that women should change to fit in, she made the mistake of trying to analyze the issue in terms of only the group she was looking at. Her thesis did not explain widespread harassment in, for example, offices where the sexes have in common a familiarity with white-collar office work. Another book, which looked at Jewish immigrant women workers in the early 1900s in a mostly Jewish New York environment, attempted to explain the sexual harass-ment of those women by somehow relating it to the men's Jewishness. This, too, failed. Sexual harassment is not about Jewish men in 1900 New York, or Italian men in 1860, or American men in 1980, or British men in the 1700s, for harassment cuts across countries, cultures, classes, language and time. It is about all of these men and of course many more. Sexual harass-ment is about men—period.[39]

Women in America first entered coal mines in the 1970s. In Kentucky two women were stripped, greased, and sent out of the mine in that condi-tion as an initiation rite. As company officials were implicated, charges were filed against the company itself. The defense contended that what had happened was part of a standard initiation for all new miners, which was true. The women argued that greasing obviously had different ramifi-cations for a woman than a man. A decision was rendered in this case in favor of the women when the Kentucky Human Rights Commission or-dered the company to pay each woman $2,000 for her humiliation and em-barrassment. As women entered the American coal mines it was noted, keeping old stereotypes alive, that "in many cases, the morality of any woman who would work in the mines is severely criticized."[40]

One of these new female miners said of her male coworkers and super-visors, "They're just going to sexually abuse us until we drop out of the com-petition. I've been told I can make more money lying on my back at the pit mouth than working back in the mine." Mary, a miner, complained that the section foremen were the biggest problem. In particular one kept harassing her aggressively, telling her to "put out or get out." Her boss told her regularly that the only way she was going to advance on the job was by extending sexual favors to him. During one overture he grabbed her by the collar and physically shook her. When she approached the union with a sexual harassment grievance, Mary was told it was not an issue that could be handled through the grievance procedures. Mary's attorney, Penny Crandell, said, "The union has taken the position that this issue is not some-thing it's going to fight for. When the union says it's helping women, it just doesn't wash. The women are on their own."[41]

Amanda was a 4 feet 11 inches, 100-pound miner who had experienced harassment from a number of miners. One would get around to where nobody could see him and then expose himself to her. On one occasion the foreman brought in some pictures of a nude prostitute. He showed them around to the men, who then asked Amanda if she wanted to take a look. She refused. Already that evening the foreman had been harassing Amanda. Later she was shoveling alone when he suddenly came up behind her, grabbed her, and pinned her arms to her side. Then he wrapped one leg around her so she could not kick him and started "to fool with my parts." She bit him, which caused him to pick her up and slam her into a wall. Amanda reported all this to the shift supervisor, who promised to keep that man away from her by assigning him to another area of the mine. Another time she was physically roughed up by another foreman during a harassment incident. She reported this to the shift supervisor, who promised to also keep this worker at an opposite end of the mine. No union grievances were filed, or attempted, because fellow miners advised her against such actions. Other harassments Amanda was subjected to included being followed to her car, tailed home, and called at home. Added Amanda, "Also I was a stray, with no protection. Most of the women got jobs at the mine because they had brothers, husbands or boyfriends there. I didn't even know a coal miner when I was hired."[42]

Darla Baker started work as a coal miner in 1977 at a mine near Wheeling, West Virginia. Her employer was Consolidated Coal Company of Pittsburgh, the largest coal company in the United States, which in 1981 employed a total of 242 female coal miners in its 17,000-strong work force. Baker must have known that things might not go well when she was hired because the personnel director told her she would have to "take a lot of shit from her coworkers." To drive home the point the personnel man added that a pretty girl like Baker could expect to be "grabbed by the ass and boobs" and that "there's nothing I can do to stop it."[43]

At work one day a coworker attacked her and tried to rape her underground. Escaping the initial assault, Baker ran to an underground lunchroom where eight miners and one supervisor were taking a lunch break. The attacker followed her into the room and tried again to rape her. She was able to fight him off, but none of the men tried to help her. They all just laughed through the entire incident. The supervisor took no action. When she told a second supervisor, he just laughed. When she found another senior supervisor, he took action by seeing to it the attacker never worked with her again. However, the attacker was never punished, nor was there any official investigation into the attack by the company or the union. Then the retaliation started. Baker went out to the parking lot to find the tires on her car slashed. Rumors spread among the male miners that she had a bed hidden deep in the mine where she worked as a prostitute. Her new nickname, "Deep Throat Darla, the blow job miner," was written in chalk all over the mine. Bringing all of this to the attention of management, she was told, "Now don't start no shit, Darla, or you'll be blackballed out of coal mining where women don't belong anyway."[44]

Female coworkers suffered similar indignities. Diane Smith explained, "These comments are not isolated events happening once a week or month, but something we have to live with every single day we work. We've complained to the personnel manager, but he just laughs and so do the local United Mine Workers' Union leaders. It is a condition of our jobs and no matter what we try it never goes away." A small peephole was discovered that the men used to spy into the women's change and shower room. It was filled in the day it was discovered, but nothing else was done. There was no investigation. After the peephole became common knowledge, but before the women actually were able to locate it, the harassment increased as the men accused the women of knowing about the peephole and openly "parading" in front of it "to turn us on." The women miners had gotten suspicious that a peephole must exist after the appearance on walls of very specific graffiti, such as calling so and so "scar back" (the woman had had a back operation) and saying so and so had "inverted nipples."[45]

Harassment plagued women miners for several years before complaints started to be aired publicly. Initially most of these women were unaware that other miners were experiencing the same thing and chose to remain silent. Also working against speaking out were embarrassment and the fear of a backlash from coworkers and company officials. However, the problem finally did surface, and at a 1980 national conference of women coal miners the participants identified sexual harassment as one of the major problems facing women in the coal industry. They resolved that an in-depth survey be undertaken. In 1981 the Coal Employment Project (CEP), a nonprofit organization in Oak Ridge, Tennessee, completed this survey on sexual harassment in the coal mines, the industry's first. Of the women who responded to the survey, 17 percent reported they had been physically attacked while working underground. Another 53 percent had been propositioned by a boss on at least one occasion, 76 percent had been propositioned by their coworkers, and 63 percent said they knew of other women at their mine who had experienced similar instances of harassment. Ten percent said they had been searched for cigarettes in a sexually suggestive manner—because smoking is banned underground, physical searches of all miners are recommended by law. This survey concluded that female miners were not alone in being harassed. According to the CEP, all women workers experienced about the same amount of harassment, but female miners appeared to be recipients of "more physical abuse."[46]

A survey done at the end of the 1980s found things unchanged for miners. Interviews found many male coal miners and bosses who expressed the idea that female miners were promiscuous because they were willing to work with men in a rough environment. One male boss said, "A woman would have to be a certain breed of woman to go down there in the first place, not a lady. . . . It'd be something out of the bars or whatever." Coal miners earned around $670 a week in 1988, while females in mining towns employed in restaurants, motels, and retail stores made approximately $160–$220 per week. Female miners were found to be "extremely reluctant" to file a harassment complaint as they worried that pursuing such an action could lead to retaliation on the job and bring their sexual reputation into the public eye as an issue. They also understood complaints were difficult to win without the testimony of witnesses, who would themselves have to jeopardize their positions in the mines.[47]

For some women harassment was bad enough they had to quit jobs. It was vivid enough to be remembered decades later. Barbara and Brenda were both teenagers in early–1960s England. Barbara worked in a drugstore where the manager "was a creep . . . who'd come in and smack your bottom." She quit. Brenda was a stock clerk in a garage who left because "the stores manager started getting a bit fresh." Both of these women mentioned these incidents in the early 1980s when they were being interviewed about their work lives in general. Although no questions directly involved sexual harassment, the women brought it up spontaneously.[48]

In 1979 in Australia when a young woman complained that her employer had harassed her, it was discovered that over a six-month period he had employed 42 young women, yet the federal government's Commonwealth Employment Service continued to send job applicants to him. Shelf fillers in Australian supermarkets and department stores normally worked the night shift. At one time it was almost exclusively a male job, however, by 1980 more and more females were being employed in those jobs. One of these women remarked, "I don't think too many women are keen on working on a shift where there are so many males. It's not always easy unless you have the right sort of sense of throwing it back at them. If you know how to take the stirring that goes on you're okay, but it puts most people off."[49]

"Endemic" was the word used to describe sexual harassment in Australia Post workplaces in May 1992. Surprisingly this was confirmed by an official of the corporation. Sexual harassment is illegal in Australia and has been federally since 1984. The matter was publicized by the Women's Electoral Lobby (WEL), which claimed the harassment had made working life hell for some female postal workers. WEL had received complaints from distressed women postal workers who were afraid to file an official complaint with the Anti-Discrimination Board. In a letter to the New South Wales general manager of Australia Post, WEL accused male workers of "behaving like gangsters, great Australian braves." An unnamed women's officer with the corporation confirmed that sexual harassment went on all the time in the company. According to Pam Simons, the New South Wales WEL coordinator, harassment was worst on the early morning shift when male and female postal workers sorted the mail unsupervised. "Men talk loudly and graphically about their sexual exploits, prostitutes and women's bodies. The sex talk went on all day, every day at some post offices. Women should not have to put up with it," Simons said. "They find it distressing and hostile." One female postal worker told a reporter that her 13 male colleagues regularly pretended to reach orgasm simultaneously and made sexual grunts all day. They talked constantly about sex, including descriptions of their exploits of the previous night. The men also simulated sex. Although they had never touched her, after four years of this behavior she could no longer tolerate the atmosphere. Her male colleagues told her she would have to fit in as they were there first. A supervisor told her, "Stop fighting, children." She was also told she was imagining things. The men also said she was harassing them because they could not talk the way they wanted. When she checked into the possibilities of a transfer, female workers in four other post offices told her the problem was even worse at their workplaces. When she complained to a female postmaster, an equal employment officer showed the men a video about sexual harassment. The woman herself was sent to a psychologist to learn how to work with blue-collar men. After the video the men's behavior worsened. Finally the woman was transferred to a larger post office, where women were not so outnumbered by men and the problem of verbal harassment was said to not exist. WEL urged Australia Post to "remove the scourge" and reminded the company that it was illegal and that the company was therefore obliged to do so. Australia Post promised that it would investigate the situation.[50]

Seven female linotype operators who worked in the *Detroit Free Press* composing room filed suit against the newspaper in 1984. They alleged harassment by some of the paper's 122 male composing room employees over a ten-year period from the mid–1970s to the mid–1980s. Incidents of harassment included one woman being told by a coworker that "her cunt smelled like an alley cat, and he wished he had a machine gun and he would kill her and get her out of there." Later the same man brought a can of dog deodorant to the workplace, "which he sprayed as she went by." Pictures of masturbating women from *Hustler* magazine were left in one woman's locker and positioned in other areas so she could not avoid them. One man sometimes ran around the composing room pretending to ejaculate, while another made a cardboard penis that he held between his legs and waved around. Another worker used to rant, "God damn fucking son-of-a-bitchin' women ain't worth, aren't good for nothing but spreading their fucking legs and getting screwed." When one woman left her machine to complain after listening to that day after day, her superintendent told her, "That's probably your fault." Many of the accused men were either the women's union representatives or workers who had risen into management.

In defending itself, the paper argued that management lacked control since the union contract allowed only fines or discharges but not suspensions. The paper also resorted to attacking the credibility of the women. Mary Ann Arsenault, one of the plaintiffs' attorneys, said the company argued that "every woman either swears, passes around dirty pictures, or in some other way was asking for the treatment she received." Only after the suit was filed did the newspaper post a policy on harassment and specify that complaints be brought to management for investigations. In November 1987 a federal jury ordered Detroit's second largest daily to pay $159,000 in damages to five of the plaintiffs. Late the next month the company paid more than $185,000 (interest, court costs, and legal fees were added on). The five plaintiffs decided to split the money among all seven women. Shortly after the suit was filed a union official told one of the seven that "you're going to get your $50,000 and then you are going to get your throats cut."

Returning to work after the decision, the women said explicit sexual harassment had stopped, although some found the atmosphere in the composing room to be tense and "sometimes brutal." One said, "We walk in and people turn their backs." Coverage of the episode by the paper in its own pages was sparse, with a total of four stories printed from 1984 to 1987. Most detailed was the one right after the court decision. All foul language was edited out; all specific examples of harassment were reduced to a brief summary. Among quotes removed was this one from a plaintiff: "I really know how a rape victim feels — the 'Free Press' first made me prove that I was abused, and then made me prove that I didn't ask the person to abuse me." City editor Chip Visci described it all as "good editing," claiming the story played prominently. Actually it was in the middle of page three. Visci did regret one slipup; an in-print reference to the plaintiffs as "defendants."[51]

When hearings were held in 1990 by the New York City Commission on Human Rights and that city's Office of Labor Services about discrimination in the construction industry, a parade of witnesses came forward to testify about sexual harassment on the job. One was black carpenter Shirley Hemmings, who testified, "On every construction job I have been harassed by men. They would ask me to go out with them; they would constantly tell dirty sexual and racial jokes and make derogatory remarks about women and black persons."[52]

At a 1991 meeting of Women at Work, a two-year-old Pasadena, California–based support group for women in the trades, organizer Gina Fierman Hunt asked the three dozen or so women present how many had been sexually harassed on the job. Every hand went up. Females then made up about 2 percent of construction trades workers. Even though all had been victimized, most said they had never filed a grievance or a suit with the state's Department of Fair Employment and Housing. Retribution and ostracism discouraged such action. Electrician Linda Jofuku had a bucket of water dumped on her one day by coworkers who wanted to see her wet T-shirt. Another time she was lying on her back installing a garbage disposal when she felt the handle of a hammer and a coworker's hands groping between her legs. She quit a few weeks later, remarking, "It's very difficult to fight for yourself when you're isolated, when you're the only woman. You feel there's something wrong with you." Men in the trades denied a problem existed. John Scott, director of an electrical apprenticeship program in San Francisco, said, "We anticipated problems on the job site with harassment, but just the opposite turned out," meaning the females were "pampered." Calvin Emery, manager of Plumbers Union Local 78 in Los Angeles, remarked, "All the old stuff you may have heard about years ago doesn't happen any more."[53]

The New York City Fire Department was also a hostile place for females to be employed. Katrina Cannon was sworn in as one of the city's first firewomen in 1982. Initially assigned to a Brooklyn station, she was subjected to harassment, resulting in two firemen being disciplined after one had tried to punch her and the other had used obscene and threatening language and made gestures at her. As a result Cannon was transferred in January 1985 to Engine Company 274 in Flushing, Queens. However, the harassment continued at the new location. This time the case made its way to Judge Charles Sifton of the federal district court in Brooklyn. Sifton termed the treatment of Cannon a "public disgrace," declaring, "This is a shocking image of a city agency unable to respect the directive of a court and unable to protect the civil rights of the employees of this agency." Finding Cannon had been subjected to "inexcusable" sexual harassment on the job, the judge issued an order that further harassment could lead to jailing and fining the perpetrators. After complaining about harassment at the Queens location, Cannon had been ordered transferred to a job elsewhere. Sifton issued an order to the Fire Department not to transfer her without her consent, leaving her on the job as a firefighter in Queens. The judge scorned the department for not acting forcefully against her harassers and instead dealing with the problem by trying to transfer Cannon.[54]

A few days later Brenda Berkman, a spokeswoman for the 28 firewomen on the 10,000-person force, commented that sexual harassment pervaded the department. She also charged that department officials did little or nothing to correct the problem. When a recent case (not Cannon's) about sexual harassment was reported in the newspaper, one firewoman found a clipping of the article fastened to the bulletin board with a knife.[55]

In October 1986, just two months after the Cannon case came to light, fireman Greg McFarland was fined $15,000 and suspended from the New York City Fire Department without pay for six months. Upon his return he would be on probation for one year. This action was taken after McFarland was found guilty of sexual harassment and intoxication on duty following an incident involving firewoman Ella McNair. She was in the process of scraping from the wall with a knife a news clipping she felt was derogatory to females. McFarland tried to prevent her from doing so. In the ensuing wrestling match he cut McNair on the finger with the knife. For seven-year firefighter McNair this was just the latest in a long string of harassments. At least six male members of her station, Engine Company 207, all of whom had been connected to other incidents involving her, were slated to be transferred to other units. A new captain had also been named to command the company. When an administrative law judge had heard the case the preceding August, he had recommended that the fire commissioner discharge McFarland. McNair was outraged when she heard that the department's decision did not involve discharge because she felt the financial penalty would be mostly offset by collections firemen had taken up for their comrade. McFarland termed his penalty "harsh." Fire commissioner Joseph Spinnato defended his penalty, which he called "severe," by saying he had not wanted to take any action that would have a "divisive effect" on the department. Acknowledging that incidents of harassment were still being reported by firewomen, Spinnato commented, "It is no secret that we have had some problems in the department between the sexes." Nicholas Mancuso, president of the Uniformed Firefighters Association, claimed the department made a "political scapegoat" out of McFarland.[56]

For Katrina Cannon harassment continued unchanged. In October 1991 she went public with her charges of continued harassment, which had not let up in the nine years since she had joined the department. She told of having her tires slashed, garbage dumped on her bed at the station, a mousetrap placed in her boots, her boots slashed, and verbal abuse dumped on her. All these incidents had occurred since 1986. She was still stationed with Engine Company 274 in Flushing, Queens, one of 35 females on a force of 8,668. Cannon had complained many times to Fire Department and city officials but to no avail. As a black she saw the behavior as racist as much as sexist.[57]

Only four days after Cannon leveled her latest charges, the Fire Department announced that it had granted transfers to five men at the station and that more transfers would be coming. The five were among 21 firemen and officers—all but 2 of the males assigned to 274—who had requested a new assignment. Reporters were unable to speak to these men as they said the fire commissioner did not want them to talk to the media. It was reported that the men considered Cannon to be too difficult to work with.[58]

8
Clerical Workers

One of the stranger cases concerning the sexual harassment of female clericals involved the U.S. government. In 1862 the Treasury Department created a division to take over from private firms the printing of some of the national currency. This division was headed by Spencer M. Clark, who hired about 300 women for the division over the following months. On April 29, 1864, Representative James H. Brooks of New York rose on the floor of the House of Representatives to charge that the Treasury Department had been transformed into a "house for orgies and bacchanals." The next day Representative James A. Garfield (later president), citing Brooks's remarks, called for an investigation. A select committee convened on May 3, 1864, with Garfield in the chair and Brooks the most conspicuous of the other eight members, to begin what would be almost two months of hearings to investigate alleged general mismanagement and immorality in the Treasury Department. Specifically targeted was Clark's division, where women were said to have been hired on the basis of pulchritude instead of efficiency. According to witnesses, after hours Clark plied some of these women with oysters and ale and made "improper" overtures. One former employee claimed Clark had tried to buy her favors for $100 and when she turned him down increased the offer to $1,000; she turned him down again. Employees Ella Jackson, Jennie Germon, and Laura Duvall all testified they had spent the night with the married Clark on one or more occasions. Germon said she was invited to Clark's house when Mrs. Clark was away several times before she reluctantly succumbed. Sometimes Clark allegedly took a woman to a hotel for the night. A "disinterested" source, Ada Thompson, who lived in the same house as Jackson and Germon, corroborated some of the employees' testimony from what she herself had seen and heard.[1]

The politics of this particular situation started to emerge in December 1863 when more than $30,000 of currency destined for burning was stolen from the Treasury Department. Secretary of the Treasury Salmon P. Chase wrote Secretary of War Edwin M. Stanton asking him to direct Colonel Lafayette C. Baker to investigate and arrest the culprit. Chase wanted this done quietly and without scandal as he hoped to run for the presidency on the Republican ticket in the near future. In due course Baker arrested Stuart Gwynn, a midlevel Treasury official. Because overwhelming proof was lacking, Gwynn was thrown in jail on Baker's suggestion that this would lead Gwynn to confess. It did not and after six weeks the Treasury Department ordered Gwynn released from jail. The newly freed man immediately launched a lawsuit against Baker. The colonel rushed to the Treasury Department to find out if it would back him up. The best he received was a noncommittal reply. Angered by this lack of support, Baker insinuated he might have to bring forward more lurid items if he was not supported. He still received only a vague answer. A week later Baker produced affidavits from the women just mentioned outlining their allegations. These he took to the Treasury Department. Officials questioned Clark, who vehemently denied all charges. As far as the Treasury was concerned, this matter was then closed. Shortly after that the affidavits turned up mysteriously in the hands of Representative Brooks.[2]

In the midst of the committee hearings Duvall died. An autopsy by physicians claimed to find "incontestable evidence of unsullied virtue of the deceased." On June 30, 1864, the committee cleared the Treasury Department of gross immorality charges, saying in part, "The committee are fully persuaded that those charges were, in part, the . . . result of a conspiracy on the part of Colonel Baker and the female prostitutes associated with him, by the aid of coerced testimony, to destroy the reputation of Mr. Clark, and . . . to justify his authorized arrest of one of the officers in the printing bureau." In the committee's opinion Baker had coerced testimony from the women by going to one saying she had better sign the affidavit admitting to immoral conduct since her friends had already done so and had implicated her. Then he went to the second woman with the same story and so on. Thompson's testimony, it was claimed, was bought with money.[3]

After the matter was all over Baker continued to claim "whitewash." He was probably right. Why did the committee call the women prostitutes, particularly Duvall, since she had supposedly died a virgin? Why would any of these women sign affidavits for Baker if none had done anything? Baker used no threats of violence against them. It is impossible to say now just what happened then, but the case has parallels with the Clarence Thomas hearings over a century later. In both cases the victims were abused and smeared by an openly hostile congressional committee that had made up its mind before the hearings started. In both cases female victims were tarred with specific sexually promiscuous labels as well as being branded liars in general.

When the Chicago, Burlington, and Quincy railroad hired Minnie Rockwell as a clerk and telegraph operator on December 3, 1869, she became the first female operating employee on the line. Antagonistic to this experiment from the start, her superior complained immediately for her incompetence and said that "worst of all, Miss Rockwell had apparently become a curiosity, attracting the attention of a 'rowdy element' who disrupted the running routine of the station." Although the reasons for her departure went unrecorded, Rockwell was gone by January 1870.[4]

After a long search for a job as stenographer a woman answered an ad from a doctor in New York City in 1908. The woman's search seemed over when he offered her the job at a good salary. However, she related, "as I was leaving his office, feeling that at last I was launched safely upon the road to a good living, he said casually, 'I have an auto, and as my wife doesn't care for that sort of thing. I shall expect you to accompany me frequently on pleasure trips.' That settled the doctor, I never appeared. After that experience I was ill for two weeks; a result of my hard work, suffering and discouragement."[5]

Jobs advertised in the papers often turned out to be something other than expected. It was a common enough problem that Charlotte Ayers, using the name Nancy Blythe as a cover, answered a number of ads and reported her experiences in a three-part series in the *New York Times* in 1909. Reporting on six different job ads she answered, Ayers found most to be for commission sales work for the distribution of pamphlets and so on, positions that were not advertised that way and that promised more income in the ads than they would in fact deliver.

Two of the jobs involved sex. One of them was to sell real estate lots on commission. Mr. Robinson, the employer, told her, "I must treat the matter in the same way a man would, and learn to accept little courtesies from men in the same spirit. If I'm asked to dinner and perhaps to the theatre, I must accept in the interests of business. Funny way to do business isn't it? But he seemed to think it was all right." In those days a gentleman would not think of asking a woman out without a chaperone. The second job involved selling a new safety razor on commission. As the employer moved his face very close to hers during the interview, he said, "A pretty women like you ought to have no trouble at all in getting orders. All the buyers are men. They'll ask you out to dinner if you'll give them the opportunity, and if you can't nail an order under those circumstances you're not as smart as you look." Then the employer suddenly changed his mind and said, "By Jove! It's a damn shame for a girl as sweet as you are, with those eyes and that form, to have to work at all. I'll tell you what I will do. Come around tomorrow and I'll make you my private secretary for a week or two, until we see how things turn out."[6]

Naomi L. had to quit a position as a bookkeeper in the early years of this century when the boss started to get "too personal, too friendly." At the same time Miriam M., although a law school graduate, remained stuck in low-level jobs. "Some jobs where I was," she recalled, "if you didn't get on the couch with the boss, you didn't get on." One position was assisting a lawyer who was a friend to her brother. This attorney "had no hesitancy about making sexual advances to me. I would never tell my brother about it," Miriam observed. "Well, maybe now I would have."[7]

Apparently the situation for clerical workers was worse in other countries. Clara Mueller-Jahnke went to work as a 16-year-old clerk in Berlin in 1876. However, the job did not last long because "sexual harassment by her boss drove her back home to Pomerania."[8] Nor was this an isolated case for in the 1890s the German women's movement was agitating for a number of improvements, including an end to sexual harassment at work. The Berlin Clerks' Aid Association (BCAA) directed its most radical campaign against sexual harassment in the workplace. Leaders of the BCAA joined other feminists to focus public awareness on the issue and to urge social and legal reform. The radical group Youth Protection began to offer legal aid to employees who were victims of harassment. In 1897 alone six cases were brought to court in Berlin. Agnes Herrmann, secretary of the BCAA, explained that since a civil suit for insult was the only recourse, women usually either tolerated advances from their employers or quit their jobs, thereby losing their source of income and the likelihood of obtaining a favorable reference. It was Herrmann's view that on-the-job sexual harassment was not an "uncommon exception," although the public remained unaware because clerks feared publicity and because, witnesses usually being absent, there was often no evidence other than the victim's word. Herrmann demanded that harassment become a criminal offense just like rape. Speaking at a women's congress in Berlin in 1896 on the working conditions of women clerks, she charged they were subject to "immoral attacks on the part of numerous superiors." By 1897 the BCAA had taken more active steps by removing from its employment list companies whose managers or owners were suspected of improper behavior as well as discussing ways of dealing with the problem in its journal. This group reported harassment suits brought against employers and offered legal services. When one case was lost in court, Berlin newspapers took the opportunity to bash the female workers by hysterically claiming the BCAA was a "workers' association with socialist tendencies."[9]

Berlin Women's Weal called a public meeting in January 1898 in an effort to further publicize the issue. Fraulein Markowsky, a clerk, told those assembled that "gentlemen have persecuted the girls, often with immoral propositions." She also demanded the criminal code be changed to protect clerks from harassment. No change was made in the criminal code, but the revised commercial code of 1900 made employers responsible for sexual harassment in the workplace and permitted victims to resign with several weeks' pay. None of this had any effect on harassment, which continued unabated. As the issue became faction riddled, the BCAA withdrew from a public role in addressing harassment while concentrating on keeping the issues raised within clerical circles. Association journals in various cities continued to report cases, while some, including the one in Berlin, maintained the practice of keeping lists of undesirable employers. The journal of the Catholic Alliance also reported cases of sexual harassment. But other than reporting the existence of the problem in this fashion and warning young women to be alert to its dangers, the Catholic Alliance did nothing.[10]

More typically women were blamed for what happened in offices. As women moved into the clerical world during the period 1890–1915 in the United States, many writers thought the proximity of the two sexes at work made the businesslike running of the office next to impossible. Janette Edgmont placed the blame for this squarely on women as well as the responsibility for changing it. Women, she wrote, "in an office are disconcerting. They demand more privileges than men. Whenever a girl happens to be in an office, there is always too much discussion, and when there are two or three girls, the male clerks will compare the blonde with the brunette, and the discussion is apt to last a little too long." Another writer called stenographers "venturesome butterflies masquerading as stenographers." Fesseden Chase assembled a pamphlet consisting of newspaper articles and illustrations about the stenographer and her employer. It was Chase's view that "in the cozy den or private 'studio' of her employer, temptations and opportunities are constantly arising, and the susceptible employer is easy picking for the girl of brilliant plumage with tender glances that fascinate and lure. It is only a step from the tender glances to the satisfying kiss, and we cannot escape the fact that the 'private-office' girl is generally quite willing to kiss and to be kissed, in order to secure special favors and perhaps an increase in her salary from her susceptible employer." Chase's objective appeared to be to show that many offices were little more than brothels, with many clericals no better than prostitutes. Still other writers objected to "the pretty typewriter," as typists were once briefly called. Virtuous stenographers were said to complain that "no girl can live a consistent Christian life and hold a business position." Even though not everybody viewed these women as immoral seductresses, many did. This was a common and dominant image.[11]

Of course the reality was that the women were being victimized. Dr. W. Montague Geer was the vicar of St. Paul's Chapel in New York City. He had received a number of letters from working women outlining their plight. One letter from a female with five years of office experience stated in part, "Sometimes I have been with a firm but two or three weeks when I was subjected to gross insults. I have had improper proposals made to me in not one place, but in three or four offices until I looked forward to it as a matter of course." Another letter writer told Geer, "There are so few offices which are fit for girls to work in. Not one business man in five is a fit character." She had also been personally harassed at work. In response to the situation outlined in these letters, Geer announced in January 1907 that he had organized a group called the Stenographers' Club whose meetings were to be held during the noon hour in St. Paul's Chapel. The purpose of the group was to provide a place for working women to come during their lunch hour to ensure their safety from harassers. Women who spent all or part of that period in their work locations were regularly harassed. The first meeting of the group drew 65 stenographers and "typewriters." At the opening Geer declared, "All sense of honor and chivalry in the hearts of many employers and their [male] clerks is dead." For unspecified reasons Geer then began to backslide, trying to play both sides. The cleric said a businessman told him, "You don't know what temptations we business men are subjected to." Geer admitted women could be temptresses, saying, "Then again, many of these young girls are like kittens—playful and naturally affectionate."[12]

Two days later the *New York Times* printed two letters to the editor on this topic. Each letter claimed to be from a businesswoman. Each said she had never had any such experiences. One of them wrote, "I fear that where the discourtesy is not imaginary the girls bring it upon themselves."[13]

Two days after that the newspaper published an editorial on the matter. Although it stated that the issue had provoked "many letters," the paper printed only the two just mentioned, both of which denied the existence of sexual harassment in the workplace. But then this was the position of the paper. The editorialist felt there was really no safety reason for the Stenographers' Club, although it might be valuable for comfort or socializing. The editorial patronizingly pointed out that a woman should not generalize her experience to the entire world. Of the issue the editorial concluded, "It all depends on the woman. We do not like to dwell on that fact, but fact it is, and while some women would be safe anywhere, others are everywhere in danger—and not always through their own fault, either, though perhaps it usually is, more or less."[14]

Once in a while harassment changed the entire course and direction of a woman's life. One such was Alice Woodbridge, a New York activist of the 1890s era who worked at publicizing the abysmal working conditions of females. She was catalyzed in that direction by the fact that at various times she had held jobs that had promised her a lucrative future. However, she had been obliged to give them up "because of insulting proposals from employers."[15]

Little of this image of the female office worker as vamp and seductress had changed by the 1920s, when one writer said of the clerical worker that "her eyes would be fixed on matrimony, and the corporate president would be unable to resist the pathetic and lonely sight of his secretary." Another observer warned against the employment of females as reception clerks since "nine out of ten girls are temperamental. On one day they are likely to flirt with every male visitor. On another day they are likely to be flippant."[16]

Once again the reality was the polar opposite. Clarence J. Collins, claiming to be an investment broker, advertised in a paper in New York City for a stenographer in April 1925. More than 80 females responded. Apparently at least one of them formally complained for on April 20 one of the applicants was policewoman Elizabeth Michael. As she was waiting in the outer office for her turn to be interviewed, several women came out of the office declaring they had been "insulted." When her turn came Michael went inside, where Collins threw his arms around her. She arrested him on the spot. In court he was sentenced to six months in the workhouse.[17]

The problem of females being harassed when they applied for jobs appears to have been pervasive and long-lived. In a history of female police, Chloe Owings wrote in 1925 that one of the duties of New York City policewomen was the investigation "of employers who act in an indecent manner toward young girls applying for work." At the same time Chicago policewomen also investigated ads offering employment to women. Just before the outbreak of World War II an article profiling New York City policewomen noted that one of their responsibilities was to watch newspaper ads placed by men for females to model or to do office work.[18]

In 1949 a story profiling New York policewomen told of two female officers who investigated a complaint of sexual harassment against a tailor who was advertising for a cashier. One went inside the shop to apply for the position. When the tailor harassed her, the pair of officers arrested him.[19]

In April 1922 a new women's group, the League of Women Victims of Men, successfully held its first meeting at Nice, France. Little was known about the group, but it was thought the movement started in London. Most of those attending the Nice meeting were English speakers. Mere dislike of men was not sufficient reason to join the group; a valid cause had to be provided. Some members were jilted fiancées, but "the foundation members consisted chiefly of women who said they had lost employment through sex jealousy."[20]

Conde Nast, publisher of *Vogue*, *Vanity Fair*, and other magazines, was a harasser of employees for decades beginning at least in the 1920s. Many young women desired to work for his well-known magazines either as staff or as models. Nast's biographer reported, "The office itself was in effect both an escort service and a feudal village, with Nast possessing 'droit du seigneur.' Any unmarried woman drifting down the corridor was fair game." An associate of Nast said of the female employees, "He hires them, sires them, and fires them." Mothers warned their daughters "to watch out for Mr. Nast. He was known to be not safe in taxis." Some of the more conservative members of his society set termed him "a philanderer and a corruptor of morals." Nast's biographer reported on the effects of Nast harassing female employees, saying that "no member of the staff complained that her job had been threatened in this way; at least one, however, is known to have found the situation intolerable and resigned." As he got older and older the females got younger and younger. "He lunged predictably in taxis," it was said. Just before he died in 1942, aged 69, his health was so poor that before he made his "automatic pounce" he had to take a pill.[21]

Some writers have been able to see the reality of the situation. Looking at the history of clerical employment in England, Gregory Anderson noted that in the early 1900s, the presence of females in offices created the opportunity for their sexual exploitation, which was made easier by their subordinate role in the workplace. Often, he said, it was a case of "submit or get out. The vulnerability of women to sexual harassment within the closed world of the paternalistic counting house corresponded closely to the dangers facing female servants in domestic households."[22]

Reformer Jane Addams was concerned that the work settings and the meager wages paid clericals created situations where women accepted money and gifts in exchange for sexual favors. If a woman was the sole female in an office, she was deprived of the social restraint afforded by the companionship of other working women. This isolation constituted a danger that could lead the woman into a "vicious" life, felt Addams, for "perhaps no young woman is more exposed to the temptations of this sort than the one who works in an office where she may be the sole woman employed and where the relation to her employer and to her fellow-clerks is almost on a social basis." When Clara E. Laughlin examined the conditions of Chicago working women in 1913, she reported that many who worked in offices and stores supplemented their wages. She wrote, "Many girls who work in offices and stores spend one or two or three nights a week in some shabby 'resort' and earn the difference between shabby insufficiency and the ability to compete with or even dazzle the girls who work beside them." Clara told the story of Eugenia, who left one disreputable employer for another, but was fired from that company for refusing to go to dinner with her boss.[23]

Office rules for women employees, as outlined in books from the 1920s to 1950s, almost never mentioned sexual harassment. Instead they painted a picture in which females were informed that men were better bosses, that women had to display absolute loyalty by complaining about nothing, that women tended to be somewhat hysterical, and that any sexuality appearing at work was the sole responsibility of the fickle, emotional, female employee.

By this time the office was where the typical, average, American-born woman aspired to find employment. Factory work had been given over to newly arrived immigrant women or those with little education, as had domestic service.

Writing in 1946, Anna Baetjer stated that the consensus was that women workers were more efficient under male supervision because a male boss represented authority and because the distance between the two sexes helped maintain discipline. Also noted was that "some industries claim that women are more difficult to supervise than men, that they are more sensitive to criticism and that they offer more personality problems both in their attitude toward the supervisors and in their relationship to other workers."[24]

A few years earlier in that decade Gulielma Fell Alsop stated that it was easier for a woman to work under a man "unless she flirts with him and tries to make love to him." In her view most successful modern organizations were based on a cooperative male-female association, citing doctors and nurses in hospitals as an example. Alsop advised her female office worker-readers, "Do not contradict, do not criticize, do not make disparaging comparisons, do not complain. If thoughts of criticism, contradiction, comparison or complaint arise in your mind, shut the door of speech on them." Apparently Alsop never considered that a boss could, or would, sexually harass his workers. Her sympathy went to the at-home wife of the boss because "the husband has to go off to business where twenty sirens work under him at his behest."[25]

Loyalty was a virtue strongly stressed by Edith Johnson in her book of advice to women working in the business world. Raising the issue of a female worker whose boss's wife might question her husband's employees about calls from strange women or visits to his office from other women, Johnson advised, "Whatever happens in a man's office, whether it be right or wrong, must be regarded as private business never under any circumstances to be revealed." If the employee was ever called upon to participate in any dishonorable transaction (Johnson gave no examples but presumably meant something like lying to cover the boss's activities), "she should seek employment elsewhere and let the matter be a closed book."[26]

Beth Bailey McLean called loyalty to the company an employee's first responsibility. "Loyalty means that you don't discuss troubles and problems with outsiders." When McLean looked at the male-female interactions in a typical office she said of the males, "They are friendly and enjoy the association but they are not courting you nor do they expect you to misjudge their interest." Laying the groundwork for a woman to doubt the implications of behavior at work, McLean said that a lot of women were apt to be too easily hurt, they took criticism as a personal affront, they held a grudge, and they brooded over mistakes and hidden meanings. Be cheerful through it all for, wrote McLean "the cheerful woman who hides her fears, her hurt feelings, her troubles, who smiles and enjoys her co-workers finds that her circle of friends becomes legion."[27]

For industrial consultant Donald Laird writing in 1942, women were in the work force primarily to get a husband. He quoted one expert as saying the average female worker "aims at a state of existence in which she can see more of men and can see men more intimately" and another as saying, "Although she may not flirt openly in the office or factory, romantic questings and daydreams do flit through the woman employee's head much more than is commonly realized." Laird claimed that four days before the onset of menstruation a woman experienced "heightened sexual excitement reflected in daydreams, flirtatious conduct." Generally speaking he found women flirtatious and fickle at any time of the month for later he wrote in his book, "They will encourage the man and then unexpectedly turn him down and have nothing further to do with him in order to keep from becoming enslaved to a person they envy." An older male boss might be best for he might, thought Laird, cause less of this "surging resentment" as he naturally took the place in a woman's mind of her father. With such a low opinion of women one wonders why Laird would employ them at all. His answer was blunt and unequivocal; "because they are cheaper."[28]

Writing in 1935, Frances Maule counseled women employees that it was within the bounds of propriety to work after hours at the office with the boss even though it would not be all right to go to a man's apartment at any hour unchaperoned. "You must not run around with the Chief—or any of the other high men executives," chastised the author. "The girl of good breeding is recognized in business, as elsewhere, by the amount of self-control, dignity and good humor she is able to show under trying circumstances."[29]

Maule naïvely stated, "And just as it is a point of honor with the men to refrain from meaningless dalliance—or dalliance that means only the one thing—with the young women in the office, so, on the part of the women it shall be—and is with the ones who know their office book of etiquette—a point of honor to refrain from turning loose their feminine allurement upon defenseless and susceptible males." Young women were said to proceed on the assumption that any female who was not bad looking just "naturally" came in for a good deal of "quite harmless masculine attention that is not intended to be taken too seriously." According to Maule, when faced with such behaviors the woman was "to pretend not to see them, or else to continue to act as if they were not serious. The rules of the game for his side provide that he should drop that line at once, without making it necessary for the girl to take up a stand against him" if she indicated she was not interested.[30]

At least Maule recognized that sexual harassment took place. She admitted that infrequently the rules of the game were ignored and that a man could be so far gone in his "infatuation" that he lost all control and behaved like the "wicked would-be seducer" of a movie. If these circumstances occurred, emphasizing that such were very, very rare, Maule said, "sometimes there is no alternative but flight.... Occasionally a girl does have to give up a perfectly good job in order to extricate herself from a situation for which she is entirely blameless." There was no other option, as Maule made clear by commenting, "The one thing a girl absolutely cannot do is to carry troubles of this sort to anybody higher up. Unjust? Yes. But that is the way it is." A girl was expected by her employer to be competent to handle this sort of situation by herself. "The front office does not want to be put in the position of having to take sides, to sit in judgment, and, possibly, to risk losing a valuable man or a good customer. And if the girl makes the mistake of taking her trouble to one of her superiors, she is very soon made to realize that it is one of those things that just isn't done."[31]

To illustrate her advice Maule told the story of Jocelyn, who was "just too beautiful, too lavishly endowed with the life force, to be allowed around a business office." Starting out as a typist, Jocelyn was soon promoted to secretary to one of the executives, who immediately began to pester her for dates and so on. Frightened, Jocelyn took this story to the employment manager who had hired her. This put him in a bind because "the executive in question was important." So the personnel officer solemnly chastised her as a "very vain and silly little girl, who had mistaken mere fatherly kindness for evil intent." Then he sent her back to her job with the admonition that she had better learn to paddle her own canoe. Not surprisingly the executive continued his harassment. Jocelyn was finally forced to quit.[32]

Maule devoted more space in her book to warning girls not to fall in love with their bosses and certainly not to show it if they did. In the author's mind this was a far more frequent event than the sexual harassment of female employees. Maule gave examples of steps a kindly boss might take to discourage such emotion in his female underling. As a somewhat drastic measure he might even have to fire her.[33]

When in 1979 a Victoria, Australia, branch of the public service union the Administrative and Clerical Officers Association invited members who had been harassed at work to contact a female union official, she quickly received 26 complaints. Several women reported missing out on promotions because they refused to comply with sexual demands. Other women sought transfers to escape harassment. In one instance a female resigned from the Commonwealth Public Service as a result of sexual pressure.[34]

When Indira Chauhan surveyed women clerical workers in the city of

Bhopal, India, in the 1980s, she found much sexual harassment. "A 'difficult' woman may not be confirmed or may be denied a promotion. A doe-eyed stenographer, who was as good at shorthand and typing as any man, was sacked summarily when she pleaded her inability to accompany the boss to a conference in Kashmir," reported Chauhan. An 18-year-old girl working as a school typist was kissed by the proprietor within a week of taking the job. At one company the managing director told an interviewee that he was looking only for "sweet and juicy girls." Chauhan concluded that in the case of white-collar female workers the most vulnerable were typists, receptionists, and telephone operators. Most of them were not well off financially, with the result that the income they did earn was crucial. Most did not report their harassers for fear of job loss and for fear of being stigmatized socially. In offices where males outnumbered females harassment occurred more usually in the form of obscene remarks or touch. Coercion seemed more prevalent in small firms than in large companies.[35]

In another book published the same year Chauhan studied females in Nagpur, India, who lived in special lodging houses for working women compared to those still living at home. Employers regarded the former group of women — called hostelers — with greater suspicion than those who lived at home. Employers worried that these females were more interested in having "a good time" than in doing their work. Some of the hostelers told Chauhan that they did not tell their employers that they stayed at hostels. Women whose place of abode was known at work had to conduct themselves with "care and caution, particularly while dealing with male colleagues." Male coworkers often displayed a double standard of behavior toward females living in hostels and those living at home. More sexual harassment was directed at the hostelers. Most of the women hoped for promotion, and for this they had to display behavior that the hostelers themselves described as "controlled coquetry" or something between that and flirtation. They had to be polite, yet diplomatic, "allowing the menacing male boss to take liberties only to a certain extent and not beyond." None admitted to having entered into sexual relations to obtain a raise. Most claimed they had gained their promotion by being polite and repulsing sexual harassment. This process was described as "very tiring, tedious and causing a great deal of mental anguish by those who had experienced it."[36]

During October 1989 the Second Bar Association of Tokyo, Japan, held a phone-in for women to air their grievances about sexual harassment. So heavy was the response that the phone lines were jammed for six hours. At the end of that time 137 formal complaints were registered. Almost 40 percent were from women who told of being compelled to have sexual relations with their superiors at work. Ten of these cases were later reclassified as rape or attempted rape.[37]

With the collapse of the Soviet Union and the rise of private business in Russia sexual harassment was considered in 1993 to be "business as usual." Lena Guzeeva, a senior university student, related how at interviews for jobs in private businesses employers looked female applicants up and down. If the employers did not like what they saw, they did not hire the women. If they did, they let applicants know that their responsibilities might include those of a prostitute. Women who had made it to high positions in private firms told of being given ultimatums by their bosses such as "Sleep with me or quit."[38]

While Roberta Goldberg was trying to organize female office clerks in Baltimore, Maryland, in the early 1980s, she found sexual harassment that ranged from verbal comments to physical contact. Often statements made to the women contained just enough innuendo to make it difficult to accuse someone of harassment. Although there were then some legal avenues for women to pursue if they had been sexually harassed, Goldberg felt that "for the most part men do not have any fear of reprisal." Commented one woman clerk, "Every man feels it is his right to constantly make suggestive remarks, sexual references or even to touch and hug in a way that can be interpreted innocently. Women who try to tolerate this are abused, those who reject it are considered snobby." According to Goldberg, none of the women was pleased with that sort of attention. All viewed it as negative, but they replied to it with a variety of responses ranging from attempting to ignore it, to pretending to take it as a compliment, to making outright verbal complaints, to threatening to report the harassment. Most agreed that whatever the response, it only put off the harassment for short periods; there was little or no advantage for a female office worker regardless of her response. One clerk was subjected to harassment on a virtually daily basis. She explained how she dealt with it as she reported for work each morning: "I wonder what type of harassment he's going to give me today? But I feel like this: when he's harassing me and if I decide to quit, and I'm out there on the employment line, he's the one that's smiling because he still has his income to pay his bills, where I don't." So she put up with the situation.[39]

The New York City Transit Authority formally prohibited sexual harassment in 1986. The first employee to be disciplined was Ronald Contino in 1992, when he was drawing a $120,000 salary as a senior vice-president for surface transit. When he had been with the Sanitation Department in 1987 as an assistant commissioner he had been reprimanded for failing to thoroughly investigate charges of sexual harassment. During January 1992 while recovering from surgery Contino made a conference call to 40 staffers to congratulate them on their work during his absence. Then he told 1 of 3 females present in the group, Velva Edwards, to rent a room big enough for all of them because when he returned he would demonstrate his recovery by having public sex with Edwards and another female staffer. These two women complained; as a result Contino was demoted to a position where he developed proposals to increase worker productivity. Transit Authority president Alan F. Klepper commented, "I did not think that a single incident, as serious as it was, justified terminating him." Contino earned $110,000 a year in his demoted job.[40]

David Lanier was mayor of Dyersburg, Tennessee, for 14 years before being elected chancery judge in 1982 (his term will expire in 1998). In December 1992 he was convicted of violating the civil rights of five women by sexually assaulting them at the small-town courthouse. Reinforcing evidence from the past that job hunting itself, not just jobholding, was a dangerous undertaking, Lanier was convicted of twice forcing a woman to perform oral sex on him in his office. She had come to see him about a job, she also had a child custody case pending before him in the courts. The judge was also convicted of grabbing the breasts or buttocks of courthouse employees. Lanier was acquitted on several counts of the indictment, including a charge that he fondled a courthouse clerk for 30 minutes as she sat beside him while his court was in session. He did acknowledge having sex on the floor of his office with one of his accusers but insisted it was the woman's idea. Lanier remained free on bond and under court order to stay away from his accusers while awaiting sentencing. The state's disciplinary board for judges was investigating Lanier, who was removed from the bench in August 1992 pending the outcome of the case. The board's report would go to the Tennessee legislature, which had the power to impeach him.[41] In April 1993 Lanier was sentenced to 25 years in prison, fined $25,000, and ordered to pay the government $1,500 a month while imprisoned if he drew a pension. Lanier remained free on bond pending an appeal. He continued to draw his $85,000 salary as a judge.[42]

A few weeks after Lanier was sentenced the New York State Commission on Judicial Conduct began a closed-door hearing into harassment allegations leveled against Judge Carmen J. Cognetta, Jr., one of Staten Island's two family court jurists. Some 30 to 50 women were subpoenaed to give testimony on harassment incidents dating back six years. The hearing was initiated after allegations were made by a female lawyer who also gave information about other victims, who included female court officers, lawyers, and clerks. Reportedly Cognetta used crude and obscene language to solicit sex, touched the breasts of a court employee, and told others that he had sexually explicit dreams about them. Cognetta denied all the charges.[43]

During the transition period for Bill Clinton from president-elect to president one name mentioned as a possible nominee for U.S. solicitor general was Philip A. Lacovara, general counsel for the Wall Street investment banking firm Morgan Stanley and Company. That possibility ended

early in 1993 when it was announced that Lacovara was leaving the company, having been the subject of an investigation into sexual harassment
charges. These charges were leveled by three female employees of the
company, one being his secretary. The secretary, through use of a body
wire and tape recorder, made a surreptitious recording of remarks she
considered harassing. Morgan Stanley called in outside counsel to conduct
an investigation, which, sources said, substantiated at least one of the
women's charges, resulting in Lacovara being forced out. Even though
Lacovara and Morgan Stanley confirmed that a harassment investigation
had taken place, both denied that any allegations had been substantiated.
The company denied that any electronic evidence had been obtained by
anyone and claimed that Lacovara's decision to leave predated the allegations. Lacovara called the charges "a false and malicious effort at blackmail" leveled by two women who had been dismissed and a third who was
being fired. He was one of two Morgan Stanley officials who signed a 1991
memo to employees restating that the firm had a policy against sexual
harassment.[44]

One of the government's highest-ranking immigration officers in the
Los Angeles area was Arthur Alvarez, port director at Los Angeles International Airport until November 1992, when he was reassigned to other duties
after allegations surfaced that he had sexually harassed female subordinates. About half a dozen female Immigration and Naturalization Service
(INS) employees told police that Alvarez harassed them sexually, including
one who said he touched her improperly. Enough evidence existed for
authorities to file criminal charges of sexual battery against Alvarez for
touching the one employee, but police were reportedly consulting with the
FBI about how to pursue the matter. An FBI spokesperson said he had no
knowledge of the case. James Humble-Sanchez, president of the union that
represented INS employees, said that Alvarez, who oversaw about 200
employees, "was basically using his position to apply pressure on females
to elicit sexual favors."[45]

America's foremost medical research facility, the National Institutes
of Health (NIH) in Bethesda, Maryland, came under fire in a report released
by an outside firm in May 1993. The research facility had commissioned
the report a year earlier when black employees had alleged widespread
discrimination in the acquisitions management division, part of the Office
of Administration. In addition to citing racism, the report noted that an
"ole-boy–younger women network" had existed for years in which the object for some male managers was sex in exchange for "high performance
ratings and/or promotions." The report said five women in the division had
been propositioned for sex by managers. One secretary was harassed "so
much she could not get her work done." Women had not spoken out
because the supervisors they would have had to tell were among the

harassers. In response to this report the NIH commissioned another outside firm to conduct a study to determine whether the NIH could reprimand supervisors named in the first report.[46]

Los Angeles mayor Tom Bradley ordered a survey taken of city employees to find out the extent of harassment in the wake of the Clarence Thomas hearings. Undertaken by the Commission on the Status of Women, this report was released in September 1992. Of the city's 11,722 female employees, 4,887 (42 percent) responded. Of the respondents, 37 percent said they had been harassed in their jobs the previous year. The percentage of complaints was highest from women employed in public safety and security departments such as police, fire, and airport safety, where 48 percent said they had been harassed. Ten percent of the victims reported being harassed at least once a month. Perpetrators were colleagues, supervisors, and, occasionally, members of the public. Most women did not complain; only about 21 percent made informal complaints to supervisors. Half of those said their supervisors took no action, and some managers told the woman to put up with the harasser because "that's just the way he is." Only 5 percent made a formal complaint to a department head or some agency. Many complaints came to nothing as there were no witnesses. Some women reported they had not been told what had become of their complaint.[47]

As a rule these Los Angeles employees preferred to rely on their own instincts rather than informally or formally complain. One clerk who filed a formal complaint in the Building and Safety Department said she was prepared for repercussions from her supervisor but not for the response from a coworker, who demanded she have sex with him in exchange for his testimony. She told him to get lost, and "now he's a witness against me." Others who complained reported that bosses or coworkers became unfriendly toward them, with a few being branded as troublemakers. Under the pressure of this report Bradley suggested the hiring of an ombudsperson to streamline city employee sexual harassment complaints. At the November 1992 City Council meeting that considered this proposal more than 100 members of the Women's Action Coalition noisily demonstrated against sexual harassment and against council member Nate Holden, then accused of sexual harassment himself. The recommendation to hire a sexual harassment coordinator passed unanimously, including a yes vote from Holden. However, Holden did argue that those who filed harassment complaints should be subject to perjury action if their accusations proved false.[48]

One reason female employees working for the city of Los Angeles might be reluctant to complain can be seen in the city's response to harassment charges against City Clerk Elias Martinez. Allegations were first raised in 1991 when a clerk-typist charged Martinez had fondled or touched her on three occasions and three other female employees said they had been ogled or subjected to suggestive questioning. The matter became public in December 1992 when after an investigation had been conducted Mayor Tom Bradley recommended that Martinez be fired. Martinez denied the charges, calling one of his accusers an untrustworthy employee and a "known drunk." Everyone else misunderstood his friendliness, he added, while Bradley was after him for political reasons. An investigator for the city Personnel Department concluded that clerical employees "have been made extremely uncomfortable by the behavior of Mr. Martinez, and its pervasiveness is generally acknowledged." Months passed, with the City Council taking no action to vote on Bradley's termination recommendation. Sometimes it was the council president who ordered postponements; sometimes it was Martinez. Two of his delays were so his lawyer could take vacations. On one occasion two Latino members of council, Richard Alatore and Mike Hernandez, simply walked out of a meeting, presumably in sympathy with fellow Latino Martinez. Alatore denied he had tried to stall, but Hernandez conceded he had walked out to slow the case down. Many felt stalling was designed to take the matter past June 30, the last day in office for the retiring Mayor Bradley, in hopes of leniency from a new mayor. Of course the stalling was also beneficial to Martinez in that he continued to draw his full $116,000 salary. Deputy Mayor Mark Fabiani was upset by the delays, saying, "It's unfortunate that these women who had the courage to come forward have been left dangling in the wind. This is a case that sends a message to all women in the city about how the mayor and City Council handle sexual harassment rules. This delay does not provide a comforting answer." Finally in June 1993 the City Council voted 10 to 3 to fire Martinez, with Holden abstaining. However, the appeal by Martinez to the Civil Service Commission will drag the case out, with Martinez remaining on full salary.[49]

The family-oriented, heavily attended MCA/Universal Studios Hollywood tour was hit by a harassment suit filed late in December 1992 in Los Angeles by former employee Wendy-Sue Rosen. She accused managers of harassing her for sex, of displaying pornographic photos in work areas, and of grabbing and pinching her breasts and buttocks. Rosen worked for the tour in various capacities over 13 years, the last as an auditor at the attraction's box office. In her suit Rosen alleged that Carey Doss, manager of parking services, and Herman Mogollan, manager of tour operations, had repeatedly harassed her, once trapping her in an office where Doss masturbated in front of her. Complaints to the superiors of these men were ignored. "Upper management is well aware of what these guys are up to and have chosen to do absolutely nothing about it," said Rosen. "When I complained all they did was try to force me to quit. The guys who harass and assault the women don't get punished. In fact they get promoted. It's nothing but a sick boy's club." Rosen had resigned from her job the previous February under pressure. Allegedly Mogollan offered her paid vacations in exchange for sex, asked her to show him her breasts, and rubbed his erect penis against her body. Rosen said sexual harassment was pervasive on the theme park grounds, with the large number of teenaged girls hired each year a particular target. Dan Stormer, her attorney, said he had interviewed almost a dozen other MCA female employees who also said they were harassed while working at the park. He also had photos of nude male employees surrounding what he said was an unwilling and naked female employee. These photographs were reportedly posted in plain view in an employee area of the theme park.[50]

Penny Muck once worked as a secretary at Geffen Records in Los Angeles. The lawsuit she filed in 1991 alleged sexual harassment at that company and opened up a litany of horror stories of harassment in the music industry. In her suit Muck charged that over the period of July and August 1991 Marko Babineau, then general manager of Geffen's DGC label, repeatedly masturbated in front of her, fondled her breasts and buttocks, forced her to touch his penis, and once jammed her face into his crotch. Muck recalled one occasion in July when Babineau, leaned over her desk, unzipped his pants, and masturbated in front of her. "All of a sudden, he just starts doing it. He's got this crazy look in his eyes . . . and he's saying 'Watch me! Watch me!' . . . Immediately this big fear shoots through my whole body and I'm saying 'No! No!' but I don't know what to do."[51]

Babineau denied all the charges. However, on September 4 he resigned his job. In the official statement released at that time Geffen claimed Babineau resigned in order to spend more time with his family. The following March Geffen admitted it had terminated Babineau as a result of investigations into Muck's allegations. On September 12 Muck signed a complaint with the California Fair Employment and Housing Commission as well as with the federal Equal Employment Opportunity Commission (EEOC). She filed a civil lawsuit in November 1991 and then resigned from Geffen. Muck had also complained that Geffen executives ignored a long history of harassment complaints against Babineau made by other women employees years before her own alleged harassment began. Geffen adamantly denied this charge. Yet sources at Geffen told the *Los Angeles Times* that "Babineau had sexually harassed other female employees as far back as 1984 when he became head of promotion at Geffen Records." One woman said, "When I went to the legal department and complained the question was never what to do with the men, but what to do with the women." This woman and other sources at Geffen related that two females had previously been transferred to other departments after complaining about Babineau. In 1990 he was promoted to general manager of Geffen's new label DGC when Geffen Records was sold to MCA.[52]

Four months after being terminated by Geffen, Babineau opened his own promotion company. Reportedly he was hired by artist managers as an independent promoter to obtain radio airplay for records released by the Radio Active and Geffen labels. Both labels were distributed by MCA.[53]

When Muck's charges and lawsuit became well publicized in 1991, reverberations were felt throughout the music industry as other cases from around that period began to be made public. Within weeks Capitol Records fired an executive in the royalty department following an in-house sexual harassment investigation. Both RCA and Island labels acknowledged receiving harassment complaints from employees. Several women interviewed by the *Los Angeles Times* related stories of being slapped on the buttocks in the office, fending off superiors before evening concerts, and meeting demands in limousines for oral sex. Most of this harassment, they said, came from men who worked in the promotion department. Women in the industry had taken to organizing informal groups to warn each other of "bimbo hounds."[54]

Among the incidents uncovered was that of Jeff Aldrich, one-time senior vice-president of artists and repertoire for RCA Records who was fired in 1991 after the company conducted a sexual harassment investigation of itself. Several female employees at RCA alleged Aldrich harassed them. A month after he had been fired RCA rehired Aldrich as an independent consultant. He continued in that capacity for six months until he left New York City to join Los Angeles–based Giant Records. In July 1991 Mike Bone, president of Island Records, was named in a lawsuit by Lori Harris, Bone's former administrative assistant at the label, as having sexually harassed her. Bone made sexual advances to her in July 1990. She refused to comply and was fired by Bone the next day. Bone resigned from Island in December 1990 to become co-president of Mercury Records. Island and Mercury were both owned by PolyGram. One secretary said her boss demanded that she touch his genitals to see if she "fit in." When she complied, the boss insisted she continue the practice, threatening to tell what she had already done if she refused to continue. Another secretary was told after complaining to her harasser, "If you can't stand the heat of being pretty then take a . . . can opener to your face." Employed by the law firm of Mitchell, Silberberg, and Knupp and head of the music department there, attorney Abe Somer negotiated what was thought to then be the biggest ever music deal when he signed the Rolling Stones to a multiple album deal in 1974 with Atlantic Records. In 1990 both Somer and the company were sued for assault and battery by a young clerical worker. In her suit she claimed Somer "threatened physical contact in the form of lewd sexual contact, actually engaging in such improper contact and touching and physical abuse . . . without plaintiff's consent." This suit was settled out of court, reportedly for a six-figure sum. In that same year another clerk reached an out-of-court settlement with Somer over a sexual harassment complaint. After the assault suit was filed Somer's status at the firm was changed from partner to "of counsel," meaning he was no longer an employee. Nor did he continue to maintain an office at the firm's premises.[55]

On November 1, 1991, Bone was dismissed by Mercury just two days before the *Los Angeles Times* published a revealing article about harassment in the record industry. The timing of Bone's departure was just a coincidence, stated Mercury. At the time of Bone's appointment several females in the record business had protested Bone's return as an industry executive. Harris settled her suit against Bone out of court in November 1991 for a reported five-figure sum.

In July 1992 Bone started work as a sales and marketing executive at Def American Records, a subsidiary of Time Warner. Heidi Robinson, head of media relations of the Burbank-based label, acknowledged reports that several of the company's 12 female employees objected to working with Bone. Tammy Bruce, president of the Los Angeles chapter of the National Organization for Women, remarked, "The message that Warner is sending to women is that they just don't care about us. . . . What they are telling women is that they think sex harassment is irrelevant and that we are useless and it doesn't matter how we feel." Around the time Bone was taken on by Def American, that label was employing Marko Babineau as an independent producer to promote the label's number one single "Baby Got Back," by Seattle rap artist Sir Mix-A-Lot. This association also drew protest from female employees.[56]

Muck settled her suit against Geffen Records and Babineau out of court in November 1992 for a reported $500,000. In settling, Geffen stressed that it admitted no guilt, nor did it acknowledge any criminal wrongdoing in the matter. Just one day after this agreement was announced Geffen was hit by another sexual harassment suit, this one by former Geffen promotions director Christina Anthony. She charged she had been verbally and physically harassed between 1984 and 1990 by Babineau, who, among other things, allegedly unzipped his pants and displayed his penis. Anthony said that top label executives were each personally informed of the harassment, yet did nothing to stop it. "I was sexually harassed, intimidated and terrorized while working at Geffen Records," she said. Because management refused to intervene, Anthony said she was forced to resign. Her attorney, Dan Stormer, noted his client was not the first to complain to label executives about harassment, but "despite that, they continued to deal with a man who represents the worst in sexual politics." Named in the suit as being apprised of the harassment but doing nothing to stop it were Geffen president Edward Rosenblatt, administrator controller Jim Walker, former president Eric Eisner, and former promotion chief Al Coury.[57]

9
Serving and Nurturing Roles

Working in a retail store in the United States in the early part of this century was just as hazardous to women as any other workplace. Much debate took place at the end of the last century and into the early part of this one over the fact that women who worked in stores had to stand all day, as many as 12 hours in a row. In due course it was mandated that chairs be provided so females could sit down between customers and other duties. This victory came about because it was widely believed that standing all day somehow made it more difficult for women to become mothers.

The image of the women who worked in stores was the same as everywhere else; they were loose and immoral. In 1897 one woman picked domestic work over store employment because when she saw "the looks of the girls in the large stores and the familiarity of the young men, I preferred to go into a respectable family."[1]

Investigative journalist Helen Campbell was told by a department store manager in the 1880s, "I dare say they're [his employees] put upon. They're sassy enough, a good many of them, and some of the better ones suffer from their goings on . . . and these women that come in complaining that they ain't well-treated, nine times out of ten it's their own airs that brought it on. It's a shop girl's interest to behave herself and satisfy customers."[2]

Early in the 1900s a floorwalker who had worked in several large department stores over four years insisted to a congressional investigation of women's working conditions that of the approximately 1,000 women he had supervised over those years, 80 percent "were guilty of habitual immorality." When pressed more closely, he admitted he had personal knowledge of only one actual immoral episode. In that instance "a girl had charged that nine men in that particular store had been involved with her in improper conduct, a charge which investigation proved was true." Even here the floorwalker attributed blame to the girl and not to the men. The Wisconsin Vice Commission found that working conditions contributed to immoral behavior due to the mingling of the sexes at the workplace with "promiscuous familiarity." The commission added, "It must also be stated that the requirement that women employees shall stand all day and the active nature of the day's work cause a severe nervous strain, leading to fatigue and weakening of the will power by the time the day is ended."[3]

Although a link between prostitution and women in the workplace has often been implied, it has invariably been to suggest that prostitutes entering the nonsex industry workplace lower the moral standards, corrupt the men, and so on. The evidence is that working women have often been forced into prostitution due to the inadequacy of their wages or pressures from employers. In 1888 a prostitute in Minneapolis told a reporter, "I tried for three years to support life on the wages I was paid as a cashier in a big store. . . . I gave up the struggle at last." At the turn of the century a retail worker made $3 to $6 per week, while the minimum wage needed to survive in a big city like Chicago was around $8 per week. A prostitute could reportedly make $50 or more in the same amount of time.[4]

In Chicago around 1910 a woman, C. S., told investigators of the impossibility of living on $3 a week. "My employer, who is now in the penitentiary, induced me to go wrong when I told him I could not live on $3 a week." She continued, "When I was fifteen years old I found work in a candy store. My employer worked his will by threatening to discharge me. Afterwards he proposed that I flirt with young men who patronized the store. 'It will help business,' he said. I was forced to divide my earnings from this source with my employer." M. C. related that "I was getting $3 week and I found this insufficient for the support of my mother and myself. When I appealed to my employer he laughed at me and invited me to enter upon the life I am now following. I did."[5]

At that time in Pittsburgh an investigator looking into the conditions of women employed in stores learned that many saleswomen did leave stores in desperation over low wages to become prostitutes. They did not earn enough in retail work to feed and house themselves. She reported, "Male supervisors and floorwalkers took advantage of their plight and urged individual women to give them 'concessions.' If a woman refused, her job was in jeopardy." Rosa was employed at a ribbon counter. She had a mother and two sisters dependent on her. "She began while still in the store to 'make money on the side.'" Management discovered this and fired her. She then entered a house of prostitution. Vera worked as a cashier at a store where she made "concessions to her employer" to augment her wages. Later she left the store and also entered a house of prostitution.[6]

As simple an act as going to the toilet was often fraught with peril and anxiety for women who worked in stores and factories. Permission had to be asked for and obtained before an employee could go to the toilet. One worker told Helen Campbell, "You have to ask a man for leave every time it is necessary to go upstairs, and half the time he would look and laugh with the other clerks. I'd rather be where there are all women. They're hard on you sometimes, but they don't use foul language and insult you when you can't help yourself." Campbell added this was a fairly common happening wherein females had to run the gauntlet of men and boys after asking permission to go to the toilet. Many "sensitive and shrinking girls" refused to go to the toilet at work, bringing severe illnesses on themselves solely from the dread of running this gauntlet, argued Campbell. She added, "All physicians who treat this class testify to the fact that many become severely diseased as the result of unwillingness to subject themselves to this ordeal."[7]

Discussing her early life in the women's labor movement, Maud Nathan spoke of the difficulties for New York City store clerks in the 1890s when she said, "Floor walkers in the old days were veritable tsars; they often ruled with a rod of iron. Only the girls who were 'free-and-easy' with them, who consented to lunch or dine with them, who permitted certain liberties were allowed any freedom of action, or felt secure in their positions. . . . A complaint lodged against a floor-walker or against the head of a department—superior officers—was almost invariably followed by dismissal of the one who made the complaint."[8]

Reporting on those same store clerks 20 years later, investigative reporter Sue Clark noted, "The girls in the stores are importuned, not only by men from without these establishments, but also, to the shame of the managements, by men employed within the stores. The constant close presence of this gulf has more than one painful aspect. On account of it, not only the poor girls who fall suffer, but also the girls who have the constant sense of being on 'guard.'" Clark worried that all of this would lead them into prostitution.[9]

When Edward Hillman, manager of Chicago's Hillman's Department Store, testified before the Illinois Vice Commission around 1910, he attempted to put his store in the best light, but in doing so he indirectly exposed the extent of harassment at his store, which supposedly cared about such matters. He testified that seven floorwalkers had been dismissed by his firm for trying to "exert an evil influence over the girls." In addition other State Street stores were warned of these men in order to put a check on their activities in the loop district. These firings came following complaints made by employees. When asked if he knew it was common knowledge that a large number of department store girls reportedly led immoral lives, Hillman replied that he did not, saying, "I believe department stores take more interest in their help than do any other employers of labor. We have men and women detectives watching for 'mashers.' One got such a thrashing by a house detective yesterday that I actually was sorry for him."[10]

Distinguished journalist George Seldes recalled in his memoirs his early years in journalism working on the Pittsburgh *Leader*. He wrote in

1910 or 1911, "The son of the owner of one of the largest department stores believed that, like medieval lords who had 'the rights of the first night' with the bride of every one of his serfs, he had the right to rape every pretty salesgirl. When I reported his court hearing, my city editor for the first time in my life, gave me a sheet of carbon paper and said to make a copy. I made it. It was sent immediately to the business department. It was not printed." However, within a few days the *Leader* and all the other Pittsburgh newspapers printed double that store's usual Sunday advertising. The price per page of advertising was also increased. No Pittsburgh paper even mentioned this rape story.[11]

One of the more exhaustive studies of women's working conditions in department stores was conducted in 1895 by the New York State legislature. Dr. Jane Robbins testified about these employees—who told her stories they would not tell factory inspectors or the legislative committee— that they "are roughly talked to by the foremen and the shop is a very bad place for them. . . . The stores are very bad places for young girls at an age when there is greater danger of their being corrupted, it is a well known fact that the majority of the women who become outcasts are led into doing wrong before they reach 18."[12]

One unidentified witness had been employed in Macy's at the management level for more than 30 years before voluntarily quitting. He told investigators that when one of the cash girls had to go to the shipping department, she "was not only talked to in a shameful manner but she was thrown on the floor and the man kissed her and rubbed his whiskers all over her face; I missed the man the next day from his position, and I supposed he was discharged; I understood he was; there were a number of such cases." Asked what changes he would make if he was in charge of making the laws, he replied, "First of all I should protect the girls," for many were being "ruined." He related the story of a superintendent named Ridgeway. Cash girls were sometimes required to stay late to help clean up. One such girl said that "Mr. Ridgeway kept her and put his arm around her and kissed her and all that." The former manager got this girl to complain to higher-ups, accompanied by a female stock head. But "there was nothing done about it much, the man remained there." A year or so later Ridgeway fled New York City to avoid arrest on a different complaint of child abuse. Said the witness, "I know the man had abused a number of children." Cash girls were usually only 14 or 15 years old and made $2, perhaps up to $3, per week. It was illegal to hire them if they were younger than 14, but this law was regularly broken. These younger girls were paid even less.[13]

Many department store clerks appeared before the committee to testify. To protect them from possible reprisals from their employers, the committee did not record their names or places of employment in the almost 2,000 pages of testimony. Despite this safeguard the committee's attempts to get evidence from these women always came up empty. The tone of the testimony suggests the fear these women were testifying under. A few of them were prodded into admitting the conditions of the toilets were not the best, insufficient in number or cleanliness, or private enough. But that was the only complaint they were willing to make before the all-male committee. When asked if any sexual harassment occurred, they said no. When asked if anything was wrong with other working conditions, such as overtime and pay scales, the women testified everything was fine. They lived under a justifiable fear that any negative comments from them that got back to their bosses would mean instant dismissal — and nothing could be done about this.

As the inquiry progressed the questioners grew more and more frustrated by the lack of openness from the store employees. More often the examiners inserted their preamble about how they wanted the truth and that it was perfectly safe to be frank with them. This did not help. Committee members began to use leading questions more and more regularly, such as "Don't you mind...." "Wouldn't you rather...?" However, woman after woman insisted she did not mind working an extra four hours on a Saturday for no extra pay, that she did not mind working an extra hour to clean up for no extra money, that she did not mind at all that no chair was provided for her, that she did not deserve a higher salary or need one, and so on.[14]

At the end of the hearing Archibald Sessions, counsel to the Working Women's Society, argued that the most deplorable result of the department store system "is the effect upon the morals of young women and girls. It is said in many stores these unfortunates are purposely given wages upon which it is impossible to support life, because the alternative is always open to them of eking out their scanty pay by making a commodity of their virtue. It is well known that in Paris this is expected of the girls, and if the same thing is not the result of deliberate plans in this State, the effect is produced by the same cause."[15]

Controversy over department store work continued for some time. In terms of maligning the clerks themselves, putting all the blame on them, and relieving stores, male employees, and low wages of all responsibility, this ideology probably reached its apex in the 1910–1915 period. W. R. Hotchkin was the advertising director of Gimbel Brothers department store in 1913. He had then worked in the retail industry for 27 years. Responding in an article to the idea that department store work was bad for females, he said, "We are sometimes told that store girls flirt. Of course they do." Arguing it was not the wages or occupation but temptation that menaced virtue Hotchkin offered this solution: "Protect the girls. And again: Condemn the man with the woman." But this was the last mention he made of the man, nor did he suggest how to protect the girls. Perhaps considering that not possible, he went on to suggest that if the female could not be protected, the answer was to "supply a safe and sympathetic refuge for the girl or woman after she has first erred. A place where she can go and hide from every one when the doors of home are closed against her. Where she can go with her sin and atone for it and from which she can return to the world with a clean name and live a pure life at honest employment." With no irony intended Hotchkin considered his article to be an indignant protest on behalf of the women working in department stores.[16]

Three months later a large number of social workers, most of whom were women, joined the fray about vice among working women, especially those in department stores. These social workers argued that low wages were "scarcely ever a direct cause of the downfall of young women." They did add they did not wish to suggest that store wages were high or even sufficient. Drawing on their many years of experience and observations, these women declared that the factors that contributed to immorality among working women were weakness of mind and will, individual temperament, immoral associates, lack of religious or ethical training, injurious home influences, cramped living accommodation, lack of industrial efficiency, idleness, unwillingness to accept available employment, love of finery and pleasure, unwholesome amusement, inexperience, and ignorance of social temptations.[17]

Fourteen major department stores got together in 1915 to finance their own investigation of sexual harassment in retail employment. They concluded, "It has sometimes been stated that work in stores and factories has a demoralizing effect upon young women who are thrown into intimate contact with employers and customers who may have evil designs on them . . . but investigators found that exceedingly few of the many stories related could be traced to an extensive basis in fact."[18]

Around 1950 Arlene Tupper got a job in a men's clothing store when she was 14. The job lasted a week and a half. One of the men who had been there for years made a pass at her. Not knowing what it was all about, Arlene just went numb. "The man told the boss that I had made passes at him, so I was fired," she said.[19]

Female merchants in Chiuchin, Peru, in the 1970s, who were mostly small traders working from stalls, were "reminded of the special status of their sex by male customers' behavior toward them." Single women had to place limitations on male customers that male proprietors did not face. These females felt they had to be friendly to encourage business, but they also felt they needed to "wear a serious face" to avoid sexual harassment. Males enjoyed doing business with single female traders but often attempted unwanted advances. As a precaution these women "send clear signals that they define men as purely business clients."[20]

Because of close contact with customers, waitresses were particularly susceptible to uninvited approaches, facing harassment from employer, coworkers, and outsiders. Grace Abbott took a saloon keeper to court in 1908 on behalf of a young Bohemian immigrant named Bozema who worked for him. Her employer had "abused her shamefully and then turned her out when he found that she was to become the mother of his illegitimate child." The case was lost when the judge empathized with the man. It was with cases such as this in mind that Abbott started to organize immigrant protection associations in Chicago. Protecting immigrant girls from lecherous bosses was a major theme in her organizing efforts.[21]

Speaking to a reporter in Toronto, Canada, in 1910, a waitress said, "We have long hours, small pay and much abuse, not only from employers, but from many men who would not dare to treat their wife or sister as they do us." A second waitress complained that "some of these fellows think that if they come in and sit at your table and put a dime under the plate that you should immediately become their slave, but the girls are tired of it and will form an organization for their protection."[22]

During the same period waitresses in the United States complained about the practice of tipping, which they disliked because of what they saw as the connection between the personal relationship it implied with a customer and "insulting advances." Said one waitress in 1916, "Girls have to live on tips. . . . You have to put up with it or starve. The majority of girls . . . if they could get a good living would be glad to do without tips. . . . Advances are always made, especially in certain districts. A great number go wrong because of so many advances."[23]

Cornelia Stratton Parker performed a variety of working-class jobs circa 1920 before publishing her experiences in a book. One of these jobs was in a restaurant as a kitchen helper or pantry worker. On her first day on the job an older female employee warned her to be on her guard. At the end of her first week Parker wrote in her diary, "I couldn't stand this pace long—waiters are too affectionate." She then added, "It was in no sense personal. I mean that any girl working at my job, provided she was not too ancient and too toothless and too ignorant of the English language, would have been treated with equal enthusiasm." Parker was very naïve, calling harassment enthusiasm and affection. Much of this naïveté was gone not too long after. A later diary entry read, "But what if a girl had a couple of years of that sort of thing? . . . Sex seemed to enter in the first ten minutes. Girls are not for friends—they're to flirt with. It was for the girl to set the limits; the men had none. But eight and one-half hours a day of parrying the advances of affectionate waiters—a law should be passed limiting the cause of such exertion to two hours a day, no overtime." Worst of all for her were her experiences with a Spanish chef. Parker had to pass his stove many times a day in the course of her work. He constantly harassed her. "I came to dread it," she wrote. "Always the Spanish ex-tailor dropped everything with a clatter and chased after me. I managed to pass his confines at greater and greater speed. Invariably I heard his panting."[24]

When Dorothy Cobble looked at waitressing in the 1920s and 1930s, she found that sexual harassment plagued young and old, black and white, with male bosses not above pressuring their female staff for sex and encouraging waitresses to use their sexuality to attract customers. One waitress explained, "The boss, accustomed to looking upon his employees with the same attitude that he regards a coffee urn, does not see why he cannot use the waitress's body for other purposes than waiting on the table. After many suggestive approaches such as walking into the dressing room when she is donning her uniform, attempting caresses and so on, he states the issue bluntly, 'be nice or else'." She added that refusal of such advances was a common reason for women being unjustly discharged and was well known to any waitress who had been in the business for any length of time.[25]

At one tavern the house got a percentage of any drink men bought for a bar server, who commented, "Then they thought because they bought you a drink, they could feel you up." Customer abuse of waitresses also operated independently of the employer. Some male customers expected sexual favors in exchange for the tips. One waitress described café Romeos to a reporter by first explaining that "the wisecrack often heard in union halls . . . that you can tell a guy is middle-aged when he pays more attention to his food than he does to the waitress . . . may draw smiles all around—but never from a waitress." Detailing the seriousness of the situation, she bitterly spoke of the "boneheads . . . who can't keep their hands to themselves" and suggested that "waitresses who serve the evening trade should be issued a 38-caliber automatic as part of their uniforms."[26]

When the U.S. Congress investigated the working conditions of females in 1910, it cited four occupations as being morally dangerous for women: waitressing, domestic service, nursing, and "low-grade" factory trades. While noting the vulnerable position of these women servers—"The waitress comes in contact with men of every kind, some of whom consider a girl in her position fair game. She cannot resent their advances, for she must not offend customers. Even her refusal to accept overtures must be carefully managed"—investigators nevertheless felt that it was mostly the fault of the women, the "low"-quality females who took up waitressing.[27]

Frances Donovan worked in Chicago restaurants around 1919 to expose the life of a waitress. She sided with the men and blamed women for the sexual activity that took place in restaurants, branding them as dumb, loose, and immoral. After implying that some employees at a restaurant where she worked had venereal disease, she observed, "They appear to be happy, too, not cast down and ashamed of their degradation." Commenting on waitresses in general, Donovan offered the thought that "vulgar language and the use of profanity are the most glaring vices. . . . There is not much that is complex about the waitress and her behavior can easily be reduced to the fundamental appetites of food hunger and sex hunger. She is . . . dishonorable, loose in her sex relations." Sitting around on a break with other waitresses at one job, Donovan mentioned that nothing happened to her, that nobody made passes at her. A coworker responded, "Of course no one would insult you. Any one can tell from your looks that you wouldn't stand for it." From this Donovan concluded "that a woman is protected by her behavior even in a world of restaurants and waitresses." Ironically on the next page in her book Donovan then outlined how a man came into her restaurant every day for a week or so and pestered her for a date even though she was wearing a wedding ring. Overall from the cheapest to the most exclusive restaurants she decided, "The sex game in the waitress world is a dirty game. Even in the restaurants where the relations between the patrons and waitresses were not actively sexual, there was the constant stimulation of dirty jokes and unclean conversation."[28]

Jeanne King tried to get hired as a waitress in the 1960s at any of New York City's posh restaurants. These types of restaurants paid higher wages, generated higher tips, and hired only males. King received different excuses for not being hired: she was told that women cannot lift heavy trays and that "women can't fend off the amorous advances of men." After initiating an American Civil Liberties Union lawsuit and as a direct result of it, King became in November 1971 the first female to ever work as a waitress at New York's famed 21 Club.[29]

Asked in the 1970s about her overall experiences with sexual harassment as a waitress, King replied, "Some can be crude, look you up and down, but then they're crude when you're just walking down the street. It's a hassle with men everywhere." Waitress Ingrid responded, "It depends on where you work. You get it more as a cocktail waitress, and I think I told you once I would not work at a cocktail lounge. Because I don't want to be flirted with all the time. Other waitresses don't mind it, I didn't when I was younger, but now I get sickened by it. . . . You do get some strangers, particularly those on conventions who seem to assume right away because you're a waitress, you're a hooker."[30]

Anna Brinkley worked at cocktail and food waitressing during her college days and shortly thereafter in the 1970s. She disliked these jobs, partly because of the pay but "ultimately it always came down to some kind of crap from the male above you. Like the maitre d' would make a pass at you, and when you wouldn't do anything with him you'd get fired." She left waitressing for the better pay of the trades; she became an electrician. She was sexually harassed there.[31]

From July 1971 to July 1972 James Spradley studied the interactions of waitresses, bartenders, and customers at a bar frequented mostly by college students. This unidentified establishment was located in a large, unnamed midwestern American city and christened as Brady's Bar in the book. Spradley found a clear division of labor there, with males bartending and giving last call while females waitressed. Customers and bartenders all referred to the waitresses as "Brady's Girls," with the word *women* rarely, if ever, used. The women were also regularly called bitch and broad.[32]

A common type of harassment was the man who grabbed a waitress each time she walked past his table and persistently asked her, "Are you new here?" "What nights do you work?" "What are you doing after work?" Other regularly uttered lines included "Where have you been all my life?" "Sit down and talk to us." "Have I told you that I love you?" "Haven't I seen you someplace before?" "Wouldn't you like to sit on my lap?" Pats, pinches, grabs, and pawing also went with the territory. A customer sitting at the bar next to a waitress's station would keep crowding her on purpose, brushing up against her every time she ordered drinks. He kept grabbing her leg, asking inane questions, and then apologizing for offending her. When asked what he wanted, a common reply was "I already know what I want, I'll take you." Drink orders were often delivered with double meanings. For example, "I need a Manhattan, Hold the Cherry" or "I need a Stinger, Hold the Nuts." One night a waitress came to work wearing a one-piece jumpsuit with a zipper down the front. The bartender commented, "It'd look better if you had some tits! Who wants to pull down a zipper just to see two fried eggs thrown against a wall?" Most of the insults and harassing behavior were delivered in front of an audience, a seemingly necessary or at least desirable condition.[33]

Waitresses themselves felt they could not respond in kind with crude language. One said, "You just can't walk up and grab some guy. . . . There are very few ways that girls can get the guys back without making herself appear cheap." Another remarked, "There's no way we can get them back." According to Spradley, waitress Holly told him, "Brady's Bar was a man's world and being part of it brought an excitement all its own. You dressed for the men, served drinks to the men, laughed at jokes told by men, got tips and compliments from men, ran errands for men. Men called you sweetie and honey and sexy. Men asked you out, and men made passes."[34]

Spradley's explanation for this bar scene was totally sexist. He wrote that "the girls in the bar depend on male approval for their sense of well-being. Because of the status hierarchy the waitresses need the approval and praise of bartenders and regular customers, but the reverse is not true. . . . Before long, new waitresses, rather than taking offence, are participating in the joking behavior. . . . But the masculinity rituals would not be effective without the cooperation of the waitress. She has learned to respond demurely to taunts, invitations, and physical invasions of her personal space. She smiles, laughs, patiently removes hands, ignores the questions and moves coyly out of reach. . . . Although the girls know it is important to keep their place during these encounters, it is also clear they could act otherwise in dealing with aggressive customers." When Spradley related an account of how five male customers were joking one night about the bust size of a waitress who was present, he said, "The waitress herself is not the focus of attention in these cases; she is merely an artifact used by men to display their prowess." Spradley missed here one of the main functions of sexual harassment; the public and personal degradation of women.[35]

A restaurant owner in New South Wales, Australia, in 1979 hired and fired 18 young women over the course of a six-month period because he was convinced that sooner or later he would get one who would submit to his unsolicited sexual advances. At the same time in that country female members, most of them barmaids, of the Federated Liquor and Allied Industries Employees Union made frequent complaints to their union about advances made by owners or managers. One hotel became notorious, with its "amazing turnover" in female staff attributed to the fact that women who rejected the manager's harassment either quit or were fired.[36]

Michelle Gubbay worked as a waitress in a strip joint called The Paradise Lounge. Working as a team, waitresses and stripper-dancers were required to mix with the customers to hustle overpriced drinks. Those who were deemed less than enthusiastic in this regard by management, those who preferred not to face the groping hands and the obscene remarks, were continually hassled by management. Compare Gubbay's analysis with Spradley's. The latter portrayed women as content with sexual harassment, as actually wanting and needing it for their identity. Gubbay's vastly different, more accurate view was not filtered through the lens of male revisionism. She wrote, "Men come into the Paradise, and their distrust and objectification and hatred of women is confirmed—confirmed, mind you, it is nothing brand-new—and women working there have their anger and hatred of men confirmed." She could not think of one woman in the club who had not at one time or another expressed some form of deep and bitter hostility toward the male customers and, by extension, toward men generally. Gubbay wondered how women could not feel hostile as the men made comments at them, tried to grab and paw them, humiliated them by deriding other women, and detracted from their personhood by labeling them bitches and whores, by judging them, and by seeing them only in terms of how they pleased men. "And is this behavior of the men in the club so different from the behavior of men on the street, or the subway, in the office, in our home, in our beds?" She continued, "If ever I doubted before that men hated women, I could never doubt that again after having worked at the Paradise. There I can see and feel the hatred exuding from the men; I can see it as they sit, watching the strippers; I can feel it when they interact with me. It is a hatred of the power of women's sexuality, a disgust and a contempt for beings they see solely as sexual creatures."[37]

Barmaids in 1980s Mexico, when they were employed, were subjected to lewd comments and propositions from customers. Conventionally women were not employed in jobs dealing with the public, particularly bar and restaurant work due to its connotations with hostessing and prostitution. Women bar attendants were said by many to give an establishment a "bad name" or to "lower the tone." At one restaurant the owner refused to hire women as waitresses. He did use them at the cash desk as this was "female work," and it was also the only place in his restaurant where a woman could sit apart and be safe from harassment by male staff or, as he insisted, not "provoke" the male employees.[38]

The image of the loose woman plagued stewardesses almost from the time they first took to the air in the early 1930s. Inez Keller Fruite was one of the first eight stewardesses. She recalled that the wives of the pilots started a letter-writing campaign to Boeing Air Transport saying that the "stewardesses were trying to steal their husbands and requested their removal." The jealous wife of one pilot in Salt Lake City always met her husband at the plane. Boeing issued written regulations in 1931 to warn off stewardesses, which said, "At no time will stewardesses be permitted to carry on conversations with pilots or ground personnel on duty except on business." Likely this was more of an appeasement to the wives than a rigidly enforced regulation.[39]

Decades later Paula Kane revealed her experiences as a stewardess from 1968 to 1973 when she was employed by American Airlines. During the 1950s most airlines adopted forced retirement rules for these women, setting the age at around 32 to 35. Most women did not even last that long in the job; less than 3 percent of American Airlines stewardesses were older than 30 in 1967. Much of that turnover was likely due to the effects of sexual harassment. Kane argued that a change to a more sexual image for stewardesses dated to 1966 when advertising executive Mary Wells jazzed up Braniff's overall image, including that of the attendants. Other airlines followed this lead; some decked out their stewardesses in mini-skirts and so on. National Airlines instituted its famous "Fly Me—I'm Cheryl" campaign. This was followed by a couple of stewardess exploitation books, *Coffee, Tea or Me?* and *How to Make a Good Stewardess*. On the heels of that came Continental Airlines' 1974 "We Really Move Our Tails for You" campaign, which the airline claimed was inspired by National's reported 19 percent passenger increase after the introduction of the "Fly Me" campaign. Using an issue of the company's magazine as a vehicle, Najeeb Halaby, president of Pan American Airways, told his stewardesses in 1971, "They should be more like Japanese geisha girls, prepared to flatter and entertain the male passengers." According to Kane, all of this led to changes, with even more sexual harassment occurring on the planes. A supervisor with American Airlines laughed this all off by saying, "They might get a pat, but the girls are moving so fast they scarcely have time to get pinched."[40]

On many occasions Kane experienced having her behind patted as she walked down the aisle or being subjected to pickup attempts by passengers. During a flight from New York to Chicago TWA stewardess Judy Carroll was called by a distinguished man to get his coat from the overhead rack. When she did he pinched her on the behind. Later somebody near that man called her for something. The first man put his hand up her skirt. On an American Airlines junket for press people to promote travel to Mexico an American Airlines public relations man harassed all eight stewardesses on board. After the trip the flight director talked to the man and then informed the women they had nothing to worry about as the public relations man was not going to report them. Angered by this all eight women wrote a report about him. It was ignored. When Southern Airlines ran a charter flight in 1967, men returning to Atlanta from a pro football game harassed the stewardesses to such an extent the women had to take refuge in the cockpit, with the pilot having to make a forced landing.[41]

Two decades later a similar event took place. On December 31, 1987, an Eastern Airlines plane was preparing to travel from Philadelphia to Orlando. Shortly before takeoff Joseph Litchfield Clark made a sexually explicit remark to a stewardess. He was persuaded to take his seat. Once in the air he made a more sexually explicit remark to another stewardess and tried to physically assault her. Again he was persuaded to take his seat. Radioing ahead, the pilot made an unscheduled landing at Charleston, South Carolina, where the FBI was waiting to arrest Clark.[42]

Harassment of stewardesses came not only from the passengers but also from the pilots and copilots. Chicago was the site of a 1973 rape of a stewardess by a pilot during a layover away from their home city. The carrier, an unidentified major domestic line, refused to take any action against the pilot. When preliminary discussions on the matter got under way, the representative of the stewardess was told by a top management official who knew nothing about the case, "You've got to remember, these girls provoke this sort of thing." Finally the pilot was disciplined but not for his sexual attack, only for drinking within a 24-hour restricted period before a flight.[43]

Kane called the occupation one in which "we are supposed to be the fresh, wholesome girls who love men, the quiet concubines of the pilots, and the submissive partners to male sexual fantasies." Subservience to the image and resultant harassment took their toll on the psyches of the women who played these roles. They moved in stages from disillusionment to frustration to anger to out of the job completely. This was a corporate policy that the stewardesses called "use them 'till their smiles wear out, then get rid of them and get a new bunch."[44] Labor historian Philip Foner noted in 1980 that the Association of Flight Attendants was one of the few unions in the United States that actively struggled against the sexual harassment of its members.[45]

Images, however, die hard, especially when they serve the interest of the male overclass or underpin, explain, rationalize, and excuse its behavior. Just as stewardesses were starting to win rights, such as the elimination of age discrimination, newscaster Harry Reasoner said on television at the end of the 1960s that he preferred "young and attractive women" on his flights. He suggested the "surly union women should be replaced by soft and fluffy ones." Some 20 years later Al Neuharth, founder of the newspaper *USA Today*, called for a return to the "sky girls" he preferred to look at. He yearned for the good old days when a flight attendant was "a nurse; unmarried; under age 25; not over 5 feet 4 inches tall; and weighed less than 115 pounds." Neuharth complained that "many of the young attractive, enthusiastic female flight attendants — then called stewardesses — have been replaced by aging women who are tired of their jobs or by flighty young men who have trouble balancing a cup of coffee." From a total of 426 staffers in his newsroom, 175 quickly signed a letter stating they were "offended, outraged and embarrassed" by Neuharth's comments.[46]

Nurses have been widely viewed as promiscuous. Commenting on English nurses of the early 1800s, one author wrote that a "grave and very common charge against nurses was that of sexual promiscuity." Since they came into daily contact with male doctors, staff, and patients, these men were regarded as easy prey to such unprincipled and immoral women. In one London hospital a sister told Florence Nightingale that "there was immoral conduct practiced in the very wards" and then gave her "some awful examples."[47]

Referring to America around 1900, another writer found the existence of "stereotypes of nurses as being immoral and sexually promiscuous." The argument by this observer was that such images gained currency when hospitals in the early years had to rely on "untrained, uneducated, and unrefined women" to supply nursing services. This kind of analysis played into male hands by blaming lower-class women while refusing to see that the image of women as promiscuous has existed over time, across countries, and in many, if not all, occupational categories.[48]

The reality of nurses has of course been the opposite of the image of them. When seven nurses and six ayahs (nursing assistants) were questioned in Calcutta, India, in the 1980s, all of the nurses and four of the ayahs cited examples of harassment from patients and staff in their hospitals. Aruna Brahmachari, a 40-year-old nurse, spoke of a long history of harassment by senior staff and doctors and of a number of "promises" of marriage in return for sexual favors. Another nurse, in her mid-forties, said that when she was young "nursing was considered akin to prostitution." Traditionally such occupations were reserved for low-caste women because of the "pollution" from contact with bodily functions.[49]

A much larger survey was conducted of 720 nurses from all parts of India in the 1980s. A vast majority of nurses claimed they had personally never been victims of sexual harassment in the institutions in which they were employed. About 10 percent admitted to having been harassed. Curiously, however, when asked about the existence of sexual abuse in their institutions, 61 percent of the nurses were able to cite such cases. This reluctance to admit to personal harassment was thought due to a fear of being socially stigmatized upon such admission. Making passes, using vulgar language, pawing, and pinching were the most common forms of harassment. Sometimes a rape and kidnap were reported. In a few cases there was a murder. Generally the abusers were doctors and patients and, to a lesser extent, other staff and visitors of patients. The night shift was the most dangerous work period for the nurses. Two thirds of those victimized (either themselves or those who could cite victims) admitted they did not protest against such abuse. One third did complain, usually with little effect. In some government hospitals in Allahabad politicians who were admitted as patients harassed the nurses. When the harasser was a patient, the complaining nurses relied on rebukes; when the harasser was a doctor, these nurses reported the matter to higher authorities. In Delhi one of the nurses was continually being pressed for sexual favors by a junior doctor. Even this reporting did not alter his behavior since he had political backing and was confident of his position and power. The nurse continued to lodge protests, with the doctor finally being suspended.[50]

Indira Chauhan found similar conditions in India around the same time when she reported that nurses and female doctors in small towns and villages felt insecure. In hospitals nurses were regularly at the mercy of men. Those who resisted sexual advances often found themselves facing complaints, supervisors, and adverse remarks; these nurses were treated as if "to please every male is a part of their duty." Nurses in a hospital in Chandigarh ignored government regulations by wearing *salwar* and *kameez* instead of the prescribed blouse and skirt, which, they maintained, "exposed them."[51]

In a 1982 survey of 89 registered nurses who returned questionnaires, more than 60 percent reported having experienced sexual harassment at work in the preceding year. Typically the harasser was a physician. Five years later Alan Grieco mailed questionnaires to all licensed practical nurses and registered nurses in Boone County, Missouri. Of the 462 returned surveys, 76 percent of the respondents reported being sexually harassed in the workplace. Inappropriate behavior ranged from lewd comments to brief minor touching to mauling to rape. More severe harassment came from patients than from other groups such as doctors. Patients were reported as harassers by 87 percent of harassed nurses, 67 percent reported physicians, and 59 percent reported other staff. From informal discussions with some women who did not return the questionnaire Grieco concluded there was a variety of reasons for noncompletion, "including feelings that the problem was unremediable and avoidance of unpleasant memories." Grieco concluded his finding by suggesting that "in nursing, unlike other occupations traditionally held by women, the prevalence of sexual harassment is fairly high, and moderate to severe harassment, especially from patients, is not rare."[52]

Looking at dental assistants and hygienists in 1990, writer Colleen Reiter found many examples of harassment. One assistant said the dentist called her from the airport almost every time he returned from a trip to ask her for a ride to his house. During the ride he made sexual advances. Another complained of receiving late-night calls from her employer. The boss waited until his wife went to sleep, and then called his assistant. A nurse in a surgical practice finally quit after she was unable to handle the harassment in her office anymore. Although the dentist used to paw all the women in the office, everyone was afraid to tell the man to keep his hands to himself. When the nurse told him to behave himself, "he became furious." Reiter explained the problem to readers in the trade magazine *The Dental Assistant*, where she warned her readers what to watch for. She made the mistake of assuming that sexual harassment came out of sexual desire, rather than out of hatred of women and an attempt to control, dominate, and terrorize them. Reiter wrote, "This warning is not intended to portray all doctors as sexually starved ogres." In discussing what could be done if harassment occurred, Reiter noted that a complaint could be lodged with the district EEOC office or the state Fair Employment Practices Office but that these agencies could deal only with work sites of 15 or more employees—which excluded most dental offices and clinics. She noted a civil suit could be filed in court but also noted that the chances of winning were poor. Citing EEOC cases, she found the majority lacked sufficient evidence to merit a "hostile environment" charge and thus resulted in a "no probable cause" finding. A less traumatic way to handle the situation, thought Reiter, was to quit; however, she admitted the situation might be just as bad with a different doctor. Not to mention the departing employee was leaving behind a dentist who would probably harass his next assistant.[53]

A study of registered dental hygienists in 1990 in Washington contained data gathered from a mailing to a random sampling of 30 percent of the state's 2,138 hygienists. Of the 650 who received a mailing, 472 responded. Of the respondents, 26.3 percent, all female, reported experiencing harassment in the work setting, 54 percent of the harassers were male dentist-employers, 37.1 percent were male patients, and the remainder were coworkers and others. Thirty-five percent of the respondents said they knew other individuals who had been harassed in dental settings. Many reported that dental assistants were sexually harassed twice as often as were hygienists. Of those harassed, 37 percent took no action, staying in the job, with 25 percent quitting their employment. Back in the mid-1980s the American Dental Assistants Association included a questionnaire in one of its publications. Replies found that 43 percent of responding assistants reported experiencing harassment at work. Of those harassed assistants, 97 percent stated they were pressured to quit or were fired because they refused to comply with the harasser's demands. Despite this the study found that "the entire group of respondents did not individually view sexual harassment as a serious problem for their profession."[54]

10
Wartime Work and the Military

The two world wars of this century brought women special opportunities in and out of the service. It opened up jobs previously denied to them. It also brought them more hardships in terms of additional harassment. During World War I a special law prevailed in England that mandated that before an employee could leave certain "controlled establishments," such as munitions plants, the individual had to obtain a "leave certificate." The granting of this certificate was in the hands of a local tribunal. A number of women applied for these certificates from a certain munitions plant on the grounds that a man employed on the night shift had been "rude" to them. This was how the problem was stated by the timid and reluctant females to the three-man tribunal hearing their pleas. This body was prepared to turn down the requests until a female union official wrote down an account of what had happened at the plant and passed this to the chairman. After reading it, "he was profoundly shocked, and after some questioning as to what the shy and frightened girls had really been subjected to the case was decided in their favors."[1]

During the same period labor shortages in the United States led the federal government to create agencies to establish safe working conditions for women, to monitor male-female relationships on the job, and to oversee the introduction of females into male-dominated environments. One such agency was the United States Railroad Administration's Women's Service Section (WSS). This group found that "abusive personal treatment of women by male supervisors and foremen ranged from verbal discourtesy and incivility to physical assaults."[2]

At the auditor's office of the Southern Railroad in Cincinnati women clerks complained that four male employees tried to handle them all the time by touching their necks, pinching their breasts, and lifting up their skirts. Women who submitted without complaint were given wage increases by the office supervisor; those who protested were denied raises. At the office of the Great Northern Railroad's yardmaster in Cut Bank, Montana, the man in charge often shoved his hand down the back of a female clerk in the presence of his wife and a government inspector. The assistant chief clerk of the revision office in Richmond, Virginia, of the Chesapeake and Ohio Railroad committed so much sexual harassment that higher management finally terminated him.[3]

Most of the cases of sexual harassment reported in the Railroad Administration files were uncovered by field agents of the WSS. Only rarely did victims initiate official complaints. Fear of losing a well-paying job was a major factor in discouraging complaints. Some women acknowledged to the WSS agents that they had silently suffered the sexual advances of their bosses because these men threatened to spread ugly rumors about their character or in other ways make their work lives miserable. Railroad management was known to counter complaints by accusing the women of flirting with their bosses or wearing provocative clothing on the job. With such examples of having complaints turned against them, women had no faith in relying on railroad officials to conduct trustworthy investigations of complaints of harassment. Nor were these women any more confident in turning to the male representatives of the Brotherhood of Railway Clerks, whom they felt belittled them and their grievances. The most common responses by such victims were to swallow their pride and tolerate the abuse, minimizing it to the extent they could. They reasoned that high-paying railroad jobs under less than ideal conditions were better than lower-paying jobs that carried no guarantee that employers would behave any better. That a file of complaints existed at all was due to the work of the WSS agents.[4]

In response to a manpower shortage in Britain during World War I the Ministry of Agriculture formed a uniformed Women's Land Army in 1917. Recruits were given a short period of training of four to six weeks and then sent out to an employer that needed agricultural work done that would have gone undone otherwise. Mainly the Women's Land Army looked to single females for recruits. Selective in this recruiting, the army favored girls of "sufficiently high character to make it safe to send them out to live alone on the farms or in cottages." Between 1917 and 1919 almost half of the 43,000 recruits were rejected for these character reasons.[5]

Being part of, or associated with, the troops was no better. In March 1917 England, faced with a manpower shortage, began to advertise for women to join the newly formed Women's Army Auxiliary Corps (WAAC). This aroused persistent public fears about immorality if women played such an active role in the forces. A prevailing public sentiment was that WAAC volunteers were "suspected of both adopting masculine attributes and being rampantly sexual." Fueled by such attitudes, many soldiers made assumptions. Said one WAAC, "Some of the men we met in France were getting a bit fresh you see and of course we were very prudish . . . and we ticked them off. And they said, 'what are you? We thought you were WAACs. . . . Are you Church Army?' No, we said, we are WAACs. Do you have a sister, we said to one of them. 'Yes, but not a WAAC thank God.' . . . There must have been some gossip about us."[6]

This idea that women involved with the forces must be promiscuous was held in many countries. During World War I "scurrilous stories" about the behavior of Australian nursing sisters assigned to Egypt appeared in Australian newspapers. The same thing happened in World War II when a favorite malicious rumor spread was that "mass abortions for women in the services are going on in Adelaide."[7]

Similar branding took place against members of the American Women's Army Corps (WAC) during World War II. Enlistment in the WAC began to drop dramatically in 1943. Partly to blame was civilian apathy, "but much more important was the hostility of male soldiers, so virulent and widespread that it scared the women away." It was said WACs "spoiled" the character of any town in which they were stationed. Organized rumors, which raced through cities, were then picked up and sensationalized by the press. According to one account, these rumors included that "vast numbers of Wacs had been sent home pregnant from North Africa; 90 percent of all Wacs were prostitutes and 40 percent were pregnant; the Army doctors rejected virgins; the Army tolerated public sexual displays and soliciting; all Wacs were issued contraceptives; Wacs were recruited to improve male 'morale'."[8]

WACs were bitter that such lies could be printed. This took the pride and enthusiasm they had for the army out of them. Regarding the effects this slander had on her troops, one WAC commander said, "It raised hell. . . . Long distance calls from parents began to come in, telling the girls to come home. The girls all came in crying, asking if this disgrace was what they had been asked to join the Army for." For a time fears were that this slandering was all an Axis plot. However, an army intelligence investigation determined that the false stories were spread by "Army personnel, Navy personnel. Coast Guard personnel, business men, women, factory workers and others. Also wives, jealous civilian women, gossips and fanatics, disgruntled former Wacs but most often male soldiers."[9] Almost 100 percent of soldiers' comments on the WACs in North Africa, where they were assigned, were "unfavorable and obscene."[10]

A second account also outlined the spread of these rumors during World War II. The fact that they spread with ease among military personnel and civilians indicated just how readily people wanted to believe them. That contradictory rumors floated around simultaneously — such as WACs were all provided with contraceptives since they were promiscuous, yet at the same time hundreds of thousands of them were pregnant — gave pause to no one. During that war contraceptives were in fact issued only to men. Rumors circulated to such an extent that the president and the secretary of war were forced to issue a public defense of enlisted women.[11]

Branding of these women as promiscuous was a convenient way to justify the resulting sexual harassment. It also provided a rationale for not taking complaints seriously or responding to them. After all, how can someone sexually harass a promiscuous woman? WAC officers regularly ran into opposition from their male counterparts. Complaints against the men revolved around charges of favoritism and sexual harassment. Similar problems plagued WAAC and Women's Royal Naval Service (WREN) troops in England. WREN driver Marjorie Wardle found herself continually harassed as she chauffeured male officers around. She found Americans "particularly troublesome."[12]

Britain's Ministry of Agriculture revived the uniformed Women's Land Army during World War II. One member of the army, Valerie Moss, agreed with Wardle, commenting that "Americans were bad enough. The really dangerous ones, though, were the Poles! You didn't go anywhere by yourself with the Poles if you could help it. . . . All they wanted to do was get you behind a hedge!" After the collapse of Polish resistance, armed forces personnel from that country who fled to England were assigned to British units. Dorothy Barton and her partner were so afraid of the cowman who lived below them on the farm they were assigned to that they added an extra bolt to their door. When Barton was away for a weekend the cowman tried to break in, and the partner was forced to virtually barricade herself inside. The two women appealed to the farmer to get rid of the man. Instead he got rid of them.[13]

Jobs in factories and other areas during World War II replacing called-up men were just as hazardous. Doris White recalled the "caterwauling and whistling" that went on when she had to walk through an all-male section of her British plant to reach the stores. Generally she took a friend with her, "not wishing to go alone." As British tram conductors many women were physically abused by the public, often by passengers trying to "get fresh." These conductors were angry at magistrates, whom they felt set fines that were too low. One woman was thrown from a platform into the roadway, suffering a broken jaw in the process.[14]

American women factory workers received the same treatment. In a Detroit plane factory the men wasted so much time "whistling and ogling" that the foreman moved the women so they could not be seen.[15] At Seattle's Boeing plant in 1942 it was reported that "whistles and catcalls followed the women as they attempted to do their jobs; some workers charged that the presence of women was disturbing to the men." One male Boeing mechanic commented, "You'd think those fellows down there had never seen a girl. Every time a skirt would whip by up there, you could hear the whistles above the riveting, and I'll bet the girls could feel the focus of every eye in the place." Describing her feelings after she started wartime work in the Seattle shipyards, Lili Solomon reported, "Maybe you think it didn't take nerve for women to make that first break into the yards. . . . I never walked a longer road in my life than that to the tool room. The battery of eyes that turned on my jittery physique, the chorus of 'Hi, sister' and 'tsk-tsk' soon had me thinking: 'Maybe I'm wrong. Maybe I'm not just another human. Maybe I am from Mars'."[16]

The Royal Australian Air Force (RAAF) held a 1981 inquiry into allegations that a commanding officer at a base harassed his civilian secretary as well as several airwomen. In the newspaper account of the events real names were not used. The situation started in 1980 when commanding officer Tom, in his fifties, hired a new secretary, Valerie. Soon he ordered her to wear dresses, not pants, so he could see her legs. He pestered her for dates. At a lunch function the pair attended he made her sit next to him and then he put his hands on her bare legs under the table. On returning to the office after this function, Tom grabbed Valerie and took her standing up; he penetrated her for a minute or two but did not reach orgasm. Over the next four months he did this regularly. Said Valerie, "I was too stupid to do something about it." Tom began to call her his "whore" and "harlot" and told her to come to work wearing no underpants so she would be more accessible and to perform fellatio on him; he reminded her she could always be returned to the typing pool. Finally Valerie submitted a formal letter of complaint but not about herself. Instead it was an allegation that Tom had harassed a 19-year-old airwoman at the base. Soon afterward Valerie was removed as Tom's secretary because she was told she was unstable and was put to work in an area the employees called the leper colony. After months of delay and stonewalling the RAAF finally held a hearing in August 1981. Tom denied all the allegations.[17]

Carol B., then stationed elsewhere, testified Tom had made advances to her, pawed at her body, put his hands in her clothes, and tried once to rape her. Tom denied all this, admitting only that he might have patted her hand in the car. Former flight-lieutenant Judy S. related that he had pawed at her body. Tom admitted he had sexually propositioned Judy over the last eight years, saying, "In the old days there would have been no such thing as sexual harassment. Nowadays, of course, with all these new in-things, I suppose you could term that sexual harassment." Corporal Beth P. told that at one party a group of about 20 airwomen hung together for protection as the rumor was that Tom was out "for a kill" that night. Two male witnesses testified for the females, essentially adding to the body of evidence indicating Tom was a harasser. The RAAF decided, in findings not made public at the time, that there was no case against Tom, who had remained in charge of his base throughout the period of the inquiry and for six months thereafter. Then he was posted to another city but retired two years early. In a separate assessment the Defence Department's public service representative came to a different conclusion, deciding Valerie "had experienced some form of sexual harassment." She was offered a transfer and workers' compensation for emotional damage. One male who testified, Flight-Lieutenant O., was verbally reprimanded for testifying against an officer. He was soon transferred to another location. The second male, Flight-Lieutenant T., was given a formal "adverse" report for his "gross disloyalty" in testifying against an officer. The panel recommended a "departmental warning" be placed on him for the rest of his career.[18]

In 1978 the American WAC was merged with the army into one unit. It was a move beset with controversy. The army administration center in its 1978 "Final Report" on the changeover to females integrated into the army said, "Widespread rape is also feared in stressful situations. Women are distractive to men." During this period there were frequent episodes of females being propositioned by both junior enlisted men and enlisted supervisors in addition to sexual jokes, gestures, and leers, which occurred both on and off duty.[19]

Outside critics of integration agreed with the idea that men in war with their "animal lusts released" would rape their female comrades. A writer for the *New York Times* referred to it as the "roar of the hormones." Full integration of the army seemingly made the problem of sexual harassment more widespread, or perhaps women complained about it more frequently. At Fort Meade in 1979 a young private first class related that men would stare at her and comment on her body as she walked past. A lieutenant bombarded her with notes, asking her to go out with him. "If I didn't go out with him," she recounted, "he said I wouldn't get my leave passes." On night duty a female military police officer was victimized by her partner; she had to physically remove his hands from her body each night. Another woman who was forced to physically defend herself told the company commander. He chastised her, claiming she had brought it on herself by asking for trouble due to the clothes she wore. Reports from other army posts such as Forts Benning, Bragg, and Dix indicated a similar prevalence of harassment. At the Presidio in San Francisco a colonel in the criminal investigation branch was found guilty on eight sex-related offenses. Although the maximum sentence he faced was 21 years at hard labor, the colonel escaped with a fine of $15,000.[20]

General Mary Clarke admitted that sexual harassment was going on "at some places" but then qualified this by adding, "I personally do not consider it a great problem." Of course this outraged many women in the army, who knew perfectly well it was a major problem. Julie Drake of Fort Ord found the men around her all making lewd comments, with the company commander being the worst. "He said vulgar things about my body to other men." Cindy Hopkins of Fort Hood related how during her first week there she had men in the company push her door open without knocking, sometimes saying, "Hi, you wanna go to bed?" She had a boyfriend who would walk her to work every morning "to protect her from the whistles and insults." From the other side of the fence Sergeant Reilly of Fort McClellan warned his male recruits not to fraternize with any female recruit because they could be accused of harassment, among other things, if they did. Reilly worried that one of his men could be confronted by one of these women while he was at a low ebb and yield to them. He regarded some of these women as "immoral little tramps."[21]

Author Helen Rogan spent time at the U.S. Military Academy at West Point in the winter of 1980 talking to the female cadets. West Point admitted its first females in 1976, although a large majority of the faculty and administration vigorously fought that integration. Captain Edwards summed up his opposition to the move by saying, "Do I want my daughter to become promiscuous and callous?" During those first few years of integration at West Point most of the abuse directed at the women was sexual. Cadet Joan Reeve said that when the women were in formation, they had to stand at attention in silence. The men would then gather around them and make sexual comments that they could not respond to or get away from. The men would surmise about the women's weekends and talk about how many women they had taken to bed. Reeve said, "Just to be talked about as if you're not entirely human is a kind of terror." Alice Sullivan heard the males warn other men not to go out with the female cadets because they "carried a lot of diseases." When the women said, "Good morning, sir" to a passing upperclassman, the response was often, "Hi, whore." One man came up to Amy Branch and said, "I can see by your rosy glow you must have been fucked." When Branch complained to this man, telling him he would never say something like that to his sister, he told her he was only joking. Numerous cadets told Rogan of finding condoms overflowing with shaving cream stuffed into their beds, of receiving vibrators in the mail, of finding obscene comments written all over their walls, and of being called terrible names.[22]

One female cadet told of another who was so scared she would not leave her room at night because as soon as the men saw her, she became "a target." The result was that the frightened woman urinated into the sink at night rather than going out of her room to the toilet area. Males would often enter the female rooms at night, which had no locks on the doors or guards. Ellen Davis woke one night to find one man with his hand between her legs. This incident led to a complaint and a hearing. At those proceedings Davis was put through a lie detector test, questioned about her previous boyfriends, and asked whether she was a virgin. The assailant was allowed to graduate from West Point but was not commissioned. After a vacation break Davis did not return to the academy. According to Alice Sullivan, the reaction of the other men to this incident was "Why are you all so upset, why's she so upset? She was just finger-fucked." Due to this incident the women, who shared rooms, were not allowed to spend the night alone. If a woman's roommate was away, the remaining woman had to move in with other women for the night. Complaining bitterly, the females asked, "Why should we have to move?" Sullivan said of the overall sexual harassment at West Point and the position there of women, "We could not let the authorities know what was happening, because if we did we would be harassed further. We were victims and there was nothing we could do."[23]

Ninety-one female army members stationed in Germany were studied in 1980 by Michael Rustad. More than half told him of being subjected to at least one instance of a sexual shakedown during on-duty hours. One woman, after exchanging hellos with a man as they were leaving the mess hall, had the man suddenly comment, "Boy, do you have a cute ass. I'd like to put my wood to your three holes." Many of these women received abuse on a regular, even daily, basis from their male counterparts. Although one woman wore a wedding ring and told her harasser that she was married, he continually pestered her for dates, replying, "That's no reason. What are you — some kind of dyke or something?" Commenting on the general situation, another woman said, "There's no chance to get away unless you lock yourself in your room. They're always after you. You can't tell them to fuck-off because they'll use it against you. You don't want to be a bitch all of the time. I don't like the abusive language, gestures, or insinuations from the men. Most women have to endure pressures from male soldiers." These sexual harassments were not reported to higher command because the women feared retaliation, "especially from males of higher rank."[24]

The situation in the navy was just as bad for women. In 1992 a study of the sexual harassment of female navy officers done by retired navy commander Kay Krohne was released. It was based on research done between 1988 and 1990, the fist in-depth study of the problem in the navy. Most harassment involved off-color jokes, sexual remarks, and unsolicited physical contact. Examples of severe harassment included a navy pilot who pulled out his penis in front of a subordinate female officer, saying, "So, what do you think of that?" At a disciplinary hearing he argued that it was just a joke, that he was trying to bring some humor to a situation. In another incident a female commander was confronted in her personal quarters by a group of four men that included her commanding officer. These men put their hands up her sweater, pulled her down on the bed, and then photographed her. Before they left her quarters two of the men exposed themselves.[25]

Krohne interviewed 61 female officers, of whom 40 (65.5 percent) said they had been harassed sexually. These findings were similar to those of a 1990 Defense Department report that found that 64 percent of the females in the U.S. military had been sexually harassed. Referring to yet another study, Captain Martha Whitehead noted, "One of our recent Navy surveys showed that 75 percent of the women . . . said sexual harassment was a problem." Whitehead felt it was a bigger problem among the enlisted women than among the officers.[26]

That Defense Department study, released by the Pentagon, found that more than one third of the women experienced some form of serious harassment, including touching, pressure for sexual favors, and rape. Females made up 11 percent of the 2 million people then on active duty in the military. Of the 64 percent who had experienced some form of harassment, 71 percent said they had experienced three or more forms of harassment. The Pentagon found that 52 percent of the females surveyed had been subjected to teasing and jokes; 44 percent, to looks and gestures; 38 percent to touching and cornering; 15 percent, to pressure for sexual favors; and 5 percent, to actual or attempted rape or assault. Of those 12,500 active-duty military women surveyed, less than 40 percent believed harassment charges would be taken seriously, and 38 percent expressed fear that reporting sexual harassment would cause work problems for them.[27]

Looking in detail at eight cases of sexual harassment and the nine men involved, Krohne found that two were court-martialed and forced to resign. The seven other men received administrative discipline, although the navy refused to provide Krohne with any details of the discipline. One of those seven was a commanding officer who said to a female officer, "What did you think of my penis hanging out of my shorts yesterday?" When the woman did not respond, the officer said, "OK, well let me show you again." He then exposed himself. In her report Krohne concluded "The harassment suffered by the eight women studied in this report is the tip of a very large iceberg posing a dangerous threat to the U.S. armed forces. . . . Reprisals of one kind or another are common against women who report sexual harassment." Of the women who reported being harassed 56 percent did not file a complaint, for various reasons, including the fear of reprisals as well as general lack of confidence in the system. Even though this was 1990, some of these women were still indirectly faulting themselves as somehow responsible for the harassment. In her research Krohne found one woman who decided to gain weight to look unattractive and a second who stopped wearing makeup and started wearing uniforms that were two sizes too big in order to discourage the officer who was harassing her for sex.[28]

An independent group appointed by the Defense Department to advise it on women's issues surveyed American military bases overseas in the 1980s. During 1986 the delegation toured U.S. bases in Western Europe and reported that the army and the air force were permitting sexual abuses against women. One year later members of the advisory group toured marine and navy units in the western Pacific and reported that those services condoned sexual harassment, discrimination, and "morally repugnant behavior." This led to punishment of some male officers and orders that rules against harassment be enforced. No specifics were given. In September 1988 the group submitted its third report, this time after a tour of bases in southern Europe. The report found American military women were harassed by local men as well as by U.S. servicemen. Acknowledging that little could be done about off-base harassment by locals, the report urged that "the on-base situations can and should be monitored closely by the command leadership." Group leader Jacquelyn K. Davis said that servicewomen repeatedly complained of harassment, with "some of the incidents explicitly sexual and very offensive." After having this report for five months, the Defense Department had still taken no action. Davis noted that the department's response "has not been overwhelming. They've just thrown up their hands and said there's nothing we can do about that."[29]

Civilian employees were also subjected to sexual abuse at naval bases, particularly at Miramar Naval Air Station in San Diego, which was plagued by allegations of sexual harassment at the base during the early months of 1992. In February of that year an employee of the base exchange named Connie Kent sued the navy and three male coworkers for sexual harassment. Kent claimed she had been subjected to close to two years of unwanted sexual advances by the three men. She also charged that several supervisors had ignored her repeated complaints about the behavior of the men. On February 16 a 49-year-old employee of the base exchange, Elpidio M. Tubig, a barber, was arrested on charges of sexual battery on 19-year-old female coworker Nicole Staples, who was employed as a receptionist at the exchange's beauty salon. According to Staples, Tubig grabbed her from behind and kissed her repeatedly against her will as the two prepared to start work. This incident was reported to the Shore Patrol, which in turn called the San Diego police. Miramar spokesperson Doug Sayers tried to downplay the event to a reporter by denying it included sexual misconduct allegations—calling it simple battery—and denying Tubig was arrested. San Diego police confirmed Tubig had in fact been arrested for sexual misconduct. In still another incident former lifeguard Claire Fullerton came forward at the time of Tubig's arrest to state she had been sexually harassed by a sailor while she was employed as a lifeguard at the base pool. When that took place back in 1991, Fullerton put in a formal complaint. She was pressured, she said, by base officials to sign a statement saying she voluntarily chose not to pursue charges of sexual harassment. Fullerton did sign this but only "under duress," for she was told that if she continued to press her complaint, she would lose her job. As a single mother of two she felt forced to sign. Just three days after Tubig's arrest the navy formally threw Fullerton's complaint out. All of these incidents took place despite an official policy in the navy of zero tolerance for sexual harassment.[30]

Just three months later, in May 1992, the navy released the results of its investigation into sexual abuse and harassment at a convention of naval aviators that took place in September 1991. Navy investigators found that dozens of women had been abused instead of the handful who had initially filed complaints at the three-day convention held at a hotel in Las Vegas, Nevada, by the Tailhook Association, a private naval organization. However, despite the investigators interviewing 1,500 officers and civilians about the incident, the probers were able to identify only two suspects. This failure was attributed by investigators to the refusal of many pilots, including some with senior rank, to cooperate. A code of silence was maintained. The report told of a rowdy, drunken scene in which 14 female officers and 12 civilian women—including one minor—were abused by dozens of mostly junior navy officers. Reportedly many other women were assaulted but left the convention without ever being identified. During the convention navy and marine pilots lined the hallways of the Las Vegas Hilton and forced terrified women to run the gauntlet, grabbing at their breasts and buttocks and ripping at their clothes. The hotel was trashed to the tune of $23,000. Secretary of the Navy H. Lawrence Garrett denounced the behavior and ordered all field commanders to put their people on notice that "we will not condone sexual harassment in any form, or tolerate those who permit it to exist."[31]

The Tailhook incident and report attracted widespread media coverage and public outrage, fueled by the obvious ineptness of the navy's probe. That probe was set in motion September 7, 1991, the final night of the convention, when an admiral's aide told a fellow officer she had been assaulted that night by several marine and navy pilots in a crowded third-floor corridor that contained a group of hospitality suites rented by squadrons for holding parties. Investigators later found that on each night of the convention groups of officers in civilian dress suddenly surrounded unsuspecting females as they stepped off an elevator. The men formed gauntlets and pushed the females through, pawing at their breasts and genitals while tearing at their clothes. The aide's complaint was eventually relayed to Admiral J. L. Johnson, vice chief of naval operations, who on October 10 ordered the Naval Investigative Service (NIS) to commence an inquiry. Later that month Garrett directed another agency, the Naval Inspector General (NIG), to also investigate.

Garrett had personally attended the convention, rejecting the advice of a staff member who warned him of "indecent behavior." The navy secretary maintained that he had been on an outdoor terrace when the assaults took place in a hallway and that he had no knowledge of them until weeks later. This appeared in the first report released by the NIS on April 29. On June 16 the NIS released a supplement left out of the April report that contained testimony placing Garrett much closer to the assaults, as close as in one of the suites. Representative Patricia Schroeder of Colorado commented, "It's pretty hard to believe the missing part just happened to have his name on it. The longer this Tailhook incident hangs around the more it smells." So inept was coordination of the inquiry by the navy that it was not sure exactly how many officers were implicated in the assaults. A list of about 70 officers was ordered sent to their individual commanders, as military justice is dispensed at that level. As of mid–June the navy could say that only one person, a lieutenant based at Florida's Cecil Field Naval Air Station, had been disciplined. That unnamed individual was ordered to receive counseling. With criticism over lack of results and charges of coverup mounting, Garrett ordered the Defense Department's chief investigator, the Pentagon Inspector General, to review the navy's inquiry.[32]

The aide who first complained went public in June, when she appeared on national television to detail what had taken place. She was Lieutenant Paula Coughlin, admiral's aide, helicopter pilot, and daughter of a retired navy aviator. As she was shoved down the gauntlet she appealed, "Help me" to one man who seemed to be walking away. He turned and grabbed her breasts. Coughlin described herself during the ordeal as "the most frightened I've ever been in my life. I thought, 'I have no control over these guys. I'm going to be gang-raped'." She added, "I've been in the Navy almost eight years and I've worked my ass off to be one of the guys, to be the best naval officer I can and prove that women can do whatever the job calls for. And what I got, I was treated like trash. I wasn't one of them." The assaulters knew she was an officer because they chanted "admiral's aide" as they shoved her around. When she reported her assault to her boss, Admiral John W. Snyder, Jr., his only response was to chastise her for going to the third floor since it was well known what went on there. Snyder was later relieved of his command for failure to take any action in response to her complaint. Later it was revealed that an NIS civilian agent, Laney S. Spigener, involved in the initial investigation had pressured Coughlin to go out with him socially. A complaint by Coughlin on November 26, 1991, to his superiors led to Spigener's removal from the case after a probe. On April 15 he was suspended without pay for three days.[33]

Driven by the Coughlin television appearance, pressure on the navy intensified. The Tailhook Association, which contained both retired and active-duty naval aviators, announced it was canceling its scheduled 1992 convention in San Diego because of the controversy. Although that group and the navy had worked closely together for some three decades, the navy announced in the summer of 1992 that it had severed ties with Tailhook.[34]

Coughlin went public on June 24. On June 26 Garrett resigned as navy secretary amid the questions of his personal involvement and the navy's woeful handling of the probe. He left stating, "I accept full responsibility for the handling of the Tailhook incident and the leadership failure which allowed such misconduct to occur." When President George Bush accepted the resignation, he omitted the customary note of thanks, leading to speculation that Garrett had been forced to resign by Secretary of Defense Dick Cheney acting on Bush's orders. Later that day Coughlin was given an audience with Bush at the White House, where she was assured of a full investigation into the affair. The Pentagon Inspector General ordered all disciplinary proceedings against the 70 or so men then implicated suspended on the grounds that their superior officers might themselves be suspect.[35]

When the Pentagon released its findings on September 24, 1992, the report gave a "blistering critique" of the navy's inquiry into Tailhook. It stated that senior navy officials deliberately undermined their own investigation to avoid negative publicity, while some admirals had sabotaged their agents' efforts due to their own hostility toward women. The admiral in charge of the NIS refused to allow interviews of senior officers even after it was clear that some had witnessed improper acts and had failed to intervene. Singled out for specific criticism were three officers: Rear Admiral Duvall M. Williams, Jr., NIS commander; Rear Admiral John E. Gordon, the navy's judge advocate general (top lawyer); and Rear Admiral George W. Davis VI, the navy's inspector general.

Williams had repeatedly expressed a desire to end his investigation and at one point told a civilian he did not believe females belonged in the military. On another occasion Williams and Assistant Secretary of the Navy Barbara S. Pope had a "screaming match" in a Pentagon hallway, with the admiral offering the opinion that "a lot of Navy pilots are go-go dancers, topless dancers or hookers." On yet another occasion Williams was discussing Coughlin's statements with a female NIS officer. In the statement Coughlin had used profanity in describing what she said to her attackers. Williams commented, "Any women who would use the f-word on a regular basis would welcome this type of activity." Of Williams's handling of the investigation, the Pentagon report concluded his "overriding goal, and the motivation for his actions, was to keep the investigation within narrow limits and to dissuade investigators from pursuing issues that might lead them to question the conduct of senior officers at Tailhook '91." Gordon was scored because, although he was the navy's top lawyer, he had played no role at all in ensuring that all the relevant issues got addressed. He was also attacked for failing to provide a comprehensive report that the navy could use to correct the problem. Davis told Pentagon probers that he did not interview senior officers who had attended Tailhook or identify individuals for discipline because he felt such measures would be seen as a "witch hunt." He excused officers' tolerance for sexual misconduct by arguing that in the past navy culture had tolerated such behavior. "Frankly, I think a Navy captain who had seen that over four or five years, had seen the

Rhino room with a dildo hanging on the wall, is not going to walk in there in 1991 and change anything," explained Davis (women were goaded into a hospitality suite to drink from a dispenser shaped like a rhinocerous penis). When the report was released, Acting Secretary of the Navy Sean O'Keefe announced that he had accepted the resignations of Williams and Gordon. Davis had been reassigned.

Also criticized in the Pentagon report was the second-highest-ranked civilian, Undersecretary of the Navy J. Daniel Howard. Despite being criticized for failing to get the NIS and NIG to coordinate their probes and for providing generally weak leadership, Howard was to remain in his position. The undersecretary told investigators he felt powerless and frustrated as he could not halt the internecine warfare between the NIS and NIG, which often refused to cooperate and share information.

More testimony came to light contradicting Garrett's claims as to where he was during the assaults. Placing him close to the attack was a navy captain who took a lie detector test and was judged to be "non-deceptive." This caused the Pentagon report to conclude, "We believe the statements contradicting the secretary's affidavit cast doubt on the secretary's credibility regarding his activities on the third floor."[36]

When *Los Angeles Times* reporter Melissa Healy reviewed the situation on November 1, 1992, she found men feeling sorry for themselves and still blaming women. Male naval personnel were said to be sullen and keeping more distance between themselves and females. James Webb, a former secretary of the navy, complained of a "witch hunt" that "threatens to swamp the entire naval service." He also referred to Williams and Gordon as the junior admirals who were "taken out back and shot." Commander G. Thomas Mariner exclaimed that "good men's careers are being ruined." Some blamed women, who, they said, were using the episode to push harder for the right to a combat role in the military. Some complained that the Pentagon probers had used coercion. A retired admiral said that military people were convenient as scapegoats. One unidentified male officer counseled his charges in the service at a session on how to deal with navy and marine females. He advised having no nonnecessary conversation with them, explaining, "Those conversations that are not a part of your job are just running an unnecessary risk. And if I were the last guy in the office, I'd send any women home, too. My aim is to protect myself." The session this man led was a consciousness-raising session on sexual harassment. Reporter Healy fueled this mentality herself by writing that all navy men "quake at the mere thought of a sexual harassment charge."[37]

Of course this was all untrue. More than one full year had passed at that time, and nobody had really been punished. O'Keefe had by then declared that no further punishment would be handed out to the two admirals forced to resign. In fact both men simply retired early, in their current grades, and thus would draw a pension for life much higher than an average worker would even dream about. The usual path for retired high-ranking military officers — most retire well before 65 — is to quickly sign on as highly paid executives with companies specializing in defense contracts. Then they march back to the Pentagon, where as civilians they lobby their old military friends to keep the contracts coming.[38]

The backlash against women in the wake of Tailhook was actually in full bloom in July, at a time when the issue of allowing females a combat role was being formally considered by the government. *Washington Post* reporter John Lancaster found that Tailhook added fuel to the idea that women did not belong in the military at all, never mind discussing removing the combat restriction. He found this sentiment from conservative commentators "in a flurry of newspaper editorials and talk show chatter." Typical was Charley Reese of the *Orlando Sentinel*, who wrote, "The people who should be booted out of the service are the female officers who complained. If a grown woman can't handle some friendly drunks in a public place, then she's hardly qualified to command men in the much more serious and stressful environment of war."[39]

With regard to the cold shoulder treatment navy men extended to navy women after Tailhook, one female officer told Healy, "It's a little bit like sexual harassment. Basically it tells you that you're still the outsider." Another female officer commented, "There's a sense of 'see what you women have done?' They're still blaming the victim." Many women would not comment at all in the aftermath of Tailhook. They feared further reprisals from men. Of the period since going public, Coughlin remarked, "It's definitely taken its toll on me, made me very cynical, jaded. . . . It really has given new meaning to revictimization. . . . I've run into attitudes, people who don't acknowledge me in a room. And it beats you down."[40]

After attacking the original navy report on Tailhook, the Pentagon Inspector General went on to do its own study of the convention. This report, released in April 1993, concluded that the misconduct was even worse than had been previously suspected. A total of 83 women — 49 civilians, 22 servicewomen, 6 government employees, and 6 wives — were assaulted over the few days of the convention. The report also concluded that abuses were not significantly different from those at earlier Tailhook meetings, thereby rejecting the claim of some that Tailhook '91 was an isolated incident. In addition to pawing, mauling, and ripping the clothes off women, the aviators engaged in incidents of indecent exposure, such as streaking, mooning, and ballwalking (walking with the testicles exposed). Investigation files on at least 140 officers were referred to the military services for possible disciplinary action.[41]

A month later these investigations were still apparently ongoing. All that had taken place was the reassignment of six senior navy officers to desk jobs so they would be available — and not at sea, for example — to the personnel deciding if they should be disciplined for their role in Tailhook '91. Later in May the Tailhook Association announced that it would go ahead with its 1993 convention, scheduled for the fall in San Diego. The navy, which had supported Tailhook conventions in the past but had withdrawn support in the wake of Tailhook '91, maintained an official posture of no position on the '93 affair, while privately it "strongly encouraged members to break their ties" with Tailhook.[42]

A few days after Garrett resigned army specialist Jacqueline Ortiz testified before the Senate Committee on Veterans Affairs. Ortiz told of how while based in Saudi Arabia, in 1991, she had been forcibly sodomized by her sergeant shortly after the Desert Storm air offensive started. She immediately reported the assault to her superiors, but they did not believe her. Initially army investigators charged Ortiz with sexual improprieties after her alleged assailant, First Sergeant David Martinez, stated she had engaged in consensual sex with him. Ortiz was issued a reprimand and later removed. Further investigation, initiated after Ortiz complained to a representative revealed that Martinez had been untruthful, as determined by a lie detector test. Despite this the army had taken no disciplinary action against him. The army apologized to Ortiz. She was one of four female veterans who told the Senate panel that they were raped or assaulted by fellow soldiers but not believed by male superiors. "It's very difficult to deal with," said Ortiz. "I was very proud to serve my country but not to be a sex slave to someone who had a problem with power. . . . I would rather have been shot by a bullet and killed that way, than have to deal with what I deal with daily." Two or three days after Ortiz testified the army charged the sergeant with sexual assault and falsifying official documents.[43]

In other testimony Diana Davis, executive director of the National Women Veterans Conference, told the committee she had been raped by a sergeant several years previously when he had offered to walk her back to her barracks. When she reported the assault to her company commander, she was told to forget about it. If she pressed charges, her superiors explained, she "would ruin the young sergeant's career." Another victim was Barbara Franco, who testified she had been raped by three fellow army soldiers while on a weekend pass in Virginia Beach, Virginia, in 1975. Later she was assaulted at Fort Hood, Texas, by two soldiers. After this second assault she tried to commit suicide by taking an overdose of Valium. Three of the four assault victims who testified told of seeking aid at VA hospitals only to find those institutions having no programs to treat sexual abuse victims or inadequate programs with insensitive counselors. Ortiz found them "unresponsive" to her request for aid, as did Franco, who encountered counselors behaving the same as her harassers. "They say sexually abusive things. They stare and leer at me all the way through the door."[44]

When *Washington Post* reporter John Lancaster investigated sexual harassment in the military in the fall of 1992, he found consistent themes, including a blame-the-victim approach, indifferent or hostile commanders, retaliation against the victims, and even psychiatric exams for the accuser.

The nightmare for army paratrooper Christine Hart began in her barracks at Fort Bragg, North Carolina, where she alleged she was wakened from a deep sleep and raped by a senior enlisted man on the morning of September 21, 1991. Hart reported the assault to a staff sergeant before 7 A.M. Not until midafternoon after a long series of interviews was she escorted to a hospital for a medical exam. During the following investigation Hart claimed she felt more like a criminal than a victim, subjected to false insinuations about a prior sexual relationship with the accused and pressured to submit to a polygraph test—reported to be routine in the military for rape victims. Officials for the army said the case was investigated vigorously; however, prosecutors declined to prosecute, citing an absence of corroboration or physical evidence. In the end the authorities decided consensual sex had taken place. Hart—20 years old at the time of the assault—was charged with underage drinking and demoted, while the accused married male was disciplined for adultery.[45]

For navy lieutenant and helicopter pilot Lynn Tasker the nightmare began with her deployment to the Mediterranean in August 1989. A chief petty officer on board that supply ship showered her with unwanted attention and written pleas for sex. When Tasker failed to respond she found it was very difficult to get routine maintenance performed on her aircraft; the officer supervised helicopter maintenance work. "He became very hostile and he conveyed that hostility to the troops. All of a sudden all of the enlisted guys were against me," she said. When the ship returned home to Norfolk Naval Air Station, Tasker chanced to talk to an enlisted woman, who told her of being harassed by the same man while at sea during a March 1989 trip. She said he kissed her and unbuttoned her clothes. When this unidentified enlisted woman told her male supervisor about the incident, he told her to "brush it under the rug and keep your mouth shut." Together the two women complained to their squadron commander, who ordered the officer court-martialed on charges of indecent assault, solicitation of sex, and insubordination. Despite testimony from the two females and a copy of one of the chief's "lust letters," the jury of nine officers and enlisted personnel (only one female) acquitted the chief in March 1990. Defense lawyers argued Tasker encouraged the sailor's advances by wearing makeup and provocative gym shorts. Said defense lawyer James T. Nawrocki, now in private practice, "She used to do stuff like jog around the flight deck in these short pants. . . . She made goo-goo eyes. . . . He was stupid for what he did, but on the other hand, she enticed him and gave him ideas." Seething ever since, Tasker planned to leave the navy at the earliest possible time, April 1993, a decision she made "as soon as I heard the verdict." Of the trial and the entire procedure Tasker commented, "It was like being raped up there. I felt like they were saying as a group, 'That's what happens when you try to do something to us. We're the status quo here . . . .' It never ends. It really does not end. I'm so tired of fighting these battles, you can't know." Also bitter was the enlisted woman, who exclaimed, "We were railroaded." Still on active duty at the Norfolk base is the chief petty officer. Sometimes the two women see him around the base.[46]

When air force captain Catherine Drader was posted to a remote military listening post, Iraklion Air Station, on the Mediterranean island of Crete in September 1989, she arrived with two young sons after a divorce and custody battle. She was named chief of the personnel division at the base. In April 1990 Drader filed a harassment complaint against her boss, Colonel Richard T. Lee, who, she alleged, had made verbally offensive remarks. In an affidavit the base equal opportunity officer, Captain Mark S. Ledin, said he thought she had a legitimate complaint, stating, "I personally saw him set her up for malicious and denigrating comments during our . . . staff meetings." However, an investigator from the 16th Air Force Inspector General's Office concluded on June 4, 1990, that there was no basis to the charge and dismissed her complaint. Just one hour after being notified of this decision, Lee appeared in Drader's office to issue her an order to report for a mental health exam at a base hospital in Athens, Greece. Drader had already been informally evaluated by the base psychiatric officer, at the request of Lee, and given a clean bill of health. She refused the order, regarding it as retaliation, and also worried her ex-husband, an air force officer, might somehow use it to resume a child custody fight. Because of this refusal, Lee ordered her court-martialed. The authorities did not agree that the order was retaliation, and on December 8, 1990, Drader was convicted of disobeying an order. She was fined a sum of money and confined to the base for 60 days. Lee later admitted that when Drader filed the harassment complaint, he was "mildly irritated" and that "this complaint was not rational behavior in my view. It did play a part in my decision to order her for a mental health evaluation." Lee commenced discharge proceedings against her in March 1991 following another disciplinary action in which he reprimanded her for her failure to salute him in a few casual encounters around the base. Again Drader was put through a court-martial; again she was convicted. This time she was expelled from the service in June 1991. When Senator Lloyd Bentsen of Texas was informed of the case, he contacted the air force, which then reexamined the case. In this reexamination the military confirmed there was "substantial evidence that Drader's commander made sexist and offensive remarks in public on several occasions." However, the report added that "the allegations of reprisal were not supported by the evidence." The expulsion stood.[47]

Air Force major Debra Morrison-Orton worked as a social worker at Colorado's Peterson Air Force Base in 1990 when she filed a complaint of harassment by coworkers with the base equal opportunity office. A base-level inquiry dismissed her charges of sex discrimination, inappropriate physical contact, and lewd comments by a fellow worker, who, she said, referred to her breasts as "earmuffs." A base legal officer confirmed this finding, citing, among other things, Morrison-Orton's "shrill tone" and the "huge volume of paper" generated by the complaint. A few days later she was fired from her job. Commander of the clinic where she was employed, Lieutenant Colonel Kenneth A. Ansell said in a sworn statement that the major was "deeply into the feminist movement" and that she had "poisoned the well" by turning females at the base against their male superiors. Higher-level investigations by a senior officer a year later supported Morrison-Orton's charges and recommended correction of her personal record. This was done in June 1992 when the major worked as the assistant director of alcohol rehabilitation programs at a Florida air force base. Of this finding by a senior officer, Ansell commented that it was only "one man's opinion." He was never disciplined.[48]

In 1992 army specialist Alexis M. Colon, employed at the dental clinic at Fort Hood, Texas, formally accused several male supervisors of unwanted physical contact and repeated overtures. This triggered accusations from her coworkers that she had sexually harassed them. For this Colon was disciplined with a letter of "counseling." A few days after that Colon shot herself to death, leaving a suicide note that read, "I am too weak to face those people." The army investigation that followed blamed her suicide partly on unspecified "personal and marital" problems. The army confirmed that she had been sexually harassed at the clinic and that the working conditions there "may have exacerbated her stress and depression." Although two sergeants were disciplined as a result of Colon's complaint, no action was taken against the lieutenant colonel who had reprimanded her.[49]

All of these women were the victims of a military justice system that is weighted more heavily against them than that found in the civilian world, which is also weighted against women. Females in the military are not allowed to complain to an independent EEOC and then, if the case is found to have merit, to file suit under Title VII of the Civil Rights Act of 1964. Military females must go through the chain of command, which means direct supervisors who themselves may be part of the problem. The army and air force each have base-level equal opportunity offices, but these are not independent and do not have enforcement powers. A senior army officer and psychotherapist who had counseled many sexual harassment victims called the military system for handling such charges "a joke. It's an internal system. If a soldier complains, the unit's commander is responsible for investigating his own unit. That's crazy."[50]

Worried by the Tailhook affair and wanting to avoid anything similar, the army dispatched consultants in the summer of 1992 to investigate conditions among civilian employees at the Army Aviation and Troop Command and the Army Reserve Personnel Center. Both of these large installations were in St. Louis. Investigators looked into as many as 100 accusations of sexual harassment by senior and middle-level civilian supervisors against female civilian employees. The army refused to release the report publicly or to provide details. However, it did pronounce itself "alarmed" by the report and promised an extensive probe. One of the consultants, H. Minton Francis, said that at the aviation command he had received as many as 100 allegations of "open, vicious sexual harassment."[51]

Equally bleak for military women is the situation in the Canadian Forces. Since 1988 that country's military has had a formal policy of zero tolerance of sexual harassment. However, the Defense Department in a 1992 memo acknowledged that the widely accepted finding that most victims did not take formal action—particularly when required to report incidents to their supervisors—made it "extremely difficult to identify the actual incidence of sexual harassment in the Canadian Forces and to evaluate the effectiveness of the policy." A sexual harassment survey of 5,600 military personnel was conducted in 1992, but results were not to be released until late 1993 at the earliest. Nonetheless, various reports done by and for the military indicated harassment was far from zero. At a Canadian Forces Base (CFB) in Wainwright, Alberta, there was a case of "disgraceful and unacceptable sexual harassment" wherein several military instructors engaged in a discussion as to who would be the first to get a woman into bed. In eastern Ontario at CFB Petawawa the junior officers' handbook was termed "extremely sexist." At CFB Borden, near Toronto, four females were "subjected to four weeks of terrorism" during a training course. The women's tent was repeatedly raided, among other things. Other instructors at CFB Borden "made humiliating comments about women." Many male soldiers at CFB Chatham in New Brunswick made obscene comments to female soldiers and were openly hostile to them. In interviews some of the men inquired of the investigators as to the consequences of "punching them out." Women had complained informally to investigators of everything from insults to physical intimidation. Most did not complain formally, fearing a backlash by males if any disciplinary action was taken. Some senior officers at that base were aware of the harassment and "think it is normal and should be left alone." A report on the St. Hubert military base in Quebec stated that verbal harassment of female personnel "appears to be rampant" and is virtually ignored by senior officers. This report added that if women tried to follow the official procedures for harassment complaints, they "might suffer serious harm."[52]

11
Professional Women

No matter what occupational level a woman occupies, whether it be blue or white collar, servant or professional, she will be subjected to sexual harassment on the job. Professional women are on the receiving end of a good deal of such abuse. Geeta Chaturvedi studied 100 female administrators in India in the early 1980s. All were employed in the public sector, with 36 in state and federal government work and the other 64 employed in various school systems. Chaturvedi called these women "executives" and "educationists," respectively. One question they were asked was, "Is it true that sometimes male bosses try to take liberties with their female subordinates?" It was a matter the author referred to as "delicate." Thirty-four percent of executives and 47 percent of educationists responded yes, 53 percent of executives and 34 percent of educationists replied no, and the rest had no opinion.[1]

An educationist, not herself harassed, said she was aware of such incidents in the case of others. One executive reported she was "reverted consequent upon her failure to oblige her boss in his bid to fulfill his nefarious intentions." Respondents agreed that educationists were more likely to be subjected to "misbehavior" of male bosses than executives and that female subordinates at lower levels faced the same problem, with complaints having been received from them in many cases. These women also agreed that, male behavior notwithstanding, much depended on the firmness of the woman employee concerned. Some respondents were of the opinion that sexual harassment was less widespread in the public sector, where the incumbent's job was secure, than in the private sector, where it was described as "acute." So circumspect was Chaturvedi in her approach to this issue that the words *sex, sexual,* or *harassment* were never mentioned at all in her book.[2]

Anuradha Bhoite looked at 163 professional women in India in the mid–1980s. Specifically Bhoite studied 62 teachers, 57 nurses, and 44 *gramsevikas* (roughly, a child welfare and nutrition worker), all of whom were government employees sent into rural areas as part of rural development schemes. In the period just prior to the study harassment of female employees in villages had been the topic of serious public discussion, with a number of cases of sexual harassment of these women reported in the newspapers. The issue was also discussed vehemently on the floor of the Maharashtra legislature. The area studied by Bhoite was a rural part of Parbhani district in Maharashtra state. These women were found to be harassed by town leaders, hooligans, and their own officers (supervisors). All 163 women were quizzed on whether they had been sexually harassed. Explaining that it was difficult to gain such admissions, Bhoite said, "At the outset, it was presumed that women would not openly admit of attempt of molestation on their modesty by the officers, as they would think that such an admission would endanger their moral character. So, another question was included in the schedule to ascertain whether they know any cases of harassment or molestation of other women employees."[3]

Asked if they had been personally molested by supervisors, only 18 of the 163 (11 percent) replied yes: 7 nurses (12.2 percent), 4 teachers (6.4 percent), and 7 *gramsevikas* (15.9 percent). However, when asked if they knew of cases of harassment of other female employees, 73 (44.8 percent) replied they did. When asked if they had been harassed by either their officers or by villagers, 105 women (64 percent) said yes; 44 nurses (77 percent), 28 teachers (45 percent), and 33 *gramsevikas* (75 percent). Bhoite concluded that teaching as an occupation was held in the greatest respect as compared to the other two.[4]

Examples of harassment cited by Bhoite included Miss S. K., a *gramsevika* who wrote a letter to an executive officer complaining about her local supervisor, saying, "I fear my modesty and life are not safe here because of this officer. So I entreat you to transfer me immediately and relieve me from the clutches of this officer." Not long after that she was found burned to death in her village quarters. Miss M. G. was molested by the *sirpanch* (village headman) of the village. He tried to rape her as she slept in a courtyard. Miss S. S., a teacher, refused the advances of the *sirpanch* in another village. Shortly after she was molested on a road in broad daylight by the younger brother of the headman. Miss N. R. N., a nurse, was gang-raped by a group of *goondas* (hooligans) one evening as she returned to her base village after visiting a nearby village. According to Bhoite, if the female employees complained against the leaders in the village to their officers, the officers were unwilling to take effective action on such complaints as they feared possible interference from these villagers later on. "So, the woman employee, even though harassed, is not able to complain against goondas or leaders. She has no other go but to succumb to the pressure of these people."[5]

Audrey was a British engineer who quit one engineering job with a multinational company in the late 1980s because of harassment. A fellow employee had pretended to fall in love with her and made it obvious to everyone in the company, making it awkward for Audrey. "You cannot say that you object because basically you have still got to get on with them and work," she commented. In addition she had to ask one of her bosses to stop putting his hands on her. Working for another company was Wendy, also a British engineer. She recalled being subjected to hundreds of little harassments. One morning a coworker said to her, "You're looking nice today; you're looking really rapeable." Some offices, she found, were not content to just have calendars with nude women on them but instead had "whole walls covered in photographs that had been carefully put up — yards of photographs. And I hated walking through those offices." Various women had retaliated at times by hanging up calendars of naked men to make a point, but they had been threatened with disciplinary action for doing that, or the men would say, "We're going to take them all down soon, but if you could just take yours down first as a gesture." Of course the men never took theirs down.[6]

Back in America Kristine Utley brought a sex discrimination suit in December 1987 against the Wall Street investment banking firm of Goldman, Sachs. Utley was the only female sales associate in the money market department. She charged the work environment in the company's Boston office as being "hostile, intimidating, and sexist." To support her claim Utley produced memos that announced the arrival of new women employees — each bearing a picture of a nude centerfold. She also gave examples of printed joke sheets that routinely were distributed around the office. Typical was the following: "Why Beer Is Better Than a Woman" — because "a beer doesn't get jealous when you grab another beer" and "a beer always goes down easy." Another woman who had once worked on Wall Street for Goldman, Sachs and for Merrill Lynch commented dryly, "I really don't understand why Goldman keeps getting singled out for negative publicity. . . . They're a typical investment bank."[7]

Deborah Ann Katz, an air traffic controller for the federal government, won her sexual harassment case in 1983 against the Department of Transportation. At her job in Herndon, Virginia Katz was harassed by her supervisor, who frequently propositioned her and called her "the cow" and "the bitch." After winning her case, Katz was returned to the Federal Aviation Administration's Leesburg, Virginia, facility in January 1984. Continuing turmoil prompted her to file a complaint charging retaliation against her. Said Katz, "I did not want to go back. It's like being sent back to your parents after a court finds they abused you sexually."[8]

Cecily Coleman was fired in May 1984 as the executive director of ABC's advisory committee on voter education, which had been set up to use the resources of the company's television network to encourage citizens to vote in the 1984 presidential campaign. During her time at ABC Coleman's salary went from $40,000 to $60,000 a year, and she received a commendation from Leonard H. Goldenson, the ABC chair. Alleging she had been fired after she reported to company officials that her immediate supervisor, James Abernathy, had sexually harassed her for nearly a year, Coleman launched a multimillion dollar lawsuit. Abernathy, vice-president of corporate affairs, denied the charge. Four months after Coleman filed her lawsuit Abernathy was dismissed by ABC. The company gave no reason for this termination. According to Coleman's attorney, ABC admitted in a deposition that there were at least seven cases of sexual harassment at ABC's offices in Washington and New York between April 1, 1982, and April 20, 1984. ABC rejected all of Coleman's allegations and said her charges stemmed from her "ultimate frustration" at not obtaining regular employment with ABC (Coleman's job was temporary). The network claimed she had failed to complete some of her job duties and had deceived ABC with regard to her educational background and previous accomplishments. Stating it could find no evidence of harassment, ABC said it had tried to accommodate her by assuring her she would be insulated from Abernathy at work. According to the network, she was fired after she submitted a list of eight conditions ABC claimed it could not meet. In the summer of 1985 just before the case was scheduled to go before a judge, an out-of-court settlement was reached, with Coleman receiving an unreported amount of money.[9]

Attorneys at the law firm of King and Spalding in Atlanta, Georgia, wanted to hold a wet T-shirt contest in 1983 to feature the company's female summer associates. Reacting to in-house criticism, the firm changed course a little and instead held a bathing suit competition. The winner was offered a job with the company. Said one partner, "She had the body we'd like to see more of." The contest choice of a wet T-shirt competition was more than a little ill-timed because former associate Elizabeth Hishon's lawsuit for sex discrimination against the firm was then pending in the Supreme Court. Law writer Nina Burleigh summed up her view of sexual harassment in law offices in the late 1980s by saying, "Most women lawyers deal with sexual harassment by quitting their jobs or suffering silently." Said Joel Henning of Chicago's Hildebrandt, Inc., "Anyone who thinks that sexual harassment doesn't go on in law firms is crazy. Law firms are no worse than other workplaces, but they're no better, either." In 1988 when Henning worked at a satellite office of a major law firm, he discovered the male partners bedded female attorneys, secretaries, and paralegals; they kept score by carving notches on their desks.[10]

Female law students encounter harassment on job interviews. One researcher noted, "A lot goes on at interviews. A student will see a guy, and during the interview, he'll try to date her." Suzanne Baer, director of career and placement at New York University Law School, had a similar story to tell of a student who had accepted a part-time position with a law firm in

1987. Then she was called in by the hiring attorney and asked to go out to dinner. Ostensibly this invitation was for the purpose of learning more about the company; however, in reality it was a sexual proposition. This woman declined the job. One female attorney reported that a male lawyer at her firm liked to "jokingly" try to look up her dress if she was going upstairs or down her blouse if she happened to lean over in his presence. Harassed perhaps even more were the paralegals and secretaries at these firms, who had even less status. Career consultant Cheryl Heisler remarked, "The attitude at some firms is, as long as the female attorneys are not themselves being harassed, they're not supposed to mind if it happens to secretaries."[11]

As in every other occupation women lawyers who have been harassed are reluctant to officially complain. U.S. bankruptcy court judge Lisa Hill Fenning explained this by saying, "One of the reasons women lawyers don't report harassment is that they feel inadequate for not being able to cope with it on their own. They see it as a character defect rather than a management problem." Marina Angel, a law professor at Temple University, thought that sexual harassment in the legal workplace was an issue that had not been adequately addressed at all. She remembered being chased around desks as a Wall Street associate and said, "Let me tell you it was a problem and it is a problem, and people are not talking about it."[12]

Catherine A. Broderick was a staff attorney for the Securities and Exchange Commission (SEC) in Washington, D.C., starting in 1979. Within a week of joining the SEC, she was already spurning repeated offers of a ride home. At a 1982 farewell party for a staff member she was kissed by regional administrator Paul Leonard after he untied her sweater. Broderick observed other incidents of harassment. One SEC official had sex with a secretary, who received two promotions, $300 in cash, and a perfect evaluation. Officials at the SEC gave preferential treatment to those who submitted to their sexual advances. Those, such as Broderick, who rejected the harassment were denied promotions and job opportunities. Broderick was given a bad evaluation and then a transfer after complaining. In her lawsuit Broderick charged that she had been sexually harassed at work by her superiors and that those superiors retaliated against her when she opposed their illegal actions. Judge John H. Pratt of the federal district court in Washington ruled in 1988 that the SEC was responsible for "creating and refusing to remedy a sexually hostile work environment." He also said there was no doubt Broderick had been forced to work in an atmosphere where she was harassed. The SEC had contended she was paranoid. Pratt held that John Shad, former SEC chair and ambassador to the Netherlands at the time of the trial, and other senior officials were "not interested in the subject" of sex discrimination, noting that not one of the offending personnel was ever disciplined for his conduct.[13]

Under the terms of the suit's settlement Broderick was to be promoted two salary grades and to receive an unreported amount of back pay based on salary increases to which she would have been entitled over the previous eight years. The SEC also agreed to pay for 208 psychiatric counseling sessions for Broderick over the coming two years as well as to provide job-finding services if she decided to leave the commission. By accepting the settlement, the SEC decided not to appeal Pratt's ruling. When Pratt approved the settlement he also permanently barred the SEC from "creating or condoning" a hostile work environment for women.[14] Four months later the SEC reached an out-of-court settlement over the sexual harassment suit of former SEC employee Veronica Awkard. Terms of the settlement were not announced, but rumor had it that she received $145,000.[15]

At a meeting of law firms near the end of 1990 half of the 30 firms in attendance admitted investigating complaints of sexual harassment in their offices. Lynn Hecht Schafran, a lawyer with the National Organization for Women's Legal Defense and Educational Fund, thought female lawyers did not often complain when they were subjected to sexual harassment. "They don't even want to see the guy punished," she explained. "All they want is for it to stop and to make sure they're not going to get a bad evaluation. It takes great courage to make a complaint of this kind." A lawyer in an eastern city filed a complaint with the EEOC about harassment when she was discharged immediately after complaining about the sexual advances of a partner in the firm. This company refused to give her a reference. In a 1989 poll in Maryland 19 percent of female lawyers said they had been sexually harassed by judges.[16]

A 1992 study that surveyed judges and lawyers in the U.S. Ninth Circuit Court of Appeals, headquartered in California and covering nine western states, found that 60 percent of the 900 female lawyers reported they had been the target of unwanted sexual advances and other forms of sexual harassment during the previous five years. Perpetrators were judges, lawyers, clients, and other court personnel. Six percent said they had been harassed by judges. Seven of 34 women judges reported hearing male federal judges making disparaging comments about a female lawyer's "presumed sexual orientation." Several court employees complained that judges had shown them pornographic material from obscenity cases. A female lawyer was asked by a judge to leave the room during a settlement discussion so he could "tell a dirty joke." Behavior detailed by some of the respondents included "unwanted touching and groping under the conference table." In one case a female lawyer was tackled to the ground in her office by a male lawyer's client. When she asked the lawyer to control his client he refused. She added, "Both men said, 'You must be frigid'." A male judge said that his wife had been a practicing attorney all their married life and that "she and all other women lawyers are abused badly for no good reason." This report noted the problem was not generational as harassers were as likely to be younger as to be older.[17]

Another poll, released in 1993, surveyed 553 female lawyers. Taken by the publishing firm Prentice Hall Law and Business, it found that 56 percent of the respondents reported harassment by law firm colleagues or opposing council, 45 percent by clients, and 31 percent by judges.[18]

Another lawyer who did complain was Sheila Donahue. She did so against the New York branch of Los Angeles–based Paul Hastings, Jonofsky, and Walker. Donahue alleged that a partner in the firm, Ronald P. Mysliwiec, had subjected her and other female employees to "numerous unwelcome comments about his sexual experiences and desires" and referred to these coworkers as "toots," "honeybunch," "little girl," and other more "vulgar and derogatory" terms. In October and November 1987 Donahue told partners in the firm about Mysliwiec's conduct, but the harassment continued. A few weeks later the company retaliated by giving her a marginal performance evaluation just seven months after it had deemed her "fully acceptable." Soon after that Donahue was notified that she had no long-term future with the firm. A second woman harassed by Mysliwiec resigned in December 1987; a third was dismissed in March 1988. Donahue resigned one month later.[19]

The most celebrated case of sexual harassment in journalism may be that of Lisa Olson, who told of being confronted and harassed by nude members of the New England Patriots football team while trying to do her job as a sports reporter. What happened to Olson was not an uncommon experience for female sportswriters. What was unusual was that Olson, reluctantly, blew the whistle. Then team owner Victor Kiam made light of the whole issue with ill-advised remarks. This elevated the matter to national headlines for an extended period of time, with many people coming out of the woodwork to take sides. Many of them were antagonistic to Olson.

On September 17, 1990, Olson was in the Patriots' locker room conducting an interview with cornerback Maurice Hurst for her paper the *Boston Herald*. It was her first year on the football beat, although Olson had covered other professional sports teams in the past. According to Olson, five team members were involved. One, naked, walked over and made sexist and lewd remarks that dared her to touch his genitals. Then he suggested the other four players, also naked, taunt her. Behind him these other players made lewd gestures. Olson said this incident left her feeling "violated" and having experienced "nothing less than mind rape."[20]

Olson told *Herald* sports editor Bob Sales about the incident but did not write about it publicly at the time, explaining to Sales that she preferred the situation be handled behind the scenes with disciplinary action. After being informed of what had occurred, Patriots' general manager Pat

Sullivan conducted an investigation. The result of that was the fining of one unnamed player. Sullivan would not disclose the amount of the fine but did say it was more than the rumored $2,000. Under league rules Sullivan had authority to levy a fine of as much as one game's salary, $30,000 in the case of tight end Zeke Mowatt, generally believed to be the player fined. A second paper in that city, the *Boston Globe* heard of the incident, interviewed Olson later that first week (she did not object) and then broke the story in the *Globe* on September 21. The *Herald* had not intended to run it. The next day Kiam told a *Herald* reporter, "I can't disagree with the players' actions. Your paper's asking for trouble sending a female reporter to cover the team." One day after that Olson covered the next Patriots game, during which she exchanged words with Kiam. The owner was quoted as having been overheard saying of the sportswriter, "What a classic bitch. No wonder the players can't stand her." As a result Sales called on National Football League (NFL) commissioner Paul Tagliabue to suspend Kiam and on fans to boycott the coming weekend Patriots home game at Foxboro, Massachusetts. The Boston chapter of the National Organization for Women considered calling a national boycott of goods made by Remington Products, of which Kiam was president, saying, "Mr. Kiam does not deserve to walk away from this incident by offering a tepid apology to Lisa Olson. He, a man who enriches himself largely by selling products to women, does not deserve our business. We ask you to consider whom you support when you buy Remington products."[21]

Tagliabue announced he would appoint a special counsel to investigate the matter. Kiam denied making the remarks about Olson. His friend Jim Carr, reportedly present at the time, said what Kiam had uttered was "She's an aggressive reporter, isn't she?" Kiam's version of the harassment incident was that Olson was sitting on the floor while she spoke to Hurst, which allowed her to look at players's genitals. In this version Mowatt then approached her and said, "You seem to be so interested in it, you want to touch it?" Sullivan defended his investigation by stating, "We feel very strongly that we looked into this carefully and believe we chose the right player to fine. We apologized to Lisa as an organization, I apologized to her three separate times." Kiam also apologized to her "for any remarks which I made which may have been construed as having condoned these actions." Sales remained unsatisfied, declaring, "This is not a public relations problem. It's a human problem. We'd like a suspension of Victor Kiam and we'd like the players to be identified publicly." The team owner took out full-page newspaper ads deploring the incident, but only after the National Organization for Women announced its threatened boycott. Hostility was high against Olson in many quarters. At the Patriots home game in Foxboro at the end of September she was booed by the crowd.[22]

At the end of November the NFL released its report of the incident.

Prepared by Philip Heymann, a Harvard Law School professor, the 60-page document determined that Olson was "degraded and humiliated" primarily by three players. In response to this the NFL levied fines; $12,500 against Mowatt, whose testimony Heymann found to be "not credible"; $5,000 against Michael Timpson; and $5,000 against Robert Perryman. The New England Patriots team was fined $50,000. In a letter sent to Kiam, Tagliabue called the episode "distasteful, unnecessary and damaging to the league and others. It included a mix of misconduct, insensitivity, misstatements and other inappropriate actions or inaction, all of which could and should have been avoided." The report concluded, "No one tried to bring the humiliating activity around Lisa Olson to a stop. Neither players nor management personnel said or did anything."[23]

Seemingly the episode ended there, until February 4, 1991, when Kiam was one of the speakers at a dinner in Connecticut. The crowd was all male, 800 strong. On that evening Kiam told the following joke; "What do the Iraqis have in common with Lisa Olson? They've both seen Patriot missiles up close." A couple of days later Kiam apologized, stating, "I used bad judgment in repeating one particular joke. The comments were insensitive and inappropriate. I apologize to those who were offended." Olson declined comment at the time. Sales said of Kiam, "He of all people knows how much pain this has caused Lisa Olson and he should have known how much more pain telling this joke would cause her. It was an awful thing to have done."[24]

At the end of April Olson initiated a lawsuit for sexual harassment, civil rights violations, and emotional distress. Named in the suit were the three players fined, the Patriots team, Sullivan, and James Oldham, public relations director of the club at the time. Shortly thereafter Olson left the *Herald* and the United States to take a job as a reporter on a Sydney, Australia, paper, where she continues to work at this writing. Both papers were owned by Rupert Murdoch. An out-of-court settlement of the lawsuit was reached in February 1992. No details were made public. Olson said that originally she had not intended to sue but changed her mind after Kiam told his missile joke.[25]

Three months following that it was learned that all three players had filed appeals against their fines. Timpson dropped his appeal and paid the $5,000; however, neither Mowatt nor Perryman had paid his fine as of the end of May 1992. The Patriots team had paid its fine to the NFL. Faced with those appeals and possible lawsuits by the players themselves, Tagliabue admitted it was difficult, if not impossible, to collect fines that did not relate to play on the field. Tagliabue suggested it was unlikely either man would ever pay. Such reasoning was clearly specious as the NFL vigorously pursued players over drug abuse. Nor was it likely that a player would run up a huge legal bill over the Olson case.[26]

At the height of the public furor over the Anita Hill/Clarence Thomas charges of harassment, sportswriter Tracy Dodds came forward to say that while she and other female sports reporters empathized with Hill, they also wondered what all the fuss was about. "I can't believe the country is all agog over this," said Dodds. "We've been putting up with this for years." Dodds was then the assistant sports editor on the *Orange County Register* in southern California and president of the 400-member Association of Women in Sports Media. Some of the cases she could cite included that of a player masturbating in front of a woman reporter, another spitting on a writer's leg, and a third, while naked, presenting his penis to a reporter and asking, "Do you know what that is?" The quick-witted journalist retorted, "It looks like a penis, only smaller." Dodds once found herself in a locker room with eight nude players sitting around a table eating lasagna. "I felt like throwing up," she said. When on the road with sports teams women reporters can expect to receive nuisance calls in their hotel rooms from players in the middle of the night. Although she was a pioneer female sports reporter who broke in with the *Milwaukee Journal* in 1973 fresh out of college, the specter of harassment was still in her mind 20 years later. "To this day, when I have to go into a locker room, my stomach is in knots. I am saying, 'Please God, don't let there be a scene. Don't have someone standing naked over me'." Even though she felt sexual harassment occurred less frequently in her area than when she first broke in, Dodds added, "But it can still happen anytime." She also noted that "an overwhelmingly large number of female sportswriters do not go public with their sexual harassment. When you report it you are a strident bitch. So you roll with it, make a joke of it." Despite some popular conceptions that these female reporters liked to see naked men, Dodds and other writers considered such a scene an "offensive environment" and a "needless one." The male athletes did not have to be naked but made an issue of it. Even in the 1990s the idea of morality was brought up, with these women who dared enter male locker rooms branded by players and much of the general public as loose and immoral and in search of cheap thrills. Therefore in accordance with the male ideology of sexual harassment, these sportwriters deserved whatever they got. Dodds concluded, "But are we going to be treated with respect? That is still coming."[27]

Generally respect for women working professionally in the media was, and remains, lacking. Reporter Carolyn Weaver suggested that female journalists had as much trouble with sexual harassment as women in other white-collar professions. However, even though the press reported on harassment in government, private business, and the military, it was much more reluctant to do so when the issue hit home. Assistant managing editor of the *St. Petersburg Times*, Ben Johnson, stated, "We're behind the rest of corporate America in dealing with it.... We're not serious about it."

Nearly 40 percent of women employed at 19 American newspapers reported being harassed, according to an Associated Press Managing Editors Association survey. A University of Maryland poll reported 60 percent of 102 female journalists working out of congressional press galleries in Washington had been harassed. When the trade magazine *News Inc.* surveyed 199 newspaperwomen, most of them managers on small papers, in the fall of 1991, 44 percent reported incidents of harassment. Half of these incidents had occurred within the previous five years and 20 percent during the previous six months. Of 55 women television news directors, 55 percent said they had been sexually harassed on the job, according to a poll undertaken by the University of Missouri School of Journalism. Most respondents never reported the incidents.[28]

Harassment suits settled out of court by the parties usually contain a gag clause whereby the victim agrees to not discuss the case in any way in public. These secrecy settlements are common in all areas of society but are particularly ironic for the news media. When Lynne Carrier settled her suit against the *San Diego Tribune*, she refused the offer of an extra $10,000 to remain silent. "I told them I thought it was outrageous for a newspaper that makes its livelihood by public disclosure to have a confidential settlement," she explained. Lawyer Vicki Golden remarked, "Defendants say they won't settle otherwise, unless you keep quiet. It's pretty hard to say 'No, I'd rather take my chances to vindicate myself in court two years down the road'." Bruce Meachum of the Denver Newspaper Guild remarked, "I think it's pretty clear that it's worth more money with a high-profile case, to have confidentiality. What else would they be settled for? There's no other reason for a company to settle up front, unless they think they have a dead loser of a case."[29]

CBS settled a 1986 lawsuit brought by seven women who alleged they had been sexually harassed and sexually assaulted, in spite of their repeated requests for help from top managers, while working on the network's program "Nightwatch." The 1987 settlement included a gag clause with the proviso that if the silence was broken, the plaintiffs would have to pay back the settlement plus a substantial penalty. This payback of settlement plus is a standard part of any gag clause. Despite the newsworthiness of this case, which involved a prestigious and nationally known news organization, it received next to no coverage. The *Washington Post* reported it briefly in passing a few times, but only in the television column. One of the women involved at first agreed to talk to reporter Weaver about the case off the record but then changed her mind after a discussion with her lawyer. Six of the seven females left television news. The sole exception remained as an independent producer.[30]

Secrecy agreements allow defendants to escape to some degree the responsibility for the harassment. Since no details or specifics are ever released, the affair is left open to speculation that harassment did not take place at all or that it was not all that severe. These agreements make it much easier to blame the female instead of the defendant. Late in 1989 assistant metro editor J. Frazier Smith resigned from the *Cincinnati Enquirer* after charges by five female staffers that he had harassed them. One of them, reporter Nancy Firor, later sued the paper alleging the company retaliated against her because she had complained against Smith. Following Smith's departure management told the women they were not allowed to talk about the incidents. As the company never announced exactly why Smith had departed, rumors circulated, such as the departure was a racial thing — Smith and Firor were of different races. Firor was unable to defend herself under a gag order, so she appealed to the company to clear the air. Instead it considered her a problem, denying her a promotion. *Enquirer* editor George Blake claimed that he did not know if the women had in fact been told not to talk about the complaint and that he did not remember if his own newspaper had reported the affair. He did say the paper had long circulated a written policy against sexual harassment. A lawyer for Firor, Lynn Pundzak, stated there was no evidence of such a policy prior to the Smith charges. In fact the *Enquirer* never reported any of the story in its own pages. The story broke in the *Cleveland Plain Dealer*. Upon leaving, Smith negotiated a confidential severance agreement.[31]

Emily Dunning got her M.D. degree in 1902 and then a position at Gouverneur Hospital — the downtown New York branch of Bellevue Hospital. She became the first female appointed to a place on the medical staff of a city hospital, despite vehement protests by the staffs of those two hospitals and others. Nobody wanted to be "dominated" by a woman. On her first day on the job the house surgeon told Emily she would be on duty that night for routine catheterization in the male surgical ward. "I felt as though a stick of dynamite with a burning, sputtering fuse had suddenly been placed in my hands," recalled Dunning. Until then "men and men alone" had dealt with the afflictions of the male sexual organ. Once she treated an eight-year-old girl who was the victim of a brutal rape. At dinner the next day four of her male colleagues brought the rape up and went over all the details, asking Emily about it. Emily decided this was a plan evidently rehearsed in advance, for she commented, "Certainly anything that had to do with sexual irregularities was taboo in those days and never allowed as a subject of discussion in a mixed group."[32]

Close to a century later, in July 1991, Dr. Frances Conley, a surgeon for 25 years and a professor at Stanford University in Palo Alto, California, suddenly announced her resignation, citing what she called "gender insensitivity." One example she used was being called "honey" by male surgeons. On the need to be in control in the operating room, Conley explained, "That control is established because people respect who I am and what I can do.

If a man walks into the operating room and says, 'How's it going, honey?', what happens to my control? It disappears because every woman who is working in that room with me has also been called 'honey' by this same guy, and it means all of a sudden I don't have the status of a surgeon in control of the case being done. I have suddenly become a fellow 'honey'." Conley added, "When I was younger I would be repeatedly asked to bed by fellow doctors. This would always happen in front of an audience. It was always done for effect. . . . I have had male doctors run their hands up my leg, never in an operating room, but in meetings. It is always done for an audience. Two months ago, I stood up to leave a meeting of all men and me, and as I stood up one of them said to me, 'Gee, I can see the shape of your breasts, even through your white coat'." Rather than view this as sexual harassment, Conley preferred to describe it as sexism. A few days after tendering her resignation Conley withdrew it.[33]

Advancing on a plane from flight attendant to pilot still held dangers for women. In October 1992 Kathy Gillies, a United Airlines pilot with 12 years of experience, launched a suit against her employer alleging that during her three years with United pilots she had flown with had made sexual advances to her and sexually assaulted her. According to her complaint, Gillies was subjected continually to sexual harassment, with male coworkers asking her to have intercourse with them and telling her she resembled females in pornographic magazines. She was also tackled and sexually assaulted by a United pilot with whom she could still be assigned to fly. Gillies asked United to investigate her complaint. In a letter of reply one month before Gillies initiated her lawsuit, United said it had conducted a full probe and had found no wrongdoing. Considering this cavalier treatment, the pilot responded "I don't feel anyone should have to endure what I have endured since being employed by United Airlines. I don't feel that the company has taken my sexual harassment complaints seriously." In the letter United also told her it could not guarantee she would never be scheduled to fly with the pilot who was alleged to have assaulted her. If that should happen, United said the two were "expected to treat each other in a professional manner."[34]

Job hunting was once again shown to be a dangerous pursuit in the trial of a Burbank, California, talent agent in 1993. Wallace Kaye attracted actresses to his office who were looking for acting or modeling jobs. Once in his office Kaye locked the door and had the women perform improvised scenes of a sexual nature. During the performance Kaye touched the women on their breasts, buttocks, and vaginas. These activities took place at the Kaye Talent Agency between October 1990 and September 1992. In 1993 Kaye was convicted of sexually assaulting ten females, nine actresses, and one undercover policewoman borrowed from the nearby Glendale force to gather evidence. The ten counts he was convicted on ranged from felony

sexual battery by restraint to felony imprisonment by violence to misdemeanor battery. Judge Jack B. Tso, finding planning and premeditation in
the attacks, sentenced Kaye to five years and four months in prison, ignoring the recommendation of parole officer Gerald Magid that Kaye be sentenced to probation. Tso noted that as a talent agent Kaye held a position
of trust with his clients and that his victims were much smaller than the
six foot, more than 200 pound agent. Burbank police Sergeant David Gab-
riel took the stand to explain he wished he had not borrowed the policewoman because the assault "affected her so much I completely regret
having done it. . . . She felt some of the trauma that the victims did." Magid
said he was bothered by the testimony of Kaye's victims and wondered "if
they had lived cloistered lives and had never had a pass made at them."[35]

12

Political Men

A 1977 article indicated that sexual harassment might be rampant on Capitol Hill. A female aide to an East Coast U.S. senator said, "It's an open secret that some of our Congressmen and Senators just won't hire a woman unless they try her out." Women employed on the Hill discussed the problems of dodging their bosses and fellow staff members around desks. These women were also expected to "hostel important male constituents." Recourse for such abuse was next to impossible because Congress, with the support of President Jimmy Carter's attorney general, declared itself completely immune from all the antidiscrimination legislation it had passed for others. Women and minorities who had grievances about sexist and racist behavior were forced to rely for any redress on members' of Congress voluntary membership in, from 1988, the House Fair Employment Practices Commission and, prior to that time, the Senate ethics code, which was self-regulating.[1]

As events would show the Hill did indeed harbor much sexual harassment. Although it did not gain wide public attention until the 1990s, a number of documented cases went as far back as the 1970s. Most likely sexual harassment on Capitol Hill went back even further than that but remained undocumented and unrecorded. On March 1, 1992, the *Seattle Times* broke a story about Senator Brock Adams, then 65 and a Democrat representing Washington State, first elected to the Senate in 1986. The paper published the stories of eight unnamed women who accused Adams—a former U.S. secretary of transportation—of misbehavior, sexual harassment, and physical assault. One political activist said she was drugged and raped. Two other accusers claimed to have been molested by the senator after being drugged or offered a suspicious drink. None of these women had reported their assaults to the police. The *Seattle Times* departed from its usual standards in the use of unnamed sources because its three and a half year investigation had uncovered allegations that pointed to a pattern of "abuses of power and women." Seven of the accusers signed statements for the paper in which they said they were ready to go to court if necessary to back up their claims. Adams denied all the charges. He added he would not resign his Senate seat but serve out his term — he was up for election in November 1992. His already underway reelection campaign was considered in trouble even before this story broke because of previously publicized charges that he had drugged and molested a young female aide in 1987. Although that case was highly publicized, no charges were laid. Whatever political support Adams had began to rapidly melt away within hours of the appearance of the *Seattle Times* article.[2]

The paper's story was the result of some of the women coming forward on their own and some being tracked down by the newspaper. None would allow her name to be used. These assaults and harassments took place from the 1970s through the 1980s. Michael R. Fancher, executive editor of the newspaper, said his paper "found the women credible and their independent stories of misdeeds fit a pattern." In addition to these eight women other unnamed sources cited as familiar with Adams were quoted as saying, "The senator had long been known by his staff and associates for aggressively kissing and handling women within his reach." Back in the early 1970s when Adams was serving in the U.S. House of Representatives, a Democratic Party activist alleged that Adams invited her to a Seattle bar. The woman was recovering from a cold at the time so Adams gave her two pills, which he said were Vitamin C tablets. As they left the bar he insisted on following her home to see she got there safely. Once inside he pushed her onto a couch and raped her. The woman now thinks the pills were a drug. She did not press charges, saying, "When a guy has that much power, there's nothing you can do about it. It's very traumatic when I think about it. There's no way to prove he did this to me." A second woman related that Adams offered her some champagne laced with a red liquid. She blacked out and then awoke to find him removing her clothes. A former secretary to Adams was invited to play tennis with him when he was Carter's transportation secretary. After the game he offered her a drink with what looked like a crushed pill on the bottom. Although she threw away the drink, Adams still kissed her against her will and pawed her body before being called away to a meeting. The other accusers were a secretary employed by Adams for ten years, a lobbyist, two former aides, and a secretary at a Seattle law firm where he was a partner. To the *Seattle Times* these women described "a persistent pattern of unwanted kisses and fondling." At a public luncheon the lobbyist had to endure Adams running his hand up her skirt and keeping it on her thigh for 15 minutes while she discreetly tried to fend him off. A number of these women told their friends or family about the attacks or harassment. The newspaper verified its story with those other sources. To a greater or lesser degree all of the accusers felt they were helpless to speak out or report criminal behavior due to Adams's stature.[3]

For some of the these women their feelings about not speaking out changed after 1988. It was that year that the public first learned about Adams's alleged sexual abuse of Kari Tupper. It was also that year when the *Seattle Times* started into its slow-moving investigation. Tupper, then 24, reported to the police that on a night in 1987 she was drugged by Adams and awoke the next morning to find herself nude in the bedroom of his Washington, D.C., residence, with Adams pawing her body. Tupper worked as an aide to Adams and was also a family friend. She went to his home that evening, she said, to confront him after two years of unwanted sexual harassment. Adams admitted Tupper spent the night at his home but said it was because she was not feeling well and accepted his invitation to spend the night in a separate bedroom. He denied any assault. Tupper waited a month before reporting the incident to the police. The authorities subsequently decided not to file any charges. However, the Tupper case apparently emboldened other women to talk to the *Seattle Times*. The paper noted that several of the accusers had been contacted by Adams and his aides, including as recently as a week before the story was published, who urged them not to talk to the press. During the preceding months Adams had been campaigning as a champion of women's issues.[4]

That the media all too often trivialized, distorted, or denied such issues as sexual harassment could be seen in the coverage given by *U.S. News and World Report* when the Tupper allegations became public. The magazine began its account of that assault by saying, "The senator is not the first politician accused of hanky-panky." Rape is herein reduced to nothing more than minor hanky-panky. The latter term also normally connotes consent, as in when two people engage in something like adultery behind their spouses' backs. The assault is generalized to imply a lot of men do this, so it is okay, majority rule. Thus a serious criminal behavior is trivialized, and the implications are that the victim consented to her assault and that it could not really be an assault since so many men do this, so it could not be wrong. But then all of this should not be surprising since in 1989 males held 94 percent of the top management positions in the U.S. media. The ideas of the prevailing class will be the prevailing ideas.[5]

Dorena Bertussi came to Capitol Hill from San Diego in 1987 as a new legislative assistant to her local Democratic representative, Jim Bates. During her second week on the job he began to harass her. He asked her at different times if she was "being physically taken care of" and remarked that her breasts "really look good" and that "you look like the kind of person who likes it done rough to her. " One time she was sitting with her legs crossed, and Bertussi claimed, "he put my leg in between his and started to do a bump and grind on it, like a dog. I recoiled. I was kind of in shock." After just five months on the job Bertussi started searching for new employment. In time she found it. Then she went on to become the first woman to win a sexual harassment case against a representative. Becoming something of a spokesperson for the cause, Bertussi found herself counseling others who called her with horror stories about abuse. In some quarters the Hill was considered "the sexual harassment capital of the country."[6]

Jean Dugan, a former chair of the Capitol Hill Women's Political Caucus, commented, "What a lot of women have done is quit." The message they get is, "Keep quiet if you can't handle it. Don't knock the system." Because females working on the Hill could not take their sexual harassment complaints to the EEOC—as women employed in the private sector could by then do—the system encouraged silence in those harassed. Shari Jenifer, a staff member on the House Ways and Means Committee, interviewed dozens of current and former Capitol Hill aides, yet none would talk publicly about the harassment they had experienced. Jenifer explained their silence by saying, "If it's a choice between your pride and dignity and having a roof over your head, what are you going to chose?" When the Capitol Hill Women's Political Caucus sponsored a program around 1989 about sexual harassment, dozens of women besieged the panelists and confided secrets for three hours. One of those who spoke was Janina Jaruzelski, a House attorney, who told of a friend who had been raped by a Senate aide. The friend had been harassed for a long time by the high-level staffer. One night he cornered her in the office and started making lewd remarks. She wanted to leave, but he insisted she have sex with him. He told her if she left the room, he would get her fired or report her to the police. Then he locked the door, put a desk against it, and raped her. The woman did not report the rape to the police because she supported her senator politically and feared he would be discredited in a scandal that involved one of his top aides. Wanda Baucus, wife of Senator Max Baucus (D.–Mont.) disclosed in 1991 that she had been sexually harassed by two senators. One called her as often as three times a day when she first started working on the Hill. A few years later at a formal dinner another senator physically grabbed her under the table. A female lobbyist related how a representative invited her into his office, politely listened to her discuss a bill, then blocked her from leaving his office, and, she said, "grabbed me and shoved his tongue in my mouth. It's been eight years and my skin is still crawling."[7]

Although these women did not usually speak out, there was an informal network set up by experienced staffers whereby females warned each other of the worst harassers. It was reported that there were about 50 offices so bad that the recommendation was that they should be definitely avoided. Democrats and Republicans were equally guilty, with the male aides of these legislators sometimes being more offensive than the members because the latter had to worry about scandals ending their careers. More senior and powerful members were also viewed as potentially more dangerous since they tended to see themselves as invincible and less likely to be caught.[8]

Bertussi was angry enough over her treatment by Bates that after she left his employment she decided to talk to reporters and file a complaint. The only way to do that was through the ethics committee, which did not have any standard forms or any instructions on how to file a complaint. Persevering, Bertussi learned the rules herself. She could file a complaint herself only if she first approached three House members, asked them to sponsor her, and was turned down by each one of them. Lynn Martin, then a representative from Illinois and later labor secretary, agreed to file the complaint for Bertussi and sponsor her. That was in 1988. Martin recalled, "I've had members of Congress who didn't speak to me for years because they just didn't get it." After the complaint was filed the committee waited seven months before considering the case. The committee never talked to Bertussi directly. Instead staffers took a deposition from her and then called only two of her eight witnesses. Surprisingly the case was decided in her favor; however, the House Ethics Committee gave Bates the mildest possible punishment, issuing a letter of reproval. All Bertussi got from Bates was a seven-sentence letter of apology from him that began, "This year has been a trying time for both of us."[9]

The committee's scolding of Bates on October 18, 1989, was based on evidence that showed he had violated rules of conduct in his behavior toward two women on his staff. Instructed to apologize to the women — both had left his staff by then — he was warned that any further such action could result in a recommendation that disciplinary action be taken against him. His improper conduct was said to "deserve reproval." Reproval was a category devised by the committee several years previously for cases it believed were not serious enough to merit further action. All the more serious categories of action from reprimand to censure to expulsion required a vote of the full House before they could be imposed. On one occasion he wrapped his legs around the leg of one woman in full view of other staff members. He asked one woman if she would sleep with him if they were stranded on a desert island. Said Bates to the committee, "I think I made a mistake. I didn't really know what sexual harassment was."[10]

Life got embarrassing in the Florida state capitol in Tallahassee early in 1991 when it became public that a $47,000 secret payment had been made by the state to a woman to keep her from filing a sexual harassment suit against Fred Lippman, a democratic state representative from Hollywood, Florida. In November 1990 Lippman was named House majority leader, and that was when rumors about the payoff began to circulate around the capitol. Kathie Jennings worked as a legislative analyst for a House committee from 1983 to 1986 at the time Lippman chaired that committee. Jennings alleged that Lippman made remarks to her like "I want to be with you" and "I want to be intimate with you." Once he barged into the bedroom of the condo she rented from him and attempted to undress her. Also an alleged harasser of Jennings was Ken Sarvis, the committee's staff director. Sarvis constantly made suggestive remarks to her, said Jennings. Both men denied the charges. When Jennings threatened to initiate a lawsuit against the two men for $300,000, the House leadership authorized the $47,000 payout to the woman. One of the terms of the agreement was that Jennings was never to publicly discuss the matter. If she did, she would be required to pay double the amount — $94,000 — back. The House speaker at the time, Jon Mills, authorized the payment, telling the office of the State Comptroller only that the 1987 payout was for a legal settlement. When the matter became public in 1991, Mills commented that he felt he had done the right thing since he had saved the state money but that he now regretted the secrecy involved. Two months after this incident became public Lippman was removed as House majority leader and admonished for "very disappointing" conduct.[11]

A similar incident occurred in May 1993 and involved Fairfax, Virginia, County supervisor Robert B. Dix, Jr., elected to that post in 1991. Jacquelyn L. Pace-Herron, his former aide, alleged Dix had harassed her by jokingly suggesting she perform oral sex on him, playfully grabbing at her breasts, grabbing his crotch in her presence, and often calling her a "stupid bitch." Other women who came forward included two who had worked with Dix in 1991 at a car dealership and a reporter who had covered Dix in 1991–1992. All said his sexual comments, often about oral sex, made them feel uncomfortable. Requests by the women that he stop such behavior went unheeded. Pace-Herron received a payment of $8,600 in taxpayers' money in return for a promise not to sue Dix for sexual harassment. Dix denied all allegations but refused comment on the payment. Fairfax County executive William J. Leidinger admitted approving the payment, claiming that county policy allowed him to grant lump-sum settlements up to $25,000 for claims brought by employees without consulting the Board of Supervisors. Leidinger claimed such settlements were reached from "time to time" but refused to say how many he had approved during his administration. Officially the situation was seen as a dispute between employer and employee, with the money viewed as a severance payment. The most senior board member, supervisor Joseph Alexander, with almost 30 years' experience, could not recall ever paying severance to an employee. Like Congress, the Board of Supervisors exempted itself from personnel regulations applied to the rest of government. Aides to supervisors served at their bosses' pleasure, had no grievance rights, and could be fired on the spot without just cause. The Dix case generated more criticism over possible misuse of taxpayer money than over the charges of harassment.[12]

Given the light punishment involved in the Bates case, the Women's Political Caucus was motivated to draft its own sexual harassment policy and then ask all congressional offices to adopt it. Within a couple of years

282 offices had signed on, a little more than half. Bertussi's case also prompted the House to create the Office of Fair Employment Practices late in 1988. However, the office was so secretive that no one knew how well it was functioning or if it was hearing any harassment cases. For 1990 the only information this office released about itself was that it had received 262 discrimination inquiries. Meanwhile the Senate created its own Fair Employment Practices Office, with employees having the right to appeal a decision to federal court. This marked the first time that congressional staffers were given the right to judicial review.[13]

When the Anita Hill case was in the public eye, Bertussi noted the sudden burst of militancy against harassment on the part of female members of the House and wondered, "Where the hell were they three years ago? It just wasn't fashionable then." As late as 1990 the San Diego chapters of the National Organization for Women and the National Women's Political Caucus recommended or endorsed Bates, termed a liberal democrat, because his opponent was considered a staunch conservative. A feminist grumbled, "He's a slug, but he's our slug." Bates lost in the 1990 election. He maintained that Bertussi had misunderstood him and that he had never sexually harassed her. He insisted he would run again in 1992. He felt the Clarence Thomas hearings, which vindicated Thomas, would help his planned new campaign because, he reasoned, constituents would now tell him, "I understand what you went through."[14] He did not run in the 1992 general election.

Although the Anita Hill allegations did not directly involve a member of Congress, the case was played out on Capitol Hill, and it was those members of Congress who clearly showed their views of women with their treatment of Anita Hill. When President George Bush nominated Clarence Thomas in mid–1992 to fill a vacancy on the U.S. Supreme Court, the expected difficulties in getting him confirmed were thought to be his reputation as too conservative and his antiabortion views. In the event the group of senators on the Judiciary Committee who held the hearings seemed set to confirm Thomas as the proceedings ground to a close. However, as they ended a charge of sexual harassment against Thomas was aired by Anita Hill, a law professor in Oklahoma. Hill charged that Thomas had harassed her with vulgar language, sexual innuendos, pestering her for dates, and so forth. All of this took place, she alleged, a decade previous when Hill had worked for Thomas during the latter's tenure as chair of the EEOC. Since the scheduled hearings had just ended, the senators arrogantly declared that the nomination hearings were closed and that they would not be reopened just to hear these charges.

On October 6, 1992, it was reported that Hill told Judiciary Committee investigators that Thomas had harassed her while head of the EEOC. The following day she held a press conference in Oklahoma. Public response was strong, with a groundswell of anger directed at the senators on the Judiciary Committee for their refusal to reopen the hearings. This anger was fueled by the cavalier way senators implicitly labeled this whole affair as trivial by dismissing it out of hand. Finally the senators, faced by a barrage of protest, yielded and agreed to hear the charges formally in front of the committee. To save face and pretend they had not been forced to yield, the senators insisted on the fiction that Thomas had asked for the hearings to be reopened in order to clear his name.

Even though the hearings were reopened, the deck was stacked against Hill from the start. A maximum of two days was to be allocated to hearing the harassment charges, with only a couple of days allowed prior to that to round up witnesses, check facts, and so forth. Hill was savaged at those hearings by a group of senators who in the main loathed her and treated her in a contemptuous manner. Anyone who watched any of the televised hearings could not fail to be struck by the open antagonism these men felt toward her. Their minds were clearly made up before this charge was heard. Old stereotypes were dusted off and trotted out to damn Hill, directly or indirectly branding her a lying, promiscuous, hysterical, and, in a particularly ugly spin, vengeful woman who had perhaps been spurned by Thomas. A notably uncredible witness for the Thomas side claimed Hill had once sexually come on to him. These senators portrayed Hill as a "crazy, vindictive erotomaniac," as one journalist noted.[15]

The EEOC itself had come under suspicion long before this hearing, back in 1976 when the *Wall Street Journal* published a story that the EEOC had been investigated as a result of audits of its field offices. This was before Thomas's tenure as head of that agency. According to the story, reports were ordered secretly "in response to rumors alleging staff misconduct." Sexual harassment was not contained among the criminal investigation's formal charges, yet one source who read the audits but refused to be named maintained they "indicated a high level of sexual harassment within many of the EEOC regional offices."[16]

Names of two other women victims of Thomas's sexual harassment were mentioned in conjunction with the Hill hearings, but they were never called to testify. Ostensibly the reason was that no time remained; in reality they were blocked by the senators on the Judiciary Committee because they clearly put Thomas in a bad light, making it more and more difficult to justify recommending that he be confirmed to the nation's highest court. After Hill first spoke publicly one of these other women, Angela Wright, came forward to state that Thomas had harassed her at the EEOC. She had been hired in 1984 by Thomas as director of public affairs. Wright was conservative, Republican, and credible. Until then she had never heard of Anita Hill. When Wright came forward she was working as an assistant editor on the *Charlotte Observer*. Speaking to Cynthia Hogen, special counsel and member of Senator Joseph Biden's (chair of the Judiciary Committee) staff, Wright told of her harassment by Thomas at the EEOC; "There were several comments that he made. Clarence Thomas did consistently pressure me to date him. At one point, Clarence Thomas made comments about my anatomy. Clarence Thomas made comments about women's anatomy quite often. At one point Clarence Thomas came by my apartment at night, unannounced and uninvited, and talked about the prospect of my dating him." He once asked her "what size my boobs were." She said other women at the EEOC had told her that Thomas wanted to date them and that he made comments about women's bodies. In the end Wright was fired by Thomas. The White House and most of the senators on the committee did not want Wright to testify at the hearings. However, Senator Howard Metzenbaum insisted that a subpoena be issued to her, which should have ensured she would indeed testify. One of the witnesses for Thomas, who did testify publicly, claimed she had heard a rumor that Wright was fired over an incident in which she was rude to an EEOC commissioner and was slapped by that person. After this was well publicized and reported in the press three former EEOC employees tried to reach the committee to refute it as false. They were passed from one person to another, with no member of the committee or any of the aides involved formally taking down their statements.[17]

Wright provided Biden's staff with the names of several women she said would confirm her statements. Only a single phone call was placed to each one. Rose Jordain returned the call. She had once worked for Thomas at the EEOC, knew something of the Wright/Thomas relationship, and was prepared to testify. Jordain stated of Wright, "She confided to me increasingly that she was . . . uneasy with the chairman because of the comments she told me he was making about her figure, her body, her breasts, her legs, how she looked in certain suits or dresses. . . . One time she came into my office in tears, said she had bought a new suit . . . and he had evidently quite a bit of comment to make about it and how sexy she looked in it and that kind of thing, and it unnerved her a great deal. She became increasingly nervous about being in his presence alone." Both Wright and Jordain were ready to testify and would have, even in the early hours of the morning if necessary. But the committee stalled for time and then closed the hearings at the end of the second day without calling either to the stand. Explaining that they were out of time, committee members added that not testifying was all right with Wright and Jordain. Copies of Wright's statements were released to the press, but only at 3 A.M., which was too late for the morning newspapers. Apparently Jordain's testimony was never released, nor did it form part of the official transcript of the hearings — it was not necessary to publicly testify to have a statement become a part of the official record. Jordain was interviewed by Senate committee staffers, and her statement was to have been distributed to the entire Senate, yet many key aides said they never saw it or even heard of Jordain. In the hearing aftermath the *Washington Post* ran no stories on Wright or Jordain. The *New York Times* assigned a team of reporters to check, but after two weeks of work the project was dropped and no story appeared in the *Times*. Clarence Thomas was confirmed in the full Senate on October 15, 1991, by a vote of 52 to 48. On October 23 Thomas took his seat on the Supreme Court.[18]

One of the many media defenders of Clarence Thomas was Juan Williams, a journalist for the *Washington Post*. After an article on the op-ed page claiming Anita Hill had no credible evidence to support her charge, Williams became a widely quoted defender of the jurist. At about the same time he was scoring Hill and being cited by others, his own newspaper was conducting an investigation of him after several female employees complained he had harassed them with sexually explicit and hostile comments. On November 2, 1991, the *Washington Post* announced Williams had been disciplined for his conduct and that he would apologize to the staff. Initially the paper was not going to release the Williams story publicly at all, planning to keep it secret, but a protest by 50 female employees against this decision caused the paper to change its mind. Executive editor Leonard Downie, Jr., said, "The complaints were found to be serious and, as Juan acknowledges, he was disciplined for his conduct and intends to apologize to the women he offended." Details of the disciplinary action were not made public.[19]

Another who was virulent in condemning Hill was Far Right media personality and commentator John McLaughlin, who could be seen on television shows such as "The McLaughlin Group." A panelist on that program, Fred Barnes, said on the show on October 12, 1991, that he thought Hill's motives for inventing her story were "frustration, revenge and shame." Under this bizarre and ludicrous theory Hill left Thomas's employ after being rejected by the jurist to go to a lesser law school, embarrassed by everything. Along the way Hill dreamed up the harassment story to tell friends so she could hide her humiliation at not doing very well.[20]

According to Jack Germond, another regular panelist and McLaughlin associate, McLaughlin's response to Hill was that "he went absolutely berserk trashing Anita Hill and defending Clarence Thomas. But I don't know if that's ideological. He tends to side with the men." And like Juan Williams, McLaughlin had an ugly past based on a 1988 lawsuit filed against him for sexual harassment. Linda Dean, his former executive assistant, filed that suit alleging that he told her he "needed a lot of sex" and "a mistress" and that he touched her "intimately and against her will." Dean claimed she was forced to quit her job because she resisted the harassment. Another female employee accompanied him to Ireland in 1986 to interview the prime minister. After a dinner, according to this woman's sworn deposition from the Dean case, McLaughlin asked the woman to come to his hotel room to pick up some papers. When she prepared to leave he blocked her path and said, "Aren't you going to kiss Daddy goodnight?" After she protested he let her go. The next night while the pair worked he started to strip down to his shorts. When she said she wanted to leave he ordered her to stay. On another trip he blocked this woman's exit from his room, pressed her against a wall, and attempted to kiss her. She managed to slip out of the room. "I bet you like it on top," he said to her. After a few months she quit. A different employee found McLaughlin holding a piece of fruit under her chin. "How would you like to bite my banana?" he said to her, according to three former employees who witnessed the incident. Women employees were said to have quit McLaughlin's employ in droves. Following the filing of the suit by Dean, McLaughlin sent a memo to his employees telling them to not discuss the case. On the advice of lawyers he settled out of court for an unreported sum, estimated at $250,000. McLaughlin denied all the accusations as well as the estimated settlement figure.[21]

In the Hill-bashing vendetta the *National Review* reached north of the border to bring a well-known Canadian right-wing extremist female journalist in to do a guest editorial. This woman discerned a sinister, take-over-the-world plot buried in the scenario. It was much more than simply leftists attempting to smear Thomas to keep a conservative off the bench. Seeing "extreme feminism" as a "state religion in America," this commentator felt people were being disentitled to their own sexuality and that a dismantling of a free society "may be part of the feminists' agenda as they rearrange social structure." She finished up by stating that Hill had no relevance to Thomas whatsoever, except "that anyone crazy enough to ask her out is not fit to be a Supreme Court Justice."[22]

Anita Hill became, and remains, the seminal sexual harassment victim precisely because of the vicious treatment she was subjected to. Initially her complaint was not going to be heard at all, thereby symbolizing the way men dismiss women, disregard their concerns, and refuse to respond in any meaningful way to crimes and violence in which all or most of the victims are women. Although Hill was a credible, forthcoming witness, as were her witnesses, while Thomas and his were not, it was Hill who was not believed. She was attacked for not coming forward to complain at the time, a charge brought against harassed women in different countries and time periods. Implicit in this charge is the assumption that if something really bad had occurred, the victim would have complained at the time and that since nothing was reported, the matter could not be serious and will be dismissed. This attitude showed a complete insensitivity to a group long oppressed and exploited by men. It touched a chord of response in any woman who understood the dynamics of power, class, and gender. Typically a harasser is an older male in a supervising position. The female is younger, in an inferior position, makes less money, and is always in danger of being fired. Given the difficulties involved, females are not to be blamed for failing to come forward at the time. Rather they are to be congratulated that they have the fortitude to come forward at all. For all these reasons Hill became a rallying point for women.

One who accurately assessed the Hill case was writer Robert Parry, who noted that longtime sources with ties to the Thomas crowd at the EEOC said that even some of Thomas's friends believed the charges were true. Republicans on the panel who questioned Hill set out, with the explicit approval of Bush, "to raise Anita Hill's negatives." Republican senators Alan Simpson, Orrin Hatch, and Arlen Spector attacked her as a "sicko" who wanted to destroy a good man who had spurned her. Aided by the Bush Justice Department, the GOP senators conducted a long and exhaustive data base search, finally unearthing an obscure legal case that mentioned pornographic film star Long Dong Silver. Hatch also waved a copy of the book *The Exorcist* which contained a reference to a pubic hair in a glass of gin. Hill alleged Thomas had talked of Silver and of a pubic hair on his Coke can. The implication was that Hill made up that material, perhaps from the sources cited by the senators. What did Hill have to gain by lying? Nothing. What did Thomas have to gain by lying? Everything. The Hill hearing was not convened to get at the truth or to openly consider whether Thomas was suitable material for the Supreme Court. The purpose of the hearing was simply to discredit and smear Hill. It worked. It was not the place for Hill to challenge the prerogatives of Bush to do as he wished.[23]

Just prior to the Hill hearings the Cleveland-based advocacy group for working women, Nine to Five, received about 200 calls a week from females with problems, mostly on pregnancy and related issues. After the hearings phone calls jumped fivefold to 200 per day, virtually all about sexual harassment. Group director Karen Nussbaum said, "People were almost bewildered. You mean this is sexual harassment? You mean I could do something about this?" When Nine to Five later checked back with women who had called them during the hearings, the organization found that those "discouraged" and "encouraged" by the episode were split 53 percent to 47 percent, respectively. Callers revealed they were mainly fending for themselves, either putting up with being harassed or leaving their job. One waitress caller worked in a Midwest restaurant where she had been dueling with her boss for months. He began by asking to fondle her breasts. Other waitresses had been fired for refusing to yield. Although this waitress had been able to put him off until then, she said that "every day it doesn't happen is a reprieve. Every day I worry about getting fired." She supported herself and three children. Another caller was a convention planner from the Southeast who spent 12 years at a large company working her way up from clerk to vice-president. During her four years as an executive she faced a continual barrage of sexual advances. As much of it happened at departmental meetings her supervisors were aware of it. "They let me know that if I wanted to play hardball, I had to handle it." One man was particularly merciless. Among other things, "he went around taking pictures of women's rear ends," she said. Confrontation had no effect, so after a year and a half she complained officially. "I waited because I had to work with this man. I didn't want him to get fired. I just wanted the harassment to stop." The harasser left the company in an unrelated layoff. The woman left to work independently. After immersing herself in the literature of harassment, she began to speak on the topic. She found that "women are the hardest to convince. I have many friends—women—who thought Hill was off her rocker. They are told it can't happen."[24]

The Connecticut Women's Educational and Legal Fund and the State Commission on Human Rights and Opportunities released a report of the results of a phone line set up to take calls from harassment victims in that state for five days from December 6 to 11, 1991, two months after the Hill hearings. A total of 128 calls were received, 125 from women; 2 of the 3 men called to describe the experience of women they knew. Leslie Brett, director of the fund, said, "A lot of the sex harassment was pretty gross and blatant." One caller described harassment that dated back 50 years. Several others related that shortly after complaining, they were either demoted or fired. Sixty-two of the callers reported extreme forms of harassment such as grabbing or assault. "The depth of pain and emotion we heard on the phone was pretty disturbing," noted Brett. One woman told of men in her workplace grabbing their crotches and thrusting their hips at her as she walked past. Another told how her male boss described her underwear to her coworkers, indicating that he was somehow spying on her in the change room. Several said the Hill hearings caused them to remember and relive incidents in their own lives. This report found, "The harassers tended to be older, better educated and earning considerably more than the women they were harassing." Two thirds of the harassers were the victim's supervisor or a company executive. About 30 percent of these harassed women filed a formal complaint either internally at the company or externally at an outside agency.[25]

Near the end of October 1992 New York City mayor David Dinkins announced the appointment of Randy Daniels as deputy mayor for public and community affairs, to assume the post on November 2. Only hours before the announcement of this appointment, Dinkins's staff received a tip that Daniels had been a sexual harasser. Nevertheless, Dinkins proceeded after a discussion with Daniels. Neither the mayor nor his staff contacted Andrew J. Stein, who employed both Daniels and his accuser at the time of the alleged incident. The charge dated to 1987, when Daniels allegedly made unwelcome advances to Barbara Wood, threatening her job if she did not have sex with him. Wood complained to Stein at the time but did not press formal charges. Stein was the City Council president, with Daniels employed as his press secretary and Wood employed as Daniels's assistant. As the controversy heated up Daniels acknowledged he had gone to Stein's office to tell people there that if they were circulating the harassment charges, he would fight back; he also denied all charges. About ten months after Wood's complaint to Stein, Daniels left the staff to take another job. The National Organization for Women criticized Dinkins for making the appointment after learning of the accusation, which the organization maintained, showed insensitivity as well as reinforcing the idea that harassment charges were not taken seriously. Some called the entire episode political, viewing Stein as a possible future mayoral candidate and speculating that Stein leaked the story to damage Dinkins. Stein denied leaking the story, adding that he eased Daniels out of his job after Wood came to him with her complaint. Dinkins responded by asking the City Department of Investigation to look into the harassment charges. A scheduled rally in Harlem in support of Daniels was abruptly canceled. An aide to Daniels said pressure was being applied by City Hall for the newly named deputy mayor to step down. The next day Daniels did indeed step down. By then Stein had said he believed Wood when she brought him her complaint but admitted he did nothing except hint to Daniels that he look for another job.[26]

A little over a week later Wood, then a television reporter, publicly told her side of the story as she felt her character was at stake and she wanted to set the record straight. She said she had not leaked the story. In their workplace Daniels used to brush by her often in their small work area, proclaimed himself her mentor, and asked her out on dates. She grew more and more uncomfortable. One night he walked her to the subway, where he propositioned her graphically and explicitly. After this rebuke Daniels withheld work from her, refused her assignments, and ignored her. Wood's uncle, Bob Teague, a news reporter, visited Daniels to complain. After that visit Daniels said to Wood, "Do you think your uncle can scare me? He can't scare me." Wood finally quit. Stein's staff encouraged her to file a formal complaint; however, she did not as she had once complained about harassment from a coworker at RKO radio back in 1983. Wood found that procedure demeaning and felt herself questioned in a humiliating way. Daniels continued to deny, claiming her story was "sick, it's pathetic, she's lying." Countered Wood, "It's all about power. Randy Daniels pressured me to have a relationship with him outside the work place so that I could have a good relationship inside the work place. He held my job over my head."[27]

On the other coast Los Angeles City Council member Nate Holden came under fire in October 1992 when Carla Cavalier, a former staffer of Holden's, instituted legal action against him that charged sexual harassment. Cavalier quit her post of field deputy in April that year after being employed for four years. She contended that she had been subjected to demeaning, sexually laden remarks from Holden and men on his staff from her first day on the job. She started as a receptionist. According to her statement, Holden's conduct ranged from suggestive comments at work to fondling. The more she resisted the worse the situation got. The harassment took place almost daily in Holden's City Hall office and every time she saw Holden after she was promoted to deputy in one of his field offices. Cavalier resigned in April after her supervisor told her she would be fired for being "rude and insulting" to Holden if she did not resign. Asked why she had not complained during the four years, she replied that she feared losing her job. "I was afraid of being blacklisted. I was afraid of the consequences," explained Cavalier. At one point she sought advice from the city's commission on the Status of Women and worked up the nerve to sign a complaint. However, she backed out after hearing people talk in a very negative way about a woman who had accused another council member's chief deputy of harassment.[28]

At a press conference Holden denied the charges, claiming that they were politically motivated at a time when he was thinking of running for mayor of Los Angeles. He also alleged that Cavalier's lawyer, Melanie Lomax, concocted charges as revenge because he had not attended a City Council meeting that Lomax deemed important. He vowed to file a defamation suit against Cavalier. A senior aide to Holden said Cavalier was fired because of repeated complaints by constituents about her demeanor. "Cavalier's body language and attitude were not conducive to good relationships," said Geneva Cox, although she would not specify what she meant. Cox added that she concluded after listening to staffers discuss the Hill hearings that Cavalier "had a negative attitude about men." Holden claimed he hired her only because she was out of work and he knew her family. "I don't think she could type," he said. After promoting her, he found "she couldn't get in step."

Other evidence then began to surface. Betty Pleasant-Miller was Holden's press secretary until she resigned in August. She quit in disgust, she said, over Holden's treatment of younger female staffers. Although she herself had not been harassed, she watched as other women were. Holden classified Pleasant-Miller as a disgruntled former employee who resigned after she was threatened with being fired.

Another woman, who did not want her name used, told of being harassed by Holden, of his rubbing her thigh, of being regularly required to fend off attempts to grab her and attempts to massage her back. This woman quit her job after six months, saying, "I hated it. Every day was hell."

Holden denied both stories. Sergeant Dominic Licavoli of the Los Angeles Police Department, a friend of Cavalier's, said she confided in him about Holden's behavior before she left his employ. "I encouraged her to bring it out in public, but she felt she couldn't win against a powerful politician like Nate Holden," said Licavoli, who described Cavalier as credible and concerned about the constituents. Lomax contended that other unnamed women had corroborated Cavalier's charges and that Holden had been specifically named as a harasser in a recent anonymous survey of city employees on sexual harassment conducted by the city's Commission on the Status of Women. That survey remained unreleased, with Lomax demanding it be made public.[29]

Elaborating on the lawsuit, Cavalier explained that her case was repeatedly rejected by lawyers, many of whom did business with the city and feared offending Holden. Due to this it took six months after resigning before she went public. Cavalier had not previously known Lomax, only calling her after seeing her on television. Harassment by Holden was, according to Cavalier, widely known and discussed at City Hall and mostly tolerated. "I did a lot of soul searching before I did this," she said. "The only thing that keeps me going is I know I'm telling the truth."[30]

A couple of weeks later the anonymous woman who alleged harassment by Holden went public and commenced legal action against him. In her statement Connie Collins said she was subjected to demeaning remarks, including requests for sexual favors, from Holden and some of his male staffers. According to Collins, she had complained verbally to Holden, to coworkers, and to others in City Hall during her six months on the job but never filed a formal complaint. Holden denied the charges and said that she had never complained to him. One of the reasons Collins came forward was that she became angry after Holden attacked Cavalier. "What he did to me, to Carla, to numerous other women was wrong. This guy is a repeat offender and he needs to be stopped in his tracks."[31]

The following month Holden announced he would be a mayoral candidate in 1993. At a council meeting more than 100 members of the Women's Action Coalition, formed in the wake of the Clarence Thomas hearings, demonstrated against him. When he met with the group members he told them that Cavalier and Collins had made advances to him, saying, "It was just the reverse. . . . I can prove that they hit on me." However, a spokesperson for Holden said the women would not listen and termed their attitude as "hostile." The group said it would continue to campaign against Holden, promising to do "everything in our power to prevent him from becoming mayor."[32]

Another charge against Holden surfaced in January 1993 when another former employee, Marlee Beyda, charged him with harassment in a lawsuit. According to Beyda, Holden touched her buttocks, legs, and

stomach; forced kisses on her; put her hand on his penis while he masturbated; performed other lewd acts; and promised her job advancement in
exchange for sexual favors. The harassments, she said, took place on at least
50 occasions during her nearly one and a half years of employment, which
ended in September 1992. Holden called her charges "all lies," accusing
Beyda and her attorney of blackmail by demanding a settlement in return
for not pursuing the complaint. Los Angeles police officials said they investigated the blackmail accusation and found it "not to be true." Of Beyda,
Holden also claimed he had rejected her advances; "I had to run around
my desk to get away from her. . . . I think she had a crush on me."[33]

The situation got nastier the following month when Holden filed a
countersuit for slander and libel against Cavalier. In March members of the
Women's Action Coalition attended a public council meeting to protest the
lack of an investigation into the charges against Holden. They waited for
nearly four hours to be called on during the public comment portion of the
meeting. But then Holden abruptly left the council chambers, causing the
meeting to be adjourned for lack of a quorum. Angry at this turn of events,
the dozen or so women marched down the hall to his office chanting, "Stop
sexual violence! Break the code of silence!" Holden and aides locked their
door, turned out the lights, and refused to come out. The women remained,
pounding on the door until police were called to disperse them. On the
very day these women were denied the right to be heard the Los Angeles
City Council had celebrated Women's History Month. A few days later the
women were back at another council meeting. When one of them asked
the council to formally investigate the harassment charges, council member Zev Yaroslavsky asked council president John Ferraro whether such
"personal accusations" did not violate council rules. Ferraro then announced
that if the next speakers used any names in their comments about sexual
harassment, they would be "cut off." At the meeting's close council member Ruth Galanter told the women that under the city charter council was
powerless to investigate one of its own, that elected officials were answer-
able to no one except the voters, and that any council member could
violate city rules with impunity, provided such violation was not a criminal
act. As soon as the Women's Action Coalition members stepped outside
the council chambers, five of them—identified by Holden and staff—were
arrested, handcuffed, and taken away by police on suspicion of disturbing
the peace on the day of the previous council meeting. With two lawsuits
in process against Holden, and more expected, the City of Los Angeles is,
and will be, a defendant. Even though the city claimed to be powerless to
act against Holden, it may very well pay for his behavior. In the April election Holden finished well down the pack in the field of 24 running for
mayor, garnering a single-digit vote total.[34]

On November 3, 1992, Senator Robert Packwood won reelection to the

Senate from Oregon. The Republican had at that time served 24 years in the Senate, acquiring along the way the reputation of being a champion of women's issues. Perhaps fortunately for him electorally, a sexual harassment story that had first surfaced in October was too incomplete to be publicly aired before election day. Thus the public did not learn of the charges until late in November when the story was too late to have any effect on the voting. Packwood displayed the classical tactics of a harasser. First he completely denied the allegations. Then he attempted to impugn and smear the women making the charges, presumably relying on his greater power and public visibility to carry the day. Finally he tried to pass this behavior off—which he had already denied totally—as the fault of something else; in this case he tried to blame alcohol, even though most of the alleged harassment had taken place when alcohol was not involved. Then he tried to dismiss the charges as a political move against him.

The *Washington Post* began investigating the story early in October after Florence Graves, a freelance journalist, contacted the paper with information gathered for an article in another publication about sexual harassment on Capitol Hill. According to former staff members and lobbyists, Packwood, from his earliest days on the Hill, had been making uninvited sexual advances to women. Accounts were collected from ten women, independently of each other, who said his approaches were uninvited and unreciprocated. In some cases the behavior took place when he had been drinking. Several said he was abrupt, grabbing them without warning, kissing them forcefully, and continuing until they made it very clear they were not interested or they pushed him away. None of the women claimed the senator had punished them for rejecting him, but nonetheless several did quit their jobs within months of being harassed. None made formal complaints, fearing that nobody would believe them and that their careers might suffer. Several former employees stated that Packwood's behavior created an atmosphere of tension and resentment in the workplace, particularly in the late 1970s and early 1980s. More experienced employees advised newer female staffers to avoid working alone after hours with the senator.[35]

The earliest account of harassment went back to 1969, when Julie Williamson was employed in Packwood's Portland office. One afternoon early in that year the senator walked in and kissed her on the back of the neck. She told him never to do that again. He followed her to another room, where he grabbed at her clothes, pulled on her ponytail, stood on her toes, and tried unsuccessfully to remove her girdle. She quit her job within weeks. During the mid–1970s Jean McMahon met with Packwood on two separate occasions to discuss writing a speech for him. Of the second meeting McMahon said, "I can remember being chased around the table and being grabbed and kissed once." Two people stated she told them of the senator's advances at the time. Paige Wagers was a clerk in the senator's Washington office in 1976 when he called her into his office. After locking the door behind her, he embraced her, stroked her hair, and forcefully kissed her on the lips. She said, "It was very clear that it was a sexual thing. It was very hard to get him to let go of me." After the incident Wagers was told such harassment had happened before. She was warned not to go into his office alone. Five years later Wagers, then employed by the Labor Department, was subjected to a second tussle with Packwood in a room in the Capitol building. Five people recalled being told by the woman of one or the other incident. Friends advised Wagers not to complain because she, instead of the senator, would be the one to suffer. In 1982 an unnamed 21-year-old clerical on Packwood's staff was invited into his office to talk. He pulled her out of her chair, tried to kiss her, and stuck his tongue in her mouth. Explaining why she did not complain she remarked, "I wasn't important enough for anybody to believe. . . . I didn't know where to turn. I didn't know who to complain to, and he would probably just deny it, have me fired, and that's all that I needed at the time." According to 22-year-old college intern Maura C. Roche, when she was in his inner office in the fall of 1989 Packwood read from a binder several sexually explicit jokes to her. The senator and his wife, Georgie Packwood, separated in 1990 and divorced in 1991. When apprised of these charges she responded, "I have been aware of these allegations for many years. It does not come as any surprise to me."[36]

When the *Washington Post* first contacted the senator's office in October about the charges, the first response came from Packwood's chief of staff, Elaine Franklin, who claimed that they were all politically motivated and that the newspaper's inquiry was a "witch hunt." The first meeting between the paper and the senator took place on October 29, when he was confronted with six specific accounts. Packwood denied everything, even claiming not to remember McMahon at all. He was given time to respond as he said he wanted to review his records to gather any information that might "tend to detract from the credibility" of the females identified to him. Early in November the senator sent the *Post* statements about three of the accusers. He and his staffers had asked people who knew some of the women to write statements about them. None of these statements dealt with the specific incidents but were essentially character assassinations. Some suggested that some of the women were attracted to Packwood, may have invited his advances, or were untruthful. Several contained potentially embarrassing descriptions about purported aspects of the accuser's personal lives and sexual backgrounds.[37]

One statement regarding Julie Williamson was submitted by Ann Elias, a friend of Julie's and wife of James A. Elias, who had run Packwood's 1968 campaign. Ann offered the opinion that Julie had wanted a romantic relationship with the senator. Missing from the statement was the fact that an upset and distraught Julie had come to Ann Elias's apartment in 1969 to tell her that Packwood had sexually harassed her that day. When a *Post* reporter asked Ann about this, she acknowledged the visit had been made. She did not include it in the statement because, she said, she had not been asked for details.[38]

Another of those harassed was Mary Heffernan, founder of the Oregon chapter of the National Abortion Rights Action League. During a visit to the senator's office in the early 1980s, he grabbed her and kissed her. She did not complain because she felt she could not afford to alienate a key senator. Mabsie Walters, former president of Heffernan's group, revealed that Packwood called her on November 9 to ask about Heffernan. The senator asked her if it was not true that Heffernan had had a nervous breakdown. Walters said not that she had ever heard. Heffernan stated, "There is absolutely nothing like that in my history." Walters did not understand the reason for that conversation until two weeks later when she saw the *Post* article, which caused her to conclude about Packwood, "I believe he was looking for detrimental information about one of the alleged victims." It was also revealed about Julie Williamson that a Packwood friend warned her in the spring of 1991 that her private life would be made public if she accused the senator. Allegedly Ann Elias phoned Williamson in May to deliver the warning that she best not go public. Elias, when contacted, declined to comment.[39]

As the sheer number of accusers increased, the Packwood strategy shifted. On November 20 the senator issued a vague statement that included a kind of apology. It read, in part, "I will not make an issue of any specific allegation. . . . If any of my comments or actions have indeed been unwelcome or if I have conducted myself in any way that has caused any individual discomfort or embarrassment, for that I am sincerely sorry." The statement stopped short of admitting he had made any uninvited sexual advances.[40]

Pressure for the senator to resign came from the Oregon Democratic Party as well as various women's groups. Maintaining his silence, Packwood had an aide inform the media that he would not resign. Franklin issued a statement that tried to gloss over her boss's crude and ugly smear tactics. It read, in part, "It is not now his intention to publicly discredit or criticize the women or their allegations." Some women leaders, believing Packwood to be a women's issues advocate, called for only mild action. Judith Lichtman, president of the Women's Legal Defense Fund, recommended only an investigation by the Senate Ethics Committee, and Harriet Woods, president of the National Women's Political Caucus, suggested that a confession and apology by Packwood might be sufficient.[41]

At the end of November Packwood issued a statement that claimed

drinking may have partially explained his behavior. He then entered an alcohol treatment facility to be evaluated, saying, "If I take the proper steps
I hope my past conduct is not unforgivable." At least two of his victims,
Roche and Williamson, were not satisfied with the senator's latest ruse.
Said Williamson, the statement "appears to be an attempt to blame his behavior on alcohol," but "in the situation I was in, there was no alcohol involved. . . . I would like to see Bob Packwood removed from a position
where he can harm women."[42]

Coming to his defense was James Glassman, editor of Capitol Hill's
Roll Call newspaper, who called some of the allegations stale due to their
age. Glassman suggested the matter be referred only to the Senate's newly
created Office of Fair Employment Practices instead of the Ethics Committee. Both groups were self-policing bodies; however, in the former case
the investigation was carried out in secret. Neither group did any more
than administer a wrist slap. Packwood, like all members of Congress, was
exempt from being charged with sex discrimination under Title VII of the
Civil Rights Act of 1964. Congress had exempted itself from that measure,
and others, at the time of passage.[43]

On December 1 the Senate Ethics Committee announced it would
open a preliminary inquiry into the allegations against Packwood to decide
if a full inquiry would be held. At the same time Roberta Ulrich, a reporter
for the Portland *Oregonian*, disclosed that the senator had unexpectedly
kissed her on the lips the previous March. "I considered it totally improper
and inappropriate. I have been in this business a long time and never have
I had a public official do something like that," she declared.[44]

Just one day later new charges of sexual harassment were leveled at
Packwood by five more women, who filed a complaint with the Senate
Ethics Committee. Details and the names of these women were not publicly released by the Oregon Coalition Against Domestic and Sexual Violence, which filed on behalf of the women. The incidents allegedly took
place from the 1960s through the 1980s. The coalition had established a
telephone hotline to allow women who had been accosted by the senator
to come forward. It was through this method that the five new females
were found. Oregon women's groups were worried the Ethics Committee
would put on a sham hearing with no more than a mild rebuke to Packwood
at most. By filing more complaints, the coalition hoped to put the Senate
on notice that there were far more women out there victimized by Packwood than the ten previously identified.[45]

Generally women's groups adopted a harder line toward Packwood as
evidence against him continued to mount. The Oregon chapter of the National Abortion Rights Action League — which had supported his reelection bid — wanted him forced from office. Diana Lynn, the group's director
said, "If I had known, if the board had known how he had been treating

women for 24 years, he would not have got the endorsement. . . . If he'd really believed in women's rights he would never have smeared the women involved." Former Oregon supreme court justice Betty Roberts echoed the thoughts of many that Packwood had engaged in a "deliberate attempt" to deceive voters by delaying publication of the charges until after the election. Roberts called on him to resign or face a possible recall effort. Worries about receiving any justice at the hands of the Ethics Committee continued to increase. Fred Wertheimer of Common Cause urged that an independent investigator be appointed. The most serious penalty the Senate could impose—expulsion—had not been invoked by the Senate in more than 100 years. Retired Oregon supreme court justice Hans Linde expressed those fears when he offered the opinion that if Packwood was seated and the Senate went "ahead with the investigation, I would think it extremely unlikely that punishment later would be anything more than censure."[46]

Yet another accusation emerged later that month when Tiffany Work alleged Packwood fondled her buttocks and improperly touched two other teenage girls in 1973 when Work was 13 years old. The teens had been hired to pass out campaign literature. In a statement Packwood termed this latest charge "an outrageous lie."[47]

On December 10 Packwood held his first press conference on the issue. While refusing to discuss the allegations in detail or to comment on his efforts to smear his accusers, he did apologize and said, "My actions were just plain wrong and there is no better word for it. . . . I just didn't get it. I do now. . . . The important point is that my actions were unwelcome and insensitive. These women were offended, appropriately so, and I am truly sorry." He maintained the Work charge was a lie and stated he would not resign from the Senate. Sensing the profound cynicism and manipulation inherent in the senator's remarks, Patricia Ireland, president of the National Organization for Women, called for him to step down. "I certainly think he has abused his public trust," she said. Harriet Woods now took a much more militant line, saying of his press conference, "I thought he was trying to save his political life but was not yet dealing with the lives of the women he victimized."[48]

More problems for Packwood arose at the beginning of January 1993, when two of his staff members resigned alleging they were ordered to solicit campaign funds, an action they considered unethical or illegal. Senate rules allowed two or three specially designated staffers to receive, solicit, and distribute campaign funds, but neither of the two accusers was so designated.[49]

An umbrella organization of women's and other groups, the Oregonians for Ethical Representation, mailed a petition to the Senate Rules and Administration Committee in mid–December requesting Packwood not be formally seated on January 5 with the new Congress but barred as he had won the election by "fraud on the voters." The chair of that committee, Wendell H. Ford, issued a statement that the request would be considered by the full Senate after it reconvened. By then, of course, Packwood and all the others would be formally seated.[50] About two dozen members of the National Organization for Women demonstrated in front of the Capitol on January 4 in a last-ditch unsuccessful attempt to prevent Packwood from being formally seated the following day.[51]

More allegations charging Packwood with sexual harassment had brought the number of women accusing him up to a total of 23 by February 1993. The secret investigation into the matter by the Senate Ethics Committee remained ongoing at this writing. The findings of this investigation were not expected until at least late 1993.[52]

The disgraceful and shabby treatment of Anita Hill angered and enraged many women. One was Carol Moseley Braun of Illinois, who stated that was the reason she entered the race for her state's Senate seat. After defeating incumbent Alan J. Dixon in the Democratic primary, she went on to victory in the November 1992 general election, thus becoming the first black female U.S. senator. Even before being formally seated on the following January 5, Braun's behavior had raised grave doubts. After having campaigned on a "single working mother" image, she moved into a $3,000-a-month Chicago lakefront penthouse, reportedly receiving special treatment in the lease and paying below-market value. While most newly elected senators were using the time between election and formal seating to prepare for their roles, Braun was spending most of that time on an overseas vacation. As a result when she took office she had not hired a chief of staff, relying on almost a dozen holdovers from the defeated Dixon's staff to run her office. On that vacation she took her son and campaign manager, Kgosie Matthews, flying back on the expensive Concorde and then from New York to Chicago on a private plane owned by an Illinois lawyer. Braun paid for none of this traveling until, under pressure, she agreed to pay the lawyer three first-class fares for the final leg of the trip.

Most important was the fact that two female staffers alleged that Matthews had sexually harassed them while campaign manager. Initially Braun said she and Matthews were just "best friends." Finally she admitted they were dating. As a result of the harassment allegations Braun hired a lawyer—whom they both admitted was a staunch supporter—to investigate. This probe was conducted in secret; with no results being made public. Braun did say that this probe showed the allegations had no merit. Braun also denounced her two former aides. A perhaps understandably embarrassed women's movement remained unusually quiet. Neither Harriet Woods nor Patricia Ireland offered any criticism. Ireland went so far as to brush off some of the charges as politically inspired. Had a male senator dealt with harassment charges leveled against his manager in the same fashion as Braun had, he would have been severely and justifiably scored, particularly by women's groups.[53]

Alaska state senator George Jacko phoned the Juneau police at 4:30 A.M. one morning. He identified himself as a state legislator and asked the police to help him get into the motel room of a female legislative aide. When the dispatcher asked why, Jacko refused to explain, saying only that it was confidential. The police declined to assist. The call came only after repeated knocks on the motel room door and requests to the desk clerk for a key had yielded no results. Soon other allegations of harassment surfaced against Jacko. An aide for another state senator received a note from Jacko in which he offered to change his vote on a bill in exchange for a date. Another female was followed home by Jacko when she was a 17-year-old page. Jacko forced his way into her home and left only when a roommate appeared. Women picketed the capitol steps in Juneau, demanding a more speedy investigation. Police in Juneau are reportedly at work on the case. Jacko denied all charges, refused to discuss any allegations, and offered the thought that he might have a drinking problem.[54]

Louisiana state representative David Armstrong of New Orleans kept a temporary residence in Baton Rouge at the Howard Johnson Plaza-Suite Hotel while the legislature was in session. That is, until the hotel banned him in May 1993 to protect its female staff from Armstrong's repeated sexual harassments. Prior to the ban hotel manager Rick Smith said he had stopped sending housekeeping employees to the room alone as several told of Armstrong greeting them wearing little clothing, or of being naked, or making various sexual gestures, and of inviting them to join him in sexual activities.[55]

With great fanfare in June 1991 the provincial government of Ontario, Canada, appointed Carlton Masters as agent general in New York, the province's senior official in the United States, overseeing trade and investment relations. Just one year later the Ontario government placed him on leave pending the investigation of harassment complaints. Based on interviews with Masters and several female employees in New York and Boston, the report prepared by an outside agency stated the investigators "accept the evidence of the complainants." Initially the government kept the affair quiet, attempting to negotiate with Masters. The deal was to give him an equivalent post and salary back in Toronto. The sticking points were whether Masters would have to apologize and whether he would report directly to Ontario premier Bob Rae. With no deal reached, Masters tendered his resignation in December 1992, having negotiated a severance package that included an agreement that the report remain private. Opposition political parties in the province raised such a storm of protest that Rae was ultimately forced to make the report public.[56]

13
Surveys and Laws

It is impossible to state just how prevalent the sexual harassment of women in the workplace was in the past since surveys of the problem are a recent undertaking. That it is tremendously widespread at present and the source of much needless anxiety and worse for women is attested to by these various surveys. Most concern the United States, but the surveys done of women in other countries indicate harassment varies little from one country to another, just as the way males deal with the problem — by not dealing with it at all — varies little across cultures. And although the prevalence of harassment in the past is unknown, there is nothing to indicate it was less pervasive. Given that workers had even less rights and less ability to redress grievances in the past than they do today, and given that women were farther removed from equality in the past than they are today, it seems reasonable to speculate that sexual harassment may have been a more pervasive problem in the past than at present. It seems unlikely that it would have been more infrequent in the old days.

Although the first survey of harassment did not take place until 1975, there was an earlier mention as to the extent and existence of the problem in the 1963 book *Women View Their Working World*. In it 107 women were asked about their concerns and problems at work. One item mentioned was "fresh men." In a comparison between male and female bosses those respondents said that "women bosses are never wolves."[1]

A decade later, in October 1973, 300 female workers in New York City formed a group called Women Office Workers (WOW). Within a few years more than a dozen independent organizations of office workers had arisen in cities across the country. Among the many issues of concern that they addressed was women's need to speak out against and seek protection from sexual harassment by male supervisors. WOW worked closely with another group, the Working Women United Institute (WWUI), to reveal the extent of sexual harassment in various occupations, especially among office workers, and the extent to which job security was dependent on how well the woman worker satisfied her employer as a sex object instead of as a worker. When WOW surveyed 15,000 office workers in 1975, 33 percent reported sexual abuse, including threats of dismissal if they refused to comply with their bosses's advances. The vast majority of women were not members of trade unions, but even those who were could expect no help from that quarter. According to WOW, these male-dominated unions were unlikely to provide any support for women who brought forward complaints of harassment. Among the very few unions actively fighting against harassment in the workplace on behalf of their members were the American Federation of State, County, and Municipal Employees and the Association of Flight Attendants. Even for these unions success was notably lacking. Fear of reprisals kept many women from speaking out in the first place. For those who did all too often arbitrators dismissed the complaints for "lack of evidence." In October 1975 the Screen Actors Guild set up a morals complaint bureau that was designed to arbitrate charges of harassment. Later this union wrote a prohibition against conducting job interviews outside of the office into its contract.[2]

Redbook magazine published a questionnaire on the problem, inviting its readers to fill it out and send it in. When the magazine published the results in 1976, it had received more than 9,000 replies. More than 92 percent reported sexual harassment as a problem; 88 percent reported they had personally experienced one or more forms of unwanted sexual harassment on the job; and almost 50 percent of these women said they or somebody they knew had left or been fired from a job because of sexual harassment. At Cornell University in 1975 the Women's Section of the Human Affairs Program distributed what was reported to be the first questionnaire ever devoted solely to the issue of sexual harassment. A total of 155 women responded, with 92 percent calling it a serious problem. Seventy percent of the respondents had personally experienced some form of harassment, and 56 percent of that group (39 percent of the total) reported being subjected to physical harassment. The Cornell study concluded that "75 percent of the time that the harassment was ignored it eventually worsened and about one-fourth of the women who ignored it were eventually hit with on-the-job penalties for not responding."[3]

Lin Farley, previously of WWUI, commented that "my experience indicates that, in any group of ten working women, five to seven have had experiences of this kind. That's one half to two-thirds of all the women in the work force." For some surveys this proved to be definitely on the low side. When the WWUI did a survey, it found that more than 80 percent of their respondents had experienced sexual harassment at least once, that women on lower salaries were more likely to experience physical harassment, and that if ignored, the behavior continued or became worse. But if these women did complain, they faced retaliation in the form of increased work loads, complaints about the quality of their work, and poor job evaluations.[4]

Reporting on a 1980 study of Illinois government workers, Barbara Hayler said that 59 percent of the respondents reported experiencing one or more incidents of sexual harassment in their present place of employment; these ranged from suggestive looks to sexual remarks to propositions to coercive sex. Respondents were asked to report only those incidents of unwanted sexual attention that made them feel humiliated or threatened. Fifty-two percent were subjected to teasing or sexual remarks, 41 percent received suggestive looks or leers, 25 percent were physically touched or grabbed, 20 percent were the targets of sexual propositions, 14 percent experienced repeated pressure to engage in personal relationships, 9 percent reported other miscellaneous items, and 2 percent were subjected to some type of coercive sex. As most females reported more than one type of harassment, the total is greater than 100 percent. With regard to the consequences of not cooperating or not tolerating this abuse, 6 percent of these women were denied promotions, 14 percent said a promotion denial happened to someone they knew; 3 percent were transferred involuntarily, 10 percent knew of such other cases of transfer, 3 percent were fired, 13 percent knew of other women being fired, and 7 percent quit their jobs as a result of the abuse.[5]

In a Los Angeles study released around the same time 53 percent of the women surveyed reported being subjected to sexual harassment at work. Thirty-three percent reported experiencing some type of negative consequences due to repulsing such advances, and 10 percent reportedly quit their jobs to avoid the problem.[6]

When a telephone survey was conducted of 139 unskilled female auto workers in 1982, 36 percent of those women reported having experienced harassment. A small 1981 survey of female coal miners revealed that 53 percent had been propositioned by a boss, 76 percent had been propositioned by a coworker, and 17 percent had experienced a physical attack. Looking at some of these studies, observer Suzanne Carothers concluded that traditional women's work was more likely to be characterized by, as an extreme, the threat of losing a job for refusing to comply with sexual demands. The sexually demeaning work environment was the more typical method of harassment for women working in previously all male workplaces. In white-collar environments the harassment was mostly verbal, whereas in blue-collar environments it was mostly physical — talk versus touch.[7]

One of the largest surveys undertaken on the issue was done by the Merit Systems Protection Board of the U.S. government, an office that handled the employment grievances of civilian government employees, in response to a request from Congress. This board conducted a random survey of 23,000 male and female employees in the federal workplace covering the period from 1978 to 1980. When the government released the results in March 1981, they showed that 42 percent of the female respondents had experienced some form of overt sexual harassment during the period covered by this survey. With regard to the severity of the issue a further 42 percent of those surveyed placed sexual harassment in employment in the same category of other major sex-related social problems affecting the status of women; family violence, rape, and incest. Sixteen percent of the women stated they had lost a promotion or job or had quit a government position because of the abuse.[8]

Extrapolating the findings of this study to the workplace population of 42 million women, one commentator predicted that over the following year 21,000 of those women would face rape or attempted rape in the workplace, with 20 percent of them reporting more than one occurrence; 164,000 women would be pressured for sexual favors or receive unwanted letters or calls; and 315,000 could expect pressure for dates. Another 500,000 would be subjected to unwanted touching at work, while a second 500,000 would experience suggestive looks. Seven million would have to put up with sexual remarks in the workplace. Breaking sexual harassment down into age categories, this study found that 67 percent of teen females experienced some harassment on the job, 59 percent of 20- to 24-year-olds, 53 percent of 25- to 34-year-olds, 43 percent of 35- to 44-year-olds, 33 percent of 45- to 54-year-olds, and 22 percent of those aged 55 and older. The most commonly found harasser was an older married white man who was an equal coworker. Of harassed white women 75 percent said the perpetrator was white; of harassed black women 53 percent said the perpetrator was white. The Merit Board stated that this sexual harassment cost the U.S. economy more than $10 million annually in lowered productivity, wasted training, higher staff turnover, lowered morale, and increased costs for health and psychiatric care for the victims of harassment.[9]

All women who worked had to do so with the expectation that they would likely experience on-the-job sexual harassment at some time. For many females it would be part of their daily work environment. After studying the issue, the Center for Women Policy Studies concluded that however one defined sexual harassment, narrowly or broadly, it was one of the most serious employment problems facing women. The center continued, "In the restrictions which it imposes on women, it is the means as well as the message, paralleling in the workplace methods found in society as a whole for subduing and directing the aspirations of women." The center felt this was indicated by the results of studies and court cases that showed the heavy involvement of supervisory personnel in the most serious forms of overt sexual harassment as well as the most subtle sex discrimination. "It is also shown by the indifference, unwillingness, inability, and even opposition which is often shown by management to providing relief for victims of even extreme forms of harassment, not to mention to providing a harassment-free and egalitarian work environment."[10]

When Jerry Jacobs studied the issue in the late 1980s, he concluded that women in male-dominated occupations reported more harassment than females in sex-neutral or female-dominated jobs. Harassers were both supervisors and coworkers. Half of the women in white-collar female-dominated jobs who considered switching to blue-collar male-dominated positions expected they would be subjected to harassment. In the female-dominated areas Jacobs said harassment often involved unwanted sexual advances and pressure for dates, with rejection leading to possible retaliation that included the threat of being fired. In male-dominated jobs harassment usually involved a sexually demeaning work environment that included pinups on the walls, unwanted physical contact, slurs, jokes, and the sabotage of the women's work. Jacobs noted that sexual harassment had a cost attached, having been shown to cause psychological and emotional problems, lowered job satisfaction, loss of motivation, negative attitudes toward coworkers and supervisors, a lower sense of job competence, and high absenteeism and turnover. "When harassment has the intent or effect of inhibiting women from entering male-dominated occupations or inducing them to leave, then harassment becomes a mechanism of social control that promotes sex segregation in the workplace," he added.[11]

Reporting from England in 1985, Cynthia Cockburn said that researchers found two types of sexual harassment, one for females in traditional women's work and one for those who crossed over into previously all male terrain. In the traditional occupations harassment occurred more often as hints and requests for dates that, if repulsed, were followed by retaliation. In male-dominated employment the harassment was said to be more openly hostile from the start. Cockburn felt the motive for harassment in traditional jobs was the exploitation of role and power differences, whereas in male-dominated workplaces the abuse was a defense by male workers against what they took to be an implicit challenge to their masculine power and work roles.[12]

The Merit Systems Protection Board did a second study on sexual harassment in the federal government workplace covering the years 1985 to 1987, seven years after the first survey. When the board released the results, they showed that 42 percent of the women working for the federal government said they had been sexually harassed during the two-year period, exactly the same proportion as in the previous study. Harassment came in the form of pressure for sexual favors, 9 percent; phone calls or letters, 12 percent; deliberate touching, 26 percent; suggestive looks, 28 percent; and sexual remarks, 35 percent. Just 5 percent of those subjected to harassment took official action, with the rest believing it would do very little good or perhaps make their work lives even more unpleasant. Although the results from this study closely paralleled those of the first, the cost estimate of harassment was dramatically changed. This time the Merit Board estimated the economic cost of sexual harassment from 1985 to 1987 to the United States at $267 million.[13]

Most surveys of the problem turned up a low rate of attempted rape or assault if they broke down harassment into categories. The Merit Board, which found 42 percent of its respondents had been harassed, reported the extreme form of harassment, attempted or actual rape, at 0.8 percent. In one survey 372 women were asked only if they had ever experienced a sexual assault, an attempted sexual assault, or any kind of forced oral or anal sexual activity by someone the women knew from work. Seventeen percent replied yes. Sixty-six percent of those were attempted assaults. Of the completed assaults 62 percent were sexual intercourse and 38 percent were oral or anal sex. Bosses were responsible for 49 percent of the assaults; coworkers were the assaulters in almost all other cases. Almost 20 percent of those victims quit their jobs, with 20 percent complaining through channels. Only two women both quit and complained. The disparity between the high rate of extreme harassment—assaults and attempts—found in this survey and most other studies where the rate, if given at all, was low may be at least partly explained by one researcher, who found that "many women who have been raped in the course of sexual harassment have been advised by their lawyers not to mention the rape because it would destroy their credibility."[14]

Fortune magazine surveyed some of the top 500 companies in America in 1988. This business magazine sent out a 49-question survey to 160 of those companies. Results indicated that almost 90 percent of the Fortune 500 companies had received complaints of sexual harassment during the preceding 12 months. More than 33 percent had been hit with a lawsuit, and almost 25 percent had been repeatedly sued. Sixty-four percent of company human resource managers agreed that most complaints of harassment were valid. *Fortune* compared that with the results of an 1981 *Redbook/Harvard Business Review* study in which 63 percent of top managers and 52 percent of middle managers were of the opinion that "the amount of sexual harassment at work is greatly exaggerated." Sexual harassment at work cost the typical Fortune 500 company an estimated $6.7 million a year in absenteeism, low morale, low productivity, and employee turnover. Thirty-six percent of the complaints were against the woman's immediate supervisor; 26 percent, against another person with greater power than the harassed; and 38 percent, against equal coworkers. Of the complaints 26 percent involved deliberate touching, 29 percent involved pressure for dates or sexual favors, and 1 percent involved actual or attempted rape.[15]

Even though nearly 9 of every 10 companies had received at least one complaint in the preceding year and 25 of the 160 surveyed had received six or more complaints during that time, it was still a very low number, computed out to be only 1.4 complaints per 1,000 women. However, it was company management being surveyed, not the employees themselves. Therefore only "official" complaints would be cited by these bureaucrats. Freada Klein, an organizational development expert, said, "Employees don't have confidence in the complaint structure. Every employee-attitude survey that we've conducted for the private sector shows at least 15 percent of female employees have been sexually harassed in the last 12 months." Again this is a low figure, but Klein was doing surveys for the company concerned, a fact not lost on employees who might be less likely to be honest than if a completely independent women's group was conducting the survey. The whole issue tended to be sidestepped by companies anyway, with only an estimated 9 percent including a question on sexual harassment in their workplace if and when they conducted general employee surveys. Only 4 percent of companies brought up the issue at exit interviews. Added Klein, "Women are still not complaining early enough because it's not safe to complain. Harassment tends to escalate if it's not stopped promptly. When it does escalate, the victim, is in a double bind. If she finally complains, she can be asked, 'If this has been going on for months, why didn't you come forward sooner?'" *Fortune* indicated that companies with the lowest percentage of women workers reported the highest rate of formal sexual harassment complaints. When females made up less than 25 percent of the work force, the number of complaints numbered about two per 1,000 women. This figure dropped by half when females made up more than 50 percent of the workforce. In those companies with higher proportions of females, "most complaints involve only an inappropriate comment. There are rarely cases of physical contact," stated the magazine.[16]

The *National Law Journal* surveyed 918 female lawyers in 1989. These women were employed by large law firms in Atlanta, Boston, Chicago, Cleveland, Dallas, Houston, Los Angeles, Miami, Philadelphia, New York, San Francisco, Washington, and Tampa. Thirty-three percent of those surveyed made more than $100,000 per year. Sixty percent said they had experienced unwanted sexual attention on the job. Said one, "Most women in my firm could give you examples of sexual discrimination that would curl your hair. I wish I could warn other women law students about picking my firm, but of course, I cannot." Thirteen of these women reported incidents of rape, attempted rape, or assault on the job, mostly by superiors. The majority of these lawyers who were sexually harassed ignored it or dealt with it themselves. Only 7 percent reported it to their firm.[17]

Foreign workers at the United Nations are in the United States on special visas. Once a foreign national stops working for the U.N. she or he loses that visa and has to leave the country within 30 days. At the U.N. Secretariat in the early-to-mid-1970s female workers complained that sexist remarks; comments about how women look, walk, and dress; overfamiliarity; and physical touching were typical of the behavior of men of all nationalities. Some were involved in repeated attempts to use their positions to force women into having sex with them. In mid decade a small group of women formed U.N. Employees for Equal Opportunity (UNEEQ) on a consultative status at the U.N. This group circulated a questionnaire among U.N. staffers that asked, among other things, about sexual harassment at the Secretariat. After about 25 replies from employees were received, the rest of the forms were intercepted by the administration—the U.N. internal messenger system was used. The U.N. Security Service was ordered to undertake a full investigation of the group. When Barbara Rogers, UNEEQ leader, met with Acting Chief of Staff Services Kuo-ho Ching, he complained that the part of the questionnaire dealing with sexual harassment would invite answers that could "create the wrong impression" if they found their way into the wrong hands. Finally a new group was formed, the Ad Hoc Group on Equal Rights for Women, which issued a report in 1976 based on replies to a questionnaire on sexual harassment by 875 women and men. The survey was sanctioned by the administration of the United Nations this time. Half of the respondents, who were employed in professional and clerical capacities, reported they had either personally been subjected to harassment of some type or were aware that such behavior existed within the U.N. As was usually the case most of those harassed were reluctant to formally complain for various reasons, including fear of losing their jobs, fear of antagonizing U.N. officials, and a reluctance to damage the organization's reputation. Approximately one third of those harassed complained about it. Some of those said they were made to pay a penalty for exposing their harassment.[18]

When the British National Association of Local Government Officers conducted a 1982 study in Liverpool, it found that 52 percent of the women surveyed reported having experienced sexual harassment on the job. More than 50 percent of that group experienced the abuse in their present jobs. Harassment covered a wide range of behavior, including remarks and unsolicited physical contact and touching. A survey done in London around the same time found that one out of ten 25- to 34-year-old working women complained of sexual blackmail when it came to promotion. A commission of the European Community found "a large number of women getting unwanted attention from men." In the mid–1980s, 300 working women of Bhopal, India, were surveyed. All were central or state government employees. Twenty-seven percent of the respondents reported being harassed. Noting the difference between private and public employment in India, the study stated that for government workers "cases of sexual harassment are by no means absent, but they are very rare as compared to private service where appointment and dismissal are at the sweet will of the employer."[19]

Another British survey, done by the Inland Revenue Staff Federation, surveyed hundreds of employees, most of them secretaries, in government offices in 1983 in Merseyside. Investigators found that "most women employed in government departments are likely to face sexual harassment at work." Most of the cases were not reported because a superior officer was often the harasser or because management was all male or both.[20]

In the aftermath of the Clarence Thomas hearings the London *Sunday Times* polled 200 women—100 clericals and 100 top professionals—from politics, art, and business. Forty percent said they had been sexually harassed at work at some point, 33 percent of the clericals, 57 percent of the professionals. Those harassed from the latter group included Rabbi Julia Neuberger; Joan Lestor, a Labour member of Parliament; and a number of prominent businesswomen, lawyers, doctors, and scientists. For media personality Anna Raeburn sexual harassment had been a problem since her first job, where her boss put his hand up her skirt. Years later when working at Capital Radio, she confronted a senior manager who was harassing a female switchboard operator and herself, "a feeler." One night he tried to grab her. She had to climb over a desk to get out of the room. After her complaints he stopped the behavior. Margaret Ewing, Scottish member of Parliament for Moray, said that sexual harassment took place in the Commons. "It happened to me when I was younger," she explained. "Quite a lot of the women MPs used to get fed up with these men patting their heads or bottoms. It still happens." Model Kirsten Imrie was so upset by the sexual advances of her employer that she wanted to sue. However, her lawyer told her the court would not believe she had not provoked him. She left that employer, but he made it impossible for her to collect unemployment benefits.[21]

The main British agency that handled serious sexual harassment complaints was the Equal Opportunities Commission. In the five years prior to 1991 it received only a total of 300 complaints. One hundred fifty of those reached an out-of-court settlement, 52 complaints were dropped, and 98 went to a tribunal, with 54 of those being successful.[22]

Management attitude was studied in Canada in 1992 when the results of a survey of 321 chief executive officers of companies that employed more than 1 million Canadians were released. Only a handful of the CEOs were women, but in the companies 36 percent of the work force was female, with 11 percent of senior managers being female. These CEOs were asked, "How do you view the issue of sexual harassment in the workplace?" Fifty-seven percent replied the topic had been blown out of proportion, 31 percent believed it was a "real problem," 17 percent were "somewhere in between," and 5 percent were unsure. In comparison a poll of Canadians taken in October 1991 found that 49 percent felt sexual harassment was a "real problem" that affected the quality of life for working women. The chief executives essentially dismissed harassment as not a serious threat to women when they guessed that only 22 percent of women would be sexually harassed at some point in their working lives. In that October survey 37 percent of the women polled said they had experienced sexual harassment at work. The Merit Board studies showed 21 percent of working females being sexually harassed each and every year. As in the United States the sexual harassment in Canada was estimated to cost the companies millions of dollars each year. Ruth Corbin, vice-president of the organization that conducted the October poll, noted wryly of the CEO data, "The data would indicate that they are not in sync with the general population."[23]

Legal recourse for women in America against sexual harassment was slow in coming given that the behavior had been occurring for centuries. It did arrive fairly rapidly after the issue was given a formal name and became well publicized—which happened beginning in the mid–1970s with the publication of surveys on the issue and case roundups that showed how pervasive the problem was. The militancy of the women fighting harassment was, of course, fueled by the feminist movement, which was fighting to redress any number of grievances. Also deserving of credit were the women who had the courage to initiate those early lawsuits prior to the mid–1970s. Although most of those women lost their cases, a few won, and eventually an appropriate legal path was cleared. Unfortunately there is no indication that sexual harassment of women in the workplace has abated. In individual cases some women win financial settlements and job reinstatements. Most do not. The contempt men feel for women remains. Harassment is still hard to prove. It can take years of time and much expense to go through the legal system. Women living financially from week to week must still think hard and carefully about filing a complaint.

The male overclass treated the entire issue with contempt before and trivialized it by not even recognizing it in law. Now that sexual harassment is recognized in law, the male overclass merely pays it lip service, relying on many powerful factors to ensure that the vast majority of sexual harassment cases never get into a courtroom or even formally filed as complaints. Factors such as blaming the female, getting females to see harassing behaviors as complimentary, and convincing them to see themselves as constantly overreacting (the myth of the hysterical female) and that the harassment was something entirely different. At one time African-Americans had no civil rights by law. They were treated abominably by whites. That was changed by law until they had equal rights in law with whites. They were still treated abominably by whites. So far the same situation obtains with sexual harassment laws. When necessary the male overclass will change what it says but not what it thinks, feels, and does. For the vast majority of females the new laws against sexual harassment in the workplace have been nothing more than smoke and mirrors holding out much but delivering little—business as usual for the male overclass.

Some of the incidents of harassment that came to public attention in the mid–1970s—presumably helping arouse the feminist movement to lobby for the issue to be taken seriously, to be acknowledged as a major issue of concern to women, and to insist on having legal recourse to redress the problem—included an executive secretary to the head of a small business in California. He repeatedly harangued her with tales of his sexual exploits, patted her on the buttocks, and requested blow jobs. After a number of incidents in which he unzipped his pants and exposed himself in front of her, she finally quit this job, which she badly needed financially. Her employer gave her poor work references and would not support her unemployment insurance claim. In a case in a restaurant customers continually grabbed at a waitress's breasts and buttocks or pushed their hands up the short-skirted outfit she was required to wear. When she complained to the manager he told her, "This was all part of her job, that the regular customers had worked out a betting system, with a dollar-value attributed to each part of a waitress's body that they succeeded in giving a 'good feel,' and that this meant business for the restaurant."[24]

A woman factory worker complained to the plant personnel manager about coworkers repeatedly harassing her sexually. The response of the personnel man was to grab her breast. A nurse in a Washington, D.C., hospital described sexual harassment in 1975 as a "working condition between male doctors and female nurses," with patients propositioning as well. Another nurse wrote to columnist Ann Landers complaining about being constantly grabbed by male patients. Lander's response was that the nurse had to be "sending some sort of signals" to provoke these attacks. This reply drew a flood of angry letters from nurses relating similar experiences. Young actress Ann McCurry was abruptly fired in Boston in 1974 from the stage play Lenny. She alleged she had been fired at the demand of the play's male star because she rebuked his sexual advances. Even though this case drew strong feminist support, as a result of publicity, McCurry was not rehired. Actors Equity, her union, was not sympathetic to her complaints. A little later the Screen Actors Guild set up its own morals complaint board to deal with casting-couch complaints. A bank executive told the Wall Street Journal that she had been offered accounts by several prospective clients only if she would agree to "go out" with them.[25]

On a first job out of high school a young woman's 60-year-old boss used to corner her behind the filing cabinets and try to paw her body. She quit. Another young woman employed as a clerk in a retail store was horrified to learn that her boss expected her to entertain his best customers sexually. When she refused she was fired. A reporter noted that "some women have been physically forced down on couches; one woman was called into her employer's office and made to watch as he exposed himself. . . . Some women claim they were told bluntly they would have to perform sexual acts to keep their jobs." One female was threatened with rape; another, as promotion time neared, was invited by her boss to meet him for a drink in the bar of a nearby motel.[26] Author Betty Lehran Harragan stated that she believed "more women are refused employment, fired, or forced to quit salaried jobs as the result of sexual demands and the ramifications thereof than for any other single cause."[27]

In 1975 the WWUI, founded that year in Ithaca, New York, and later relocated to New York City, held a pioneering speakout in Ithaca. About 275 women turned out, with 10 percent willing to risk retaliation and embarrassment by publicly talking of their experiences of being sexually harassed. When Freada Klein, Lynn Wehrli, and Elizabeth Cohn Stuntz worked as rape victim advocates, they answered hundreds of calls reporting on-the-job rapes. Said Klein, "Women would call in desperation, scared to lose their jobs, wondering what they'd done to cause the unwanted advances. But our rape-crisis center—and others—could only do so much. Whoever heard of prosecuting the boss for rape—and winning? And we couldn't respond to the less violent—but extremely traumatic—range of verbal and physical sexual assaults." In response these three women formed the Alliance Against Sexual Coercion in June 1977 in the Boston area. It was said to be the first grass-roots group devoted to providing services to victims of sexual harassment at work.[28]

Few women took their harassers to court in the 1970s, and those who did mostly lost because the courts refused to interpret sexual harassment as sex discrimination. One early case was decided in 1975 in Arizona. Two women alleged they had had to resign their jobs to avoid their superior's repeated sexual and verbal abuse. This man did the same thing to other female employees. It was held by the court that even if they were subjected to the harassment that they alleged, there was no right to relief under the Civil Rights Act. The judge called the supervisor's conduct merely a "personal proclivity, peculiarity or mannerism" for which the employer was not liable. The court also held the supervisor's behavior was not "based on sex" because the harassment might have been directed at males as well.[29]

Paulette Barnes, a payroll clerk for the federal government's Environmental Protection Agency, complained that her superior harassed her for sex with suggestions, remarks, and so forth. After she repeatedly refused him he belittled her, stripped her of job duties, and ultimately abolished her job. She sued under Title VII of the Civil Rights Act. The first court ruled against her, holding she was penalized because she refused her supervisor's sexual advances, not because of her sex. She won on appeal in a 1974 Washington, D.C., decision, but in a narrow way that did not set a general precedent.[30]

Others who fared badly in the legal system were Adrienne Tomkins, who was hired as an office worker in 1971 by the Public Service Electric and Gas Company in New Jersey. Her supervisor asked her to go to lunch with him one day to discuss a promotion. It was simply a ruse for him to make sexual advances toward her. She was detained by the supervisor against her will through the use of economic threats and physical force. Tomkins complained to her superiors about this incident, sought a transfer, and then later accepted a less desirable position with the company. Retaliation by the firm against Tomkins came in the form of disciplinary layoffs along with threats of salary cuts and demotions. Fifteen months after her assault Tomkins was fired by the company. Another was Maxine Munford, who was hired as an assistant collection manager. On her first day at work Glen D. Harris, her supervisor, made sexual suggestions to her, which she rebuffed. Harris indicated to Munford that her job might depend on her compliance. Shortly thereafter Harris told her she would accompany him on a business trip, stay overnight in the same motel room, and have sexual relations with him. Munford refused and was summarily fired. When she protested her dismissal company management supported the termination.[31]

Then the situation in the legal system began to turn around for harassed women. Back in 1970 or 1971 Diane Williams was working as an information specialist for the Community Relations Service of the Justice Department. One supervisor made continual advances toward her, which she always rejected. Then he started to criticize her work and goad her into arguments. After she complained to the agency director, the supervisor confronted her, saying, "I don't know what you are trying to do, but if it comes to a showdown between you and me, you will surely lose, because I am the director's boy." When her complaints to higher management in the agency brought no relief, she filed a formal complaint with the Justice Department. She was then fired from her job in 1972, with a note placed in her personnel file that she had been terminated because she was a malicious gossip. That information would be sent to all other government offices where she happened to apply for jobs. At a Justice Department hearing Williams was dismayed to find many of her coworkers declaring to the examiners that they had "no personal knowledge" of the situation despite the fact they had often talked with her about it. The examiner decided at this 1973 hearing there was no evidence of discrimination. Williams appealed to the courts, the U.S. district court disagreed with the examiner, finding evidence of discrimination. The judge sent the case back for a second hearing. That examiner found evidence of discrimination, but the Justice Department refused to accept his findings. Williams appealed to the courts again, with the same judge, Charles R. Richey, upholding the second examiner. Judge Richey agreed that her personnel file should be purged and that she should get back pay. It was 1976.[32]

In Denver, Colorado, Mary Heelan refused to have sexual relations with her supervisor at the Johns-Manville Corporation. This resulted in her being fired. In spite of her complaints about this and her dismissal, the company did nothing. In 1978 a federal judge of a district court ordered her reinstated with back pay, finding Heelan had been fired for refusing to have sex with her boss. For the first time in court a judge had issued a ruling finding specifically that sexual harassment in the workplace was sex discrimination under Title VII of the 1964 Civil Rights Act.[33]

It was by then established in the courts that sexual harassment that involved a tangible loss (quid pro quo harassment), such as the loss of a job if a sexual demand was not met or the refusal to hire or promote for the same reason, was illegal discrimination under Title VII. Employer liability in these cases was usually affirmed, but not always, and remained somewhat unclear.[34]

The next major step was taken on April 11, 1980, when EEOC chairperson Eleanor Holmes Norton published EEOC regulations explicitly forbidding the sexual harassment of employees by their supervisors. These rules applied to federal, state, and local government agencies and to private businesses with 15 or more employees. Under the rules employers had an "affirmative duty" to prevent and eliminate sexual harassment, which could be "either physical or verbal in nature." Three criteria were laid down to determine whether an action constituted unlawful sexual harassment. "Unwelcome sexual advances" were illegal if an employee's submission was an explicit or implicit condition of employment, if the employee's responses became a basis for employment decisions, or if the advances interfered with workers' performance, creating a "hostile or offensive" environment. Harassment on the basis of sex was declared a violation of Section 703 of Title VII of the Civil Rights Act of 1964.[35]

The concept of "hostile environment" harassment, wherein a female may not suffer economically (such as by being fired or not promoted), was affirmed by the Circuit Court of Appeals for the District of Columbia in 1981 when the court reasoned that a company could harass a woman with impunity by deliberately stopping short of discharging her under the narrow quid pro quo standard. The U.S. Supreme Court in *Meritor Savings Bank v. Vinson* (1986) unanimously affirmed that both types of sexual harassment were prohibited under Title VII. A victim of sexual harassment did not need to demonstrate specific economic harm. This ruling upheld the EEOC guidelines. Those guidelines made an employer liable for the acts of its agents and supervising employees as well as for the acts of coworkers and customers if nothing was done after a complaint was brought to the employer's attention. However, even though the Supreme Court definitely held the employer liable in the case of quid pro quo harassment, it stopped well short of holding an employer automatically liable for hostile environment liability. By the end of 1988 more than 38,500 sexual harassment cases had been filed with the federal government since the 1980 implementation of the EEOC guidelines.[36]

When a victim of harassment brought suit through the EEOC and Title VII, she was limited in the amount of money she could claim to the sum she had lost or been denied such as back pay if fired, salary difference if denied a promotion, medical payments if the harassment caused her to seek health care, and so on. No punitive damages could be sought or awarded. This route was the easiest for women as they incurred no legal fees. Suing civilly meant that punitive damages could be awarded in any amount but that legal costs could also be great. Under the Civil Rights Act of 1991 companies could be held liable for compensatory and punitive damages in sexual harassment claims. For businesses with 15 to 100 employees this amount was capped at $50,000; for companies with more than 500 employees the cap was $300,000.[37]

This step forward for those subjected to harassment, by allowing them punitive and compensatory damages when they proceeded through the Civil Rights acts, is under potential jeopardy due to the decision of the U.S. Supreme Court to review the case of Teresa Harris. From 1985 to 1987 Harris worked as a rental manager for a company that leased forklifts. Her employer, Charles Hardy, once called her a "dumb-ass woman," commented on her clothes, and suggested that she and other female employees pick up objects he had dropped on the floor and that they retrieve coins from his front pants pockets. Complaints by Harris to Hardy failed to stop the behavior. Later Hardy suggested to her that they go to a Holiday Inn to negotiate her raise. Upset and angry Harris quit and sued, contending she had been forced out of her job. She lost, with a judge deciding that even though Hardy was vulgar and crude and Harris may have been genuinely offended, the atmosphere was not so poisoned as to be abusive and intimidating to her. The judge's decision was upheld all the way to the U.S. Sixth Court of Appeals. The Supreme Court agreed to hear Harris's appeal to clarify the definition of sexual harassment to determine whether it need only be behavior that offends a female or whether she must be psychologically damaged by it as well. The Court could in essence change the standard for harassment from that which would offend a "reasonable victim" (virtually all females, of course) to that which would offend a "reasonable person" (which would also include the viewpoint of males, potentially making it even more difficult to win a harassment case in court).[38] Late in 1993 the Supreme Court held for Harris 9 to 0 that a complainant did not have to prove psychological inquiries to win a harassment case.

Australia specifically outlawed sexual harassment in the Sex Discrimination Act of 1984. Cases have also been successfully pursued through the Equal Opportunity Tribunal under the New South Wales Anti-Discrimination Act of 1977. In a 1984 case, Hill v. Water Resources Commission, sexual harassment was held to be discriminatory and preventing it a management responsibility. Also in New South Wales some forms of sexual assault, such as pinching and grabbing, were covered by the Crimes (Sexual Assault) Amendment Act of 1981.[39]

Japan got its first sexual harassment suit late in 1989 when a woman filed a suit seeking damages from her former boss and the publishing company she worked for, claiming "his sexual innuendos forced her to leave the company and give up her career." In April 1992 a Tokyo judge awarded her $12,400 in a ruling that for the first time recognized verbal sexual discrimination as illegal in the Japanese workplace. Although the term *sexual harassment* was not used, the judge recognized sexual discrimination as illegal. Reportedly Japanese women traditionally remained silent about such unwanted behavior from males.[40]

The topic of sexual harassment—abbreviated to *sekuhara* in Japan—became a hot topic in that country around the time of the lawsuit, but this was primarily due to the number of suits filed by women in America against the Japanese subsidiary companies that employed them. Japanese women's magazines featured stories of *sekuhara* victims. Soon the media featured the views of men who offered comments such as "Sexual small talk just eases office relations," and "Women should take sekuhara as a sign that they're still appreciated by men." In spite of the landmark legal case at least one liberal newspaper felt Japan was still not taking the issue of sexual harassment in the workplace very seriously.[41]

Some Japanese bars that specialized in providing hostesses for men took *sekuhara* for their name. The author of a magazine column for female clerical workers said she opposed lawsuits over harassment except in cases of rape or assault. When the female who won the lawsuit first took her complaint to two arbitrators—a male and a female—they told her she should be flattered by the man's attention. For the Japanese women's movement, which was tiny compared to those in other countries, the issue of harassment had arisen only in the previous three years. Women's groups and women in general said that sexual harassment by men was the norm in the workplace. Yukiki Tsunoda, a lawyer in the foregoing case, said, "Sexual harassment is a big problem in Japan." Two other cases about a year earlier in Japanese courts had found for the females. In one a woman received damages after claiming a colleague had threatened her when she refused to go to a hotel with him. The other woman was awarded damages after testifying a man had assaulted her on a business trip. Females won in those actions because the men did not show up in court. In the publishing case the action was vigorously contested, and the behavior consisted entirely of verbal harassments that were not direct threats.[42] In the wake of that case a poll taken by the Labor Ministry of Japan reported that 43 percent of females in management complained of sexual harassment.[43]

In France, it was claimed, "sexual harassment of women workers by their bosses is believed to be widespread. It has now been outlawed." A new clause added to the penal code in 1991 made sexual harassment a criminal offense punishable by up to a year in prison and or a fine of Fr 100,000 ($16,000) "to subject by order, constraint, or pressure favors of a sexual nature" from subordinates at work. According to many women's groups, this new proviso was not as good as it was made out to be. They complained the law was too vague and limited—it did not apply to co-workers of equal rank, for example. These groups felt the law did not make it very easy for women to get redress for harassment. France was the second country in the European Community, after Spain, to enact specific legislation on the issue. In Britain and Ireland there was clear judicial acceptance that sexual harassment could constitute unlawful sex discrimination, but no specific law as such.[44]

Studies done in the EC indicated that about half of all women workers in EC countries had experienced minor sexual harassment such as pats, jokes, and caresses, with 25 percent having been subjected to strong physical or verbal pressure and 3 percent having been victims of violent physical attacks. A majority of women had suffered harassment more than once, with the most frequent victims being women who were most vulnerable socially or occupationally, such as the separated, divorced, or widowed, as their dependence on jobs was greater. Members of groups with little social acceptance or integration, such as women with disabilities, ethnic minorities, and lesbians, were also frequent victims of harassment. These studies also showed that females competing with males at high management levels or those in traditionally male occupations were more exposed to harassment than the average female. A commission of the European Community issued the Code of Good Conduct or Practical Guide aimed at businesses, workers, and unions to cut down on harassment. The guide explained that sexual harassment could be physical, verbal, or "relational"—behavior such as showing pornographic photos, making gestures, whistling and so on. This commission, which existed to help member countries protect employees in the workplace, issued a recommendation to define sexual harassment as follows: "Any behavior that has a sexual character or that is based on sex, related to the dignity of women and men in the work place, is unacceptable if: It is unwanted and the person at whom it is directed finds it offensive; the acceptance or rejection of this behavior motivates, explains, or implies a decision affecting professional advancement or employment, keeping one's job, one's salary, or other conditions affecting the person at whom it is directed, and such behavior creates an atmosphere of intimidation, hostility, or humiliation for the person at whom it is directed."[45]

The situation for working women in India was bleak in 1992. Although there was a provision for prosecuting a harasser under section 509 of the Indian penal code, Madras attorney Geetha Ramaseshan said, "Hardly any superior officer has been charged under the section, and even the police are most reluctant to book cases under this section. The relatives and friends of the victim convince her that if she makes a noise, it will tell upon her character." Many females were said to remain silent after being harassed in order to not appear "uncool" and unable to cope with the pressures of the modern world. One of the few who spoke out and won in court was government official Ela Chaudhuri. The court passed "severe strictures" on her harasser, another government official. However, according to one 1992 account, the prevalence of sexual harassment in the workplace was actually increasing, assuming new and subtler forms; "there is virtually no working woman who has not experienced it at some stage of her career." A woman advertising executive in New Delhi commented, "In the 10 years I've worked in this office, things have deteriorated. There are more women in the office now, but there's also more harassment." Men's reaction to harassment complaints ranged from disbelief to amusement to outright condemnation—of the females. The resulting frustration could be seen in the case of a young Madras clerk who had suffered daily harassment by the head clerk for months in silence: one day she picked up the office register and whacked him over the head. This action was met with "open approbation" from her male coworkers. Most at risk were women employed in clerical jobs and in nursing. One woman executive noted, "The harassment is not couched in terms of refusing a raise or anything like that. It's more, 'Baby, if you can't take this dirty joke or sexually explicit story, you shouldn't be here'."[46]

Men in Kenya avidly followed the Clarence Thomas hearings on television and in the newspapers. They felt sorry for him and wanted him to win. As for Anita Hill, they termed her a "man destroyer." A typical comment from them was "He must have refused to marry her or something like that." For the most part these men insisted that Kenya did not even have a name for such behavior, and that such behavior did not occur in Kenya. Rose Waruinee, an attorney, pointed out that the penal code had a provision under which anybody who "insults the modesty of any woman or girl" was guilty of a misdemeanor and liable to one year in prison. This was a long-standing proviso apparently harking back to a more puritanical time. Member of Kenya's Parliament Grace Ogot was flabbergasted with the idea that harassment did not exist in Kenya. She said she had received many complaints from females harassed in places of work. "They are supposed to go out on 'dates' prior to interviews, others are failed in exams and some minors have been raped," explained Ogot. At an early 1990s meeting of Kenyan women with more than 60 in attendance, one of them asked the group, "Can anyone here who has never been sexually harassed in one way or another please raise her hand?" Nobody did.[47]

14
Legal Myths and Realities

With legal machinery in place to deal with sexual harassment complaints and with the issue openly acknowledged and discussed in the media as a major and serious problem, one might assume that the situation is improving for women so victimized. Unfortunately the reality is far from that. Acknowledging and openly discussing a problem did not mean that it was solved or in the process of being solved. Poverty, to cite one example, has been so treated and discussed for a very long time, yet it remains a serious problem. Under Reagan and Bush poverty in American actually got worse. Naturally enough the media play up the miniscule number of women who win large settlements in civil suits, thereby giving weight to an unsupported assumption that it is both easy and lucrative to successfully pursue a harassment action through the system. Yet as attorney Joe Wiley noted, plaintiffs are successful in less than 5 percent of all sexual harassment cases. And not all of those few win big.[1]

The Civil Rights Act of 1991, which President Bush signed into law on November 21 of that year, held out the promise of allowing victims of harassment to gain more in monetary compensation by allowing them to sue for punitive damages for the first time and to have jury trials. Prior to that time they were limited to back pay for unjust termination, and so on, when they proceeded through government channels such as the EEOC and the Civil Rights Act of 1964. Jury trials were not allowed. Pursuing a complaint that way meant there were few legal costs involved compared to the high legal costs in civil suits, which allowed jury trials and unlimited punitive damages. Under the 1991 Civil Rights Act such damages, while permissible, were capped at $50,000 for companies employing 15 to 100 workers and at $300,000 for businesses employing more than 500 people. This cap applied to women, people with disabilities, and religious minorities but not to racial and ethnic minorities, which were allowed uncapped damages. Thus it was possible that a black woman working for a company employing 50 workers who had been harassed sexually and then fired could claim a maximum of $50,000 in damages. If that same woman had been harassed because she was black — but not because she was a woman —

and then fired, she could claim an unlimited amount in damages. Not surprisingly this capping has been a bone of contention in women's groups. The Civil Rights Act of 1991 did not apply to cases already in process on or before the November 21 bill signing, nor did it apply to sexual harassment that took place before that date, no matter when the action was brought. Nor, in fact, did the bill have incorporated into it a specific effective date. Marcia Greenberger, co-president of the National Women's Law Center, was one of many women agitating for uncapped punitive damages. She argued that the point of punitive damages was to lay a serious cost on discrimination, which then motivated employers to eliminate it. With full damages allowable, Greenberger felt people would not have to go to court as harassment would not exist. Others argued that full damages would simply open the floodgates to such suits.[2]

The idea that if sexual harassment was more costly to companies, it would somehow vanish or seriously abate is not new. Nor is it true. Harassment is already costly in terms of staff turnover, medical leaves, training expenses, lowered productivity, and so on. If companies acted solely by making rational economic choices, then harassment and other discriminatory practices would long ago have ceased, and we would not have or need all the antidiscrimination laws that we now have, and need, but that are not effective. Even when high costs of harassment are associated with a specific suit, it does not cause a company to alter its course or eradicate harassment, as the following examples will show. No cost is too high to pay when the white supremacist capitalist patriarchy perceives itself challenged. In the end all such costs are passed on to the consumer, to the taxpayer, in one way or another. Clearly this is true for public companies and agencies that do not exist to make a profit. It is equally true for private companies. The latter sometimes take public steps, such as terminating a harasser, but when this does happen it is usually perceived as a necessary public relations move. Often such people are simply recycled through the industry (as noted in the music business) or promoted. As another example of high costs not terminating repulsive and offensive behavior consider the Los Angeles Police Department, which in fiscal 1991–1992 paid out $20.2 million in claims, settlements, and jury verdicts for police brutality. This was before a settlement was reached with Rodney King and the many other suits since filed by brutalized Angelinos who were apparently emboldened to come forward after the King beating. Violence by Los Angeles police is well known and has been documented many times, most recently in the Christopher Report in the wake of the King beating. Payouts will likely rise dramatically in Los Angeles over the coming years. Yet little or nothing is done to reverse the situation. Large payouts are a problem for other police forces as well, such as those in Detroit and New York City.[3]

Sometimes when a woman brings a sexual harassment case the problem is that nobody wants to hear. Catherine Duffey, a former inspector for the Agriculture Department in New Jersey, found herself harassed by a supervisor at work. He unzipped his pants and made a suggestive remark. Verbal abuse followed, which continued over time. A couple of weeks later she quit. At her exit interview in the summer of 1991 she indicated that she had been subjected to harassment. However, no one at the department ever asked her about it. Next she wrote letters to her legislators and in general persisted in an effort to get an investigation launched. When the department finally did, in October, Duffey found herself under scrutiny for insubordination. Early in the following year the U.S. Agriculture Department acknowledged the investigation was over but that it had not yet reached its decision.[4]

Sometimes the powers that be hear the complaint but do not take it seriously. Chrysler fired a male employee from its parts plant in Beaver Dam, Wisconsin, in January 1989 after he touched a female coworker's breasts. An investigation by the auto company disclosed that the man had a history of sexual assault and harassment in the workplace. The man appealed his termination to an arbitrator. The latter ruled the employee should be reinstated, not because he found no harassment had occurred but because it was not an "extremely serious offense, such as stealing or striking a foreman." An appeals court upheld the arbitrator's ruling in April 1992. Chrysler appealed to the U.S. Supreme Court, which in the fall of 1992 declined to review the case.[5]

Sometimes the problem is to be found in who actually hears the complaint. John A. Stewart had been the equal opportunity officer for Jacksonville Shipyards in Jacksonville, Florida, and was that company's industrial relations manager in 1986 when the National Organization for Women sued the firm. The suit centered on complaints by welder Lois Robinson that coworkers had harassed her by making sexual remarks and by posting nude pictures. Federal district court judge Howell W. Melton in his 1991 ruling on that case said, "Stewart is liable for the hostile work environment to which Robinson was subjected. He held responsibility for the day-to-day administration of the sexual harassment complaint machinery. Its failure is his failure." On March 2, 1992, Stewart started work as the head of affirmative action — overseeing efforts to hire and promote women and members of minority groups — for the city of Jacksonville. The next day a local newspaper reported the just cited court case. Later the same day Stewart resigned under pressure from Mayor Ed Austin. Stewart insisted that Austin knew of his involvement in the lawsuit. Austin stated that, although he had been aware of the suit, he had not known its "full depth."[6]

Virginia Delgado worked from 1979 to 1983 — when she was fired for nonperformance — at the Naval Systems Engineering Command in Alexandria, Virginia. Her boss was John C. Joseph, deputy director of the Equal

Employment Office there. After being fired, Delgado took her case to court alleging Joseph had sexually harassed her. She won a judgment in court against the navy, which awarded her back pay but not reinstatement. Judge James C. Cacheris held that Joseph, "in violation of EEO regulations, discouraged five or six women from bringing discrimination complaints" and that "the record is replete with his derogatory attitude toward women." As in all such cases an agency was the defendant, not an individual, in this case the Navy, not Joseph. Defense of Joseph was paid for by the navy and cost an estimated $200,000, a sum that included Delgado's back pay. Joseph was not disciplined. He then earned $65,000 a year and continued to be in charge of preventing sexual harassment and discrimination among the command's 22,400 employees. In addition he reviewed allegations of discrimination from field offices and conducted equal employment opportunity training sessions for new supervisors. After being fired, Delgado, then 53, was unable to find any work to pay near the $25,000 she had earned as a civil servant.[7]

Michele Cassida's problems began in 1984 when she started work at the Operative and Systems Integration Division at the U.S. Army's Fort Carson, Colorado, facility. All parties in this case, and the previous one, were civilian employees of the military. Coworker John W. Brackett, married with four children, asked her out. She refused. He persisted and it got worse. A later finding by the EEOC held that Brackett "subjected her to years of unrelenting antagonism, exhibited both verbally and physically," and that when he was promoted to supervisor "[he] attempted to use that authority to damage" Cassida professionally. Kelly P. LaCombe, another coworker, also harassed Cassida by blowing her kisses, brushing up against her breasts with his elbow, bumping into her buttocks, and touching her knees with his hands. Finally Cassida filed an internal complaint of harassment against Brackett. The man assigned to investigate was LaCombe. First LaCombe assured her that Brackett would not bother her again. Then LaCombe grabbed her and kissed her, "tongue in mouth." Cassida filed a formal complaint against the army, citing both men. An outside army investigator found that the two men had indeed created "an offensive working environment." Six weeks after that finding was released by the army's Civilian Appeal and Review Agency, Colonel Melvin C. Jenks, Fort Carson's garrison commander, rewrote the army's performance standards. He amended base standards to read, "One substantiated EEO complaint is considered acceptable within the rating period." Previously one had been unacceptable. Army spokesperson Major Barbara Goodno called this policy change "inappropriate." The rewrite allowed Brackett and LaCombe to receive good evaluations. The former also received a $1,146 bonus, and it was noted in LaCombe's file that he promoted "a good work environment." Neither man was disciplined.

An angry Cassida appealed to the EEOC, which confirmed she had been harassed. This probe also found LaCombe had harassed other women for it concluded after gathering statements from four other women that "women expressed embarrassment, discomfort and anger at being touched. These women all stated that they said nothing because of his position." LaCombe testified that Cassida solicited sexual advances by the way she dressed and acted, testimony the EEOC declared to "lack credibility." In its report the EEOC strongly criticized the army for its "inexplicable failure to acknowledge or give weight to clear and credible evidence of patterns of harassment by both officials. . . . We find the agency's remedies should include consideration of disciplinary action against the guilty officials." Eventually the army sent the two men to a harassment-prevention class and suspended LaCombe for one week without pay. He continued to supervise 86 people, including 27 women.[8]

When a complainant wishes to file a harassment suit against the government agency that employs the harasser, the complainant must first take the matter to the agency's internal equal employment opportunity officer, who tries to resolve disputes informally. If that fails, the victim can then go to the independent EEOC. Findings by the EEOC are only recommendations; they are not binding. They also exclude workplaces of less than 15 employees, which omits, for example, most people who work in dental practices. If the complaint is adjudicated in federal court, the judge can levy binding sanctions against the company, not against the harassing individual, within the compensation limits mentioned previously. In many ways the agency is the final judge of its own guilt. Any disciplinary action against harassing individuals is solely up to the agency. When the EEOC studied its 1989 cases, it found that agencies rejected the EEOC's findings of discrimination 58 percent of the time. This included harassment cases and discrimination cases based on all other criteria, such as age, race, sex, and disability. One reporter concluded that "more often than not the agencies found guilty of discriminations do not discipline the individuals responsible for the misconduct." Decisions by the EEOC were not binding on private companies either.[9]

Sometimes women file a complaint, apparently win, but really lose. Hairdresser Verna Flanagan of Richmond, California, was subjected to years of taunts and abuse at the barbershop where she worked in the late 1980s. Her breasts were pinched by employees as clients watched; she said the harassment was "constant." Eventually she lost her job, and her marriage broke up. Flanagan sued the barbershop and was awarded $30,000 in 1990 by the state Fair Employment and Housing Commission. However, she never collected anything because the state supreme court ruled the commission had no power to collect damages. "Until this day I do not work; I have no money. This is something that never goes away," explained the

woman as she testified in November 1991 before a special California legislature hearing sponsored by the bipartisan women's caucus to hear tales of
sexual harassment. The hearing underscored how little effective redress
victims of harassment had. Going through civil courts was too costly for most
women, and the state commission, like the EEOC, had only limited power.
A bill that would have enabled victims to collect cash damages from their
employers over and above direct loss was vetoed by Governor Pete Wilson
earlier that year. Milan D. Smith resigned from the Fair Employment and
Housing Commission to protest that veto, saying, "There's basically nothing
that can be done unless you can afford an attorney." The women who
testified at that hearing ranged from attorneys to waitresses to a pipefitter
to a neurosurgeon. They explained that employers rarely took their complaints seriously. Complaining at all, said several, was "career suicide."
Harassment ranged from constant degrading remarks to male coworkers
displaying their genitals to being threatened with the loss of their jobs if
they did not consent to sex. Melissa Clerkin was one of two former Long
Beach, California, police officers who had jointly been awarded $3.1 mil-
lion in a civil suit for being harassed on the job. As the award was still under
appeal she had not then collected anything. She was retired from the force
on a stress disability. "Every aspect of our life was put on trial. I've had to
file bankruptcy. I have about $2 in my purse. I have to say I wouldn't really
recommend this to anybody."[10]

Carol Zabkowicz was a young mother with two children who was
employed as a laborer in a household appliance company warehouse near
Milwaukee when she filed a harassment action in 1982. For almost five
years she had continually reported to her manager and supervisor an onslaught of sexual abuse from coworkers who, called her sexual names,
dropped their pants in front of her, and posted pornographic caricatures
of her around the building. She won her suit, being awarded $2,700 in back
pay for the time she was absent from work on medical leave due to the
stress threatening her pregnancy. At times the family had to call for police
protection because of anonymous threats. When her neighbors were contacted by the deposition attorney, they were asked what kind of wife and
mother she was and if she had any extramarital affairs. During her own
deposition she was asked questions such as "Do you wear a bra?" "What
is your breast size without a bra?" "What is your sex life with your husband?" Five months after she won her suit the warehouse was closed down.
Of the ordeal as a whole Carol declared, "My husband suffered, my
children, my parents, though they all supported me."[11]

Jean Jew was a medical neuroscience researcher and faculty member
at the University of Iowa College of Medicine. She endured severe harassment and discrimination from one senior-level male academic and from
several male colleagues at her own level. Throughout the time Jew was

harassed she repeatedly but unsuccessfully tried to get her superior to put an end to a stream of crude remarks, posted pornographic cartoons of her, and rumor that she was moving up by providing sexual favors. In 1983 she filed a formal complaint within the university system. After their probe a panel of faculty members decided her allegations were true. However, the university refused to act on this finding. Jew then hired a lawyer, sued the university, won, and was awarded damages. The university still refused to comply with her request that the "primary instigator of the harassment," a professor of anatomy, be transferred to another department. Explained Jew, "This means I'm working in an environment that is still very hostile." Unless she could produce a witness or evidence that he was continuing to harass her, the university maintained the environment was not hostile. Jew commented on her experience, "I can't say that I would advise all women to do this. I was uniquely advantaged because I had tenure . . . a salary that enabled me to retain an attorney. I did not have a family, spouse or children that would call for me to sacrifice. How many women are in that position?"[12]

Linda Frost was employed as a school liaison for delinquent boys in San Bernardino County, California. Around 1986 her boss, Charles Terrell, San Bernardino County superintendent of schools, began to use their lunchtime meetings to complain of unmet sexual needs. For a time she ignored him, but he approached her at work and called her at home. Once while they were away at a conference he lured her to his hotel room, where he displayed himself naked beneath an open robe. Demanding sex, he exclaimed, "You work for me. I own you." Frost extricated herself only after she threatened to kill herself. Next came obscene late-night phone calls. Then he threatened to fire her if she did not yield to him. When she complained to supervisors, nothing at all was done except to advise Frost to transfer or quit. Only then did she retain a lawyer. The municipal government of San Bernardino assembled a defense team of several attorneys, and stalled the proceedings, eventually spending hundreds of thousands of dollars in legal bills before settling for $235,000. "It was all taxpayers' money," Frost said. "It was money that should have been spent in the classrooms for my kids." This was a common way of dealing with the problem around the country. James Wiederschall, who represented the office of the superintendent, commented, "If anybody should be looked at in terms of why all this money was spent, talk to Mrs. Frost and her attorney, because they are the ones who did it." Frost only sued when her in-house complaints met with inaction, indifference, and retaliation. Lynne Bernabei, an attorney who had represented plaintiffs in many harassment cases, remarked, "With the government, it's the taxpayers' money so they don't give a damn. They fight every single case as long, and delay it as much, as they can. There's no economic incentive to settle, because there's a deep pocket there." As a part of the settlement Frost quit her job. The ranch for troubled boys, Verdemont, where she had been employed closed for lack of funds. Superintendent Terrell remained in his $102,882 a year post.[13]

In the mid–1980s Pat Swanson worked for Elmhurst Chrysler Plymouth in a small community 40 miles northwest of Chicago. While employed there she was sexually harassed by dealership co-owner Roger Meacham, who dropped his pants in front of her, made lewd remarks about her breasts, and threw paper clips down her blouse. All these behaviors were witnessed by Swanson's colleagues. On many occasions Meacham came up behind Swanson in the hallway and thrust his hand up her skirt, grabbing her between the legs on the thigh. None of her many protestations caused Meacham to stop. When he fired Swanson in December 1984, she was convinced it was because of her objections to his harassing. Soon, however, she heard from friends that he was publicly saying in their small town that Swanson was an "undependable" employee. It was then for the first time she told her husband and two close friends of the harassment. Together they decided to file a complaint with the EEOC. During the two years it took to be heard Swanson was unable to obtain work in the town, which she assumed was because her former boss had put out the word. One reason she had not complained in the past was that, as she explained, "I knew this man was powerful in the car business in this area, and he could have kept me from getting a job." From all appearances he did anyway. During that two-year wait Swanson suffered from anxiety, stress, and migraines and gained 50 pounds. She was about 46 when fired. At the trial lawyers for Meacham defended their client by asking, "Why would this man come after an overweight, older female with visions of grandeur?" A federal court found she had been harassed but awarded her $1. In 1989 the U.S. Court of Appeals for the Seventh Circuit upheld the federal court, finding that Swanson had been sexually harassed by Roger Meacham. However, it ruled that because she had been discharged from her job for reasons unrelated to the harassment, Meacham was the winning party in the suit. Thus Swanson had to forfeit her $1 award and pay Meacham his court costs of $2,600. Each month thereafter Swanson sent Meacham a check for $50, saying, "In my eyes, I'm sending the check to my attacker."[14]

The story of the harassment of Securities and Exchange Commission lawyer Catherine Broderick was outlined in a previous chapter. Broderick won her case in court, with SEC having spent a total of $1.3 million because of that suit: $240,000 for legal bills, $128,000 for back pay to Broderick, $97,000 for a consultant to investigate the matter, and $840,000 for a consultant to help the agency improve its equal employment opportunity program. None of the three attorneys whom the court found had harassed Broderick was disciplined; one has since been promoted. Nor were any other employees who together created the hostile environment found to exist by the courts disciplined. The SEC said there was no punishment because a subsequent investigation it conducted using private attorneys (presumably the $97,000 consultant) concluded there was "insufficient evidence" to support a finding against the three men.[15]

References

Chapter 1

1. Sandra S. Tangri, "Research on Women's Work and the Family at the Urban Institute," in Anne Hoiberg, ed., *Women and the World of Work* (New York: Plenum Press, 1982), p. 174.

2. Andrea Dworkin, *Right-Wing Women* (London: Women's Press, 1983), p. 67.

3. Barbara Drygulski Wright, *Women, Work and Technology* (Ann Arbor: University of Michigan Press, 1987), p. 262.

4. Michael Korda, *Male Chauvinism* (New York: Random House, 1972), pp. 105–106.

5. Lin Farley, *Sexual Shakedown* (New York: McGraw-Hill, 1978), p. 42; Darlene Clark Hine, *Black Women in White* (Bloomington: Indiana University Press, 1989), p. 50; Rosalyn Baxandall, ed., *America's Working Women* (New York: Random House, 1976), p. 93.

6. Robert W. Smuts, *Women and Work in America* (New York: Columbia University Press, 1959), p. 88.

7. Lynn Y. Weiner, *From Working Girl to Working Mother* (Chapel Hill: University of North Carolina Press, 1985), p. 26.

8. Mary Christine Stansell, "Women of the Laboring Poor in New York City, 1820–1860" (Ph.D. diss., Yale University, 1979), p. 107; Eleanor Gordon, *Women and the Labour Movement in Scotland, 1850–1914* (Oxford: Clarendon Press, 1991), p. 78.

9. Susan Estabrook Kennedy, *If All We Did Was to Weep at Home* (Bloomington: Indiana University Press, 1979), pp. 101, 103.

10. Zahida Birjis, *Women at Work* (Lahore: National Institute of Public Administration, 1964), pp. 14, 35.

11. Elizabeth Faulkner Baker, *Technology and Women's Work* (New York: Columbia University Press, 1964), p. 6.

12. Baxandall, *America's Working Women*, pp. 92–93; Linda Rubinstein, "Dominance Eroticised," in Margaret Bevege, ed., *Worth Her Salt* (Sydney: Hale & Iremonger, 1982), p. 167.

13. Mary Conyington, "Relations Between Occupation and Criminality of Women," in U.S. Congress, Senate, *Report on Conditions of Women and Child Wage-Earners in the United States*, 19 vols., 61st Cong., 2d sess., Document #645 (Washington, D.C.: GPO, 1911), vol. 15, pp. 53, 65, 81, 114.

14. Ibid., pp. 87–88, 105–108.

15. George Brushaber, "Lust on the Job," *Christianity Today* 35 December 16, 1991, p. 21.

16. "Sex at Work," *Times* (London), October 19, 1991, p. 13A.

17. Helen Gurley Brown, "At Work, Sexual Electricity," *Wall Street Journal*, October 29, 1992, p. A22.

18. "Wandering Hands," *The Economist* 325, December 5, 1992, p. 27.

19. Gretchen Morgenson, "May I Have the Pleasure?" *National Review* 43, November 18, 1991, pp. 36–37ff.

20. Jane E. Workman, "The Role of Cosmetics in Attributions About Sexual Harassment," *Sex Roles* 24 (June 1991): 759–769.

21. Suresh Kanekar, "Sex-Related Differences in Perceptions of Sexual Harassment of Women in India," *Journal of Social Psychology* 113 (February 1993): 119–120.

22. Nicholas Davidson, "Feminism and Sexual Harassment," *Society* 28 (May/June 1991): 39–44.

Chapter 2

1. Barbara Mayer Wertheimer, *We Were There* (New York: Pantheon Books, 1977), p. 21; Julia Cherry Spruill, *Women's Life and Work in the Southern Colonies* (New York: Norton, 1972), pp. 314–317.

2. Spruill, *Women's Life and Work*, pp. 322–323.

3. Ibid., pp. 321–322.

4. Ibid., pp. 323–324.

5. Peter Kolchin, *Unfree Labor* (Cambridge, Mass.: Belknap Press, 1987), pp. 112–113.

6. Monica Perrot, *A Tolerable Good Success* (Sydney: Hale & Iremonger, 1983), p. 36; Katrina Alford *Production or Reproduction* (Melbourne: Oxford University Press, 1984), pp. 166–167.

7. Perrot, *A Tolerable Good Success*, p. 32.

8. Ruth Teale, *Colonial Eve* (Melbourne: Oxford University Press, 1978), p. 21; Alford, *Production or Reproduction*, p. 166.

9. Alford, *Production or Reproduction*, p. 168; Hilary Weatherburn, "The Female Factory," in Judy Mackinolty, ed., *In Pursuit of Justice* (Sydney: Hale & Iremonger, 1979), p. 22.

10. Kay Daniels, "Prostitution in Tasmania During the Transition from Penal Settlement to 'Civilized' Society," in Kay Daniels, ed., *So Much Hard Work* (Sydney: Fontana, 1984), pp. 34–35.

11. Perrot, *A Tolerable Good Success*, p. 37.

12. Alford, *Production or Reproduction*, pp. 168–169.

13. D. R. Banaji, *Slavery in British India* (Bombay: Taraporevala, 1933), pp. 18, 26–27, 215, 223, 252.

14. Aban B. Mehta, *The Domestic Servant Class* (Bombay: Popular Book Depot, 1960), pp. 12, 14.

15. Frederick Law Olmstead, *A Journey in the Back Country* (New York: Putnam's Sons, 1907), pp. 93, 96; Frederick Law Olmstead *A Journey in the Seaboard Slave States* (New York: Dix & Edwards, 1856), p. 640.

16. Jacqueline Jones, *Labor of Love, Labor of Sorrow* (New York: Basic Books, 1985), p. 37; Olmstead, *A Journey in the Back Country*, p. 92.

17. Leslie Howard Owen, *This Species of Property* (New York: Oxford University Press, 1976), p. 197.

18. Judith K. Schafer, "Open and Notorious Concubinage," in Darlene Hines,

ed., *Black Women in American History: From Colonial Times Through the Nineteenth Century* (Brooklyn: Carlson, 1990), vol. 4, pp. 1192–1194.

19. Jones, *Labor of Love*, pp. 20, 38.

20. Charles L. Perdue, Jr., *Weevils in the Wheat* (Charlottesville: University Press of Virginia, 1976), p. 207.

21. Harriet A. Jacobs, *Incidents in the Life of a Slave Girl* (Miami: Mnemosyne, 1969, reprint of 1861 ed.), pp. 23–25, 29, 44–45, 50.

22. Owen, *This Species of Property*, p. 212; Perdue, *Weevils in the Wheat*, p. 117; Jones, *Labor of Love*, p. 38.

23. Perdue, *Weevils in the Wheat*, pp. 117, 245, 257, 301, 332.

24. John W. Blassingame, *Slave Testimony* (Baton Rouge: Louisiana State University Press, 1977), pp. 156, 221, 400, 506, 540.

25. Herbert G. Gutman, *The Black Family in Slavery and Freedom, 1750–1925* (New York: Pantheon Books, 1976), p. 80.

26. Ibid., pp. 393–394, 399.

27. Jones, *Labor of Love*, pp. 94–95.

28. Dolores E. Janiewski, *Sisterhood Denied* (Philadelphia: Temple University Press, 1985), p. 52.

29. Jones, *Labor of Love*, p. 157.

30. Robert Edgar Conrad, *Children of God's Fire* (Princeton: Princeton University Press, 1983), pp. 177–178.

31. Ibid., p. 130.

32. Ibid., pp. 274–281.

Chapter 3

1. Antonia Fraser, *The Weaker Vessel* (London: Weidenfeld & Nicolson, 1984), p. 151; E. S. Turner, *What the Butler Saw* (London: Michael Joseph, 1962), p. 14.

2. Turner, *What the Butler Saw*, pp. 56–57.

3. Ibid., pp. 57–59.

4. Ibid., p. 69.

5. Anna Clark, *Women's Silence, Men's Violence* (London: Pandora, 1987), pp. 40–41.

6. Ibid., pp. 40–41, 57–58.

7. Sarah C. Maza, *Servers and Masters in Eighteenth Century France*, (Princeton: Princeton University Press, 1983), pp. 89, 130–131.

8. Turner, *What the Butler Saw*, p. 91.

9. David M. Katzman, *Seven Days a Week* (New York: Oxford University Press, 1978), p. 216.

10. Lynn Y. Weiner, *From Working Girl to Working Mother* (Chapel Hill: University of North Carolina Press, 1985), p. 66.

11. Daniel E. Sutherland, *Americans and Their Servants* (Baton Rouge: Louisiana State University Press, 1981), p. 70.

12. Mary Conyington, "Relations Between Occupation and Criminality of Women," in U.S. Congress, Senate, *Report on Conditions of Women and Child Wage-Earners in the United States*, 19 vols. 61st Cong. 2d sess., Document #645 (Washington, D.C.: GPO, 1911), vol. 15, pp. 74, 87.

13. Weiner, *From Working Girl*, p. 66.

14. Turner, *What the Butler Saw*, pp. 225, 244.

15. Clark, *Women's Silence*, pp. 106, 108.

16. Madeleine B. Stern, *Critical Essays on Louisa May Alcott* (Boston: Hall, 1984), p. 52.

17. Mary Jo Maynes, "Gender and Class in Working-Class Women's Autobiographies," in Ruth-Ellen B. Joeres, ed., *German Women in the Eighteenth and Nineteenth Centuries* (Bloomington: Indiana University Press, 1986), p. 239.

18. Rachel G. Fuchs, "Pregnant, Single, and Far from Home: Migrant Women in Nineteenth-Century Paris," *American Historical Review* 95 (October 1990): 1007, 1020–1021.

19. John R. Gillis, "Servants, Sexual Relations, and the Risks of Illegitimacy in London, 1801–1900." *Feminist Studies* 5 (Spring 1979): 143, 160.

20. Lana Rakow, ed., *The Revolution in Words: Righting Women, 1868–1871* (New York: Routledge, 1990), p. 73.

21. Helen Campbell, *Prisoners of Poverty* (Boston: Roberts Brothers, 1887), p. 234.

22. Karen Tranberg Hansen, *Distant Companions: Servants and Employers in Zambia, 1900–1985* (Ithaca: Cornell University Press, 1989), pp. 90–97, 106–110.

23. Turner, *What the Butler Saw*, pp. 98, 227.

24. Allan Nevins, *Study in Power* (New York: Scribner's Sons, 1953), vol. 1, p. 4.

25. Sidney L. Gulick, *Working Women of Japan* (New York: Missionary Education Movement of the United States and Canada, 1915), pp. 54, 56.

26. Lori Rotenberg, "The Wayward Worker," in *Women at Work: Ontario, 1850–1930* (Toronto: Canadian Women's Educational Press, 1974), p. 41.

27. Campbell, *Prisoners of Poverty*, pp. 135–136.

28. Faye E. Dudden, *Serving Women* (Middleton, Conn.: Wesleyan University Press, 1983), p. 215.

29. Nathan Huggins, *Protestants Against Poverty* (Westport: Conn.: Greenwood Press, 1971), pp. 87–89.

30. Eve Ebbet, *Victoria's Daughters* (Wellington: A. H. & A. W. Reed, 1981), pp. 50–51.

31. Deidre Beddoe, *Back to Home and Duty* (London: Pandora, 1989), pp. 63–64.

32. Katzman, *Seven Days a Week*, pp. 216–217.

33. Jacqueline Jones, *Labor of Love, Labor of Sorrow* (New York: Basic Books, 1985), p. 150.

34. Verta Mae, *Thursdays and Every Other Sunday Off* (Garden City, N.Y.: Doubleday, 1972), p. 60.

35. Linda Martin, *The Servant Problem* (Jefferson, N.C.: McFarland, 1985), p. 124.

36. Rina Cohen, "The Work Conditions of Immigrant Women Live-In Domestics," *Resources for Feminist Research* 16 (March 1987): 36–38.

37. Judith Rollins, *Between Women* (Philadelphia: Temple University Press, 1985), pp. 150–151.

38. Joanne Lipman, "The Nanny Trap," *Wall Street Journal*, April 14, 1993, pp. A1, A16; Joanne Lipman, "Far from Home, an Irish Nanny Found Herself Terrified and Isolated," *Wall Street Journal*, April 14, 1993, p. A6.

39. Martin, *The Servant Problem*, pp. 115–116.

40. Yayori Matsui, *Women's Asia* (London: Zed Press, 1987), pp. 54–55.

41. Carol Andreas, *When Women Rebel* (Westport: Conn.: Lawrence Hill, 1985), p. 147; Ximena Bunster, *Sellers and Servants* (New York: Praeger, 1985), pp. 84, 179.

42. Indira Chauhan, *Purdah to Profession* (Delhi: B. R. Publishing, 1986), p. 122.

43. Marilyn Thomson, *Women of El Salvador* (London: Zed Press, 1986), pp. 19, 34.

44. "Maids Repatriated Amid Abuse Claims," *Sydney Morning Herald*, May 2, 1992, p. 13.

45. Alan Armstrong, *Farmworkers* (London: Batsford, 1988), pp. 80, 96; Pamela Horn, *Victorian Countrywomen* (Oxford: Basil Blackwell, 1991), pp. 160–161; W. Hasbach, *A History of the English Agricultural Labourer* (London: King & Son, 1920), pp. 201–202.

46. Elda Gentili Zappi, *If Eight Hours Seem Too Few* (Albany: State University of New York Press, 1991), pp. 29, 112, 140.

47. John Kenneth Turner, *Barbarous Mexico* (Chicago: Kerr, 1910), pp. 79–80.

48. Shirlene Ann Soto, *The Mexican Woman* (Palo Alto: R & E Research, 1979), p. 49; Thomson, *Women of El Salvador*, p. 34.

Chapter 4

1. Angela V. John, *By the Sweat of Their Brow* (London: Routledge & Kegan Paul, 1984), p. 31.

2. Ibid., pp. 31–32, 40–41.

3. Sally Alexander, *Women's Work in Nineteenth-Century London* (London: Journeyman Press, 1976), pp. 9–10.

4. John, *By the Sweat of Their Brow*, p. 91.

5. Anna Clark, *Women's Silence, Men's Violence* (London: Pandora, 1987), pp. 93–94.

6. Ibid., p. 95.

7. Friedrich Engels, *The Conditions of the Working Class in England* (Stanford: Stanford University Press, 1968), pp. 167–168.

8. Mary Jo Maynes, "Gender and Class in Working-Class Women's Autobiographies," in Ruth-Ellen B. Joeres, ed., *German Women in the Eighteenth and Nineteenth Centuries* (Bloomington: Indiana University Press, 1986), pp. 234, 240, 330–331.

9. John C. Fout, "The Viennese Enquette of 1896 on Working Women." in ibid., p. 57.

10. Margaret Hewitt, *Wives and Mothers in Victorian Industry* (London: Rockliff, 1958), pp. 50–51.

11. Ibid., pp. 48–61.

12. Ada Nield Chew, *Ada Nield Chew: The Life and Writings of a Working Woman* (London: Virago, 1982), pp. 99–101.

13. Susan Groag Bell, ed., *Women, The Family, and Freedom, Volume 1, 1750–1880* (Stanford: Stanford University Press, 1983), p. 202.

14. E. Patricia Tsurumi, *Factory Girls* (Princeton: Princeton University Press, 1990), p. 166.

15. Patricia Hilden, *Working Women and Socialist Politics in France, 1880–1914* (Oxford: Clarendon Press, 1986), p. 60.

16. Ibid., pp. 108, 111–112.

17. Stewart B. Kaufman, ed., *The Samuel Gompers Papers* (Urbana: University of Illinois Press, 1986), vol. 1, p. 313.

18. Mary H. Blewett, *Men, Women, and Work* (Urbana: University of Illinois Press, 1988), pp. 179–180, 182.

19. Mary Christine Stansell, "Women of the Laboring Poor in New York City, 1820–1860" (Ph.D. diss., Yale University, 1979), p. 107.

20. Virginia Penny, *The Employment of Women* (Boston: Walker, Wise & Company, 1862), p. 306.

21. Virginia Penny, *Think and Act* (Philadelphia: Claxton, Remsen & Haffelfinger, 1869), pp. 360–362.

22. Sue Weiler, "The Uprising in Chicago," in Joan M. Jensen, ed., *A Needle, a Bobbin, a Strike* (Philadelphia: Temple University Press, 1984), p. 121.

23. Helen Campbell, *Prisoners of Poverty* (Boston: Roberts Brothers, 1887), p. 22.

24. Stansell, "Women of the Laboring Poor," p. 87.

25. Ibid., p. 108–109.

26. Campbell, *Prisoners of Poverty*, p. 87.

27. Susan Levine, *Labor's True Woman* (Philadelphia: Temple University Press, 1984), p. 56.

28. Susan Estabrook Kennedy, *If All We Did Was to Weep at Home* (Bloomington: Indiana University Press, 1979), p. 66.

29. Lin Farley, *Sexual Shakedown* (New York: McGraw-Hill, 1978), p. 42; Helen Campbell, *Women Wage-Earners* (Boston: Roberts Brothers, 1893), p. 272.

30. John Duguid Milne, *Industrial Employment of Women in the Middle and Lower Ranks* (New York: Garland, 1984, reprint of 1870 ed.) pp. 244, 246–247.

31. Florence Gordon, "The Condition of Female Labour and the Rate of Pay of Women's Wages in Sydney, 1894," in Beverly Kingston , ed., *The World Moves Slowly* (Sydney: Cassell, 1977), p. 109.

32. Philip S. Foner, ed. *The Factory Girls* (Urbana: University of Illinois Press, 1980), p. 83.

33. Harriet H. Robinson, *Loom and Spindle* (New York: Crowell, 1898), p. 61.

34. Tsurumi, *Factory Girls*, p. 166.

35. Sharon L. Sievers, *Flowers in Salt* (Stanford: Stanford University Press, 1983), pp. 59, 62.

36. Yasue Aoki Kidd, *Women Workers in the Japanese Cotton Mills: 1880–1920* (Ithaca: Cornell University Press, 1978), p. 12; Sievers, *Flowers in Salt*, p. 62.

37. Sievers, *Flowers in Salt*, pp. 75, 210–211.

Chapter 5

1. Nancy Schrom Dye, *As Equals and as Sisters* (Columbia: University of Missouri Press, 1980), p. 67.

2. Stephen H. Norwood, *Labor's Flaming Youth* (Urbana: University of Illinois Press, 1990), p. 85.

3. Carol Groneman, ed., *To Toil the Livelong Day: America's Women at Work, 1770–1980* (Ithaca: Cornell University Press, 1987), p. 157; Philip S. Foner, *Women and the Labor Movement: From Colonial Times to the Eve of World War I* (New York: Free Press, 1979), p. 357.

4. Groneman, *To Toil the Livelong Day*, p. 158.

5. Dye, *As Equals and as Sisters*, pp. 22–23.

6. Groneman, *To Toil the Livelong Day*, p. 158.

7. Foner, *Women and the Labor Movement*, p. 357; Susan A. Glenn, *Daughters of the Shtel* (Ithaca: Cornell University Press, 1990), p. 175.

8. Mary Bularzik, "Sexual Harassment at the Workplace," *Radical America* 12 (July/August 1978): 38.

9. "Garment Strike," *Life and Labor* 1 (January 1911): 14.

10. Priscilla Long, "The Women of the Colorado Fuel and Iron Strike, 1913–1914," in Ruth Milkman, ed., *Women, Work and Protest* (Boston: Routledge & Kegan Paul, 1985), pp. 67, 74–75.

11. Paul Kellogg, "The McKees Rocks Strike," *Survey*, August 7, 1909, p. 663.

12. Foner, *Women and the Labor Movement*, pp. 422–423.

13. Jan Lambertz, "Sexual Harassment in the Nineteenth Century English Cotton Industry," *History Workshop Journal* 19 (Spring 1985): 34–36.

14. Ibid., p. 31.

15. Ibid., p. 32.

16. Ibid., pp. 33–34.

17. Ibid., p. 33.

18. Ibid., p. 34.

19. Rose L. Glickman, *Russian Factory Women: Workplace and Society, 1880–1914* (Berkeley and Los Angeles: University of California Press, 1984), p. 166.

20. Mary Christine Stansell, "Women of the Laboring Poor in New York City, 1820–1860" (Ph.D. diss., Yale University, 1979), p. 107.

21. Sarah Boston, *Women Workers and the Trade Unions* (London: Lawrence & Wishart, 1987), p. 338.

22. Eleanor Gordon, *Women and the Labour Movement in Scotland, 1850–1914* (Oxford: Clarendon Press, 1991), pp. 82, 84.

23. Lin Farley, *Sexual Shakedown* (New York: McGraw-Hill, 1978), p. 42.

24. Barbara Meyer Wertheimer, *We Were There* (New York: Pantheon Books, 1977), p. 184.

25. Dye, *As Equals and as Sisters*, pp. 22–23.

26. Nina Asher, "Dorothy Jacobs Bellanca," in Joan M. Jensen, ed., *A Needle, a Bobbin, a Strike* (Philadelphia: Temple University Press, 1984), p. 214.

27. Farley, *Sexual Shakedown*, p. 43.

28. Jennie Farley, ed., *Women Workers in Fifteen Countries* (Ithaca: ILR Press, 1985), p. 137.

29. Kazuko Ono, *Chinese Women in a Century of Revolution, 1850–1950* (Stanford: Stanford University Press, 1978), p. 119.

30. Linda Rubinstein, "Dominance Eroticised," in Margaret Bevege, ed., *Worth Her Salt* (Sydney: Hale & Iremonger, 1982), p. 174.

31. *Women at Work* (Brussels: European Trade Union Confederation, 1976), p. 124.

32. Foner, *Women and the Labor Movement*, p. 559.

Chapter 6

1. Edward Cadbury, *Women's Work and Wages* (Chicago: University of Chicago Press, 1907), p. 195.

2. Virginia Yans-McLaughlin, "Italian Women and Work," in Milton Canter, ed., *Class, Sex, and the Woman Worker* (Westport, Conn.: Greenwood, 1977), p. 112.

3. Dorothy Richardson, "The Long Day," in *Women at Work* (Chicago: Quadrangle, 1972), p. 224.

4. Ibid., pp. 260–262, 275.

5. Mrs. John Van Vorst, *The Woman Who Toils* (New York: Doubleday, Page, 1903), pp. 92, 264, 271.

6. Rose Schneiderman, *All for One* (New York: Eriksson, 1967), pp. 86–87.

7. Sydney Stahl Weinberg, *The World of Our Mothers* (Chapel Hill: University of North Carolina Press, 1989), p. 28.

8. Philip S. Foner, *Women and the Labor Movement: From Colonial Times to the Eve of World War I* (New York: Free Press, 1979), p. 462; Mary Bularzik, "Sexual Harassment at the Workplace," *Radical America* 12 (July/August 1978): 36.

9. Isaac Metzker, ed., *A Bintel Brief* (Garden City, N.Y.: Doubleday, 1971), p. 72.

10. Susan A. Glenn, *Daughters of the Shtel* (Ithaca: Cornell University Press, 1990), pp. 146–148.

11. Elizabeth Hasanovitz, *One of Them* (Boston: Houghton Mifflin, 1917), pp. 109–110.

12. Gustavus Myers, *History of Bigotry in the United States* (New York: Random House, 1943), pp. 258, 261.

13. Bularzik, "Sexual Harassment," pp. 34–35.

14. Weinberg, *The World of Our Mothers*, p. 184.

15. Susan Estabrook Kennedy, *If All We Did Was to Weep at Home* (Bloomington: Indiana University Press, 1979), p. 145.

16. Dolores Elizabeth Janiewski, "From Field to Factory: Race, Class, Sex and the Woman Worker in Durham, 1880–1940" (Ph.D. diss., Duke University, 1979), pp. 97–98; Dolores E. Janiewski, *Sisterhood Denied* (Philadelphia: Temple University Press, 1985), pp. 97, 216.

17. Carol Groneman, ed., *To Toil the Livelong Day: America's Women at Work, 1770–1980* (Ithaca: Cornell University Press, 1987), p. 166; Foner, *Women and the Labor Movement*, p. 404.

18. Ordway Tead, *Instincts in Industry* (Boston: Houghton Mifflin, 1918), pp. 33–34.

19. U.S. Congress, Senate, "Glass Industry," in *Report on Conditions of Women and Child Wage-Earners in the United States*, 19 vols., 61st Cong., 2d sess., Document #645 (Washington, D.C.: GPO, 1911), vol. 3, p. 389.

20. Lynn Y. Weiner, *From Working Girl to Working Mother* (Chapel Hill: University of North Carolina Press, 1985), p. 73.

21. Robert W. Smuts, *Women and Work in America* (New York: Columbia University Press, 1959), p. 118.

22. Norbert C. Soldon, ed., *The World of Women's Trade Unionism* (Westport, Conn.: Greenwood Press, 1985), pp. 38–39, 63, 178, 207.

23. Jenny Morris, *Women Workers and the Sweated Trades* (Hants, England: Gower, 1986), pp. 74–78.

24. Shirlene Ann Soto, *The Mexican Woman* (Palo Alto, Calif.: R & E Research, 1979), p. 7.

25. Margaret E. Burton, *Women Workers of the Orient* (West Medford, Mass.: Central Committee on the United Study of Foreign Missions, 1918), pp. 56, 64–65.

26. Rose L. Glickman, *Russian Factory Women: Workplace and Society, 1880–1914* (Berkeley and Los Angeles: University of California Press, 1984), p. 142.

27. Ibid., p. 185.

28. Ibid., p. 143.

29. Ibid., pp. 142, 205–206.

30. Ibid., p. 206.

31. Jan Lambertz, "Sexual Harassment in the Nineteenth Century English Cotton Industry," *History Workshop Journal* 19 (Spring 1985): 36–39.

32. Liston Pope, *Millhands & Preachers* (New Haven: Yale University Press, 1942), p. 159.

33. Mary H. Blewett, *The Last Generation* (Amherst: University of Massachusetts Press, 1990), pp. 111, 163, 251.

34. Ibid., pp. 38–39, 152, 154.

35. Ruth Meyerowitz, "Organizing the United Auto Workers," in Ruth Milkman, ed., *Women, Work and Protest* (Boston: Routledge & Kegan Paul, 1985), pp. 241, 251.

36. Nancy F. Gabin, *Feminism in the Labor Movement* (Ithaca: Cornell University Press, 1990), p. 28.

37. Ruth Milkman, *Gender at Work* (Urbana: University of Illinois Press, 1987), p. 40.

38. Emily Honig, *Sisters and Strangers: Women in the Shanghai Cotton Mills, 1919–1949* (Stanford: Stanford University Press, 1986), pp. 107–108, 113, 121.

39. Ibid., p. 144.

40. E. Patricia Tsurumi, *Factory Girls* (Princeton: Princeton University Press, 1990), p. 167.

41. Hilary Standing, *Dependence and Autonomy* (London: Routledge, 1991), pp. 147, 174.

42. Iris Berger, *Threads of Solidarity: Women in South African Industry, 1900–1980* (Bloomington: Indiana University Press, 1992), pp. 4, 71–72, 82–83.

43. P. R. Rohini, *My Life Is One Long Struggle* (Belgaum, India: Pratishabd, 1983), p. 10.

44. Ibid., pp. 55, 77–78.

45. Victoria Byerly, *Hard Times Cotton Mill Girls* (Ithaca: ILR Press, 1986), p. 121.

46. Laurie Coyle, "Women at Farah," in Joan M. Jenson, ed., *A Needle, a Bobbin, a Strike* (Philadelphia: Temple University Press, 1984), p. 231.

47. Kay Deaux, *Women of Steel* (New York: Praeger, 1983), p. 122.

48. Susan Yeadle, *Women's Working Lives* (London: Tavistock, 1984), p. 74.

49. Sabeena Hafeez, *The Metropolitan Women in Pakistan* (Karachi: Royal, 1981), pp. 175–176.

50. Carol Andreas, *When Women Rebel* (Westport, Conn.: Lawrence Hill, 1985), p. 133.

51. Cathy A. Rakowski, *Women in Nontraditional Industry: The Case of Steel in Ciudad Guyana, Venezuela* Working Paper #104 (East Lansing: Michigan State University, November 1985), pp. 3, 5.

52. Ibid., pp. 9–10.

53. Ibid., p. 10.

54. Ibid., pp. 14–15.

55. Berger, *Threads of Solidarity*, pp. 283–285.

56. Aihwa Ong, *Spirits of Resistance and Capitalist Discipline* (Albany: State University of New York Press, 1987), pp. 4, 177, 179, 182, 187.

57. Ibid., pp. 167, 211–212.

58. Linda Rubinstein, "Dominance Eroticised," in Margaret Bevege, ed., *Worth Her Salt* (Sydney: Hale & Iremonger, 1982), pp. 165, 169.

59. Marilyn Thomson, *Women of El Salvador* (London: Zed Press, 1986), p. 19.

60. Daphne Patai, ed., *Brazilian Women Speak* (New Brunswick: Rutgers University Press, 1988), p. 218.

61. Wendy Lee, "Prostitution and Tourism in South-East Asia," in Nanneke Redclift, ed., *Working Women* (London: Routledge, 1991), p. 88.

62. Emily Honig, *Personal Voices: Chinese Women in the 1980s* (Stanford: Stanford University Press, 1988), pp. 278–280.

63. Sylvia Chant, *Women and Survival in Mexican Cities* (Manchester: Manchester University Press, 1991), pp. 93, 96–97.

64. Stan Gray, "Fight to Survive—The Case of Bonita Clark," *Canadian Dimension* 20 (May 1986): 15–20.

65. Katherine Lanpher, "A Bitter Brew," *Ms.* 3 (November/December 1992): 36–38.

66. "Women and Children First," *Multinational Monitor* 14 (January/February 1993): 30–31.

Chapter 7

1. Jeffrey W. Riemer, *Hard Hats* (Beverly Hills: Sage, 1979), pp. 92–93.

2. Jean Reith Schroeder, *Alone in a Crowd: Women in the Trades Tell Their Stories* (Philadelphia: Temple University Press, 1985), pp. 71, 257–258.

3. Ibid., pp. 10, 80, 83, 84, 199, 214.

4. Ibid., pp. 134–135, 170.

5. Ibid., pp. 126–127.

6. Molly Martin, ed., *Hard-Hatted Women* (Seattle: Seal Press, 1988), pp. 11, 25, 179.

7. Ibid., p. 78.

8. "The Tombs," *New York Times*, January 16, 1870, p. 3.

9. "Policewomen," *New York Times*, March 31, 1880, p. 4; "Police Matrons," *New York Times*, October 1, 1890, p. 4; "Police Matrons Needed," *New York Times*, December 25, 1890, p. 8.

10. Lin Farley, *Sexual Shakedown* (New York: McGraw-Hill, 1978), pp. 54–55.

11. Susan E. Martin, "Sexual Politics in the Workplace," *Symbolic Interaction* 1 (Spring 1978): 51, 56–57.

12. Amarjit Mahajan, *Indian Policewomen* (New Delhi: Deep & Deep, 1982), pp. 95, 149.

13. Roger Graef, *Talking Blues* (London: Collins Harvill, 1989), pp. 203, 208, 211, 383–384.

14. Peter Horne, *Women in Law Enforcement*, 2d ed. (Springfield, Ill.: Charles C. Thomas, 1980), pp. 127–128.

15. Susan E. Martin, *On the Move: The Status of Women in Policing* (Washington, D.C.: Police Foundation, 1990), pp. 140–141, 144–145.

16. "Three Awarded $2.7 Million in a Sexual Harassment Suit," *New York Times*, November 12, 1990, p. B8; "Court Criticizes Police Department in a Sex Case," *New York Times*, July 28, 1992, p. B3; Patricia Davis, "Complaints of Sexism Detailed," *Washington Post*, August 3, 1992, pp. B1, B5.

17. Joseph P. Fried, "Transfer Linked to Harassment, Police Say," *New York Times*, October 17, 1992, p. 28.

18. Patt Morrison, "Female Officers Unwelcome—But Doing Fine," *Los Angeles Times*, July 12, 1991, pp. A1, A27–A29.

19. "Officer's Suit Says She Was Raped, Then Fired," *Los Angeles Times*, December 18, 1992, p. B3.

20. Karen Klabin, "Lewd Conduct," *LA Weekly*, 15 March 5, 1993, pp. 14, 16.

21. Ibid.; Sonia Nazario, "Forced to Be Reckoned With," *Los Angeles Times*, June 5, 1993, p. A12.

22. "Officers of the Law Should Know Better," *Los Angeles Times*, February 1, 1991, p. B6.

23. Faye Fiore, "Sheriff's Dept. Concedes on 2 Sex Bias Suits," *Los Angeles Times*, December 4, 1992, pp. A1, A36.

24. Roxanna Kopetman, "Long Beach Policewomen Call Sexual Harassment Endemic," *Los Angeles Times*, September 28, 1991, p. B3.

25. N. F. Mendoza, "Crossing the Thin Blue Line," *Los Angeles Times*, May 11, 1993, p. F7.

26. Dan Weikel, "Sexual Harassment Suit Filed Against Police," *Los Angeles Times*, September 25, 1992, p. A35; Nancy Wride, "Women Alleging Sex Harassment Cite Reprisal Fear," *Los Angeles Times*, September 28, 1992, pp. A3, A18.

27. Nancy Wride, "Police Chief Named in Harassment Suit to Retire," *Los Angeles Times*, October 15, 1992, pp. A3, A29.

28. Nancy Wride, "Newport Beach Police Chief, Aide Put on Leave over Rape Allegations," *Los Angeles Times*, October 16, 1992, pp. A3, A36.

29. Nancy Wride, "Police Officials Sue Newport Beach over Harassment Inquiry," *Los Angeles Times*, November 13, 1992, pp. A3, A34.

30. Dan Weikel, "4 More Women to Join Suit Against Police," *Los Angeles Times*, December 2, 1992, pp. A3, A28.

31. Jodi Wilgoren, "Inquiry Finds Merit in Sex Harassment Suit," *Los Angeles Times*, December 16, 1992, pp. A3, A31.

32. "Face It Squarely—Deal with It," *Los Angeles Times*, December 17, 1992, p. B6.

33. Dan Weikel, "Police Chief Fired in Newport Beach," *Los Angeles Times*, December 23, 1992, pp. A3, A22; "Moving to Right a Wrong," *Los Angeles Times*, December 24, 1992, p. B6.

34. Dan Weikel, "Campbell Calls Firing Part of a Conspiracy," *Los Angeles Times*, December 24, 1992, pp. A3, A16.

35. Jodi Wilgoren, "Newport Beach Won't Pay Fired Officers' Legal Costs," *Los Angeles Times*, January 29, 1993, p. A29; "Newport Beach Settles 4 Harassment Cases," *Los Angeles Times*, February 4, 1993, p. A17; Jodi Wilgoren, "Newport Beach Settles with Fired Police Chief, Captain," *Los Angeles Times*, June 11, 1993, p. B8.

36. Shelby Grad, "Irvine Orders Probe of Police Sex Charges," *Los Angeles Times*, June 24, 1993, p. B8.

37. Lynne Duke, "Law Enforcers Grapple with Diversity," *Washington Post*, January 27, 1993, pp. A1, A12.

38. Mary Lindenstein Walshok, *Blue-Collar Women* (Garden City, N.Y.: Doubleday, 1981), pp. 230–232, 239–240, 259–260.

39. Susan A. Glenn, *Daughters of the Shtel* (Ithaca: Cornell University Press, 1990), pp. 42–43.

40. Allanna M. Sullivan, "Women Say No to Sexual Harassment," *Coal Age* 84 (August 1979): 84.

41. Ibid., pp. 75–76.

42. Ibid., pp. 77–78.

43. Raymond M. Lane, "A Man's World," *Village Voice*, December 16–22, 1981, p. 15.

44. Ibid., pp. 15–16.

45. Ibid., pp. 17, 20–21.

46. Allanna M. Sullivan, "Women Endure Job-Related Sexual Abuse," *Coal Age* 86 (August 1981): 80–81.

47. Kristen R. Yount, "Ladies, Flirts and Tomboys," *Journal of Contemporary Ethnography* 19 (January 1991): 396, 402, 404.

48. Susan Yeandle, *Women's Working Lives* (London: Tavistock, 1984), p. 74.

49. Linda Rubinstein, "Dominance Eroticised," in Margaret Bevege, ed., *Worth Her Salt* (Sydney: Hale & Iremonger, 1982), p. 173; Carol O'Donnell, *The Basis of the Bargain* (Sydney: Allen & Unwin, 1984), p. 151.

50. Adele Horin, "Sex Antics Upset Female Postal Staff," *Sydney Morning Herald*, May 14, 1992, p. 2.

51. Rosanne Less, "Words Against Women: The Detroit Story," *Columbia Journalism Review* 26 (March/April 1988): 6, 8.

52. Leonard Buder, "Bias Is Rampant in Construction, Hearing Is Told," *New York Times*, March 13, 1990, p. B4.

53. Michael J. Ybarra, "A Man's World," *Los Angeles Times*, April 30, 1991, pp. E1, E7.

54. "Judge Blocks Bias by Fire Companies," *New York Times*, June 14, 1986, p. 32.

55. Suzanne Daley, "Female Firefighters Charge Inaction on Sex Bias," *New York Times*, June 18, 1986, p. B2.

56. "Firefighter Fined in Sex Harassment Case," *New York Times*, October 3, 1986, p. B2.

57. Dennis Hevesi, "Firefighter Again Makes Her Harassment Charge," *New York Times*, October 18, 1991, p. B3.

58. Joseph P. Fried, "After Harassment Charge, Her Fellow Firefighters Transfer," *New York Times*, October 22, 1991, p. B1.

Chapter 8

1. Charles F. Cooney, "Nothing More . . . Than a Whorehouse," *Civil War Times Illustrated* 21 (December 1982): 40–42.

2. Ibid., pp. 42–43.

3. Ibid., p. 43.

4. Walter Licht, *Working for the Railroad* (Princeton: Princeton University Press, 1983), p. 216.

5. Mary Bularzik, "Sexual Harassment at the Workplace," *Radical America* 12 (July/August 1978): 25.

6. Charlotte Wharton Ayers, "Help Wanted—Female," *New York Times*, August 1, 1909, pt. 5, p. 2; Charlotte Wharton Ayers, "The Help Wanted Sharks and Their Prey," *New York Times*, August 15, 1909, pt. 5, p. 9; Charlotte Wharton Ayers, "The Would-Be Worker and the Enticing Ads," *New York Times*, August 8, 1909, pt. 5, p. 6.

7. Sydney Stahl Weinberg, *The World of Our Mothers* (Chapel Hill: University of North Carolina Press, 1989), p. 108.

8. Juliane Jacobi-Dittrich, "The Struggle for an Identity," in Ruth-Ellen B. Joeres, ed., *German Women in the Eighteenth and Nineteenth Centuries* (Bloomington: Indiana University Press, 1986), p. 327.

9. Carole Elizabeth Adams, *Women Clerks in Wilhelmine Germany* (Cambridge: Cambridge University Press, 1988), pp. 43, 59–60.

10. Ibid., pp. 60–61.

11. Lisa M. Fine, *The Souls of the Skyscraper* (Philadelphia: Temple University Press, 1990), p. 59.

12. "Stenographers' Club Starts with 65 Girls," *New York Times*, January 17, 1907, p. 7.

13. "Business Women Protest," *New York Times*, January 19, 1907, p. 6.

14. "Women in Offices," *New York Times*, January 21, 1907, p. 8.

15. Maud Nathan, *The Story of an Epoch-Making Movement* (Garden City, N.Y.: Doubleday, Page, 1926), pp. 15–16.

16. Margery W. Davies, *Woman's Place Is at the Typewriter* (Philadelphia: Temple University Press, 1982), p. 85.

17. "He Hugged a Policewoman," *New York Times*, May 1, 1925, p. 11.

18. Chloe Owings, *Women Police* (Montclair, N.J.: Patterson Smith 1969, reprint of 1925 ed.), pp. 132, 163.

19. Stanley Frank, "Some Cops Have Lovely Legs," *Saturday Evening Post* 222, December 24, 1949, p. 39.

20. "Women Victims of Men Organize at Nice," *New York Times*, April 3, 1922, p. 1.

21. Caroline Seebohm, *The Man Who Was Vogue* (London: Weidenfeld & Nicolson, 1982), pp. 156–157, 161, 292, 361.

22. Gregory Anderson, *The White Blouse Revolution* (Manchester: Manchester University Press, 1988), pp. 22–23.

23. Fine, *The Souls of the Skyscraper*, p. 58.

24. Anna M. Baetjer, *Women in Industry* (Philadelphia: Saunders, 1946), p. 33.

25. Gulielma Fell Alsop, *She's Off to Work* (New York: Vanguard, 1941), pp. 161, 167, 234.

26. Edith Johnson, *To Women of the Business World* (Philadelphia: Lippincott, 1923), p. 82.

27. Beth Bailey McLean, *The Young Woman in Business* (Ames: Iowa State College Press, 1953), pp. 56, 62–63.

28. Donald A. Laird, *The Psychology of Supervising the Working Woman* (New York: McGraw-Hill, 1942), pp. 26–28, 92, 113, 119.

29. Frances Maule, *She Strives to Conquer* (New York: Funk & Wagnalls, 1935), pp. 24–25.

30. Ibid., pp. 155–157.

31. Ibid., pp. 157–158.

32. Ibid., p. 159.

33. Ibid., pp. 159–163.

34. Linda Rubinstein, "Dominance Eroticised," in Margaret Bevege, ed., *Worth Her Salt* (Sydney: Hale & Iremonger, 1982), p. 166.

35. Indira Chauhan, *Purdah to Profession* (Delhi: B. R. Publishing, 1986), pp. 121–122.

36. Indira Chauhan, *The Dilemma of Working Women Hostelers* (Delhi: B. R. Publishing, 1986), pp. 43, 45–46.

37. "Discomfort Women," *The Economist*, November 25, 1989, p. 36.

38. Elizabeth Shogren, "Russia's Equality Erosion," *Los Angeles Times*, February 11, 1993, p. A10.

39. Roberta Goldberg, *Organizing Women Office Workers* (New York: Praeger, 1983), pp. 74–75.

40. "Transit Authority Demotes Executive in Sex Harassment," *New York Times*, March 1, 1992, p. 37.

41. "Tennessee Judge Convicted of Rights Violations in Sexual Assaults at Courthouse," *Los Angeles Times*, December 20, 1992, p. A9.

42. "Judge Given 25 Years in Prison for Sex Assaults," *Los Angeles Times*, April 13, 1993, p. A18.

43. Robert D. McFadden, "Harassing Charge Leveled at Judge," *New York Times*, May 23, 1993, p. 16.

44. Andrew Blum, "Lacovara Leaves Amid Complaints," *National Law Review* 15, January 25, 1993, pp. 3, 32.

45. Patrick J. McDonnell, "INS Official Is Target of Sexual Harassment Probe," *Los Angeles Times*, January 28, 1993, p. B3.

46. Veronica T. Jennings, "Sex Fueled Promotions at NIH Unit, Report Says," *Washington Post*, May 8, 1993, pp. A1, A6.

47. Alicia Di Rado, "37% of Women in City Jobs Cite Sex Harassment," *Los Angeles Times*, September 23, 1992, pp. A1, A15.

48. Laurie Becklund, "Female City Employees Use Variety of Tactics to Fight Harassment," *Los Angeles Times*, September 24, 1992, pp. B3, B8; James Rainey, "Sex Harassment Ombudsman OKd," *Los Angeles Times*, November 14, 1992, p. B3.

49. James Rainey, "Action on City Clerk Case Delayed Again," *Los Angeles Times*, May 20, 1993, pp. B1, B3; James Rainey, "Council Votes to Fire Official for Sex Harassment," *Los Angeles Times*, June 3, 1993, pp. B1, B4.

50. Chuck Philips, "$10-Million Suit Claims Harassment by Managers at Universal Studios Tour," *Los Angeles Times*, December 18, 1992, pp. B1, B3.

51. Chuck Philips, "'Anita Hill of Music Industry' Talks," *Los Angeles Times*, March 5, 1992, pp. F1, F13.

52. Ibid., p. F13; Laurie Becklund, "Sexual Harassment Claims Confront Music Industry," *Los Angeles Times*, November 3, 1991, p. A18.

53. Philips, "'Anita Hill of Music Industry' Talks," p. F13.

54. Ibid.; Becklund, "Sexual Harassment Claims," pp. A1, A18.

55. Ibid., pp. A18–A19.

56. Chuck Philips, "Controversial Record Exec Hired by Def," *Los Angeles Times*, July 21, 1992, pp. F1, F7.

57. Chuck Philips, "Geffen Firm Said to Settle Case of Sex Harassment," *Los Angeles Times*, November 17, 1992, pp. F1, F4; "Harassment Lawsuit," *Los Angeles Times*, November 18, 1992, p. F2.

Chapter 9

1. Lynn Weiner, *From Working Girl to Working Mother* (Chapel Hill: University of North Carolina Press, 1985), p. 64.

2. Helen Campbell, *Prisoners of Poverty* (Boston: Roberts Bros, 1887), p. 175.

3. Mary Conyington, "Relations Between Occupations and Criminality of Women," in U.S. Congress, Senate, *Report on Conditions of Women and Child Wage-Earners in the United States*, 19 vols., 61st Cong., 2d sess., Document #645, (Washington, D.C.: GPO, 1911), vol. 15, pp. 95–96; Weiner, *From Working Girl*, p. 45.

4. Weiner, *From Working Girl*, p. 48.

5. Thomas H. Russell, *The Girl's Fight for a Living* (Chicago: Donahue, 1913), pp. 127–128.

6. Barbara Mayer Wertheimer, *We Were There* (New York: Pantheon Books, 1977), p. 240.

7. Campbell, *Prisoners of Poverty*, p. 181; Helen Campbell, *Women Wage-Earners* (Boston: Roberts Brothers, 1893), p. 221.

8. Maud Nathan, *The Story of an Epoch-Making Movement* (Garden City, N.Y.: Doubleday, 1926), p. 7.

9. Sue Ainslie Clark, *Making Both Ends Meet* (New York: Macmillan, 1911), p. 28.

10. Russell, *The Girl's Fight*, pp. 92, 95, 97.

11. George Seldes, *Witness to a Century* (New York: Ballantine Books, 1987), p. 48.

12. *Girls of the Department Store: Report and Testimony Taken Before the Special Committee of the Assembly Appointed to Investigate the Condition of Female Labor in the City of New York.* (New York: Garland, 1987, reprint of 1895 ed.), pp. 96, 100.

13. Ibid., pp. 967–968.

14. Ibid., pp. 1111, 1121ff.

15. Ibid., p. 1948.

16. W. R. Hotchkin, "An Indignant Protest on Behalf of the Shop Girl," *New York Times*, March 30, 1913, pt. 5, p. 2.

17. "Low Wages Do Not Drive Girls Astray," *New York Times*, June 22, 1913, pt. 2, p. 10.

18. Lin Farley, *Sexual Shakedown* (New York: McGraw-Hill, 1978), p. 42.

19. Jean Reith Schroeder, *Alone in a Crowd: Women in the Trades Tell Their Stories* (Philadelphia: Temple University Press, 1985), p. 205.

20. Susan C. Bourque, *Women of the Andes* (Ann Arbor: University of Michigan Press, 1981), p. 131.

21. Mary Bularzik, "Sexual Harassment at the Workplace," *Radical America* 12 (July/August 1978): 36.

22. Wayne Roberts, *Honest Womanhood* (Toronto: New Hogtown, 1976), pp. 21–22.

23. Sarah Eisenstein, *Give Us Bread But Give Us Roses* (London: Routledge & Kegan Paul, 1983), pp. 28–29.

24. Cornelia Stratton Parker, *Working with the Working Woman* (New York: Harper & Bros., 1922), pp. 193, 212–215.

25. Dorothy Sue Cobble, *Dishing It Out* (Urbana: University of Illinois Press, 1991), p. 44.

26. Ibid., pp. 44–45.

27. Conyington, "Relations Between Occupations and Criminality," pp. 74, 87.

28. Frances Donovan, *The Woman Who Waits* (Boston: Gorham, 1920), pp. 27, 145, 216–218.

29. Louise Kapp Howe, *Pink Collar Workers* (New York: Putnam's Sons, 1977), p. 142.

30. Ibid., pp. 127–128.

31. Schroeder, *Alone in a Crowd*, pp. 190, 199–200.

32. James P. Spradley, *The Cocktail Waitress* (New York: Wiley, 1975), pp. 12, 15.

33. Ibid., pp. 20, 60, 96, 97, 116.

34. Ibid., pp. 16, 23.

35. Ibid., pp. 92, 117, 133.

36. Linda Rubinstein, "Dominance Eroticised," in Margaret Bevege, ed., *Worth Her Salt* (Sydney: Hale & Iremonger, 1982), pp. 166, 170.

37. Rosalyn Baxandall, *America's Working Women* (New York: Random House, 1976), pp. 342, 343, 348.

38. Sylvia Chant, *Women and Survival in Mexican Cities* (Manchester: Manchester University Press, 1991), pp. 78, 82.

39. Georgia Panter Nielson, *From Sky Girl to Flight Attendant* (Ithaca: ILR Press, 1982), p. 12.

40. Paula Kane, *Sex Objects in the Sky* (Chicago: Follett, 1974), pp. 52–54, 102, 103, 104.

41. Ibid., pp. 13, 14, 104.

42. "Sexual Harassment Arrest on Jet," *New York Times,* January 2, 1988, p. 10.

43. Kane, *Sex Objects in the Sky,* pp. 62–63.

44. Ibid., pp. 13, 20.

45. Philip S. Foner, *Women and the American Labor Movement: From World War I to the Present* (New York: Free Press, 1980), p. 558.

46. Kane, *Sex Objects in the Sky,* p. 20; Martin A. Lee, *Unreliable Sources* (New York: Carol, 1990), p. 229.

47. Lee Holcombe, *Victorian Ladies at Work* (Hamden, Conn.: Archon, 1973), p. 70.

48. Darlene Clark Hine, *Black Women in White* (Bloomington: Indiana University Press, 1989), p. 49.

49. Hilary Standing, *Dependence and Autonomy* (London: Routledge, 1991), p. 52.

50. N. Shantha Mohan, *Status of Nurses in India* (New Delhi: Uppal, 1985), pp. 60, 85.

51. Indira Chauhan, *Purdah to Profession* (Delhi: B. R. Publishing, 1986), p. 122.

52. Alan Grieco, "Scope and Nature of Sexual Harassment in Nursing," *Journal of Sex Research* 23 (May 1987): 261–265.

53. Colleen Reiter, "Sexual Harassment in the Dental Practice," *The Dental Assistant* 59 (January/February 1990): 18–19.

54. Cynthia Garvin, "Sexual Harassment Within Dental Offices in Washington State," *Journal of Dental Hygiene* 66: (May 1992): 178, 181, 184.

Chapter 10

1. Ordway Tead, *Instincts in Industry* (Boston: Houghton Mifflin, 1918), p. 35.

2. Maurine Weiner Greenwalk, *Women, War, and Work* (Westport, Conn.: Greenwood Press, 1980), p. 98.

3. Ibid., pp. 98–99.

4. Ibid., pp. 99–100.

5. Alan Armstrong, *Farmworkers* (London: Batsford, 1988), p. 164.

6. Elizabeth Crosthwait, "The Girl Behind the Gun," in Lenore Davidoff, ed., *Our Work, Our Lives, Our Words* (London: Macmillan, 1986), p. 178.

7. Patsy Adam-Smith, *Australian Women at War* (Melbourne: Nelson, 1984), pp. 285–286.

8. Helen Rogan, *Mixed Company* (New York: Putnam's Sons, 1981), p. 141.

9. Ibid., p. 142.

10. Ibid.

11. Susan M. Hartmann, *The Home Front and Beyond* (Boston: Twayne, 1982), p. 39.

12. D'Ann Campbell, *Women at War with America* (Cambridge, Mass.: Harvard University Press, 1984), p. 34; Gail Braybon *Out of the Cage* (London: Pandora, 1987), pp. 205–206.

13. Braybon, *Out of the Cage*, pp. 206–207.

14. Ibid., pp. 207, 209.

15. Campbell, *Women at War*, p. 125.

16. Karen Anderson, *Wartime Women* (Westport, Conn.: Greenwood Press, 1981), p. 47.

17. Adele Horin, "A Military Problem," *The National Times*, July 25–31, 1982, pp. 8–9.

18. Ibid., pp. 10–11.

19. Michael Rustad, *Women in Khaki* (New York: Praeger, 1982), pp. 147, 193–194.

20. Helen Rogan, *Mixed Company* (New York: Putnam, 1981), pp. 27, 243.

21. Ibid., pp. 244–246.

22. Ibid., pp. 21, 195–196.

23. Ibid., pp. 196–197.

24. Rustad, *Women in Khaki*, pp. 147–152.

25. H. G. Reza, "New Study Indicates Wide Sex Harassment in Navy," *Los Angeles Times*, February 10, 1992, pp. A1, A3.

26. Ibid.

27. Eric Schmitt, "2 Out of 3 Women in Military Report Sexual Harassment Incidents," *New York Times*, September 12, 1990, p. A22; John Lancaster, "In Harassment Cases, His Word Outranks Hers," *Washington Post*, November 15, 1992, pp. A1, A20.

28. Reza, "New Study."

29. Richard Halloran, "Study Finds Servicewomen Harassed," *New York Times*, February 21, 1989, p. A18.

30. H. G. Reza, "2 Tell of Sex Harassment at Navy Base," *Los Angeles Times*, March 12, 1992, p. A23.

31. "Probe Found Navy Attacked More Women," *Sydney Morning Herald*, May 2, 1992, p. A23.

32. Eric Schmitt, "Citing Scandal, Navy Group Cancels Annual Convention," *New York Times*, June 18, 1992, p. B11; Melissa Healy, "Pentagon Blasts Navy's Tailhook Investigation," *Los Angeles Times*, September 25, 1992, pp. A1, A36–A37; Eric Schmitt, "Pentagon Takes Over," *New York Times*, June 19, 1992, p. A20.

33. John Lancaster, "A Gauntlet of Terror, Frustration," *Washington Post*, June 24, 1992, pp. A1, A4; Neil A. Lewis, "President Meets Female Officer in Navy Incident," *New York Times*, June 28, 1992, p. 12; "Navy Investigator Removed from Inquiry on Assault," *New York Times*, July 9, 1992, p. A14.

34. Melissa Healy, "Pentagon Blasts Navy's Tailhook Investigation," *Los Angeles Times*, September 25, 1992, p. A36.

35. Neil A. Lewis, "President Meets Female Officer in Navy Incident," *New York Times*, June 28, 1992, p. 12; Eric Schmitt, "Navy Chief Quits Amid Questions over Role in Sex-Assault Inquiry," *New York Times*, June 27, 1992, pp. A1, A7; Melissa Healy, "Navy Secretary Resigns over Tailhook Incident," *Los Angeles Times*, June 27, 1992, pp. A1, A20.

36. Eric Schmitt, "Scathing Report Cites Hostility Toward Women," *New York Times*, September 25, 1992, pp. A1, A20; Melissa Healy, "Pentagon Blasts Navy's Tailhook Investigation," *Los Angeles Times*, September 25, 1992, pp. A1, A36–37.

37. Melissa Healy, "Tailhook Still Rips Through Navy, Marines," *Los Angeles Times*, November 1, 1992, pp. A1, A12, A14.

38. Melissa Healy, "No Further Punishment for 2 Admirals," *Los Angeles Times*, October 27, 1992, p. A16.

39. John Lancaster, "Reports of Sexual Assaults Add Fuel to Debate over Women in Combat," *Washington Post*, July 14, 1992, p. A3.

40. Melissa Healy, "Tailhook Still Rips," pp. A1, A12, A14.

41. Michael R. Gordon, "Pentagon Report Tells of Aviators' Debauchery," *New York Times*, April 24, 1993, pp. 1, 9; Melissa Healy, "140 Officers Faulted in Tailhook Sex Scandal," *Los Angeles Times*, April 24, 1993, pp. A1, A6.

42. H. G. Reza, "6 Officers in Tailhook Case Get Desk Job," *Los Angeles Times*, May 14, 1993, p. A3; "Tailhook Assn. Plans First Convention Since Scandal," *Los Angeles Times*, May 27, 1993, p. B8.

43. Melissa Healy, "Woman Reservist Tells of Sexual Assault," *Los Angeles Times*, July 1, 1992, p. A5; "Sergeant Held in Sex Assault After Senators Hear Accuser," *New York Times*, July 4, 1992, p. 8.

44. Elaine Sciolina, "Military Women Report Pattern of Sexual Abuse by Servicemen," *New York Times*, July 1, 1992, pp. A1, A16.

45. Lancaster, "In Harassment Cases," pp. A1, A20; John Lancaster, "After Barracks Attack, She Felt Like a Criminal," *Washington Post*, November 15, 1992, p. A21.

46. Lancaster, "In Harassment Cases," pp. A1, A20; John Lancaster, "It Started with a Note," *Washington Post*, November 15, 1992, p. A20.

47. Lancaster, "In Harassment Cases," pp. A1, A20; John Lancaster, "It Ended Her Service," *Washington Post*, November 15, 1992, p. A20.

48. Lancaster, "In Harassment Cases," pp. A1, A20.

49. Ibid.

50. Ibid.

51. Eric Schmitt, "Army Investigating Scores of Complaints of Sex Harassment," *New York Times*, October 29, 1992, pp. A1, A9.

52. Geoffrey York, "Sex Harassment Called Rampant on Military Bases," *Globe & Mail*, March 11, 1993, p. 1.

Chapter 11

1. Geeta Chaturvedi, *Women Administrators of India* (Jaipur, India: RBSA Publications, 1985), p. 206.

2. Ibid., p. 207.

3. Anuradha Bhoite, *Women Employees and Rural Development* (Delhi: Gian, 1987), pp. 17, 67.

4. Ibid., pp. 71, 94, 97, 99.

5. Ibid., pp. 102, 127–129.

6. Ruth Carter, *Women in Engineering* (London: Macmillan, 1990), pp. 95–96.

7. Anne B. Fisher, *Wall Street Women* (New York: Knopf, 1990), pp. 12–13.

8. Miranda S. Spivak, "Uncle Sam's Cabin," *Ms.* 17 (November 1988): 84.

9. "Sexual Harassment Case Nears Trial," *New York Times*, June 24, 1985, p. C14; "ABC Settles Harassment Suit," *New York Times*, July 3, 1985, p. C20.

10. Nina Burleigh, "Breaking the Silence," *ABA Journal* 75 (August 1989): 46, 48.

11. Ibid., pp. 48, 51.

12. Ibid., pp. 48–52.

13. Gregory A. Robb, "Judge Finds S.E.C. Attorney Was Sexually Harassed at Job," *New York Times*, May 14, 1988, p. 11.

14. "S.E.C. Harassment Suit Ends," *New York Times*, June 17, 1988, p. B4.

15. "Harassment Suit Settled by S.E.C.," *New York Times*, September 3, 1988, p. 8.

16. David Margolick, "Curbing Sexual Harassment in the Legal World," *New York Times*, November 9, 1990, p. B5.

17. Saundra Torry, "Study Finds Sexual Harassment Prevalent in Western U.S. Courts," *Washington Post*, August 5, 1992, p. A2; "Survey Finds Sex Bias, Harassment in Federal Courts," *Los Angeles Times*, August 5, 1992, p. A17.

18. Philip Hager, "Women Lawyers Get Advice on Countering Sexual Bias," *Los Angeles Times*, March 5, 1993, p. B8.

19. Margolick, "Curbing Sexual Harassment."

20. Gerald Eskenazi, "Harassment Charge Draws N.F.L.'s Attention," *New York Times*, September 27, 1990, pp. B11, B15; Dave Anderson, "The Only Issue Is Human Decency," *New York Times*, September 30, 1990, sec. 8, p. 6.

21. Eskenazi, "Harassment Charge"; Gerald Eskenazi, "Investigator to Look into Harassment," *New York Times*, September 28, 1990, p. A21.

22. Eskenazi, "Harassment Charge," pp. B11, B15; Dave Anderson, "The Right Place for Women," *New York Times*, October 4, 1990, p. A28.

23. Thomas George, "Patriots and 3 Players Fined," *New York Times*, November 28, 1990, p. B11.

24. Thomas Rogers, "Kiam Apologizes After Joking About the Olson Incident," *New York Times*, February 17, 1991, p. B17.

25. "Olson to Sue Patriots," *New York Times*, April 25, 1991, p. B20; "Olson Settles Suit," *New York Times*, February 25, 1992, p. B11.

26. Gerald Eskenazi, "N.F.L. Has Never Collected Some Fines in Olson Incident," *New York Times*, May 27, 1992, p. B13.

27. M. L. Stein, "Female Sportswriters and Sexual Harassment," *Editor & Publisher* 124, October 26, 1991, pp. 8, 40.

28. Carolyn Weaver, "A Secret No More," *Washington Journalism Review* 14 (September 1992): 23–27.

29. Ibid., p. 25.

30. Ibid.

31. Ibid., pp. 26–27.

32. Emily Dunning Barringer, *Bowery to Bellevue* (New York: Norton, 1950), pp. 112–113, 115, 184.

33. Elizabeth L'Hommedieu, "Walking Out on the Boys," *Time* 138, July 8, 1991, pp. 52–53.

34. Otto Strong, "United Pilot Files a Sexual Harassment Suit," *Los Angeles Times*, October 14, 1992, p. D2.

35. Julie Tamaki, "Talent Agent Sent to Prison in Sex Assaults," *Los Angeles Times*, June 10, 1993, p. B3.

Chapter 12

1. Karen Lindsey, "Sexual Harassment on the Job," *Ms.* 6 (November 1977): 48.

2. John Balzar, "Sex Charges Bring End to Brock Adams' Career," *Los Angeles Times*, March 2, 1992, p. A1.

3. Ibid., p. A16.

4. Ibid.

5. Martin A. Lee, *Unreliable Sources* (New York: Carol, 1990), pp. 229, 234.

6. Rochelle Sharpe, "Capitol Hill's Worst Kept Secret: Sexual Harassment," *Ms* 2 (January/February 1992): 28.

7. Ibid., pp. 29–30.

8. Ibid., p. 29.

9. Ibid., pp. 28, 31.

10. Michael Oreskes, "Ethics Committee Scolds Lawmaker," *New York Times*, October 19, 1989, p. A24.

11. "A Secret Payment Stirs Up Florida," *New York Times*, February 17, 1991, p. 31; "Florida House Majority Leader Is Replaced," *New York Times*, April 17, 1991, p. A20.

12. Peter Baker, "3 More Voice Complaints Against Dix," *Washington Post*, May 21, 1993, pp. D1, D2; Peter Baker "Leidinger Approved Payment," *Washington Post*, May 22, 1993, pp. D1, D2.

13. Sharpe, "Capitol Hill's Worst Kept Secret," p. 31.

14. Ibid.

15. Lynda Edwards, "GAG Rule," *Spy* (March 1992): 40, 42.

16. Lin Farley, *Sexual Shakedown* (New York: McGraw-Hill, 1978), pp. 18–19.

17. Edwards, "GAG Rule," pp. 40, 43–45.

18. Ibid., pp. 42, 46, 50.

19. "Thomas Defender Apologizes," *New York Times*, November 3, 1991, p. 31.

20. Robert Parry, *Fooling America* (New York: Morrow, 1992), p. 308.

21. Jacob Weisberg, "The Devil in John McLaughlin," *Esquire* 118 (November 1992): 80, 82.

22. Barbara Amiel, "Feminist Harassment," *National Review* 43, November 4, 1991, pp. 14–15.

23. Parry, *Fooling America*, pp. 305–310.

24. Barbara Presley Noble, "The Fallout from Hill-Thomas," *New York Times*, February 2, 1992, sec. 3, p. 23.

25. Jacqueline Weaver, "Survey Finds Workplace Remains Harassment Site," *New York Times*, March 22, 1992, sec. 12, p. 8.

26. Jane Fritsch, "Dinkins Keeps His Distance as Aide Responds on Harassment," *New York Times*, October 24, 1992, p. 11, Robert D. McFadden, "Rally for New Dinkins Aide Halted as Criticism Mounts," *New York Times*, October 26, 1992, p. B12; "Sex Harassment and Men in Power," *New York Times*, October 27, 1992, p. A16.

27. Deborah Sontag, "City Hall Sex," *New York Times*, November 8, 1992, p. 22.

28. Andrea Ford, "Former Aide Defends Actions in Accusing Holden of Harassment," *Los Angeles Times*, October 9, 1992, pp. B1, B3.

29. Andrea Ford, "2 Women Back Claims of Harassment by Holden," *Los Angeles Times*, October 8, 1992, pp. B1, B3.

30. Ford, "Former Aide."

31. Andrea Ford, "2nd Woman Says Holden Harassed Her," *Los Angeles Times*, October 21, 1992, p. B3.

32. James Rainey, "Sex Harassment Ombudsman OKd," *Los Angeles Times*, November 14, 1992, p. B3.

33. James Rainey, "3rd Ex-Holden Worker Charges Harassment," *Los Angeles Times*, January 21, 1993, pp. B1, B4.

34. "Holden Countersues 3 Women Accusers," *Los Angeles Times*, February 19, 1993, p. B2; James Rainey, "Police Detain Five Women over Protest at Holden Office," *Los Angeles Times*, March 24, 1993, pp. B1, B3; Robin Abcarian, "Who Has Courage to Speak Out on Harassment?" *Los Angeles Times*, March 28, 1993, pp. E1, E3.

35. Florence Graves, "Packwood Accused of Sexual Advances," *Washington Post*, November 22, 1992, pp. A1, A26, A27.

36. Ibid.

37. Ibid., pp. A26, A27.

38. Ibid., p. A26.

39. "Packwood Apologizes After Sex Harassment Is Charged," *Los Angeles Times*, November 23, 1992, p. A8; "More Packwood Allegations Revealed," *Los Angeles Times*, December 6, 1992, p. A24.

40. Graves, "Packwood Accused," p. A1.

41. Paul Houston, "Democrats in Oregon Want Packwood Out," *Los Angeles Times*, November 24, 1992, pp. A1, A22.

42. "Packwood May Undergo Alcohol Testing," *Los Angeles Times*, November 29, 1992, p. A34.

43. William J. Eaton, "Sen. Packwood Enters Alcohol Abuse Facility," *Los Angeles Times*, December 1, 1992, p. A20.

44. William J. Eaton, "Ethics Panel Beginning Packwood Inquiry," *Los Angeles Times*, December 2, 1992, p. A19.

45. Richard C. Paddock, "New Harassment Allegations Surface in Packwood Case," *Los Angeles Times*, December 3, 1992, p. A27.

46. Alexander Cockburn, "A Spotlight on Single-Issue Cynicism," *Los Angeles Times*, December 20, 1992, p. M5; Brad Knickerbocker, "Women's Groups Shun Packwood Due to Sexual-Misconduct Charges," *Christian Science Monitor*, December 8, 1992, p. 3.

47. "Packwood Denies New Sex Allegation," *Los Angeles Times*, December 9, 1992, p. A22.

48. William J. Eaton, "Packwood Apologizes, Vows Not to Resign," *Los Angeles Times*, December 11, 1992, p. A4.

49. "2 Say They Quit Packwood over Fund Raising," *Los Angeles Times*, January 4, 1993, p. A17.

50. "Petition Calls for Senate to Refuse to Seat Packwood," *Los Angeles Times*, December 16, 1992, p. A27.

51. William J. Eaton, "103rd U.S. Congress Meets Today," *Los Angeles Times*, January 5, 1993, p. A12.

52. "Packwood Faces 13 More Accusers," *New York Times*, February 8, 1993, p. A10.

53. William J. Eaton, "Freshman Braun Raises Some Eyebrows," *Los Angeles Times*, January 6, 1993, p. A5.

54. David Hulen, "Sexual Harassment Flap Tops Agenda of Alaska Lawmakers," *Los Angeles Times*, March 2, 1993, p. A5.

55. Chuck Shepherd, "News of the Weird," *Los Angeles Reader*, 15: June 18, 1993, p. 54.

56. Margot Gibb-Clark, "Report Backs Charges of Harassment," *Globe & Mail*, April 5, 1993, pp. A1, A4.

Chapter 13

1. Lin Farley, *Sexual Shakedown* (New York: McGraw-Hill, 1978), p. 20.

2. Philip S. Foner, *Women and the American Labor Movement: From World War I to the Present* (New York: Free Press, 1980), p. 558.

3. Farley, *Sexual Shakedown*, pp. 20, 22.

4. Caryl Rivers, "Sexual Harassment," *Mother Jones* 3 (June 1978): 22; Mary Owen, *Working Women* (Melbourne: Sisters, 1979), p. 78.

5. Barbara Sinclair Deckard, *The Women's Movement*, 3d ed. (New York: Harper & Row, 1983), pp. 408–409.

6. Ibid., p. 409.

7. Suzanne C. Carothers, "Contrasting Sexual Harassment in Female- and Male-Dominated Occupations," in Karen Brodkin Sacks, ed., *My Troubles Are Going to Have Trouble with Me* (New Brunswick: Rutgers University Press, 1984), pp. 220–222.

8. Sandra S. Tangri, "Research on Women's Work and the Family at the Urban Institute," in Anne Hoiberg, ed., *Women and the World of Work* (New York: Plenum Press, 1982), p. 174.

9. Raymond M. Lane, "A Man's World," *Village Voice*, December 16–22, 1981, p. 16.

10. Tangri, "Research on Women's Work," p. 175.

11. Jerry A. Jacobs, *Revolving Doors* (Stanford: Stanford University Press, 1989), pp. 151–153.

12. Cynthia Cockburn, *Machinery of Dominance* (London: Pluto Press, 1985), p. 203.

13. Miranda S. Spivak, "Uncle Sam's Cabin," *Ms.* 17 (November 1988): 84.

14. Beth E. Schneider, "Put Up and Shut Up: Workplace Sexual Assaults," *Gender & Society* 5 (December 1991): 537, 539, 540–541, 543, 546.

15. Ronni Sandroff, "Sexual Harassment in the Fortune 500," *Working Woman* 13 (December 1988): 69, 71–72.

16. Ibid., pp. 71–72.

17. Tamar Lewin, "Women Say They Face Obstacles as Lawyers," *New York Times*, December 4, 1989, p. A21.

18. Kim Kelber, "The UN's Dirty Little Secret," *Ms* 6 (November 1977): 51, 79.

19. Jan Lambertz, "Sexual Harassment in the Nineteenth Century English Cotton Industry," *History Workshop Journal* 19 (Spring 1985): 29 Indira Chauhan, *Purdah to Profession (Delhi: B. R. Publishing, 1986), pp. 122–123.*

20. "Sex and the Uncivil Servant," *Times* (London), June 27, 1983, p. 2.

21. Caroline Lees, "Sex Harassment," *Sunday Times* (London), October 20, 1991, sec. 1, p. 1.

22. Ibid.

23. Bertrand Marotte, "Women Gaining More Attention in Workplace," *Vancouver Sun*, March 7, 1992, p. A1.

24. Karen Lindsey, "Sexual Harassment on the Job," *Ms.* 6 (November 1977): 48.

25. Ibid., pp. 74, 76.

26. Rivers, "Sexual Harassment," p. 22.

27. Lindsey, "Sexual Harassment," p. 50.

28. Ibid.; Rochelle Lefkowitz, "A Grass Roots Model," *Ms* 6 (November 1977): 49.

29. Susan E. Martin, *On the Move: The Status of Women in Policing* (Washington, D.C.: Police Foundation, 1990), p. 16.

30. Robert W. Schupp, "Sexual Harassment Under Title VII," *Labor Law Journal* 32 (April 1981): 240–243.

31. Ibid., pp. 244–245.

32. Rivers, "Sexual Harassment," pp. 21, 24.

33. Schupp, "Sexual Harassment," p. 245; Foner, *Women and the American Labor Movement*, p. 559; Deckard, *The Women's Movement*, pp. 176–177.

34. Martin, *On the Move*, p. 17.

35. Foner, *Women and the American Labor Movement*, p. 559.

36. Martin, *On the Move*, pp. 17–18; Sandroff, "Sexual Harassment," p. 69; Deckard, *The Women's Movement*, pp. 176–177.

37. James J. Oh, "Internal Sexual Harassment Complaints," *Employee Relations Law Journal* 18 (Autumn 1992): 228.

38. David G. Savage, "Court to Clarify Definition of Sex Harassment," *Los Angeles Times*, March 2, 1993, pp. A1, A9.

39. Carol O'Donnell, *Getting Equal* (Sydney: Allen & Unwin, 1988), p. 125.

40. "Discomfort Women," *The Economist*, November 25, 1989, p. 36; "Verbal Sex Bias Suit First in Japan," *Honolulu Advertiser*, April 17, 1992, p. B8.

41. Mikiko Taga, "Scoffing at 'Sekuhara'." *World Press Review* 39 (February 1992): 26.

42. Steven R. Weisman, "Landmark Harassment Case in Japan," *New York Times*, April 17, 1992, p. A3.

43. Ted Holden, "Revenge of the Office Ladies," *Business Week*, July 13, 1992, pp. 42–43.

44. "Frenchmen, Beware" *The Economist*, July 6, 1991, p. 50.

45. Carlota Bustelo, "The 'International Sickness' of Sexual Harassment," *World Press Review* 39 (February 1992): 24.

46. Ranjana Sengupta, "A Symptom of Urban Anomie," *World Press Review* 39 (February 1992): 25.

47. Martha Mbugguss, "A Debate in Kenya," *World Press Review* 39 (February 1992): 39.

Chapter 14

1. Otto Strong, "United Pilot Files a Sexual Harassment Suit," *Los Angeles Times*, October 14, 1992, p. D2.

2. Barbara Mathias, "The Harassment Hassle," *Washington Post*, November 5, 1991, p. B5.

3. Penelope McMillan, "Effort Launched to Reduce Costs of Liability Suits," *Los Angeles Times*, December 4, 1992, p. B1.

4. "A Complaint Is a Long-Term Item," *New York Times*, February 2, 1992, sec. 3, p. 23.

5. "Chrysler Takes Harassment Case to Supreme Court," *Los Angeles Times*, September 22, 1992, p. D2; Helen Kahn, "Supreme Court Refuses Chrysler Assault Case," *Automotive News*, October 12, 1992, p. 22.

6. "City in Florida Ousts Rights Chief in Harassment Case," *New York Times*, March 5, 1992, p. A20.

7. Dana Priest, "Agencies Often Tolerate Sexual Harassers," *Washington Post*, November 29, 1991, p. A9.

8. Ibid., pp. A1, A9.

9. Ibid., p. A8.

10. Cathleen Decker, "Women Tell of Frustration in Combatting Sexual Harassment," *Los Angeles Times*, November 15, 1991, pp. A3, A32.

11. Mathias, "The Harassment Hassle."

12. Ibid.

13. Nell Bernstein, "Fighting Victims," *Mother Jones* 17 (September/October 1992): 26–27.

14. Mathias, "The Harassment Hassle."

15. Priest, "Agencies Often Tolerate," p. A9.

Bibliography

"ABC Settles Harassment Suit." *New York Times*, July 3, 1985, p. C20.

Abcarian, Robin. "Who Has Courage to Speak Out on Harassment?" *Los Angeles Times*, March 28, 1993, pp. E1, E3.

Adams, Carole Elizabeth. *Women Clerks in Wilhelmine Germany*. Cambridge: Cambridge University Press, 1988.

Adam-Smith, Patsy. *Australian Women at War*. Melbourne: Nelson, 1984.

Alexander, Sally. *Women's Work in Nineteenth-Century London*. London: Journeyman Press, 1976.

Alford, Katrina. *Production or Reproduction*. Melbourne: Oxford University Press, 1984.

Alsop, Gulielma Fell. *She's Off to Work*. New York: Vanguard, 1941.

Amiel, Barbara. "Feminist Harassment." *National Review* 43 November 4, 1991, pp. 14–15.

Anderson, Dave. "The Only Issue Is Human Decency." *New York Times*, September 30, 1990, sec. 8, p. 6.

Anderson, Gregory, ed. *The White Blouse Revolution*. Manchester: Manchester University Press, 1988.

Anderson, Karen. *Wartime Women*. Westport, Conn.: Greenwood Press, 1981.

Andreas, Carol. *When Women Rebel*. Westport, Conn.: Lawrence Hill, 1985.

Armstrong, Alan. *Farmworkers*. London: Batsford, 1988.

Asher, Nina. "Dorothy Jacobs Bellanca." In Joan M. Jenson, ed., *A Needle, a Bobbin, a Strike*. Philadelphia: Temple University Press, 1984.

Ayers, Charlotte Wharton. "Help Wanted Female." *New York Times*, August 1, 1909, pt. 5, p. 2.

_____. "The Help Wanted Sharks and Their Prey." *New York Times*, August 15, 1909, pt. 5, p. 9.

_____. "The Would-Be Worker and the Enticing Ads." *New York Times*, August 8, 1909, pt. 5, p. 6.

Baetjer, Anna M. *Women in Industry*. Philadelphia: Saunders, 1946.

Baker, Elizabeth Faulkner. *Technology and Woman's Work*. New York: Columbia University Press, 1964.

Baker, Peter. "Leidinger Approved Payment." *Washington Post*, May 22, 1993, pp. D1, D2.

_____. "3 More Voice Complaints Against Dix." *Washington Post*, May 21, 1993, pp. D1, D2.

Balzar, John. "Sex Charges Bring End to Brock Adams' Career." *Los Angeles Times*, March 2, 1992, pp. A1, A16.

Banaji, D. R. *Slavery in British India*. Bombay: Taraporevala, 1933.

Barringer, Emily Dunning. *Bowery to Bellevue*. New York: Norton, 1950.

Baxandall, Rosalyn, ed. *America's Working Women*. New York: Random House, 1976.

Becklund, Laurie. "Female City Employees Use Variety of Tactics to Fight Harassment." *Los Angeles Times*, September 24, 1992, pp. B3, B8.
———. "Sexual Harassment Claims Confront Music Industry." *Los Angeles Times*, November 3, 1991, pp. A1, A18, A19.
Beddoe, Deidre. *Back to Home and Duty*. London: Pandora, 1989.
Bell, Susan Groag, ed. *Women, the Family, and Freedom: Volume 1, 1750–1880*. Stanford: Stanford University Press, 1983.
Berger, Iris. *Threads of Solidarity: Women in South African Industry, 1900–1980*. Bloomington: Indiana University Press, 1991.
Bernstein, Nell. "Fighting Victims." *Mother Jones* 17 (September/October 1992): 26–27.
Bhoite, Anuradha. *Women Employees and Rural Development*. Delhi: Gian, 1987.
Birjis, Zahida. *Women at Work*. Lahore: National Institute of Public Administration, 1964.
Blassingame, John W. *Slave Testimony*. Baton Rouge: Louisiana State University Press, 1977.
Blewett, Mary H. *Men, Women, and Work*. Urbana: University of Illinois Press, 1988.
Blewett, Mary H., ed. *The Last Generation*. Amherst: University of Massachusetts Press, 1990.
Blum, Andrew. "Lacovara Leaves Amid Complaints." *National Law Journal* 15 (January 25, 1993): 3, 32.
Boston, Sarah. *Women Workers and the Trade Unions*. London: Lawrence & Wishart, 1987.
Bourque, Susan C. *Women of the Andes*. Ann Arbor: University of Michigan Press, 1981.
Braybon, Gail. *Out of the Cage*. London: Pandora, 1987.
Brown, Helen Gurley. "At Work, Sexual Electricity." *Wall Street Journal*, October 29, 1992, p. A22.
Brushaber, George. "Lust on the Job." *Christianity Today* 35 Dec. 16, 1991, p. 21.
Buder, Leonard. "Bias Is Rampant in Construction, Hearing Is Told." *New York Times*, March 13, 1990, p. B4.
Bularzik, Mary. "Sexual Harassment at the Workplace." *Radical America* 12 (July/August 1978): 25–43.
Bunster, Ximena. *Sellers and Servants*. New York: Praeger, 1985.
Burleigh, Nina. "Breaking the Silence." *ABA Journal* 75 (August 1989): 46ff.
Burton, Margaret E. *Women Workers of the Orient*. West Medford, Mass.: Central Committee on the United Study of Foreign Missions, 1918.
"Business Women Protest." *New York Times*, January 19, 1907, p. 6.
Busted, Carlota. "The 'International Sickness' of Sexual Harassment." *World Press Review* 39 (February 1992): 24.
Byerly, Victoria. *Hard Times Cotton Mill Girls*. Ithaca: ILR Press, 1986.
Cadbury, Edward. *Women's Work and Wages*. Chicago: University of Chicago Press, 1907.
Campbell, D'Ann. *Women at War with America*. Cambridge, Mass.: Harvard University Press, 1984.
Campbell, Helen. *Prisoners of Poverty*. Boston: Roberts Brothers, 1887.
———. *Women Wage-Earners*. Boston: Roberts Brothers, 1893.
Carothers, Suzanne C. "Contrasting Sexual Harassment in Female- and Male-Dominated Occupations." In Karen Brodkin Sacks, ed., *My Troubles Are Going to Have Trouble with Me*. New Brunswick: Rutgers University Press, 1984.
Carter, Ruth. *Women in Engineering*. London: Macmillan, 1990.

Chant, Sylvia. *Women and Survival in Mexican Cities.* Manchester: Manchester University Press, 1991.

Chaturvedi, Geeta. *Women Administrators of India.* Jaipur, India: RBSA Publications, 1985.

Chauhan, Indira. *The Dilemma of Working Women Hostelers.* Delhi: B. R. Publishing, 1986.

————. *Purdah to Profession.* Delhi: B. R. Publishing, 1986.

Chew, Ada Nield. *Ada Nield Chew: The Life and Writings of a Working Woman.* London: Virago, 1982.

"Chrysler Takes Harassment Case to Supreme Court." *Los Angeles Times,* September 22, 1992, p. D2.

"City in Florida Ousts Rights Chief in Harassment Case." *New York Times,* March 5, 1992, p. A20.

Clark, Anna. *Women's Silence, Men's Violence.* London: Pandora, 1987.

Clark, Sue Ainslie. *Making Both Ends Meet.* New York: Macmillan, 1911.

Cobble, Dorothy Sue. *Dishing It Out.* Urbana: University of Illinois Press, 1991.

Cockburn, Alexander. "A Spotlight on Single-Issue Cynicism." *Los Angeles Times,* December 20, 1992, p. M5.

Cockburn, Cynthia. *Machinery of Dominance.* London: Pluto Press, 1985.

Cohen, Rina. "The Work Conditions of Immigrant Women Live-In Domestics." *Resources for Feminist Research* 16 (March 1987): 36–38.

"Complaint Is a Long-Term Item, A." *New York Times,* February 2, 1992, sec. 3, p. 23.

Conrad, Robert Edgar. *Children of God's Fire.* Princeton: Princeton University Press, 1983.

Conyington, Mary. "Relations Between Occupation and Criminality of Women." In U.S. Congress, Senate, *Report on Conditions of Women and Child Wage-Earners in the United States.* 19 vols. 61st Cong. 2d sess. Document #645. Washington, D.C.: 1911, vol. 15.

Cooney, Charles F. "Nothing More . . . Than a Whorehouse." *Civil War Times Illustrated* 21 (December 1982): 40–43.

"Court Criticizes Police Department in a Sex Case." *New York Times,* July 29, 1992, p. B3.

Coyle, Laurie. "Women at Work." In Joan M. Jenson, ed., *A Needle, a Bobbin, a Strike.* Philadelphia: Temple University Press, 1984.

Crosthwait, Elizabeth. "The Girl Behind the Gun." In Lenore Davidoff, ed., *Our Work, Our Lives, Our Words.* London: Macmillan, 1986.

Daley, Suzanne. "Female Firefighters Charge Inaction on Sex Bias." *New York Times,* June 18, 1986, p. B2.

Daniels, Kay. "Prostitution in Tasmania During the Transition from Penal Settlement to 'Civilized' Society." In Kay Daniels, ed., *So Much Hard Work.* Sydney: Fontana, 1984.

Davidson, Nicholas. "Feminism and Sexual Harassment." *Society* 28 (May/June 1991): 39–44.

Davies, Margery W. *Woman's Place Is at the Typewriter.* Philadelphia: Temple University Press, 1982.

Davis, Patricia. "Complaint of Sexism Detailed." *Washington Post,* August 3, 1992, pp. B1, B5.

Deaux, Kay. *Women of Steel.* New York: Praeger, 1983.

Deckard, Barbara Sinclair. *The Women's Movement.* 3d ed. New York: Harper & Row, 1983.

Decker, Cathleen. "Women Tell of Frustration in Combatting Sexual Harassment." *Los Angeles Times*, November 15, 1991, pp. A3, A32.

Di Rado, Alicia. "37% of Women in City Jobs Cite Sex Harassment." *Los Angeles Times*, September 23, 1992, pp. A1, A15.

"Discomfort Women." *The Economist*, November 25, 1989, p. 36.

Donovan, Frances. *The Woman Who Waits*. Boston: Gorham, 1920.

Dudden, Faye E. *Serving Women*. Middleton, Conn.: Wesleyan University Press, 1983.

Duke, Lynne. "Law Enforcers Grapple with Diversity." *Washington Post*, January 27, 1993, pp. A1, A12.

Dworkin, Andrea. *Right-Wing Women*. London: Women's Press, 1983.

Dye, Nancy Schrom. *As Equals and as Sisters*. Columbia: University of Missouri Press, 1980.

Eaton, William J. "Ethics Panel Beginning Packwood Inquiry." *Los Angeles Times*, December 2, 1992, p. A19.

———. "Freshman Braun Raises Some Eyebrows." *Los Angeles Times*, January 6, 1993, p. A5.

———. "103rd U.S. Congress Meets Today." *Los Angeles Times*, January 5, 1993, p. A12.

———. "Packwood Apologized, Vows Not to Resign." *Los Angeles Times*, December 11, 1992, p. A4.

———. "Sen. Packwood Enters Alcohol Abuse Facility." *Los Angeles Times*, December 1, 1992, p. A20.

Ebbet, Eve. *Victoria's Daughters*. Wellington: A. H. & A. W. Reed, 1981.

Edwards, Lynda. "GAG Rule." *Spy* (March 1992): 40–47, 50.

Eisenstein, Sarah. *Give Us Bread But Give Us Roses*. London: Routledge & Kegan Paul, 1983.

Engels, Friedrich. *The Condition of the Working Class in England*. Stanford: Stanford University Press, 1968.

Eskenazi, Gerald. "Harassment Charge Draws N.F.L.'s Attention." *New York Times*, September 17, 1990, pp. B11, B15.

———. "Investigation to Look into Harassment." *New York Times*, September 28, 1990, p. A21.

———. "N.F.L. Has Never Collected Some Fines in Olson Incident." *New York Times*, May 27, 1992, p. B13.

"Face It Squarely—Deal with It." *Los Angeles Times*, December 17, 1992, p. B6.

Farley, Jennie, ed. *Women Workers in Fifteen Countries*. Ithaca: ILR Press, 1985.

Farley, Lin. *Sexual Shakedown*. New York: McGraw-Hill, 1978.

Fine, Lisa M. *The Souls of the Skyscraper*. Philadelphia: Temple University Press, 1990.

Fiore, Faye. "Sheriff's Dept. Concedes on 2 Sex Bias Suits." *Los Angeles Times*, December 4, 1992, pp. A1, A36.

"Firefighter Fined in Sex Harassment Case." *New York Times*, October 3, 1986, p. B2.

Fisher, Anne B. *Wall Street Women*. New York: Knopf, 1990.

"Florida House Majority Leader Is Replaced." *New York Times*, April 17, 1991, p. A20.

Foner, Philip S. *Women and the American Labor Movement: From World War I to the Present*. New York: Free Press, 1980.

———. *Women and the Labor Movement: From Colonial Times to the Eve of World War I*. New York: Free Press, 1979.

_____, ed. *The Factory Girls*. Urbana: University of Illinois Press, 1980.

Ford, Andrea. "Former Aide Defends Actions in Accusing Holden of Harassment." *Los Angeles Times*, October 9, 1992, pp. B1, B3.

_____. "2nd Woman Says Holden Harassed Her." *Los Angeles Times*, October 21, 1992, p. B3.

_____. "2 Women Back Claims of Harassment by Holden." *Los Angeles Times*, October 8, 1992, pp. B1, B3.

Fout, John C. "The Viennese Enquete of 1896 on Working Women." In Ruth-Ellen B. Joeres, ed., *German Women in the Eighteenth and Nineteenth Centuries*. Bloomington: Indiana University Press, 1986.

Frank, Stanley. "Some Cops Have Lovely Legs." *Saturday Evening Post*, 222 December 24, 1949, pp. 11–13ff.

Fraser, Antonia. *The Weaker Vessel*. London: Weidenfeld & Nicolson, 1984.

"Frenchmen, Beware." *The Economist*, July 6, 1991, p. 50.

Fried, Joseph P. "After Harassment Charge, Her Fellow Firefighters Transfer." *New York Times*, October 22, 1991, p. B1.

_____. "Transfer Linked to Harassment, Police Say." *New York Times*, October 17, 1992, p. 28.

Fritsch, Jane. "Dinkins Keeps His Distance as Aide Responds on Harassment." *New York Times*, October 24, 1992, p. 11.

Fuchs, Rachel G. "Pregnant, Single and Far from Home: Migrant Women in Nineteenth-Century Paris." *American Historical Review* 95 (October 1990): 1007–1031.

Gabin, Nancy F. *Feminism in the Labor Movement*. Ithaca: Cornell University Press, 1990.

"Garment Strike." *Life and Labor*. 1 (January 1911): 14.

Garvin, Cynthia. "Sexual Harassment Within Dental Offices in Washington State." *Journal of Dental Hygiene* 66 (May 1992): 178–184.

George, Thomas. "Patriots and 3 Players Fined in Olson Incident." *New York Times*, November 28, 1990, p. B11.

Gibb-Clark, Margot. "Report Backs Charges of Harassment." *Globe & Mail*, April 5, 1993, pp. A1, A4.

Gillis, John R. "Servants, Sexual Relations, and the Risks of Illegitimacy in London, 1801–1900." *Feminist Studies* 5 (Spring 1979): 142–173.

Girls of the Department Store: Report and Testimony Taken Before the Special Committee of the Assembly Appointed to Investigate the Condition of Female Labor in the City of New York. New York: Garland, 1987, reprint of 1895 ed.

Glenn, Susan A. *Daughters of the Shtel*. Ithaca: Cornell University Press, 1990.

Glickman, Rose L. *Russian Factory Women: Workplace and Society, 1880–1914*. Berkeley and Los Angeles: University of California Press, 1984.

Goldberg, Roberta. *Organizing Women Office Workers*. New York: Praeger, 1983.

Gordon, Eleanor. *Women and the Labour Movement in Scotland, 1850–1914*. Oxford: Clarendon Press, 1991.

Gordon, Florence. "The Condition of Female Labour and the Rate of Pay of Women's Wages in Sydney, 1894." In Beverly Kingston, ed., *The World Moves Slowly*. Sydney: Cassell, 1977.

Gordon, Michael R. "Pentagon Report Tells of Aviators' Debauchery." *New York Times*, April 24, 1993, pp. 1, 9.

Grad, Shelby. "Irvine Orders Probe of Police Sex Charges." *Los Angeles Times*, June 24, 1993, p. B8.

Graef, Roger. *Talking Blues*. London: Collins Harvill, 1989.

Graves, Florence. "Packwood Accused of Sexual Advances." *Washington Post,* November 22, 1992, pp. A1, A26, A27.

Gray, Stan. "Fight to Survive—The Case of Bonita Clark." *Canadian Dimension* 20 (May 1986): 15–20.

Greenwald, Maurice Weiner. *Women, War and Work.* Westport, Conn.: Greenwood Press, 1980.

Grieco, Alan. "Scope and Nature of Sexual Harassment in Nursing." *Journal of Sex Research* 23 (May 1987): 261–265.

Groneman, Carol, ed. *To Toil the Livelong Day: America's Women at Work, 1770–1980.* Ithaca: Cornell University Press, 1987.

Gulick, Sidney L. *Working Women of Japan.* New York: Missionary Education Movement of the United States and Canada, 1915.

Gutman, Herbert G. *The Black Family in Slavery and Freedom, 1750–1925.* New York: Pantheon Books, 1976.

Hafeez, Sabeena. *The Metropolitan Women in Pakistan.* Karachi: Royal, 1981.

Hager, Philip. "Women Lawyers Get Advice on Countering Sexual Bias." *Los Angeles Times,* March 5, 1993, p. B8.

Halloran, Richard. "Study Finds Servicewomen Harassed." *New York Times,* February 21, 1989, p. A18.

Hansen, Karen Tranberg. *Distant Companions: Servants and Employers in Zambia, 1900–1985.* Ithaca: Cornell University Press, 1989.

"Harassment Lawsuit." *Los Angeles Times,* November 18, 1992, p. F2.

"Harassment Suit Settled by S.E.C." *New York Times,* September 3, 1988, p. 8.

Hartmann, Susan M. *The Home Front and Beyond.* Boston: Twayne, 1982.

Hasanovitz, Elizabeth. *One of Them.* Boston: Houghton Mifflin, 1917.

Hasbach, W. *A History of the English Agricultural Labourer.* London: King & Son, 1920.

"He Hugged a Policewoman." *New York Times,* May 1, 1925, p. 11.

Healy, Melissa. "No Further Punishment for 2 Admirals." *Los Angeles Times.* October 27, 1992, p. A16.

_____. "140 Officers Faulted in Tailhook Sex Scandal." *Los Angeles Times,* April 24, 1993, pp. A1, A16.

_____. "Pentagon Blasts Navy's Tailhook Investigation." *Los Angeles Times,* September 25, 1992, pp. A1, A36, A37.

_____. "Tailhook Still Rips Through Navy, Marines." *Los Angeles Times,* November 1, 1992, pp. A1, A12, A14.

Hevesi, Dennis. "Firefighter Again Makes Her Harassment Charge." *New York Times,* October 18, 1991, p. B3.

Hewitt, Margaret. *Wives and Mothers in Victorian Industry.* London: Rockliff, 1958.

Hilden, Patricia. *Working Women and Socialist Politics in France, 1880–1914.* Oxford: Clarendon Press, 1986.

Hine, Darlene Clark. *Black Women in White.* Bloomington: Indiana University Press, 1989.

Holcombe, Lee. *Victorian Ladies at Work.* Hamden, Conn.: Archon, 1973.

Holden, Ted. "Revenge of the Office Ladies." *Business Week,* July 13, 1992, pp. 42–43.

"Holden Countersues 3 Women Accusers." *Los Angeles Times,* February 17, 1993, p. B2.

Hollis, Patricia. *Women in Public.* London: Allen & Unwin, 1979.

L'Hommedieu, Elizabeth. "Walking Out on the Boys." *Time* 138, July 8, 1991, pp. 52–53.

Honig, Emily. *Personal Voices: Chinese Women in the 1980s.* Stanford: Stanford University Press, 1988.

―――. *Sisters and Strangers: Women in the Shanghai Cotton Mills, 1919–1949.* Stanford: Stanford University Press, 1986.

Horin, Adele. "A Military Problem." *The National Times* (Australia), July 25–31, 1982, pp. 8–11.

―――. "Sex Antics Upset Female Postal Staff." *Sydney Herald,* May 14, 1992, p. 2.

Horn, Pamela. *Victorian Countrywomen.* Oxford: Basil Blackwell, 1991.

Horne, Peter. *Women in Law Enforcement.* 2d ed. Springfield, Ill.: Charles C. Thomas, 1980.

Hotchkin, W. R. "An Indignant Protest on Behalf of the Shop Girl." *New York Times,* March 30, 1913, pt. 5, p. 2.

Houston, Paul. "Democrats in Oregon Want Packwood Out." *Los Angeles Times,* November 24, 1992, pp. A1, A22.

Howe, Louise Kapp. *Pink Collar Workers.* New York: Putnam's Sons, 1977.

Huggins, Nathan. *Protestants Against Poverty: Boston's Charities, 1870–1900.* Westport, Conn.: Greenwood Press, 1971.

Hulen, David. "Sexual Harassment Flap Tops Agenda of Alaska Lawmakers." *Los Angeles Times,* March 2, 1993, p. A5.

Jacobi-Dittrich, Juliane. "The Struggle for an Identity." In Ruth-Ellen B. Jocres, ed., *German Women in the Eighteenth and Nineteenth Centuries.* Bloomington: Indiana University Press, 1986.

Jacobs, Harriet A. *Incidents in the Life of a Slave Girl.* Miami: Mnemosyne Publishing, 1969, reprint of 1861 ed.

Jacobs, Jerry A. *Revolving Doors.* Stanford: Stanford University Press, 1989.

Janiewski, Dolores Elizabeth. "From Field to Factory: Race, Class, Sex and the Woman Worker in Durham, 1880–1940." Ph.D. diss., Duke University, 1979.

―――. *Sisterhood Denied.* Philadelphia: Temple University Press, 1985.

Jennings, Veronica T. "Sex Fueled Promotions at NIH Unit, Report Says." *Washington Post,* May 8, 1993, pp. A1, A6.

John, Angela V. *By the Sweat of Their Brow.* London: Routledge & Kegan Paul, 1984.

Johnson, Edith. *To Women of the Business World.* Philadelphia: Lippincott, 1923.

Jones, Jacqueline. *Labor of Love, Labor of Sorrow.* New York: Basic Books, 1985.

"Judge Blocks Bias by Fire Companies." *New York Times,* June 14, 1986, p. 32.

"Judge Given 25 Years in Prison for Sex Assaults." *Los Angeles Times,* April 13, 1993, p. A18.

Kahn, Helen. "Supreme Court Refuses Chrysler Assault Case." *Automotive News,* October 12, 1992, p. 22.

Kane, Paula. *Sex Objects in the Sky.* Chicago: Follett, 1974.

Kanekar, Suresh. "Sex-Related Differences in Perceptions of Sexual Harassment of Women in India." *Journal of Social Psychology* 133 (February 1993): 119–120.

Katzman, David M. *Seven Days a Week.* New York: Oxford University Press, 1978.

Kaufman, Stewart B. *The Samuel Gompers Papers.* Urbana: University of Illinois Press, 1986.

Kazuko, Ono. *Chinese Women in a Century of Revolution, 1850–1950.* Stanford: Stanford University Press, 1978.

Kelber, Mim. "The UN's Dirty Little Secret." *Ms.* 6 (November 1977): 51, 79.

Kellogg, Paul. "The McKee's Rocks Strike." *Survey,* August 7, 1909, p. 663.

Kennedy, Susan Estabrook. *If All We Did Was to Weep at Home.* Bloomington: Indiana University Press, 1979.

Kidd, Yasue Aoki. *Women Workers in the Japanese Cotton Mills: 1880–1920.* Ithaca: Cornell University Press, 1978.

Klabin, Karen. "Lewd Conduct." *LA Weekly* 15, March 5, 1993, pp. 14, 16.

Knickerbocker, Brad. "Women's Groups Shun Packwood Due to Sexual-Misconduct Charges." *Christian Science Monitor,* December 8, 1992, p. 3.

Kolchin, Peter. *Unfree Labor.* Cambridge, Mass.: Belknap Press, 1987.

Kopetman, Roxanna. "Long Beach Policewomen Call Sexual Harassment Endemic." *Los Angeles Times,* September 28, 1991, p. B3.

Korda, Michael. *Male Chauvinism.* New York: Random House, 1972.

Laird, Donald A. *The Psychology of Supervising the Working Woman.* New York: McGraw-Hill, 1942.

Lambertz, Jan. "Sexual Harassment in the Nineteenth Century English Cotton Industry." *History Workshop Journal* 19 (Spring 1985): 29–61.

Lancaster, John. "After Barracks Attack, She Felt Like a Criminal." *Washington Post,* November 15, 1992, p. A21.

_____. "A Gauntlet of Terror, Frustration." *Washington Post,* June 24, 1992, pp. A1, A4.

_____. "In Harassment Cases, His Word Outranks Hers." *Washington Post,* November 15, 1992, pp. A1, A20.

_____. "It Ended Her Service." *Washington Post,* November 15, 1992, p. A20.

_____. "It Started with a Note." *Washington Post,* November 15, 1992, p. A20.

_____. "Reports of Sexual Assaults Add Fuel to Debate over Women in Combat." *Washington Post,* July 14, 1992, p. A3.

Lane, Raymond M. "A Man's World." *Village Voice,* December 16–22, 1981, pp. 1ff.

Lanpher, Katherine. "A Bitter Brew." *Ms.* 3 (November/December 1992): 36–41.

Lee, Martin A. *Unreliable Sources.* New York: Carol, 1990.

Lee, Wendy. "Prostitution and Tourism in South-East Asia." In Nanneke Redclift, ed., *Working Women.* London: Routledge, 1991.

Lees, Caroline. "Sex Harassment." *Sunday Times* (London), October 20, 1991, sec. 1, p. 1.

Lefkowitz, Rochelle. "A Grass Roots Model." *Ms.* 6 (November 1977): 49.

Less, Rosanne. "Words Against Women: The Detroit Story." *Columbia Journalism Review* 26 (March/April 1988): 6, 8.

Levine, Susan. *Labor's True Woman.* Philadelphia: Temple University Press, 1984.

Lewin, Tamar. "Women Say They Face Obstacles as Lawyers." *New York Times,* December 4, 1989, p. A21.

Lewis, Neil A. "President Meets Female Officer in Navy Incident." *New York Times,* June 28, 1992, p. 12.

Licht, Walter. *Working for the Railroad.* Princeton: Princeton University Press, 1983.

Lindsey, Karen. "Sexual Harassment on the Job." *Ms.* 6 (November 1977): 47–51ff.

Lipman, Joanne. "Far from Home, an Irish Nanny Found Herself Terrified and Isolated." *Wall Street Journal,* April 14, 1993, p. A6.

_____. "The Nanny Trap." *Wall Street Journal,* April 14, 1993, pp. A1, A6.

Long, Priscilla. "The Women of the Colorado Fuel and Iron Strike, 1913–1914." In Ruth Milkman, ed., *Women, Work and Protest.* Boston: Routledge & Kegan Paul, 1985.

"Low Wages Do Not Drive Girls Astray." *New York Times,* June 22, 1913, sec. 2, p. 10.

MacKinnon, Catharine A. *Sexual Harassment of Working Women.* New Haven: Yale University Press, 1979.

Mae, Verta. *Thursdays and Every Other Sunday Off.* Garden City, N.Y.: Doubleday, 1972.

Mahajan, Amarjit. *Indian Policewomen.* New Delhi: Deep & Deep, 1982.

"Maids Repatriated Amid Abuse Claims." *Sydney Herald,* May 2, 1992, p. 13.

Margolick, David. "Curbing Sexual Harassment in the Legal World." *New York Times,* November 9, 1990, p. B5.

Marotte, Bertrand. "Women Gaining More Attention in Workplace." *Vancouver Sun,* March 7, 1992, pp. A1, A3.

Marston, David W. *Malice Aforethought.* New York: Morrow, 1991.

Martin, Linda. *The Servant Problem.* Jefferson, N.C.: McFarland, 1985.

Martin, Molly, ed. *Hard-Hatted Women.* Seattle: Seal Press, 1988.

Martin, Susan E. *On the Move: The Status of Women in Policing.* Washington, D.C.: Police Foundation, 1990.

_____. "Sexual Politics in the Workplace." *Symbolic Interaction* 1 (Spring 1978): 44–60.

Mathias, Barbara. "The Harassment Hassle." *Washington Post,* November 5, 1991, p. B5.

Matsui, Yayori. *Women's Asia.* London: Zed Press, 1987.

Maule, Francis. *She Strives to Conquer.* New York: Funk & Wagnalls, 1935.

Maza, Sarah C. *Servers and Masters in Eighteenth Century France.* Princeton: Princeton University Press, 1983.

Mbugguss, Martha. "A Debate in Kenya." *World Press Review* 39 (February 1992): 26.

McDonnell, Patrick J. "INS Official Is Target of Sexual Harassment Probe." *Los Angeles Times,* January 28, 1993, p. B3.

McFadden, Robert D. "Harassing Charge Leveled at Judge." *New York Times,* May 23, 1993, p. 16.

_____. "Rally for New Dinkins Aide Halted as Criticism Mounts." *New York Times,* October 26, 1992, p. B12.

McLean, Beth Bailey. *The Young Woman in Business.* Ames: Iowa State College Press, 1953.

McMillan, Penelope. "Effort Launched to Reduce Costs of Liability Suits." *Los Angeles Times,* December 4, 1992, p. B1.

Mehta, Aban B. *The Domestic Servant Class.* Bombay: Popular Book Depot, 1960.

Mendoza, N. F. "Crossing the Thin Blue Line." *Los Angeles Times,* May 11, 1993, pp. F1, F7.

Metzker, Isaac, ed. *A Bintel Brief.* Garden City, N.Y.: Doubleday, 1971.

Meyerowitz, Ruth. "Organizing the United Auto Workers." In Ruth Milkman, ed., *Women, Work and Protest.* Boston: Routledge & Kegan Paul, 1985.

Milkman, Ruth. *Gender at Work.* Urbana: University of Illinois Press, 1987.

Milne, John Duguid. *Industrial Employment of Women in the Middle and Lower Ranks.* New York: Garland, 1984, reprint of 1870 ed.

Mohan, N. Shantha. *Status of Nurses in India.* New Delhi: Uppal, 1985.

"More Packwood Allegations Revealed." *Los Angeles Times,* December 6, 1992, p. A24.

Morgenson, Gretchen. "May I Have the Pleasure?" *National Review* 43, November 18, 1991, pp. 36–37ff.

Morris, Jenny. *Women Workers and the Sweated Trades.* Hants, England: Gower, 1986.

Morrison, Patt, "Female Officers Unwelcome — But Doing Fine." *Los Angeles Times,* July 12, 1991, pp. A1, A27–A29.

"Moving to Right a Wrong." *Los Angeles Times*, December 24, 1992, p. B6.

Myers, Gustavus. *History of Bigotry in the United States.* New York: Random House, 1943.

Nathan, Maud. *The Story of an Epoch-Making Movement.* Garden City, N.Y.: Doubleday, Page, 1926.

"Navy Investigator Removed from Inquiry on Assaults." *New York Times*, July 9, 1992, p. A14.

Nazaro, Sonia. "Force to be Reckoned With." *Los Angeles Times*, June 5, 1993, pp. A1, A12.

Nevins, Allan. *Study in Power.* 2 vols. New York: Scribner's & Sons, 1953.

"Newport Beach Settles 4 Harassment Cases." *Los Angeles Times*, February 4, 1993, p. A17.

Nielson, Georgia Panter. *From Sky Girl to Flight Attendant.* Ithaca: ILR Press, 1982.

Noble, Barbara Presley. "The Fallout from Hill-Thomas." *New York Times*, February 2, 1992, sec. 3, p. 23.

Norwood, Stephen H. *Labor's Flaming Youth.* Urbana: University of Illinois Press, 1990.

O'Donnell, Carol. *The Basis of the Bargain.* Sydney: Allen & Unwin, 1984.

_____. *Getting Equal.* Sydney: Allen & Unwin, 1988.

"Officers of the Law Should Know Better." *Los Angeles Times*, February 1, 1991, p. B6.

"Officer's Suit Says She Was Raped, Then Fired." *Los Angeles Times*, December 18, 1992, p. B3.

Oh, James J. "Internal Sexual Harassment Complaints." *Employee Relations Law Journal* 18 (Autumn 1992): 227–244.

Olmstead, Frederick Law. *A Journey in the Back Country.* New York: Putnam's Sons, 1907.

_____. *A Journey in the Seaboard Slave States.* New York: Dix & Edwards, 1856.

"Olson Settles Suit." *New York Times*, February 25, 1992, p. B11.

"Olson to Sue Patriots." *New York Times*, April 25, 1991, p. B20.

Ong, Aihwa. *Spirits of Resistance and Capitalist Discipline.* Albany: State University of New York Press, 1987.

Oreskes, Michael. "Ethics Committee Scolds Lawmaker." *New York Times*, October 19, 1989, p. A24.

Owen, Leslie Howard. *This Species of Property.* New York: Oxford University Press, 1976.

Owen, Mary, comp. *Working Women.* Melbourne: Sisters, 1979.

Owings, Chloe. *Women Police.* Montclair, N.J.: Patterson Smith, 1969, reprint of 1925 ed.

"Packwood Apologizes After Sex Harassment Is Charged." *Los Angeles Times*, November 23, 1992, p. A8.

"Packwood Denies New Sex Allegation." *Los Angeles Times*, December 9, 1992, p. A22.

"Packwood Faces 13 More Accusers." *New York Times*, February 8, 1993, p. A10.

"Packwood May Undergo Alcohol Testing." *Los Angeles Times*, November 29, 1992, p. A34.

Paddock, Richard C. "New Harassment Allegations Surface in Packwood Case." *Los Angeles Times*, December 3, 1992, p. A27.

Parker, Cornelia Stratton. *Working with the Working Woman.* New York: Harper & Bros., 1922.

Parry, Robert. *Fooling America.* New York: Morrow, 1992.

Patai, Daphne, ed. *Brazilian Women Speak.* New Brunswick: Rutgers University Press, 1988.

Penny, Virginia. *The Employments of Women.* Boston: Walker, Wise, 1862.

_____. *Think and Act.* Philadelphia: Claxton, Remsen & Haffelfinger, 1869.

Perdue, Charles L., Jr. *Weevils in the Wheat.* Charlottesville: University Press of Virginia, 1976.

Perrot, Monica. *A Tolerable Good Success.* Sydney: Hale & Iremonger, 1983.

"Petition Calls for Senate to Refuse to Seat Packwood." *Los Angeles Times*, December 16, 1992, p. A27.

Philips, Chuck. "'Anita Hill of Music Industry' Talks." *Los Angeles Times*, March 5, 1992, pp. F1, F13.

_____. "Controversial Record Exec Hired by Def." *Los Angeles Times*, July 21, 1992, pp. F1, F7.

_____. "Geffen Firm Said to Settle Case of Sex Harassment." *Los Angeles Times*, November 17, 1992, pp. F1, F4.

_____. "$10-Million Suit Claims Harassment by Managers at Universal Studios Tour." *Los Angeles Times*, December 18, 1992, pp. B1, B3.

"Police Matrons." *New York Times*, October 1, 1890, p. 4.

"Police Matrons Needed." *New York Times*, December 25, 1890, p. 8.

"Policewomen." *New York Times*, March 31, 1880, p. 4.

Pope, Lison. *Millhands & Preachers.* New Haven: Yale University Press, 1942.

Priest, Dana. "Agencies Often Tolerate Sexual Harassers." *Washington Post*, November 29, 1991, pp. A1, A8, A9.

"Probe Found Navy Attacked More Women." *Sydney Herald,* May 2, 1992, p. 18.

Rainey, James. "Action on City Clerk Case Delayed Again." *Los Angeles Times*, May 20, 1993, pp. B1, B3.

_____. "Council Votes to Fire Official for Sex Harassment." *Los Angeles Times*, June 3, 1993, pp. B1, B4.

_____. "Police Detain Five Women Over Protest at Holden Office." *Los Angeles Times*, March 24, 1993, pp. B1, B3.

_____. "Sex Harassment Ombudsman OKd." *Los Angeles Times*, November 14, 1992, p. B3.

_____. "3rd Ex-Holden Worker Charges Harassment." *Los Angeles Times*, January 21, 1993, pp. B1, B4.

Rakow, Lana, ed. *The Revolution in Words: Righting Women, 1868–1871.* New York: Routledge, 1990.

Rakowski, Cathy A. *Women in Nontraditional Industry: The Case of Steel in Ciudad, Guyana, Venezuela.* Working Paper #104 (Michigan State University, November 1985).

Reiter, Colleen. "Sexual Harassment in the Dental Practice." *The Dental Assistant* 59 (January/February 1990): 16–19.

Reza, H. G. "New Study Indicates Wide Sexual Harassment in Navy." *Los Angeles Times*, February 10, 1992, pp. A1, A3.

_____. "6 Officers in Tailhook Case Get Desk Jobs." *Los Angeles Times*, May 14, 1993, p. A3.

_____. "2 Tell of Sex Harassment at Navy Base." *Los Angeles Times*, March 19, 1992, p. A23.

Richardson, Dorothy. "The Long Day." In *Women at Work.* Chicago: Quadrangle, 1972.

Riemer, Jeffrey W. *Hard Hats.* Beverly Hills: Sage, 1979.

"Right Place for Women, The." *New York Times*, October 4, 1990, p. A28.

Rivers, Caryl. "Sexual Harassment." *Mother Jones* 3 (June 1978): 21–22ff.

Robb, Gregory A. "Judge Finds S.E.C. Attorney Was Sexually Harassed at Job." *New York Times*, May 14, 1988, p. 11.

Roberts, Wayne. *Honest Womanhood.* Toronto: New Hogtown Press, 1976.

Robinson, Harriet H. *Loom and Spindle.* New York: Crowell, 1898.

Rogan, Helen. *Mixed Company.* New York: Putnam's Sons, 1981.

Rogers, Thomas. "Kiam Apologizes After Joking About the Olson Incident." *New York Times*, February 17, 1991, p. B17.

Rohini, P. R. *My Life Is One Long Struggle.* Belgaum, India: Pratishabd, 1983.

Rollins, Judith. *Between Women.* Philadelphia: Temple University Press, 1985.

Rotenberg, Lori. "The Wayward Worker." In *Women at Work: Ontario, 1850–1930.* Toronto: Canadian Women's Educational Press, 1974.

Rubinstein, Linda. "Dominance Eroticised." In Margaret Bevege, ed., *Worth Her Salt.* Sydney: Hale & Iremonger, 1982.

Russell, Thomas H. *The Girl's Fight for a Living.* Chicago: Donohue, 1913.

Rustad, Michael. *Women in Khaki.* New York: Praeger, 1982.

Sandroff, Ronni. "Sexual Harassment in the Fortune 500." *Working Woman* 13 (December 1988): 69–73.

Savage, David G. "Court to Clarify Definition of Sex Harassment." *Los Angeles Times*, March 2, 1993, pp. A1, A9.

Schafer, Judith K. "Open and Notorious Concubinage." In Darlene Hines, ed., *Black Women in American History: From Colonial Times Through the Nineteenth Century.* Vol. 4. Brooklyn: Carlson, 1990.

Schmitt, Eric. "Army Investigating Scores of Complaints of Sex Harassment." *New York Times*, October 29, 1992, pp. A1, A9.

_____. "Citing Scandal, Navy Group Cancels Annual Convention." *New York Times*, June 18, 1992, p. B11.

_____. "Navy Chief Quits Amid Questions over Role in Sex-Assault Inquiry." New York Times, June 27, 1992, pp. A1, A7.

_____. "Pentagon Takes Over." *New York Times*, June 19, 1992, p. A20.

_____. "Scathing Report Cites Hostility Toward Women." *New York Times*, September 25, 1992, pp. A1, A20.

_____. "2 out of 3 Women in Military Report Sexual Harassment Incidents." *New York Times*, September 12, 1990, p. A22.

Schneider, Beth E. "Put Up and Shut Up: Workplace Sexual Assaults." *Gender & Society* 5 (December 1991): 533–548.

Schneiderman, Rose. *All for One.* New York: Eriksson, 1967.

Schroeder, Jean Reith. *Alone in a Crowd: Women in the Trades Tell Their Stories.* Philadelphia: Temple University Press, 1985.

Schupp, Robert W. "Sexual Harassment Under Title VII." *Labor Law Journal* 32 (April 1981): 238–252.

Sciolino, Elaine. "Military Women Report Pattern of Sexual Abuse by Servicemen." *New York Times*, July 1, 1992, pp. A1, A16.

"S.E.C. Harassment Suit Ends." *New York Times,* June 17, 1988, p. B4.

"Secret Payment Stirs Up Florida, A." *New York Times*, February 17, 1991, p. 31.

Seebohm, Caroline. *The Man Who Was Vogue.* London: Weidenfeld & Nicolson, 1982.

Seldes, George. *Witness to a Century.* New York: Ballantine Books, 1987.

Sengupta, Padmini. *Women Workers of India.* London: Asia, 1960.

Sengupta, Ranjana. "A Symptom of Urban Anomie." *World Press Review* 39 (February 1992): 25.

"Sergeant Held in Sex Assault After Senators Hear Accuser." *New York Times*, July 4, 1992, p. 8.

"Sex and the Uncivil Service." *Times* (London), June 27, 1983, p. 2.

"Sex at Work." *Times* (London), October 19, 1991, p. 13A.

"Sex Harassment and Men in Power." *New York Times*, October 27, 1992, p. A16.

"Sexual Harassment Arrest on Jet." *New York Times*, January 2, 1988, p. 10.

"Sexual Harassment Case Nears Trial." *New York Times*, June 24, 1985, p. C14.

Sharpe, Rochelle. "Capitol Hill's Worst Kept Secret: Sexual Harassment." *Ms.* 2 (January/February 1992): 28–31.

Shepherd, Chuck. "News of the Weird." *Los Angeles Reader* 15, June 18, 1993, p. 54.

Shogren, Elizabeth. "Russia's Equality Erosion" *Los Angeles Times*, February 11, 1993, pp. A1, A10.

Sievers, Sharon L. *Flowers in Salt*. Stanford: Stanford University Press, 1983.

Smuts, Robert W. *Women and Work in America*. New York: Columbia University Press, 1959.

Soldon, Norbert C., ed. *The World of Women's Trade Unionism*. Westport, Conn.: Greenwood Press, 1985.

Sontag, Deborah. "City Hall Sex." *New York Times*, November 8, 1992, p. 22.

Soto, Shirlene Ann. *The Mexican Woman*. Palo Alto, Calif.: R & E Research, 1979.

Spivak, Miranda S. "Uncle Sam's Cabin." *Ms.* 17 (November 1988): 83–84.

Spradley, James P. *The Cocktail Waitress*. New York: Wiley, 1975.

Spruill, Julia Cherry. *Women's Life and Work in the Southern Colonies*. New York: Norton, 1972.

Standing, Hilary. *Dependence and Autonomy*. London: Routledge, 1991.

Stansell, Mary Christine. "Women of the Laboring Poor in New York City, 1820–1860. Ph.D. diss., Yale University, 1979.

Stein, M. L. "Female Sportswriters and Sexual Harassment." *Editor & Publisher* 124, October 26, 1991, pp. 8, 40.

"Stenographers' Club Starts with 65 Girls." *New York Times*, January 17, 1907, p. 7.

Stern, Madeleine B. *Critical Essays on Louisa May Alcott*. Boston: Hall, 1984.

Strong, Otto. "United Pilot Files a Sexual Harassment Suit." *Los Angeles Times*, October 14, 1992, p. D2.

Sullivan, Allana M. "Women Endure Job-Related Sex Abuse." *Coal Age* 86 (August 1981): 80–81.

––––––. "Women Say No to Sexual Harassment." *Coal Age* 84 (August 1979): 74ff.

"Survey Finds Sex Bias, Harassment in Federal Courts." *Los Angeles Times*, August 5, 1992, p. A17.

Sutherland, Daniel E. *Americans and Their Servants*. Baton Rouge: Louisiana State University Press, 1981.

Taga, Mikiko. "Scoffing at 'Sekuhara'?" *World Press Review* 39 (February 1992): 27.

"Tailhook Assn. Plans First Convention Since Scandal." *Los Angeles Times*, May 27, 1993, p. B8.

Tamaki, Julie. "Talent Agent Sent to Prison in Sex Assaults." *Los Angeles Times*, June 10, 1993, p. B3.

Tangri, Sandra S. "Research on Women's Work and the Family at the Urban Institute." In Anne Hoiberg, ed., *Women and the World of Work*. New York: Plenum Press, 1982.

Tead, Ordway. *Instincts in Industry*. Boston: Houghton Mifflin, 1918.

Teale, Ruth, ed. *Colonial Eve*. Melbourne: Oxford University Press, 1978.

"Tennessee Judge Convicted of Rights Violation in Sexual Assaults at Courthouse." *Los Angeles Times*, December 20, 1992, p. A9.

"Thomas Defender Apologizes." *New York Times*, November 3, 1991, p. 31.

Thomson, Marilyn. *Women of El Salvador*. London: Zed Press, 1986.

"Three Awarded $2.7 Million in a Sexual Harassment Suit." *New York Times,* November 12, 1990, p. B8.

"Tombs, The." *New York Times,* January 16, 1870, p. 3.

Torry, Saundra. "Study Finds Sexual Harassment Prevalent in Western U.S. Courts." *Washington Post,* August 5, 1992, p. A2.

"Transit Authority Demotes Executive in Sex Harassment." *New York Times,* March 1, 1992, p. 37.

Tsurumi, E. Patricia. *Factory Girls*. Princeton: Princeton University Press, 1990.

Turner, E. S. *What the Butler Saw*. London: Michael Joseph, 1962.

Turner, John Kenneth. *Barbarous Mexico*. Chicago: Kerr, 1910.

"2 Say They Quit Packwood Over Fund Raising." *Los Angeles Times,* January 4, 1993, p. A17.

U.S. Congress, Senate. "Glass Industry." In *Report on Conditions of Women and Child Wage-Earners in the United States*. 19 vols. 61st Cong., 2d sess. Document #645. Washington, D.C.: GPO, 1911, vol. 3.

Van Vorst, Mrs. John. *The Woman Who Toils*. New York: Doubleday, Page, 1903.

"Verbal Sex Bias Suit First in Japan." *Honolulu Advertiser,* April 17, 1992, p. B8.

Walshok, Mary Linderstein. *Blue-Collar Women*. Garden City, N.Y.: Doubleday, 1981.

"Wandering Hands." *The Economist,* December 5, 1992, p. 27.

Weatherburn, Hilary. "The Female Factory." In Judy Mackinolty, ed., *In Pursuit of Justice*. Sydney: Hale & Iremonger, 1979.

Weaver, Carolyn. "A Secret No More." *Washington Journalism Review* 14 (September 1992): 23–27.

Weaver, Jacqueline. "Survey Finds Workplace Remains Harassment Site." *New York Times*, March 22, 1992, sec. 12, p. 8.

Weikel, Dan. "Campbell Calls Firing Part of a Conspiracy." *Los Angeles Times*, December 24, 1992, pp. A3, A16.

————. "4 More Women to Join Suit Against Police." *Los Angeles Times*, December 2, 1992, pp. A3, A28.

————. "Police Chief Fired in Newport Beach." *Los Angeles Times*, December 23, 1992, pp. A3, A22.

————. "Sexual Harassment Suit Filed Against Police." *Los Angeles Times*, September 25, 1992, p. A35.

Weiler, Sue. "The Uprising in Chicago." In Joan M. Jensor, ed., *A Needle, a Bobbin, a Strike*. Philadelphia: Temple University Press, 1984.

Weinberg, Sydeny Stahl. *The World of Our Mothers*. Chapel Hill: University of North Carolina Press, 1989.

Weiner, Lynn. *From Working Girl to Working Mother*. Chapel Hill: University of North Carolina Press, 1985.

Weisberg, Jacob. "The Devil in John McLaughlin." *Esquire* 118 (November 1992): 69ff.

Weisman, Steven R. "Landmark Harassment Case in Japan." *New York Times*, April 17, 1992, p. A3.

Wertheimer, Barbara Mayer. *We Were There*. New York: Pantheon Books, 1977.

Wilgoren, Jodi. "Inquiry Finds Merit in Sex Harassment Suit." *Los Angeles Times*, December 16, 1992, pp. A3, A31.

————. "Newport Beach Settles with Fired Police Chief, Captain." *Los Angeles Times*, June 11, 1993, p. B8.

_____. "Newport Beach Won't Pay Fired Officers' Legal Costs." *Los Angeles Times*, January 29, 1993, p. A29.

"Women and Children First." *Multinational Monitor* 14 (January/February 1993): 30–32.

Women at Work. Brussels: European Trade Union Confederation, 1976.

"Women in Offices." *New York Times*, January 21, 1907, p. 8.

"Women Victims of Men Organize at Nice." *New York Times*, April 3, 1922, p. 1.

Workman, Jane E. "The Role of Cosmetics in Attributions About Sexual Harassment." *Sex Roles* 24 (June 1991): 759–769.

Wride, Nancy. "Newport Beach Police Chief, Aide Put on Leave over Rape Allegations." *Los Angeles Times*, October 16, 1992, pp. A3, A36.

_____. "Police Chief Named in Harassment Suit to Retire." *Los Angeles Times*, October 15, 1992, pp. A3, A29.

_____. "Police Officials Sue Newport Beach over Harassment Inquiry." *Los Angeles Times*, November 13, 1992, pp. A3, A34.

_____. "Women Alleging Sex Harassment Cite Reprisal Fear." *Los Angeles Times*, September 28, 1992, pp. A3, A18.

Wright, Barbara Drygulski, ed. *Women, Work, and Technology*. Ann Arbor: University of Michigan Press, 1987.

Yans-McLaughlin, Virginia. "Italian Women and Work." In Milton Canter, ed., *Class, Sex, and the Woman Worker*. Westport, Conn.: Greenwood Press, 1977.

Ybarra, Michael J. "A Man's World." *Los Angeles Times*, April 30, 1991, pp. E1, E7.

Yeandle, Susan. *Women's Working Lives*. London: Tavistock, 1984.

York, Geoffrey. "Sex Harassment Called Rampant on Military Bases." *Globe & Mail*, March 11, 1993, p. A1.

Yount, Kristen R. "Ladies, Flirts and Tomboys." *Journal of Contemporary Ethnography* 19 (January 1991): 396–422.

Zappi, Elda Gentili. *If Eight Hours Seem Too Few*. Albany: State University of New York Press, 1991.

Index